Eloquence Divine

Eloquence Divine
In Search of God's Rhetoric

Phillip Arrington

James Clarke & Co

For my dear friends, Roger and Dix

James Clarke & Co
P.O. Box 60
Cambridge
CB1 2NT
United Kingdom

www.jamesclarke.co
publishing@jamesclarke.co

ISBN: 978 0 227 17688 7

British Library Cataloguing in Publication Data
A record is available from the British Library

First published by James Clarke & Co, 2018

Copyright © Phillip Arrington, 2017

Published by arrangement
with Cascade Books

All rights reserved. No part of this edition may be reproduced, stored electronically or in any retrieval system, or transmitted in any form orby any means, electronic, mechanical, photocopying, recording, or otherwise, without prior written permission from the Publisher (permissions@jamesclarke.co).

Contents

Acknowledgments | ix

Introduction | 1
1. Why God's Rhetoric? | 11
2. Invenesis—Divining Acts | 31
3. Inventing and Arguing More Covenants | 65
4. Inventing Final Covenants? | 99
5. The Shape of God's Rhetoric | 130
6. Style—How God Puts His Case | 162
7. Memory and Delivery Divine | 196
8. Can God's Rhetoric Be Judged? | 213
9. The Perils and Promises of Exploring God's Rhetoric | 246

Bibliography | 257

Acknowledgments

My deepest thanks to Michelle Lietz's invaluable assistance in preparing the final draft of this book for publication.

Introduction

Eloquence Divine grew out of some speculative remarks on God's rhetoric I delivered in Louisville, Kentucky, in March 2010, at a national conference for scholars and teachers, most from English departments' various programs in rhetoric, writing studies, and literature—some of the readers I imagine for this book. Those of us on the conference panel that morning were responding to Stanley Fish's closing remark in "One University Under God," published in January, 2005. Fish ends his article on religion's re-emerging importance with a response to a curious reporter who asked what Fish thought would follow "high theory and the triumvirate of race, gender, and class as the center of intellectual energy in the academy" in the wake of Derrida's death. Fish's answer was immediate, and unambiguous—"religion."[1]

Certainly—and Fish admits as much—the American reading public does not want for books on religion or with "God" in their titles. Their sheer abundance in any still solvent American bookstore belies the provocative title of Jon Meacham's 2009 *Newsweek* article, "The End of Christian America." Meacham makes much of a statistic cited from the American Religious Identification Survey (completed in the same year as Meacham's article) showing that almost twice as many Americans (15%) claim "no religious affiliation" compared to those making this claim roughly a decade earlier (8%).[2]

This increase hardly seems to justify Meacham's sensationalized title, but neither Meacham nor Fish mentions one often overlooked part of the academy that has been steadily growing, and taking religion's resurgence very "seriously" long before Fish's comment.

---

1. Fish, "One University Under God," par. 31.
2. Meacham, "The End of Christian America," 34.

That overlooked enclave consists of renewed interest in what has been called the "rhetoric of religion"—that "immense undiscovered country" which now invites many different "critical and theoretical approaches" and many types of knowledge, all perhaps suggesting how "universal" rhetoric and religion are "to the human condition."[3] *Eloquence Divine* hopes to contribute in its own small way to this growing area of interest, especially among English and humanities teachers and their students as well as any other teachers, scholars, and students who may share an interest in the Bible, its rhetoric, and the rhetoric of the God of that Bible, perhaps widely imagined as the supreme source of rhetoric and all else.

"Universal" or not, the relationship between rhetoric and religion was clearly recognized well before 2009. Biblical scholar and rhetorical critic David J. A. Clines quotes Martin Luther's assertion that "without knowledge of literature pure theology cannot at all endure," so Luther pleads that "young people" must "be diligent in the study of poetry and rhetoric" for theology's own sake.[4] Apparently, Clines adds, the *Dogmatic Constitution on Divine Revelation* of Vatican II agreed with Luther: "poets and rhetoricians," the *Constitution*'s 1966 statement advised, should be "handling biblical texts" because, to determine "the correct understanding" of these texts, "due attention must be paid to the customary and characteristic styles of perceiving, speaking, and narrating which prevailed at the time of the sacred writer."[5] That "due attention" had not been paid to the Bible for quite some time, Clines laments, because biblical scholars had primarily focused on "historical and philological questions," while those who *did* focus on the Bible's rhetoric simply catalogued literary "devices and mechanics." Yet, "in the English speaking world," Clines observes, it has been English professors, not biblical scholars, teaching within "the heady development of schools of religious studies in secular universities" who have been the ones trying to help students understand and appreciate the Bible as literature, as "story and poem."[6]

A professor of English myself, I have not had the privilege of teaching the Bible as literature. Yet my own interest in the Bible began long before the 2010 Louisville conference, going all the way back to my boyhood in a small, North Carolina town. Growing up in the South during the 1950s and 60s, I could not easily avoid the overwhelming presence and influence

---

3. Zulick, "Rhetoric and Religion," 125.
4. Luther, *Luther's Correspondence*, quoted in Clines, "Story and Poem," 25.
5. *Dogmatic Constitution on Divine Revelation*, quoted in Clines, "Story and Poem," 28.
6. Clines, "Story and Poem," 25-26.

of Christianity. Even so, my parents were not avid church-goers when I was young, and I stopped attending the small, canary-yellow community chapel at the tender age of eight. Neither my mother nor my father objected, or objected strongly enough.

Yet I still recall the thrill I felt the first time I saw Cecil B. De Mille's 1956 big-screen re-make of his 1926 silent movie, *The Ten Commandments*. Like many viewers, I marveled at Moses's opening of the Red Sea, the eerie green fog of the Angel of Death, God's writing the Decalogue with fingers of lightening. I paid to see that movie at least a half a dozen times as a child, and I still sometimes watch re-runs of it on TV. I also had powerful reactions to the 1961 *King of Kings* and other movies about Jesus's life—especially the more controversial ones like *Jesus of Nazareth*, *The Last Temptation of Christ*, and *The Passion of the Christ*. In short, I have been a fan of movies based on the Bible for a long time; and these films have aided in the promulgation of a version of God for many devout and secular imaginations—mine included—the God who speaks and acts with uncompromised authority, the maker of the universe, and of the human beings who argue about how that universe was made, and how we should live in it.

Still, I did not think of myself as a "Christian" in those early years, and do not now. I remain an agnostic on matters of Christian faith. By the same token, unlike some authors I have read recently,[7] I am not a die-hard apologist for scientific rationality or what is often derisively called "secular humanism." Rather, I have spent much of my life, as a student and later as a professor, in English departments. Educated as a rhetorician, I have been intent on the study of how writers and speakers try to convince and persuade others to accept what they have to say and to act or believe as a writer or speaker hopes or desires. Since Aristotle's famous but tangled lectures on the subject from over two millennia ago (and certainly even before that), many have tried to examine and understand what resources speakers and writers adopt to move and sway others. The *study* of rhetoric, then, as a subject of interest to philosophers, educators, literary critics, and theologians, among many others, is quite old, and certainly ongoing.

The specific study and criticism of the Bible's rhetoric is certainly *not new* either. It traces as far back as Saint Augustine's highly original *On Christian Doctrine*, written around 390 CE and not completed until 427 CE, three years before Augustine died.[8] A more "self-conscious," modern rhetorical criticism of the Bible, however, is thought to have begun in 1968

7. See Harris's *The End of Faith*; Hitchens, *God Is not Great*; and Dawkins, *The God Delusion*. For an intriguing counter-argument to the atheistic attack on religion, see Hedges's *When Atheism Becomes Religion*.

8. Koptak, "Rhetorical Criticism of the Bible," par. 2.

and continues to date.[9] In that important year, biblical scholars and critics were being urged to go beyond the historical study of the Bible's sources, its literary "forms," and genres, by adding to this body of knowledge more careful scrutiny and analysis of the Bible's rhetorical traits, its persuasive strategies, styles, and structures. This urging soon led to an immense range of biblical studies, many describing their work as "rhetorical criticism." Yet what constitutes or is meant by "rhetorical criticism," as well as "rhetoric" itself, remains a matter of some debate.[10] This debate has been further complicated by other apparent schisms: some critics see rhetoric as the study of argument and persuasion; some, as the art of discursive composition; others, as the study of style and figurative language. Further complications ensued from scholars' quarrels over whether to let classical rhetoric guide biblical criticism, or whether "rhetorical criticism" should be more inclusive and accepting of a variety of theoretical approaches.

The invitation to greater openness soon led some biblical rhetorical critics to tie themselves into almost the same theoretical and methodological hard knots as literary studies, often the very source from which biblical rhetorical critics had been drawing from the 1970s through the 1990s. One result of this openness to the complexities of literary theories for some has been "[t]ongues and the confusions of tongues" that "heighten the babel"[11] over what should be the site of a text's meaning—authors, readers, history and culture, or the text itself—and over the very meaning of "meaning," of logos as spoken sounds or written marks. These difficulties intensified to the extent that biblical rhetorical criticism began to overlap various theoretical, highly sophisticated approaches to narrative drawn from literary theories.[12]

Yet, despite the often fruitful babel of confusions, and despite the array of rhetorical approaches to the Bible, few have attempted to examine the persuasiveness of speeches directly assigned to the biblical "God"[13] that so

---

9. Howard, "Rhetorical Criticism in Old Testament Studies," 88.

10. For a useful outline of the various theories and approaches to rhetorical criticism of the Bible as these have been affected by theories and approaches in literary studies, see Trible, *Rhetorical Criticism*, 1–87.

11. Ibid., 55.

12. For overviews of the theoretical and methodological shifts in narrative criticism of the Bible, see Thatcher's "Anatomies of the Fourth Gospel," 1-35; Moore's "Afterward," 253–58; and Trible, *Rhetorical Criticism*, 74–79.

13. Given the focus and approach of this book, here and throughout I deviate from my publisher's rules for its house style and adopt the traditional, gendered pronouns shown in upper-case letters to distinguish clearly references to God from pronouns referring to other biblical figures, including Jesus, which are not in upper-case. This adoption of upper-case, masculine pronouns should in no way be construed as a belief in or an assertion about God's gender, except insofar as "God" is written into the Bible

many believe in and worship. Little has been done to examine this God's efforts to persuade and convince those He *directly* speaks to, Adam, say, or Noah, Abraham, and, predominately, Moses. Further, no critic has yet tried to analyze how this God tries to invent and develop His arguments in the Bible as it has come down to us, or how this God arranges those arguments, or the styles He adopts to make them, and the roles memory and delivery play in His arguments. *Eloquence Divine* is one agnostic's attempt at such a study.

Certainly, what is meant by "Bible," above, is by no means a simple matter. Historical and redaction critics have labored to demonstrate that the Bible's presumed "unity" belies "a heterogeneous collection of writings" from different times and places by largely unknown writers.[14] To presume these different writings fuse as *one* text partly grants to the Bible its *scriptural* authority. This status clearly can affect how a critic sees and approaches the Bible. It may make any critic's "relation" to the Bible's "rhetorical ambiguities" depend upon that critic's theological assumptions. As a "unity," the Bible is more like a single "book" than an "anthology" of disparate fragments, and yet this same "unity" makes it a different kind of book than, say, Melville's *Moby Dick*.[15] The issue of what sort of text the Bible happens to be can have significant impact on how a rhetorical critic should approach God's ability to arrange the various arguments He invents, the specific focus of chapter 5.

Another basic question threading through this book is how different God's rhetoric is from human persuasion. This question begs another *Eloquence Divine* tries to address, the focus of chapter 8: how successful is God's rhetoric within the broad narrative arc of the Bible? While serious studies of the Bible's rhetoric have been written for academic readers, seldom has any critic set out to examine God's rhetoric as *rhetoric*, a rhetoric that may be approached and understood *internally*, from within the different texts in which these speeches and actions appear to persuade other biblical figures, following the basic, traditional parts of rhetoric itself—invention, the central concern for chapters 2 through 4, arrangement (again, chapter 5), style, examined in chapter 6, and the seemingly least applicable rhetorical canons, memory and delivery, explored in chapter 7.

This book, then, does *not* attempt to describe or analyze the historical and cultural contexts, to the extent they can be reconstructed, surrounding those texts which assign direct speeches and actions to God or Jesus, or to

---

as metaphorically gendered.

14. Warner, "Introduction," 2–3.
15. Josipovici, *Book of God*, 11–12.

speculate about the largely unknown writers of these texts or who these writers *actually* sought to persuade in writing them. *Eloquence Divine* attempts to examine what God and Jesus say and do for the audiences *they* address and try to persuade *within* the several texts I have selected for analysis.

Certainly, for the devout, the rhetorical success of the biblical God is beyond question and does not require any analysis, rhetorical or otherwise. Millions of Christians around the world believe in the biblical God's words. Many evangelicals seem to accept His language as indisputable, literal, inerrant truth, or believe God actually wrote the Bible which only some still may manage to read. Others believe in this God's truth, even though they do not completely accept the literal sense of every biblical utterance that God or any figure of the Bible makes. Even more, untold numbers of people from all walks of life, in every country, will have converted to some form of Christianity before this sentence ends.

For all that, some would castigate American Christians who have not bothered to read the Bible, much less to consider the role God's rhetoric may play in it. Stephen Prothero laments that, unlike European college students, their American counterparts profess faith in a God but do not really understand what they have so much faith in. In America, Prothero chides, "religious ignorance is bliss."[16] Prothero's own book begins by recognizing a central "paradox" for America's numerous religionists: as a nation, we are "both deeply religious and profoundly ignorant of religion."

Yet the rhetoric of the Christian Bible's God has been incredibly successful in drawing adherents for a very long time, a success certainly worth pondering for several reasons. First, human beings are not *always* the Christians they claim to be, for the very meaning of what it is to be a "Christian" remains as contentious as ever, as contentious perhaps as what "rhetoric" or "rhetorical criticism" means. Evil and suffering have not disappeared from the world; and other religions, with other views of God, still compete with the image of the biblical God widely shared among America's devout, regardless of how familiar they are with the Bible in which He appears or how inerrant they believe the Bible to be. More complications arise from there being different versions of this God and His truth among various Christian denominations, versions somehow gleaned from the Bible, or different versions of the Bible, or from sermons and homilies based on these versions, or from cultural depictions and portrayals of God and Jesus, popular and otherwise. Adding to these complications, meanwhile, are those skeptics and atheists who vie for their share of attention in the public discourse about

---

16. Prothero, *Religious Literacy*, 1.

religion, and who employ their own rhetoric to denigrate belief in *any* god, Christian or no.

God has been provocatively treated as the central literary protagonist of the Hebrew Bible.[17] Jesus, too, has also been treated as a literary character.[18] And while indebted to these and other studies of the Bible, literary, historical, and rhetorical, this book's scope is both narrower and broader in its attempt to examine the rhetoric *used* by the God who appears so pervasive in American culture—that God who speaks and acts as the primary agent within the wide, narrative contours of the Bible so many Americans accept as sacred. In other words, whatever this God may mean or be to any Christian, and irrespective of His ontological status as "real" or "fictional," *Eloquence Divine* attempts to consider God *as a rhetor*, as the divine agent who persuasively and eloquently intervenes in the world, and in the worlds of other figures in the Bible through His speeches and actions. This perspective of God obviously depends upon a metaphor, not as a figurative device, but as a way to probe the advantages and limits of such an approach, a heuristic to explore how far a "rhetorical" analysis of this God's speeches and actions can go. In offering this rhetorical view of God, I certainly do not intend to challenge the faith of the devout or aid and comfort skeptics and non-believers. I offer this book as one, albeit tentative, way to examine God's eloquence for what that examination may tell us about Him as much as what it may tell us about our own, merely human eloquence.

Eloquence Divine, then, attempts to fill, or help to fill, a notable gap in what other rhetorical critics of the Bible have so far attempted. As a rhetorical critic, I claim *no expertise* in the ancient languages in which the Bible was written or in the social, political, or historical contexts that surround this many-layered text. Because of these admitted deficiencies, I am certain that I have not lived up to the recommendations that some rhetorical critics of the Bible have outlined and endorsed.[19] Instead, I focus on the Bible most Americans have grown up with and what God says and does *in* that Bible. I do, of course, selectively draw upon those biblical specialists and historians as well as other biblical rhetorical critics for their knowledge and insights in analyzing the various dimensions of God's rhetoric. But this book is largely about and based on what God and, later, Jesus are shown to be arguing in the English Bible we now have, not its historical sources, the ancient languages

---

17. See Miles, *God*.

18. See Bloom, *Jesus and Yahweh*. Like Miles, Bloom treats God as well as Jesus as literary protagonists.

19. For these recommendations, see Trible, *Rhetorical Criticism*, 91–106.

of those sources, or the rhetorical aims of whoever wrote the different texts unified as one Bible.

Those in the humanities, educators and their students, graduates and undergraduates, interested in rhetoric, persuasive language, religion, and the Bible are the ones most likely to be interested in this book's explorations. The chapters ahead attempt what so far as I know has not yet been attempted—a candid examination of the biblical God's rhetoric in as many facets as the canon of rhetoric invites—in the hope that readers, whatever their beliefs or theoretical preferences, can gain greater understanding of how one, fairly popular version of God strives through His eloquence to affect His human audiences in the Bible.

For some Christians, and perhaps for some atheists and agnostics, even to refer to the biblical God *as a person* is already to indulge in the anthropomorphic fictions that the Bible has propagated for centuries to influence the imaginations of the American public. Yet to see the biblical God *as a rhetor* cannot possibly evade or ignore the presumption of God's *personhood*, since that quality remains very much embedded in the popular imagination of believers and non-believers alike and since, to be the Bible's central rhetor, I *presume* this God speaks, commands, argues, pleads, and tries to persuade those He addresses. Whatever else God may or may not be for any of us, He is *written* into the Bible and assigned speeches and actions whose rhetorical qualities I hope to explore.

To accomplish the primary goal of this study demands a selective approach. No biblical rhetorical critic should be expected to deal with *all* of this text's complexities or *all* that God says in it. So I confine my study only to some of the speeches God and, later, Jesus deliver—many of which may be familiar to readers even if they have not read the Bible—and some of God's and Jesus's specific gestures and actions. I focus quite specifically on the "covenant-rhetorics" God argues for, as well as His fairly frequent asides and soliloquies, speeches apparently addressed to Himself alone. However, I must *omit indirect speeches about or commentaries on what God or Jesus says or does by other figures in the Bible*—the speeches or writings of the prophets, say, and Paul's works. Even given this restriction, this study can only be illustrative and suggestive, not exhaustive, in scope.

To shape these explorations, I rely on the traditional division of rhetoric into its five major parts—invention, arrangement, style, memory, and delivery. Each of these parts or stages allows readers to see God's rhetoric from a different angle. They also provide an outline of the starting points for the various chapters of the book. With those parts in mind, I have tried to describe, analyze and, in some cases, assess those speeches biblical narrators have directly attributed to God. These traditional parts of rhetoric shape the analysis in each chapter while certain direct speeches of the biblical God and Jesus provide the textual focus.

By the end of *Eloquence Divine*, I hope that readers will have gained considerably more knowledge about God's use of rhetoric in all of this art's most applicable parts. If the Bible is "the most significant book in the history of our civilization," "[c]oming to understand what it is, and is not, is one of the most important intellectual endeavors that anyone in our society can embark."[20] One reason the Bible has been and remains "significant" is because of its rhetoric, the power of its eloquence. *That* rhetorical power, I contend, begins with the Bible's central rhetor, God Himself—how and why He argues as He does, when, and to whom. A study of this biblical God's rhetoric may affirm His special relationship to those who believe in Him; but, at the same time, it may underline how similar to and different from humans' His rhetoric can be.

---

20. Ehrman, *Jesus, Interrupted*, xi–xii.

1

Why God's Rhetoric?

Entitled to Trouble

The title and sub-title of this book draw together several incongruous, and difficult to define, terms whose very linkage may surprise some or perplex and outrage others. Despite the emergence of a more self-consciously modern rhetorical criticism as far back as 1968, and despite Margaret D. Zulick's effort in 2009 to outline various theoretical and critical approaches to the "rhetoric of religion,"[1] Wayne C. Booth observes that, prior to 1991, his efforts to locate sources that link "rhetoric" and "religion," "causally or independently," turned up only one author, Kenneth Burke,[2] an author Zulick also mentions as her first "fellow traveler" in academic studies of rhetoric and religion,[3] a traveler whose fellowship I welcome to this book as well.

Booth reports that his library's card catalogue had many sources on rhetoric, classical or modern, on "Religion and Science" or "Science and Religion," but only Burke's 1961 book, *The Rhetoric of Religion*, seemed useful to Booth's own effort to examine whether rhetoric and religion, however defined as terms, were "*essentially and constitutively* wedded . . ."[4] Booth concedes that while the library catalogue categories are by no means definitive, he believed that, as of 1991, "it [was] safe to say that most thinkers . . . ,

---

1. Zulick, "Rhetoric and Religion," 125–38.
2. Booth, "Rhetoric and Religion," 63.
3. Zulick, "Rhetoric and Religion," 125.
4. Booth, "Rhetoric and Religion," 63.

including rhetoricians and theologians," would "consider" the "question" he was asking "peculiar" at best.

The "peculiarity" of Booth's question intensifies if the terms become, not "rhetoric and religion," but "rhetoric and God," or "eloquence and God." My initial Google search of "God and rhetoric" a few years ago identified hundreds of thousands of items, but a cursory scan of the first few hundred of these suggested that most were largely concerned with the effects of rhetorical appeals to this or that deity, to the uses of "God" in different kinds of human rhetoric, some pious and inspirational, some more vitriolic and even violent. Only a few seemed focused on conjoining God and rhetoric per se. In many ways, perhaps, the paucity of relevant sources on the Internet is not entirely surprising. The words "God," "eloquence," and "rhetoric" are seldom heard in the same breath or found in the same sentence, unless it is to condemn or praise one over the other.

Scholars of rhetoric may agree with Booth that one reason for the paucity of sources is that "rhetoric," as a word and as a humanistic art, has had a confusing history, its "reputation" as a "subject" rising and falling over the centuries almost as much as philosophy's,[5] to which rhetoric is—and was—more often connected than to religion. That, at least, is how Booth saw the matter in 2004. In 1991, though, he argued that the "two slippery words" and "domains" of rhetoric and religion suffered "parallel" declines from the sixteenth to the early part of the nineteenth centuries, declines largely if not entirely precipitated by the rise and adulation of scientific thinking.[6] Yet, as I mentioned in my introduction, biblical rhetorical criticism derives from one of the Catholic Church's major intellects, Augustine, and re-emerged as early as 1968. Why Booth was unable to discover these beginning points, or was unwilling to admit he had found them, either in 1991 or 2004, remains a separate question I am not prepared to answer.

It is certainly true that, as a term, "rhetoric" is almost always negatively charged in the minds and speech of those outside its rich, diverse scholarship. Even among those in the broadcast media, the word is often simply equated with "bullshit,"[7] and just as often used as the weaker term in such popular binaries as "rhetoric/reality," "rhetoric/action," "rhetoric/fact," or "rhetoric/reason (rationality)." So, except for a handful of scholars and critics, quite a few people believe, if they will not openly say so, that "rhetoric," or Cicero's grander synonym, "eloquence," are high-sounding,

---

5. Booth, *Rhetoric of Rhetoric*, 1.

6. Booth, "Rhetoric and Religion," 66.

7. On this point, see Tietge, "Rhetoric Is not Bullshit," 229; Fredal, "Rhetoric and Bullshit," 243–59.

WHY GOD'S RHETORIC? 13

pompous names for superficial ads or politicians' almost always mindless slogans or, worse, mindless speeches. Many seem fully unaware that debates over "rhetoric's" meaning and its value as an "art" and subject of study trace back as far as Plato, if not before.

"God," of course, remains a gloriously ambiguous word whose most ancient etymology for Jacques Derrida came from *deiwos*, meaning "celestial light."[8] But, as any candid theologian or historian of the Bible will soon concede, this etymology has by no means limited how human beings have thought about or imagined God—even to the point of insisting, often violently, that no images of God or even of God's prophets should be permitted, much less encouraged.[9] The ambiguity of the word, along with the various ways humankind has imagined "God," may very well be the reason, as Booth believed in 1991, that religion and rhetoric have followed parallel, descending trajectories, since any defense of a "God" as people imagine Him must resort to rhetorical, not scientific "proofs," for justification.[10]

No study of God's rhetoric, and certainly not this one, would or should impose upon itself the task of examining *every* concept or image of God human beings have invented. This book, rather, focuses on the biblical God, at least that version which has embedded itself in America's popular imagination. This God appears as a total, unified, omniscient, omnipotent personality, capable of speech, of assuming a commanding presence in many forms, as voice, as words, as text, as the Word, as theophanies, actual, perceptible manifestations of God's presence through lessor divine beings—angels, for example—and through direct interventions in and manipulations of the natural order of the world that scientists themselves seek to know and understand. This biblical God, along with His putative "son," Jesus Christ, whose historical existence so many believe in, dominates and appears to unify that vast array of stories, poems, genealogies, and chronicles that make up the so-called "Old" and "New" Testaments—Testaments derived from copying, re-copying, redacting, and splicing together different texts and oral traditions over centuries by the imperfect, human hands of various authors and editors, living in various locales and historical periods, to make what many take to be the grand narrative of the sacred Holy Bible.

The biblical God who emerges out of these textual layers composed by various and, in most cases unknown, authors—this God, whatever else He may be for believers and non-believers alike—does *exist* in and *as* texts

---

8. For this etymology, see Derrida, *Acts of Religion*, 46.

9. For a useful, and readable, introduction to the changing concepts and images of God across Christianity, Judaism, and Islam, see Armstrong, *History of God*.

10. Booth, "Rhetoric and Religion," 71.

that no one, not even the most hardened atheist or dogmatic skeptic, will be quick to deny as empirical givens. What this God does and says in this narratively shaped text of many narratives, of many disparate, non-narrative texts, will obviously vary from translation to translation, Bible to Bible, denomination to denomination. This study, though, will rely on the biblical God as He is shown to speak and act in the Revised Standard Edition of the Bible, based as it was on the King James Bible, based it was on earlier English Bibles, the Geneva and Bishop's Bible, reaching back to William Tyndale's monumental, if incomplete and controversial, translations of the Old and New Testaments.

This God has been inferred for centuries by many people from the various uses of the word in the many different texts that biblical scholars and historians have studied. In those texts, clearly, "God" has different meanings and evokes a variety of images and metaphors—so much so that, from a strictly historical-textual perspective, no one, unified deity can really be identified in the Bible itself, much less a single, unified narrative in which this God can be said to participate. Yet that is not the "God" that most people say they believe in or say they even doubt or deny. That "God" is seen, rightly or wrongly, as a *person*, the predominate actor in the "story" the Bible supposedly tells. It is this "God" that constitutes the focus of this book, the God who speaks and acts *as if* He is a rhetor.

If this God, among many others, and this God's rhetoric, is to be explored, what is to be meant by "rhetoric" when applied to His speeches and actions? What definitional criteria may be justifiably applied to this God, and does considering Him as the primary rhetor of the Bible diminish or otherwise denigrate His divine status? These are difficult questions certainly, but they cannot be avoided in a book such as this.

Certainly, as I have already said, part of the difficulty arises from largely pejorative views of *rhetoric* itself and the many ways "rhetorical criticism" has been defined and practiced. These pejorative views have been a legitimate part of rhetoric's long history as a humanistic art of study, going back to Plato's famous attacks. Scholars of rhetoric would probably be the first to admit that these negative views are not entirely to be ignored; and, for all that scholars have argued or will argue to the contrary,[11] the negative coloring cannot be so easily bleached away because it persists even now.[12]

---

11. Tietge, "Rhetoric Is not Bullshit," 229–40; Fredal, "Rhetoric and Bullshit," 243–59.

12. This linkage can still be found in Frankfurt's popular little essay, *On Bullshit*, 16–19. Frankfurt goes on to refine his definition of "bullshit" as a blatant "lack of connection to a concern with truth . . . this indifference to how things really are . . . the essence of bullshit," 33–34.

In fact, one of the reasons it is possible to *know* that rhetoric has a *history* as a subject may be because its meaning and value have changed over the centuries, and because various theorists and historians have debated over these changes, and have used rhetoric in these debates, regardless of their positions on the art itself.

Toward a Working Definition of "Rhetoric"

Even so, it would be foolish to try to explore the biblical God's rhetoric without at least a working definition for this word as it will be used in the chapters ahead, and without justifying each part of that definition. Few scholars of rhetoric, or even religious rhetoric, will think the definition below seems particularly novel or "original," since it has been largely derived from rhetoric's lengthy and various traditions, classical and contemporary. In the pages ahead, then, "rhetoric" will refer to *any verbal, visual, or material means, or any combination of these, selected to influence, affect, or change another's actions, attitudes, or beliefs, including violence or threats of violence.*[13] "Rhetorical criticism," based on this definition, refers to *any critic's efforts to describe, analyze and, where possible, assess the means human rhetors adopt to achieve these ends.* As should become clear below, neither the definition of "rhetoric" nor "rhetorical criticism" assumes a necessarily insuperable dichotomy between intentionally affective ends and the means, logical, affective,, stylistic, or otherwise, chosen to try to accomplish those ends.

Both definitions, admittedly, apply to only *human* rhetoric, even though some theorists would likely insist that rhetoric's *essential* meaning as an "art" *must exclude* violence, threats of violence, or other means—money, sex—to force or impose influence, affect, or change on human beings.[14] This insistence is not without compelling justifications. Violence or its threat significantly deviates from the long-standing belief that rhetoric's "art" consists in a human rhetor's finding and inventing reasons to convince or persuade one or more people. There is little "art" in getting a spouse to agree with one's views on extra-marital sex if a shotgun is being held to that spouse's head. In such a case, the shotgun renders the need to offer reasons and evidence otiose. Similarly, there is little to no "art" in forcing a group of people

---

13. This definition derives primarily from Burke's *Rhetoric of Motives*, 43, and Booth's *Rhetoric of Rhetoric*, xi, though neither included violence in their definitions. Further citations to Burke's *Rhetoric of Motives* are to the 1969 reprint.

14. This seems to be Booth's position in *Rhetoric of Rhetoric*, xi. It is also Perelman and Olbrechts-Tyteca's view in *New Rhetoric*, 55. Further citations to Perelman and Olbrechts-Tyteca's *New Rhetoric* are to the 1969 reprinted translation.

or an entire nation to do another nation's bidding if the aggressor nation's military, armed with superior weaponry, seeks to impose its will rather than attempting to use verbal means to persuade.

Many scholars of rhetoric are likely to assume that the "artistry," the "eloquence," in what a speaker or writer argues, lies, to use Kenneth Burke's word, in "inducing" people to do a rhetor's bidding without "forcing" them upon threat of harm or annihilation.[15] This distinction, between persuasion and coercion or force, has been maintained at least since Aristotle separated "artistic" or "artificial" proofs from "inartistic," "inartificial" ones.[16] Basically, then, as an "art," rhetoric has depended on *more* than a person's or group's insistence on being right on this or that issue while everyone else is wrong. For rhetors, inducing human beings to believe or act has always required more than mere insistence, even when brandishing weapons of violence or threatening violence, and more than the audible volume of the words used to insist on compliance or obedience. It takes much more than simply having and expressing an "opinion" on some urgent matter. What that "more" *is* is, in fact, rhetoric's "art." Readers or auditors must, however, be *free to resist* a rhetor's arguments and appeals, or even a rhetorical critic's analyses and descriptions of these, no matter how adept a speaker or writer or critic may be, and no matter how well-armed for possible violence. That freedom, too, is *essential* to rhetoric's art. Resisting a machine gun, obviously, may be lethal. But some do resist, so even direct violence is not always persuasive against every one.

Aristotle, it must be remembered, judged an argument "inartistic" if it was, say, based on evidence elicited through "torture."[17] Arguments based on evidence from torture was to Aristotle "inartificial" because these arguments did not require from rhetors much in the way of intellectual and verbal resources to be invented. Evidence from torture or eyewitnesses does not demand a rhetor *make* anything at all; and for Aristotle arguments were, in the end, *humanly made constructs*. Arguments from torture evidence and from witness testimony remained *parts* of Aristotle's rhetoric. But these parts had little to do with rhetoric's "art." Oddly, Aristotle does not explicitly mention violence or the threat of violence as a means to convince and persuade an audience.

Yet the proposed working definitions of rhetoric and rhetorical criticism above cannot realistically exclude violence or threats of violence, just

---

15. Burke, *Rhetoric of Motives*, 43.

16. Aristotle, *"Art" of Rhetoric*, trans. Freese, 1.ii.14, ii.2. Further references are to this translation.

17. Aristotle, *Rhetoric* 1.ii.14, ii.2.

as it cannot exclude torture, if rhetoric's *full range* of persuasive resources are to be included within its meaning, and if a critic of rhetoric is to describe and analyze those resources. This recognition has certainly not escaped attention.[18] So it seems at least plausible that Aristotle might have considered violence, or threats of violence, as "inartificial" proofs that a rhetor *could use* to convince and persuade an audience if all other means had failed.

Certainly, this working definition of rhetoric highlights "artificial" proofs, much as Aristotle and many other theorists of rhetoric have. However, a more comprehensive view of rhetoric cannot *completely rule out* "inartificial" proofs—like confessions from torture or even actual, imminent violence. The historical record of the human species would rise up to contradict such exclusions, and the challenge would certainly be justifiable. Human history shows all too well that violence or its threat has been—and will continue to be—used to convince and persuade those who refuse to bend to other means of persuasion. The six gun thought to have tamed the American West was often called "the old persuader" for this very reason. Weaponries of all kinds, whatever their advertised purposes, have been invented and justified precisely for the explicit or implicit purpose of persuasion.

So human rhetoric, according to the proposed definition, *does*—and *often must*—include inartificial proofs, including violent acts and or threats of the same, so that it may at least pass a basic "reality" test. Threatening harm or annihilation often appears rhetorically motivated, so persuasion, even if predicated on an audience's freedom to resist or ignore a rhetor's artistic arguments, can blur into coercion so that there is scant space between them. Human rhetors and, as I will later show, the biblical God, may resort to violent force or its threat to accomplish persuasive aims. Rhetoric seems perfectly capable of inflicting both symbolic and actual harm against human beings, and it would seem overly naïve to suggest otherwise.

Both violent rhetoric and rhetorically motivated violence, then, seek to persuade by force. Each desires to subdue whoever or whatever resists what is claimed and argued. That much admitted, it is certainly possible that an audience may still risk resistance. This audience may be destroyed in the process, but it may also choose to fight back, to meet rhetorically charged violence with its own rhetorically charged counter-violence. An audience may also choose to surrender to the rhetoric of violence. Or it may allow itself to be harmed or destroyed rather than be coerced to do or believe what a rhetor desires. Just as human history does not lack examples of wars and insurrections driven by rhetorical motives, so it also does not lack examples

---

18. On this point, see Fish, "Doing What Comes Naturally, 517; Hunter, "Considering Issues of Rhetoric and Violence," 2–8; Foley, "*Peitho* and *Bia*," 173–81.

of individual or collective martyrdom whose choice of self-sacrifice has rhetorical motives of its own. In either case, an audience *still chooses* what it will do when facing violent rhetoric or the rhetoric of violence. Fighting back and self-sacrifice remain as choices. So, in the end, no rhetorical act, whether driven by arguments or by guns and tanks, or both, can be assumed to be *absolutely persuasive* in its effects. A wholly persuasive rhetoric, it seems, remains an utter impossibility even if violence is permitted among its means.

The proposed definition, however, is intentionally and largely centered on rhetoric as an art using symbolic media to affect others. Not all rhetoric aspires to use resources artfully, since artless, shoddy rhetoric clearly exists, and some of its practitioners are often ready to reach for force and violence instead of arguments to achieve their goals when the artlessness of their rhetoric fails or its deficiencies are exposed. Nevertheless, my rather broad definition does seek to meet the criteria for a more "self-conscious" rhetorical criticism of the Bible emphasized by a number of scholars.[19] That is, in stressing the "verbal," symbolic nature of this art, the proposed definition acknowledges that rhetoric has traditionally centered on spoken *and* written language, often with no bright line separating the two since speeches were often written before they were orally delivered. But that emphasis cannot remove or simply ignore other, extra-verbal strategies a critic may discern in any rhetorical act.

Further, in highlighting the rhetorical *intent* of a speech or a text to influence, affect, or change other people's actions, beliefs, or attitudes, my definitions would emphasize the deliberate use of verbal symbols for this purpose. The chosen purpose or intent seeks and hopes for the intended effect—conviction and/or persuasion—in the person or group addressed. *But a rhetor's intended purpose in and of itself does not and cannot guarantee in advance the effect sought, even if a rhetor resorts to "inartistic" means such as torture or violence.*

Human rhetors, by my proposed definitions, try to accomplish a purpose, to alter or change an existing state of affairs that can, in fact, be changed by rhetorical means (not all existing states would be subject to such rhetorical efforts). A conflicted state of affairs may arise in what people are doing or not doing, believing or not believing, valuing or not valuing, feeling or not feeling, thinking or not thinking. To use the word "change" is not to suggest or imply some "progressive" ideology being smuggled into this proposed definition. "Change" in and of itself does not *necessarily* imply "progress"; a change argued for may very well be "regressive." Additionally,

---

19. Howard, "Rhetorical Criticism in Old Testament Studies," 103-4.

a rhetor may argue to change an audience considering the adoption of some "progressive" proposal because that rhetor supports an even more "progressive" one.

Still, the definitions proposed do not limit rhetoric or rhetorical intent, today or in the past, to verbal symbols alone or to deliberate intentions. That, too, would be naïve and, for many critics of rhetoric, wholly undesirable. Human beings have many ways of reaching and trying to affect other human beings. They can construct images (static and dynamic) which imply rhetorical motives. They can make gestures with the same motives in mind. They may even project their rhetorical motives onto material objects, hoping to affect others through them. Almost anyone can think of a painting, song, or a movie that has affected her deeply, influenced her attitudes greatly, or even changed her mind. The rhetorical intent of certain hand gestures, too, may be seen on any congested freeway in America. And what would corporate capitalism do if it could not persuade consumers—or at least *believe* it persuades them—on what to wear, what to eat, what to drive, or where to live? In short, all that anyone can *buy and own* may reveal that person's own rhetorical motives, conscious or unconscious, quite apart from the deliberate rhetorical motives of those who sell these goods and services. The point is, efforts to influence and change others, and the means used for these purposes, *can no longer be limited to spoken or written words.*

Given the breadth of the definitions above, rhetoric's "art" would necessarily encompass a wide range of goals and strategies, from the honorable, noble, and beneficial to the dishonorable, deceptive, and unfair, even to the violent (see the diagram below).

Rhetorical Spectrum

+ + +	~~ ~~ ~~ ~~~	-- --- ---- -----
Reasoned arguments	Polemic　　Propaganda	Lies　Smears　Violence

The spectrum above assumes a relatively wide qualitative range, so as to include shoddy, artless rhetoric as well as violence or its threat, though this inclusion clearly departs from some scholars' definitions. Rhetoric's "art" certainly remains for human and, as we will see, divine rhetors *primarily* a symbolic (verbal or visual) medium, but that same art may sometimes exceed symbolic media and pass over into the "non-artistic," extra-symbolic strategies.

The left side of the spectrum acknowledges that human and divine rhetors would depend on rhetoric to solve problems, resolve conflicts, reach decisions, reinforce values and beliefs, and convince and persuade others to cooperate in achieving certain goals. But the right side of the spectrum recognizes rhetoric may also divide, enflame, and pit one person or group against another person or group. It may also try to "destroy" individuals or entire groups—symbolic destruction in the case of caricature, satire, smear-jobs, or character assassination or actual destruction in the cases of direct violence.

The large, gray middle of the spectrum (signaled by the wavy lines) suggests that both human and divine rhetors can advocate for a particular, partisan point-of-view not always heard or attended to (polemic). Ruling bodies (governments and other institutions of power) may further depend on rhetoric as propaganda to try to control persons, groups, or entire nations by presenting only that governing person or body's point-of-view as "true" while distorting, suppressing, or lying about any other opposing points-of-view.

Placing some types of rhetoric to the "left" by no means suggests a political ideology here, any more than placing others to the "right." Yet some may wonder why the diagram is a *spectrum* rather than a hierarchical flow-chart, with the more benign types of rhetoric at the top and descending downward, toward lies, smear-tactics, and violence. Such a hierarchical arrangement is certainly implicit in the spectrum as well as in my working definitions of rhetoric and rhetorical criticism. While I readily concede these points, the shape of a spectrum simply allows for the theoretical possibility of fully justifiable violent rhetoric or the rhetoric of violence.[20] The spectrum must acknowledge the necessary threats of violence, and weapons of violence embodied in military and police forces charged with maintaining law and social order without which modern nation-states could not exist. The actual and possible excesses of violence or violent rhetoric as rhetorical strategies do not and cannot preclude or render illusory valid uses of these strategies in such circumstances that would threaten a state's existence or the existence of its population. A similar point could be made about revolutionary violence or counter-violence that may result from unjust excesses of state-sponsored violence.

Human beings adapt their rhetorical intentions and means according to the situations and the person or persons to be affected. Human rhetors

---

20. See Arendt's important work on this point, *On Violence*.

can focus on one person, as the biblical God often does, or a large group, as that God also does, though less frequently. Human rhetors may even address their arguments to themselves, as the biblical God does as well. Wherever and whenever conflicts, tensions, or uncertainties exist or arise about what humans *should* think, feel, believe, or do about any given issue, rhetoric soon emerges and can spread across the spectrum, from reasoned argument to more debased, artless forms. In some cases, a rhetor may even have to *invent* the conflicts, tensions, and uncertainties that require argumentation. In other situations, the conflicts and tensions are on-going, emerging then abating, only to re-emerge again.

As later chapters will show, the conflicts and uncertainties that typically and necessarily lead human beings to *invent* rhetoric are, in the biblical God's case, much harder to discern and elucidate. The "issues" or "controversies" that emerge out of human conflicts, by definition, assume *two or more* opposing ways to think, feel, or act about any decision on any state of affairs. Such issue-driven rhetoric may be expected once the biblical God can address an audience other than Himself, but even His rhetoric invented to address human others does not always yield easily to rhetorical analysis of what issues may prompt that rhetoric.

Human rhetoric may take many forms, from written arguments and opinion-articles, to advertisements, cartoons, to direct mail, e-mail, billboards, fliers, blogs, and websites—all the way down to the clothes worn or gestures made. Even scientists, often hostile to rhetoric in any form, rely on rhetorical strategies to persuade their colleagues of findings and conclusions.[21] Various institutionalized religions have for a very long time exploited multi-media forms to promote and support the various deities they worship. Yet, while the rhetoric of the biblical God relies predominately on "artistic" proofs, spoken or written, in His attempts to argue and persuade, this same God, as the chapters ahead show, will also turn to violence or threats of violence and to theophanies, physical but indirect manifestations of His power and control, to try to achieve His goals.

Readers may wonder, of course, why my working definitions of rhetoric and rhetorical criticism make no mention of "truth," either as an end or goal, or as an ideal that rhetors should aspire to reach in what and how they argue. To be sure, the question of "truth" has never been far from

---

21. For the considerable degree to which scientists depend on rhetoric, see Ziman, *Real Science*, 251–53; Swales, *Genre Analysis*, 112, 124–27; and Gross and Levitt, *Higher Superstition*. Graduate programs in rhetorical study at some universities also offer courses in what is often called "the rhetoric of science and technology." For some sense of this subdivision of rhetoric, see Harris's *Landmark Essays on Rhetoric of Science*, and Gross and Gurak's "The State of Rhetoric of Science and Technology," 241–351.

any definition of rhetoric, at least since Plato's famous critiques. Further, it is certainly reasonable to expect "truth" to be important to any study of God's own rhetoric. Yet "truth," when it comes to rhetorical criticism of the Bible, remains "notoriously elusive."[22] It is no easy task to decide what sort of truth-criteria may or should be applied to any given human rhetorical claim, be that claim philosophical, mathematical, historical, and so forth.

Debates over what sort of truth-criteria should be used has been ongoing in the newly emerging field of argumentation theory and informal logic. For a very long time, logical validity and "objective" knowledge have been invoked as the best criteria for judging arguments, at least until argumentation theories introduced what some consider to be a far too "relativistic" criterion of audience-acceptability.[23] Yet, as some argumentation theorists have observed, even if an audience finds a rhetor's premises and conclusions "acceptable," and even if a theorist embraces acceptability as a more humane, socially and historically sensitive criterion, that theorist has already likely presupposed some kind of truth-criterion within what constitutes "acceptability" itself.[24] Thus, it may be better simply to maintain truth-criteria along with acceptability-criteria in judging arguments, so long as a theorist allows for "degrees of truth" in a rhetor's individual premises and conclusions. This problem will re-emerge fully in chapter 8, on judging God's rhetoric *as* rhetoric.

Yet rhetorical discourse, as defined above, encompasses more than the premises and conclusions expected to constitute the most basic kind of argument. Appeals to logos, to human reasoning, have never completely dominated conceptions of rhetoric. Even Aristotle's classical treatment of the art allows for other persuasive appeals, since Aristotle, unlike his teacher, was fully aware that a rhetor sometimes had to argue what was probably true or what an audience would accept as probably true, since the absolute truth in some cases was impossible or too time-consuming to discover.[25]

When a critic tries to examine rhetorical persuasion in the Bible, however, the question of truth-criteria becomes even more complicated, and complicated further still if the rhetorical persuasion a critic seeks to describe and analyze belongs to God Himself. These complications can be seen in the differences between historical criticism's notion of biblical truth and rhetorical criticism's notion of that same truth, however that criticism

---

22. Warner, "Introduction," 5–6.
23. On these debates, see Boger, "Subordinating Truth," 187–238.
24. Johnson, *Manifest Rationality*, 195–98.
25. Aristotle, *Rhetoric* 1.i.11–14, ii.3–8.

is understood and practiced.²⁶ Yet a rhetorical critic, regardless of approach, would do well to consider "biblical texts" as "live options" whose "persuasive strategies" could be treated as "undercutting those texts avowed or implied concern with truth" or as "mutual reinforcement" of that truth.²⁷ Much would depend, then, not only on the biblical text selected for rhetorical analysis but the specific persuasive strategies adopted in that text. That at least will be the principle guiding the approach to the "truth" of God's rhetoric in this book.

So What's Rhetorical about God?

So far, I have tried to explain and justify the various parts of the proposed, and deliberately broad, definition of rhetoric as a human "art," and rhetorical criticism's responsibilities to analyze and, if and where possible, to assess this art. I have also suggested that parts of the definition apply as much to human rhetoric as to the biblical God's, suggestions to be explored in the pages ahead. Yet, while some may agree with much that has been said about the art of *human* rhetoric and *human* eloquence, they may not be so quick or eager to agree that rhetoric has anything to do with the biblical God. As countless believers would insist, God, though imagined as a person, an agent, is definitely *not* human. So how, they may wonder, can even this admittedly sweeping definition of human rhetoric ever apply to the oxymoronically *nonhuman person* the biblical God is imagined to be?

This is certainly a reasonable question. In fact, it is one of the central questions this book tries to address: Do our ideas about human rhetoric, which have developed over centuries, have any bearing on the central divine being of the Christian Bible? If so, what sort of bearing?

Some have asserted that "*all* religious writing may be seen as 'rhetorical' in the sense that it [the writing] attempts to change behavior (and convince)."²⁸ From this assertion it would then follow that "the entire Bible is rhetorical, and biblical rhetorical critics can study the arguments of any biblical author to discern the means of persuasion used."

This book does not, of course, attempt to deal with "*all* religious writing" or the "entire Bible" or every "biblical author" in that Bible, assuming these authors are identifiable at all. Further, it may very well be an

---

26. For examples of these different views of truth in biblical rhetorical criticism, see Trigg, "Tales Artfully Spun," 117-32 and Kennedy's "'Truth' and 'Rhetoric' in the Pauline Epistles," 195-202.

27. Warner, "Introduction," 8.

28. Howard, "Rhetorical Criticism in Old Testament Studies," 103.

overstatement to claim that the entire corpus of all sacred works, all texts at least seen by those who accept them as "sacred," are rhetorical in nature even in the broad sense of the definitions proposed here. It may be more accurate to assert that all religious writing "attempts to change behavior" and "convince" those whose behaviors or minds, according to any given faith, need changing. But that purpose might more readily apply to those not already converted to a given faith, or those who, although converted, no longer comport themselves according to that faith and must be convinced to do so again.

It may be hyperbolic as well to claim a rhetorical intent, as defined above, for every part of any sacred text, including the Bible, or any author, known or unknown, of any part of the Bible. In some instances, it is impossible to know who the "author" of any given part of the Bible was, or even to recover much of the context for such an author. Further, whoever may have written some of these parts, and whatever the immediate context for any part may have been, there seems to be no compelling reason to limit the biblical authors' intentions to persuasion alone, since language in general, and biblical language in particular, may serve other intentions or aims, be they referential, expressive, or literary.[29] It is certainly true that the Bible, like any other sacred text, may be wielded as a rhetorical artifact against non-believers or believers of a different faith if perceived as threats. Yet this wielding does not automatically mean every part of the Bible or any other sacred text relies on the "means of persuasion" that rhetoric has sought to name and codify over the centuries.

In the pages ahead, my focus will *not* be on the persuasive means of any *one* biblical narrator or author, since it seems impossible to know with much certainty who actually recorded or imagined the speeches or acts attributed to God in the Bible. Such knowledge may never be available. What *is* available, however, are speeches and acts these authors *directly attributed to God*. The question then becomes whether a critic can usefully describe or even assess those speeches and actions as rhetorical in the sense defined above. To what extent are the verbal and non-verbal means the biblical God adopts rhetorically motivated?

In taking *some* (but by no means *all*) of this God's *direct* speeches and acts in the Bible as the focus of my study, I must assume that these speeches and acts, as represented in the textual *reality* of the Bible itself, are the work of many authors and many editors, all fully human and prone to be tendentious in the texts and oral traditions they worked from and pieced

---

29. On this point, see Kinneavy's taxonomy of discursive aims in *A Theory of Discourse*.

together into the "story" the Bible purports to tell. Scholars and historians have worked tirelessly to understand how the Bible that so many believe in, even if they have not read much of it, came into existence. The study offered here assumes the value of this historical and textual scholarship and relies on it in the chapters ahead. However, *this book makes no claim to contribute to this specialized scholarship*. I will not be weighing in on whether the Priestly Author or the J writer or the Redactor wrote this or that passage God speaks.[30] Rather, this book is meant for those interested in the interconnections among rhetoric, language, and religion, since they would very likely be the ones most interested in the degree to which the biblical God of the popular American imagination is, along with Jesus, the dominant rhetor of the Bible.

The limited space of one book on this quite vast subject, as I have said, prohibits analyses of the many *indirect reports* of what God says or does that can be found in the works of the prophets and others. Even this restriction compels a further one, since this study cannot dwell on or analyze *every* utterance God makes in the Bible. Some will be mentioned in passing. Others will be examined more thoroughly. Similar restrictions will apply to the speeches and actions of God's ostensible son, Jesus Christ, whose life and teachings this study will consider as the biblical God's last argument, His peroration as it were. There, the analysis will work from the Four Gospels of Mark, Matthew, Luke, and John, and not Paul's or other authors' efforts to interpret Christ's teachings or its history.

Various scholars and critics of rhetoric have already written about and analyzed many different parts of the Bible and the many different rhetorics adopted by many different Christian denominations—so many in fact it would be impossible to list them all. So, in an exploratory study of this kind, I mention some scholars and critics more than others because their insights are more clearly relevant to this book's focus and approach. Yet very few who have studied the rhetoric of the Bible have been particularly eager to examine God's own appeals, how He invents and elaborates them, arranges the case he makes from them, the styles He adopts, or whether memory and delivery play any part in His rhetoric. These are the classical, and sometimes controversial, parts of rhetoric as they have been passed down from ancient times to the present.

Yet no rhetorical study has made systematic use of these parts to understand God's own eloquent pleadings internal to the Bible itself.

---

30. See Friedman's very readable, informative but still highly speculative book, *Who Wrote the Bible?*

One might, of course, argue that exploring the biblical God's rhetoric through the lenses of traditional rhetoric is guilty of the same ignorance and negligence as those rhetorical critics who do not or have not drawn from more modern theories of argumentation.[31] These modern theories of argument have been seen as applicable to any kind of human reasoning and verbal communication and thus "are not bound to a specific culture." Yet some rhetorical critics maintain that it is best to study the Bible's rhetoric, since it embodies "ancient modes of reasoning . . . [,] in the light of Greco-Roman rhetorical tradition," even though it is uncertain that even the authors of the New Testament, much less the Old, would have been familiar with Aristotle's, Cicero's, or Quintilian's rhetorical concepts and terms.[32] Those who call for applying more modern theories of rhetoric to the Bible further contend it "is misleading" to assume *rhetoric*, *persuasion*, and *argumentation*, all contested terms, are basically interchangeable. This assumption can be refuted through "any form of argumentation analysis . . ." that shows these terms are not so easily conflated.[33] Finally, adopting more modern theories of argumentation to analyze the Bible would allow critics and scholars not only the ability to describe the ancient reasoning in such a text but also a way to assess the soundness of its reasoning and the degree to which biblical authors engage in fallacious arguments.[34]

These arguments certainly impinge upon and raise questions about the efficacy of the traditional canon this book assumes to examine the biblical God's rhetoric. By the same token, however, this book, despite its use of the classical tradition's names for rhetoric's parts, does not necessarily restrict itself to any one model of argumentation, classical or modern. As the chapters to come will show, God's rhetoric is by no means always fallacy-free or even always logical, if judged in the most basic human terms. In addition, the approach I take here allows for a broader recognition of the biblical God's rhetorical appeals, to His ethos, His listeners' emotions and passions, not to mention the styles He adopts for various purposes. In the chapters ahead, *rhetoric* is to be seen as a more encompassing art than the term *argument* or *argumentation* suggests.

However, one of the unaddressed advantages of the classical tradition of rhetoric, which also happened to be adopted by Christian thinkers like Augustine, lies in its reach. As an approach to God's rhetoric, it does not restrict itself only to His reasoning, His appeals to logos. As I have already

---

31. Thurén, "Is There Biblical Argumentation?" 77–78.
32. Ibid., 79, 81.
33. Ibid., 82–83.
34. Ibid., 90–91.

said, the biblical God is not reluctant to use "inartificial" or "non-artistic" means to try to secure His persuasive ends. Nor are His means of persuasion, His strategies, limited to symbolic media, to words spoken or written. Much will be said in the pages ahead about God's recourse to theophanies as a way to argue and persuade others.

Is Speaking of God's Rhetoric an Insult to God?

Is the approach taken here, by an admittedly agnostic rhetorical critic, certain to displease those more devout and accepting of the Bible's doctrines and values? That is by no means my intent. Even the evangelical faith of Pastor Dave Mallinak is by no means disturbed to conjoin the biblical God to the art of rhetoric. In a 2006 web-posting, Pastor Mallinak boldly asks his Christian readers to consider whether rhetoric is "Christian or pagan."[35] He is as well quick to condemn most of today's rhetoric—even "the rhetoric of modern Christianity"—as "very pagan," as "nothing more than relativistic drivel." Yet even he concedes rhetoric's inevitability, since "[a]ll men use rhetoric," even Christians.

The Pastor even argues that rhetoric was not invented by pagans like Socrates, Aristotle, or the sophists. It was not even invented by Adam, who spoke "artfully, even poetically" after God created Eve.[36] Rather, as he sees it, "God created the world with rhetoric." What is more, the Pastor adds, even before God created the world through rhetoric, rhetoric existed in God's mind, as does all of human history. Since "God used rhetoric, uses rhetoric, and demands that [Christians] use rhetoric," the Pastor calls upon Christians to "reclaim it" as "theirs by divine right" and use it to spread Christianity and to glorify God.

A very different response to the legitimacy of exploring the biblical God's rhetoric may be found in Eric Gans' 1998 web-posting. A French professor and scholar, Gans argues that linking God to rhetoric "does no discredit to religion."[37] Rather, "the association of God with persuasion through language provides an insight into the anthropological reality of both God and language"—"language" being the basis of Gans' own work in generative anthropology. To Gans, any attempt to reduce God to language—and thus to rhetoric—also subordinates language to God; for Gans wants his readers to ask what it is in human beings that makes them "gullible enough to accept the rhetorical appeal to God" if it is not "something

35. Mallinak, "Is Rhetoric Christian?" par. 2.
36. Ibid., par. 4.
37. Gans, "Rhetoric of God," par. 2.

inherent in the human use of language" itself. In asking this question, Gans urges his more secular readers to "understand God neither as Being nor even as Language (whether the divine Logos or the fetishized postmodern version) but as rhetoric," since "for believer and unbeliever alike, God is accessible only through the signs by means of which he persuades us of his presence."[38] In the most profound sense imaginable, then, and even from the "Hebraic perspective" of the Christian Old Testament, and its felicitous rival, the Tanakh, God's own "creation is a rhetoric, a literal speech act." God, as George Steiner phrases it, breathes and "speaks the world."[39]

As the next chapter will show, however, God's world-generating rhetoric is a more complicated idea than at first appears. Yet Pastor Mallinak, Professor Gans, and Professor Steiner all believe, obviously for different reasons, that God and rhetoric are not and never have been at odds, as words or ideas. All seem to suggest that to say "God" is to say "rhetoric" at the same time. While that casual conflation seems misleading at best, if writers so different in their own rhetorical stances and readerships, and separated by variable time-spans, can agree that it is no blasphemy to think or speak of "God," "eloquence," and "rhetoric" together, there really seems to be no compelling reason why the exploration of the biblical God's rhetoric should upset anyone open to considering this question and all that it implies.

In one sense, my exploratory efforts represent what Wayne C. Booth called for in 1991, and again in 2004, though not exactly as Booth may have intended—a "rhetorological" study. By this term as used in 1991, Booth had in mind the "comparative rhetorical study" of different human rhetorics that would "inevitably" lead a rhetorologist to "theology" and to the consideration at the very least of the God who made human beings "rhetorical creatures, ever attempting to increase our chances of critical understanding through symbolic exchange."[40] In 2004, Booth defined "rhetorology" (as opposed to "rhetrickery") as the "deepest form of [Listening Rhetoric]; the systematic probing for 'common ground,'" and described the "rhetorologist" as the person who seeks through listening to different, contrasting arguments the "often disappointed" goal of "mutual understanding."[41]

It is highly doubtful that Booth would have envisioned a book such as this one, since he had in mind the comparative study of two opposing, human rhetorics, both being grounded in God's speaking the world into existence. Yet, inasmuch as the biblical God's own rhetoric is sometimes

---

38. Ibid., par. 6, 8.
39. Steiner, *Grammars of Creation*, 33.
40. Booth, "Rhetoric and Religion," 71–72, 77.
41. Booth, *Rhetoric of Rhetoric*, 11.

WHY GOD'S RHETORIC? 29

at odds with human rhetoric, and inasmuch as this book hopes to show in what ways human and divine rhetorics overlap, *Eloquence Divine* seeks as well a "mutual understanding" through systematically comparing the biblical God's rhetoric to the system of rhetorical study as old as Aristotle, if not older. A rheterological study of this sort seems all the more necessary because Americans have lived through more than a decade during which time they have all witnessed the increasing, sometimes violent visibility of religions in our world, in our politics, and in our social institutions. It seems necessary, too, because, as human beings who use and are used by rhetoric, and who are in fact "gullible," even to Booth's "rhetrickery," scholars and critics are all the more obligated to understand the biblical God's own rhetoric, and how His uses resemble and depart from humans'.

The chapters ahead admittedly depend on "pagan" rhetorical categories—invention, arrangement, style, memory and delivery—not because they are necessarily "pagan" and therefore certain to offend the devout (though this outcome is by means assured), but because these categories have been and continue to be useful ways of analyzing human rhetoric. Applying them to a divine being who speaks and acts in the Bible may very well expose both the advantages and limitations of approaching this God as a rhetor.

Some think these pagan categories outline the "process" a rhetor should follow to produce an argument and achieve the desired effect (conviction/persuasion) on listeners. Others believe this rhetorical "process" also explains how writers produce any type of written text.[42] The extent to which these categories in fact do suggest a "process" that pagan rhetors followed when they prepared to argue in courtrooms, public assemblies, or other venues is certainly open for debate. So, too, is its extension into a general model of a writing "process."

Still, scholars of rhetoric have long agreed that invention, arrangement, style, memory, and delivery are and have been the received parts of rhetoric—a tradition passed down over the centuries, taught, learned, and followed by many speakers and writers, pagan and Christian alike. Even if

---

42. For those who favor identifying rhetoric and writing as a "process," see Murphy, "Rhetorical History as a Guide to the Salvation of American Reading and Writing," 3–12; Kinneavy, "Restoring the Humanities," 19–20; Lunsford and Ede, "On Distinctions Between Classical and Modern Rhetoric," 37–49; Young, "Paradigms and Problems," 29–47; and Arrington, "Traditions of the Writing Process," 2–4, 9–10. For more critical responses to this linkage, see Knoblauch and Brannon, *Rhetorical Traditions and the Teaching of Writing*; Knoblauch, "Modern Composition Theory and the Rhetorical Tradition," 3–4, 11–16; Sommers, "Revision Strategies of Student Writers and Experienced Adult Writers," 328–29; Halloran, "Tradition and Theory in Rhetoric," 234; and Arrington's analysis of these and other works in *Rhetoric's Agons*, 321–41.

the authors of the Bible, known and unknown, never received any training in or exposure to classical rhetoric, this fact would not necessarily mean they could not compose rhetorical speeches for the biblical God to make, or that these speeches could not be understood or examined in much the same way as other rhetorical speeches from human and "pagan" authors.

Again, how far these categories can assist us in understanding God's rhetoric remains to be seen and shown in the chapters ahead. In ancient times, a Greek or Roman rhetor could turn to the issue at hand to gain some sense of how to invent a case to argue. But how does the biblical God do that, as God? What sorts of appeals does He make to His auditors? Who are His auditors? These questions are the difficult starting points for the next several chapters which explore God's inventiveness as a rhetor.

2

Invenesis–Divining Acts

Senses of Invention

If we take God as the dominant rhetor of the Christian Bible, and if invention is the first canon for human rhetoric, then we may start by asking whether it makes any sense at all to examine this God's inventiveness. What issue would this God seek to address? What would prompt Him to find and make arguments and appeals, and to whom would this God make them? These questions would be plausible starting points for a study of a *human* rhetorical act. However, these same questions, if applied to God's first words in Genesis, confront many obstacles. In some important ways, this God would seem completely impervious to these very questions.

The title of this chapter, "*Invenesis*," is my own small invention—a neologism that fuses two closely related words, "invention" and "genesis." But, as a neologism, and however overly clever it may appear, the coinage's purpose is to suggest that the first book of the Christian Bible bears a title explicitly connected to the first part of rhetoric, and to my initial concern here—to explore if and how God invents arguments, if He indeed does. Genesis is not only the first book we read in the Bible as it is traditionally arranged. As almost any dictionary will make immediately clear, the name of this book refers to origins, beginnings, the initial acts of generation or formation. In other words, the Bible starts as far back as any book possibly can, just as the traditional first part of human rhetoric—invention—starts as far back as this art is usually taken.

As a word, "invention" is more typically associated in America with gadgets or machinery that fall under the aegis of science—or at least "applied" science. Yet, as early as 1925, Alfred North Whitehead recognized that the most dramatic invention of the nineteenth century was neither gadget nor machine but the invention of the scientific method of invention itself.[1] On this method of invention all other inventions depended—machines, medicines, space exploration, telecommunications, and, alas, military weaponry. Ways to invent all of these marvels presume science's careful, skeptical scrutiny, rigorous rules and procedures, and the method's quite powerful capacity to verify and replicate the same results quite apart from any scientist's beliefs, religious or otherwise. Yet Lewis Mumford would hasten to remind us that as early as the seventeenth century, scientists believed the invention of devices was their "duty."[2] In that century, scientists themselves certainly valued their dutiful inventions, no matter how useful or beneficial (in many cases, they were neither). Some, Mumford adds, valued such inventions so highly—especially machines—they became a surrogate religion.[3]

Most dictionaries, however, record a sense of "invention" more relevant to rhetoric, and to God's rhetorical inventiveness, than machinery. The *Concise Oxford Dictionary* explains that to "invent" means to "create by thought," to "originate." More pejorative meanings—to "concoct," "contrive," or "falsify"—follow the honorific ones. Even so, critics of rhetoric typically think of the English term as derived from its Latin and Greek cognates, *invenire*, and *heuresis*, "to come upon, find, or discover." The physical acts of searching, hunting, and finding, to which the Latin and Greek words referred, were eventually extended to describe more cerebral activities—the search for an idea or, in the case of rhetoric, for what to say and what to argue in response to any issue or controversy. Once "invention" became so extended into the cognitive and verbal domains and practices of rhetoric, it would be distinguished among classical thinkers as the "first of the five traditional parts of rhetorical theory . . . the finding and elaboration of arguments."[4] But what the God of the early chapters of Genesis says and does poses rather immediate complications for a critic who seeks to examine God's rhetorical inventiveness.

---

1. Whitehead, *Science and the Modern World*, 96.
2. Mumford, *Technics and Civilization*, 53.
3. Ibid.
4. Lanham, *Handlist of Rhetorical Terms*, 91–92.

The Up's, Down's, and Rounds and Rounds of Rhetorical Invention

These complications are the primary focus of this chapter; but, admittedly, some of them also happen to arise from how rhetorical "invention" has been defined, explained, and variously appraised over the centuries. Before we make any attempt to consider God's inventiveness in the Bible, it is important to consider, if only briefly, the fluctuating views of invention once it was appropriated to name the first phase of rhetoric's "art." To speak of "invention" as the "traditional" "first part" or "stage" of rhetoric perhaps does not account for or anticipate the many estimates of invention's value over the 2,300 years people have been thinking about this art.

Aristotle may be reasonably credited with making invention important, largely because it is so central to his definition of rhetoric "as the faculty [power, ability] of discovering [in other words, "inventing"] the possible means of persuasion in reference to any subject whatever."[5] "This," he emphasizes, "is the function of no other of the arts, each of which is able to instruct and persuade in its own special subject." Discovering all the "possible means of persuasion," however, seems a weighty, difficult goal at the outset for any human rhetor. Aristotle included within those "means" a rhetor's ability to identify what appeals a rhetor would need to invent—the well-known, often repeated triad of logos, pathos, and ethos. Not *all* of these strategies, apparently, had to be invented for *every* argument, since Aristotle understood that the means discovered to achieve the persuasive end could very well depend on the kind of issue a rhetor addressed, the kind of rhetoric (forensic, deliberative, or epideictic) a situation invited or permitted (the seemingly kairotic dimension of invention), the audience to be persuaded, not to mention the available facts—if there were any—for any *given* case.

Even though Aristotle explains all three types of appeals in his variously revised lectures on the subject, for Aristotle rhetoric's *logos* conspicuously remains the inventive core—especially a rhetor's ability to construct "enthymemes, which are the body of proof . . ."[6] "Proofs," or arguments, he further concludes, "are the only things in . . . [rhetoric] that come within the province of art; everything else is merely an accessory." Since Aristotle, such proofs have long been considered enthymemes, or brief arguments with a single premise and a conclusion drawn from it or inferences from accepted premises or from any existing evidence. These invented "proofs" were sometimes only *likely, not absolutely, true*, since an enthymeme often omits some

---

5. Aristotle, *Rhetoric* 1.ii.2.
6. Aristotle, *Rhetoric* 1.i.3.

part of the argument that a rhetor assumes an audience knows or willingly supplies. Yet the one exigent factor about the enthymemic proofs was they were not to be as complex as syllogisms, since a rhetor usually addressed audiences who would not or could not follow lengthy, complicated chains of reasoning.[7]

From Aristotle's perspective, then, the biblical God's rhetorical inventiveness would at least depend on His ability to invent enthymemic proofs, brief arguments. God, then, would be expected to make reasonable utterances, whether these utterances fit the typical form of enthymemes or not. For Aristotle assumes that rhetoric is *made*, that arguments are made; that what a human rhetor must have the power or ability to *make*—what in fact a rhetor *must make* if rhetoric is to be an "art" at all—are arguments, claims, reasons, relevant examples, real or hypothetical, maxims, and analogies. Citing witness testimony, relevant or existing laws, or evidence from torture confessions or manipulating an audience's emotions to support an argument—none of these rhetorical strategies requires a rhetor to make anything at all because these "inartificial" or "inartistic" proofs remain outside the internal, largely intellectual, artistry of making arguments.[8]

Obviously, we can reasonably wonder if anyone *before* Aristotle ranked the invention of such proofs so highly, or emphasized another view of invention entirely. Aristotle mentions "previous compilers" of rhetorical "arts," most now lost to us; but these manuals, he complains, "provided . . . only a small portion of this [rhetoric's] art," saying next to nothing about finding enthymemes or other proofs to convince listeners—the *inventive* core of rhetoric.[9] Instead, Aristotle's predecessors "chiefly devote[d] their attention to [such] matters outside the subject" as "arousing prejudices, compassion, and anger, and similar emotions" seldom connected to the subject argued.[10] Ironically, Aristotle eventually raids and loots those very compilers, spending many pages to explain how rhetors can appeal to different types of audiences' emotions and values. Yet it also seems fair to suppose that rhetors' passionate pleas would have to be "invented" quite as well as their logical proofs. A rhetor would have to discover which values and emotions to appeal to in each case, and to invent ways to induce others to feel these emotions or to consider weighting certain values over others.

Long before Aristotle emphasized a rhetor's invention of reasonable arguments, Gorgias had encouraged his paying clients, aspiring rhetors, to

7. Aristotle, *Rhetoric* 1.i.10–14, ii. 3–7.
8. Ibid.
9. Aristotle, *Rhetoric* 1.i. 3.
10. Ibid.

find and exploit the very powerful effects of vivid visual and verbal images. In his *Encomium of Helen*, Gorgias observes that soldiers may be routed by fear and desert a battlefield when they see a more well-equipped enemy.[11] This terrifying sight could make them completely forget the punishments they would otherwise have to endure for their desertion and cowardice. Likewise, a rhetor can make human beings yearn for a beloved person or place simply through conjuring a verbal image of that person or place. In fact, Gorgias's own definition of logos (his term for "rhetorical speech") famously highlights this art's verbal power to excite an audience's perceptions, emotions, and beliefs: "Speech [*logos*] is a powerful lord . . . [I]t can stop fear and banish grief and create joy and nurture pity."[12] Gorgias does not mention in this passage or in this speech whether a rhetor must *actually and truly feel* the emotion or passion he hopes to arouse in an audience. He also does not mention whether the values or passions invoked are ones the audience *should* hold. Gorgias believes, rather, that all attempts to persuade depend on a rhetor's ability to shape a deceptive argument. What matters to Gorgias is whether rhetors can get audiences to *believe* what they argue so their listeners will act as those rhetors desire. Powerful, evocative verbal images are precisely what rhetors needed to invent for whatever effects they seek to have on an audience.

As we will soon see, the biblical God invents such powerful images, including images of His own power, theophanies. Yet Aristotle's famous teacher, apparently disturbed by Gorgias's and other sophists' disregard for arguments based on knowledge, on rational truth, insisted on a rhetor's *knowing* such truth on any given subject to be argued. This insistence may explain why Plato has Socrates urge rhetors to become adepts at philosophy's dialectical method of invention—a method through which a rhetor could find the truth *before* arguing a proposition. Inventing—that is, finding—that truth was essential for Plato if rhetoric was to be classified an "art."[13] A rhetor had to determine what his audience knew and what they were uncertain about and then had to generalize from the dispersed, variable evidence he possessed to invent a true statement to defend. This true statement could then be parsed, divided, and parsed again, with each part defined and mutually supportive of the other parts. All *this* was, theoretically, supposed to precede a rhetor's initial utterance.

---

11. Gorgias, *Encomium of Helen*, trans. Kennedy, 46. Further citations are to this translation.

12. Ibid., 45.

13. See Plato's *Gorgias*, trans. Woodhead, 463a–c; *Phaedrus*, trans. Hackforth, 259e, 265a–e, 266a–b. Further citations are to these translations.

The God of Genesis's opening chapters should not need any such method to discover the truth prior to His utterances, since a defining trait of His utterances and His ethos is widely believed to be His own undisputed truthfulness. Aristotle, unlike his teacher, was not as sure if a mere human rhetor *had to find* or *could ever find* any absolute truth, divine or otherwise, before arguing *every* issue. It was often enough if a rhetor could simply find proofs that were probably or generally true.[14] This difference of opinion between Plato and his student does not entirely vanish in the centuries to come.

Yet, if Aristotle deserves credit for placing invention at the center of rhetoric, it was his Roman followers who elevated it. As a young man, Cicero wrote that invention was the "most important" of all of rhetoric's parts and devoted an entire book to it.[15] In his later work, *De Oratore*, Cicero emphasized how much rhetors had to know or find out before they translated their discoveries into an eloquent, fluid style.[16] Romanized Spanish teacher of rhetoric Quintilian also followed Cicero, his mentor, and Aristotle in emphasizing invention's value as the first canon of rhetoric.[17]

This value, though, did not go unchallenged. By the sixteenth and seventeenth centuries, some thinkers wanted to leave the classical past behind to follow the potentials and promises of the then emerging sciences. In the process, invention was reduced in importance or entirely stripped out of rhetoric's "art," eventually reduced from five to only two parts—style and delivery. Francis Bacon, often seen as one of the heralds of modern science, did not believe rhetors could be said to invent much at all, compared to what scientists could. Rather, rhetors merely recalled what they already knew to argue, hint, or insinuate.[18]

Crucial to this recall was the system of *topoi* or "places" wherein arguments could be discovered. Aristotle had already made a list of these *topoi*, general and specific, in his *Rhetoric*; and Cicero followed Aristotle's lead, making some adjustments to Aristotle's sytem.[19] Bacon, like his classical ancestors, saw some value in invention's *topoi*, encouraging rhetors to learn

---

14. Aristotle, *Rhetoric* 1.ii.14.

15. Cicero, *De Inventione*, trans. Hubbell, vol. 2, 1.vii. 9. Further citations are to this translation.

16. Cicero, *De Oratore*, trans. Sutton and Rackham, vol. 1, i.iv.16, v.17, xi.48–49. Further citations are to this translation.

17. Quintilian, *Institutio Oratoria*, trans. Butler, vol. 1, 1. Pr. 22, 3.ii.2. Further citations are to this translation.

18. Bacon, *Advancement of Learning*, 222–23.

19. Aristotle, *Rhetoric* 2.xxii–xxiv.2; Cicero, *Topica*, trans. Hubbell, vol. 2; Cicero's *De Oratore*, vol. 3, 1.2.xxxix–xl, 162–73.

them so they could discover what they should argue on different types of issues.[20] The *topoi*, it was believed, offered a systematic way to explore various controversies, specific and general, and to help a rhetor find which *topoi* could generate arguments from the issues and any available facts. The *topoi* did not supply specific definitions or classifications or comparisons: rhetors had to invent those. But they did seem to function as a system of prompts or cues for rhetors to look for definitions, categories, or resemblances if an issue and the given facts required these types of arguments. Accordingly, we should be able to identify and describe those *topoi* the biblical God draws upon to invent and elaborate any of His arguments.

Yet, if scholars accept Giambattista Vico's assessment, even this *topoi*-driven strategy was, by the early eighteenth century, in need of being salvaged from neglect. Instruction in how to use rhetoric's *topoi* of invention seems to have disappeared in many European universities. In his 1709 address to the University of Naples faculty at the start of the new school year, Vico will agree that scientific training or "modern philosophical critique" was important to students' intellectual development and their search for the truth in "the dark pathways of nature."[21] But he also warns his audience that too much emphasis on "speculative criticism" robs students of their chance to develop "common sense," "practical judgment," and their "imagination[s]"—all crucial if and when they addressed significant political and civic issues. To argue those issues, students must receive a balanced university education in the sciences as well as in "the practice of eloquence" (or rhetoric). And to nurture their imaginations and memories, students must once again be taught "[t]he art of 'topics'" which classical educators had valued but which in Vico's own day was being "utterly disregarded."

Vico's call for a more balanced university education, one that did not neglect rhetorical for scientific training, seems to have been largely ignored since, by 1979, some in higher education were vigorously calling for more theory and research on "rhetorical invention," including the classical *topoi*, so that teachers might help a new generation of students find and develop ideas to write about and ways to write about them.[22] In the centuries between Vico's call for reforms and the calls for more research in the late 70s, invention's value wavered, until it seemed to vanish completely from

20. Bacon, *Advancement of Learning*, 224.

21. Vico, *Study Methods of Our Times*, trans. Gianturco, 869. Further citations are to this translation.

22. Young, "Paradigms and Problems," 29–47. Other scholars, however, argue that invention did not entirely disappear in eighteenth- and nineteenth-century classrooms. See Crowley, "Invention in Nineteenth Century Rhetoric," 51–60, and her *Methodical Memory*.

rhetoric. Judging by some of the most influential textbooks on rhetoric of this period, many nineteenth century teachers—at least those whose thinking was shaped by Scottish psychologist Alexander Bain—were being told that invention *could not be taught at all*. Bain believed that those students learning to write, and those trying to teach them, faced the twin "burden of finding matter as well as language."[23] "Finding matter," as Bain put it, had long been the purpose of invention, and the topical system that Vico championed and hoped to restore.

Yet, over a century later, Bain was telling teachers, and presumably their students, that "matter" to write about must come from other "classes," particularly science classes. All any English teacher could expect to do was to help students clearly and correctly express the "matter" supplied from other subjects. In that same century, some rhetoric textbook authors would still insist that "invention" remained "the very life of the art of rhetoric," believing that students' writing might show "sensible improvement" if they had help with invention.[24] Yet many teachers seemed to have followed Bain's advice. They expected students to come into English classes already full of ideas and knowledge to write about from other academic studies.

Renewed interest in rhetorical invention had actually begun in America in the 1960s and early 70s. Some scholars even returned to and tried to revamp the ancient *topoi* of invention that Vico promoted. Some of these "heuristic" methods, as they were appropriately called, were soon translated for use in educational settings; but these pedagogical translations often ended up oversimplifying the very research upon which they were based.[25] As recently as 2008, an entire book was devoted to re-thinking invention, including different ways to understand the *topoi* in what was being called the "postmodern" era of rhetoric, while another scholar has even more recently argued that, by the 1980s, invention was no longer being theorized as within a rhetor's or writer's own head but, given the advances in electronic technologies, was being thought of as "externalized" and distributed so widely that no specific way to describe or teach invention as a set of strategies was possible.[26]

Such a view of the impossibility of instruction in invention strategies almost seems an echo of the Bain's attitude in the nineteenth century. Still,

23. Bain, *English Composition and Rhetoric*, 1146.
24. Day, *Art of Discourse*, 871.
25. See Hashimoto's thoughtful critique in "Structured Heuristic Procedures," 73–81.
26. See Muckelbauer's intriguing work, *The Future of Invention* as well as Lotier's, "Around 1986," 360–84.

it would be foolish to think that this brief narrative of invention's history captures the lengthy, complex debate over the value of this "traditional" first part of rhetoric. Invention is by no means a simple, uniform process, for rhetors, writers, or for those who teach them. Nor has it always been so esteemed as it was for classical predecessors. However, it seems beyond dispute that if invention does, indeed, encompass the finding or discovering and elaboration of what to say or argue on a subject, or how to find out what to say or argue through today's information technologies, it remains an essential phase for any rhetor or writer, past or present, regardless of what "methods" for invention were seen as the most productive at any given time for any given rhetorical theorist.

God—Inventor or Creator?

However, what may be *essential* for a human rhetor may not be so important to the biblical God of Genesis. Can this God, as He appears in the Bible, be said to invent at all? Consider the narrator's opening in Gen 1:1: "In the beginning God created the heavens and the earth. The earth was without form and void, and darkness was upon the face of the deep; and the Spirit of God was moving over the face of the waters."[27] Here, God's *first* act is meant to be seen as the origin of *all* acts to come. He seems to make everything in the world appear out of nothing, just like a magician who shows the audience an empty hat and then pulls out a living rabbit.[28] This analogy, helpful as it seems, may be misleading. Unlike the biblical God, the magician does not *make* the rabbit or the hat *out of nothing*, since both pre-exist the magician's trick as does the method for performing the trick, and all previous magicians who had performed it—so many the trick is now a cliché for any astounding feat.

The invention that human rhetors have been thought to perform resembles the magician's trick far more than God's generative fiat seems to. A human rhetor confronts an already existing issue or unresolved question, perhaps even a set of facts, so s/he must find, come upon, or discover what

27. All citations to The Holy Bible and corresponding annotations are from *The New Oxford Annotated Bible, Revised Standard Version Containing the Old and New Testaments*, ed. Herbert G. May and Bruce M. Metzger (New York: Oxford University Press, 1962, 1973). For highly detailed examination of the English and Hebrew translations of these opening lines from a biblical scholar who, while not focused on God's rhetoric, argues persuasively that the Bible can and should be read as a quasi-unified work, not a miscellany of different genres by different authors and historical periods, see Josipovici, *Book of God*, 53–75.

28. Burke, *Grammar of Motives*, 65. Further citations are to the 1969 reprint.

to say or argue to address the issues arising from these facts. In a very real sense, *some* or perhaps *all* of what is to be said or argued precedes, pre-exists, and is external to a rhetor's finding it, just as its finding precedes and presumes an actual rhetor to argue the issue. So, too, does a rhetor's audience, opponents, and the language, history, and cultural opinions and values they presumably share—all external *givens*. This is precisely why scholars refer to rhetorical *invention*, not rhetorical *creation*.

On this point, George Steiner wonders why "Indo-European languages allow, indeed solicit, the sentence: 'God created the universe'" yet "flinch at the sentence: 'God invented the universe.'"[29] Steiner quickly adds that "[t]he intricate play of differentiation and overlap between 'creation' and 'invention' has been little explored"—a project he takes on himself, though not in strictly rhetorical terms. This difference, however, has not been much explored as it relates to God's rhetorical inventiveness. So, whereas God's generative fiat may be seen as the most primal of all possible rhetorical acts, and has been seen as exactly that, by both secular and religious thinkers, it appears immediately and radically different from what a human rhetor does to invent an argument, so different we may wonder whether what this God says and does in the early chapters of Genesis can be described as rhetorical "invention" at all. Clearly not if a reader presumes God creates all out of nothing.

Finding All in Nothing, Nothing in All

If, though, the opening lines of the Bible are read *without this traditional presumption*—and some have read it that way—several possibilities emerge. First, at least God pre-exists the nothing and everything else He's described as making. So, too, does darkness, for there would be no other reason for this God to be shown calling out for "light" (Gen 1:3–5). The same could be said about the deep waters God divides (Gen 1:6–8). God's making of the heavens and earth, apparently, took place in the dark. Once He had "light," He names it "Day" and the darkness, "night" (Gen 1:3–5). The mere temporal sequence of God's acts in the Genesis narrative hints that the heavens and earth were hardly complete or perfect material. The earth was, the narrator explains, "without form and void" (Gen 1:1–2). But it, like the waters, apparently pre-exists and awaits God's initial utterances.

It has been suggested that, from the very start, the "character" of the God of Genesis confronts a reader of either the Hebrew or Christian Bible as

---

29. Steiner, *Grammars of Creation*, 16.

a palpable question mark. The God of both bibles has no history, no genealogy which might otherwise help a reader understand what He does or will do. These facts are, some think, what makes Him so radically different from other Middle-Eastern gods of the same time-period.[30]

If the biblical God is the central rhetor, He certainly appears unlike any other human who seeks to persuade another human. He seems to lack any controversy or issue to address, any "facts" that may suggest this or that *topos* of invention, and any audience to address other than Himself, since He has not yet invented any human beings. Consequently, when He speaks for the very first time, calling "light" into the world (Gen 1:3), God seems to be speaking only to Himself in a setting that seems beyond any narrator's ability to describe, so readers almost seem to be overhearing what God is saying to Himself while He works.[31]

As a rhetor, then, this God appears to have no obvious motive for His actions or His words, to the extent that His acts, words, or motives are even separable. Having no past, He does not make the world in response to other gods. He does not copulate with another god or struggle with rival gods to invent the world.[32] In the absence of other gods with whom He might be in conflict, the God of Genesis looks to be following His own moral impulses when He makes His human likenesses. Before that, though, God only needs to speak—or think—and whatever He wants is there, at the initial point of utterance, exactly as He wills it.[33] According to the anonymous narrator, He even *judges* what He makes as He makes it. The separation of earth from the seas, the generation of the stars and planets, the sun, moon, and all the animal life—each invented by verbal fiat, spoken into existence—all this God sees, readers are told, as "good" (Gen 1:6–24).

How the Genesis narrator *knows* what this God thinks of what He has made readers are not expected or invited to ask. Nor are they to wonder why God believes it is "good" for there to be something rather than nothing, or whether God was *utterly* alone before He makes the world. He seems to be all there is, except for the formless nothing out of which He makes all else. Yet it is possible to wonder if that formless nothing was *in* Him from the start. Some think that God's motive starts out "rhetorical."[34] But in what

---

30. Josipovici, *Book of God*, 56; Miles, *God*, 87.
31. Miles, *God*, 26.
32. Patrick and Scult, *Rhetoric and Biblical Interpretation*, 32.
33. Ibid., 33.
34. Ibid., 115, 32. Patrick and Scult argue that Biblical narratives are "rhetorical" in that God has been written into scripture as a divine agent intent on persuading His human likenesses to correct the imperfections they have caused in God's perfect vision by

sense it is hard to say, unless a reader infers that the issue before this God is precisely whether there should be form, substance, and order rather than the formless, disordered nothing. So, when He makes all from this nothing, whether that nothing is within or external to Him, He can be seen as praising Himself and what He has made to fill up the formless void as "good."

If the biblical God of Genesis has been added to an even older story of creation by another writer, beginning with chapter 2, verse 4, then the opening verses can be read as a rhetorical *narratio*—an introductory account to show God's power, especially the power of His words, His rhetoric. This *narratio* shows Him speaking directly, as the sole generative force, and this added narrative frames how one reads and interprets His highly human-like appearance in the Garden of Eden account—as a narrative "proof" for the initial assertions of His divine claims to universal authorship.[35] Drawing from Aristotle's rhetoric, a critic could even suggest that this additional narrative shows God inventing His own authoritative ethos. Still, in these early verses, questions remain. How does this God's self-addressed speech invent the universe, and is this speech as rhetorically motivated as His making human likenesses?

In his comments on Freud's idea of the human mind as a fractious "parliament" of different voices, Kenneth Burke refers to what he calls "self-addressed" rhetoric.[36] Classical and much contemporary thinking about human rhetoric typically presumes and emphasizes efforts to persuade an audience *external* to a rhetor. Yet Burke reminds us that a modern understanding of rhetoric since the birth of Christianity would have to include under the category of *audience appeals* "any ideas or images privately addressed to the individual self for moralistic or incantatory purposes." Human beings can be "very lax" or "very exacting" audiences for themselves. Even self-denigration, Burke remarks, can "on closer scrutiny" turn out to be a form of self-flattery.

The Genesis opening, however, suggests that we emend Burke, since God addresses Himself long before the "birth" of Christianity as such. As we will soon see, this opening speech is by no means the *only* part of the Bible where God addresses Himself as an audience. Yet, unlike Burke's description of self-addressed rhetoric in humans, God's self-address is not uttered under any kind of political or religious oppression that God, to avoid

---

following His laws and covenants and thereby recovering and sustaining the communal bond between God and Israel. For their full argument on this point, see 3–44.

35. Ibid., 113–14.
36. Burke, *Rhetoric of Motives*, 37–38.

repercussions, *must evade* through stylistic or any other type of subterfuge.[37] God need not suffer *any moral censorship* except His own; since He would be one immense, cultural resource for that censorship and for the superegoistic "rhetoric in all *socialization*, considered as a *moralizing* process."[38] Because the biblical God, like the Tanakh's, has no history, no parentage, and no rival gods who might shape or define His "self,"[39] it is almost impossible to surmise how "lax" or "exacting" this God is with Himself, or whether His speeches have "moralistic or incantatory purposes."[40] God's "self" does not seem to resemble Burke's conflicted, fractious "parliament." Nor do His speeches rely on terms and images arising from a "self" constituted by any "culture" or any physical body[41]—themes postmodern critics have, since Burke, variously explored.[42] So, whatever sort of "self" God rhetorically addresses is not really explicable in Burkean terms.

Neither is God's self-address explicable according to the comments Chaim Perelman and Lucie Olbrechts-Tyteca make about the rhetorical "conditions" of "inward deliberation."[43] Similar to ancient rhetoric's "model" of a speaker arguing to persuade an external audience, arguing with one's self presupposes a rhetor "divided into at least two interlocutors, two parties engaged in deliberation." In such cases, a rhetor may offer "reasons for his actions" to himself, conceived of "as an incarnation of the universal audience"—that is, all reasonable persons, present or not.[44] In his internal deliberations, though, God does not usually show Himself divided into opposing positions or interlocutors and, consequently, imagines Himself to be not only a "universal audience" but the author of all that is the universe.

If God's self-addressed rhetoric are "soliloquies," they further contrast sharply with Augustine's own ideas about such speeches, even though Augustine himself presumably coined the word as a "new title" for his "daring literary innovation," the *Soliloquia*.[45] Augustine invented his title by combining the Latin terms *soli* and *solus* with the Latin verbs *loqu* or *loqui*

37. Ibid.
38. Ibid., 38–39.
39. Miles, *God*, 26.
40. Burke, *Rhetoric of Motives*, 39.
41. Burke, "Words as Deeds," 168.
42. On this broad point, see Wess's *Kenneth Burke*.
43. Perelman and Olbrechts-Tyteca, *New Rhetoric*, 14.
44. Ibid., 30–31.
45. See Brown, *Augustine of Hippo*, 116; Cohn, "Outward Bound Soliloquies," 17–38; Hirsh, *Shakespeare and the History of Soliloquies*, 342.

to produce the common definition—speaking to one's self[46]—which, the *Oxford English Dictionary* tells us,[47] enters the language about a hundred years before the word was identified with stage practices for sixteenth-century dramas.[48] In *Soliloquia*, composed between 386–387 CE, Augustine developed a "rhetorical method" to dramatize his solitary, self-addressed thinking.[49] This work was a "significant precursor of [his] interior turn" in the *Confessions*,[50] his "first intimate self-portrait" of a "prolonged argument between [Augustine's] *Reason* and his *Soul*" to expose the author's "weaknesses."[51]

God's initial soliloquy shows no self weakened by divisions. He simply commands Himself to generate, to invent a world. Even so, some would rule out even this possibility for God.[52] If this God's earliest speech in Genesis consists of commands, imperatives aimed at Himself to bring forth the all out of the nothing, His utterances may seem quite unusual, if not aberrant. The command, "Let there be light," happens to be a quite eloquent English translation of two very brief Hebrew words in the Tanakh, *yhi 'or*, for which a better English translation would simply be "Light!"

This view of God's supposedly aberrant self-address, though, seems somewhat wrong-headed. All of us, I suspect, have issued commands to ourselves to perform some act or to decide some pressing issue. It is our way of urging ourselves, goading ourselves to do what needs to be or should be done. The shorter translation of the original Hebrew hints at the proverbial movie director calling out, "Lights! Camera! Action!" But these are commands a director utters to *others*, not to the director her/himself.

It seems not only possible but quite human that God should command Himself to make light or to separate the seas from dry land. Perhaps He orders Himself to perform these acts to make them happen at all, in the same way human beings often order themselves out loud not to forget a book or their briefcase as they rush toward the door for work. The biblical God of Genesis seems to need to call out to Himself what He wants to make. Perhaps He needs the words, the logos, to make the reality. Simply

---

46. Harper, "Soliloquy."
47. See "Soliloquy," *Oxford English Dictionary*.
48. Hirsh, *Shakespeare and the History of Soliloquies*, 324.
49. Staykova, "Augustinian Soliloquies of an Early Modern Reader," 121–22.
50. Ibid., 121. For Augustine's "inward" turn, see also Taylor, *Sources of the Self*, 131; Burke, *Rhetoric of Religion*, 51–58. Further citations to Burke's *Rhetoric of Religion* are to the 1970 reprint.
51. Brown, *Augustine*, 116, 111.
52. Miles, *God*, 26.

to name what He wants is certainly His most inventive act so far.[53] On this point, Burke usefully recognizes that naming's rhetorical function, to select and single out, is as essential to God's "personhood" as it is to our own, except that God's radically different personhood makes him a pure "super person."[54] This is why God solicits from believers both "negative" and affirmative hyperbolic terms that describe him as "immortal," "infinite," "impassive," or "eternal," "everlasting," "omnipotent," and "omniscient." It is why He is associated with the negative verbal command of "No" as a *"principle"* for his many acts. God's naming may be how He convinces Himself that He is the power that He is, that He is the omnipotent God many imagine Him to be, intent on proving to Himself that He has the power to be all there is.

Obviously, much is suggested by God's opening speech. Obviously, too, the narrator had to find some way to show this God making the cosmic stage for His human likenesses. However anthropomorphic the language, it places this God on the page as an "author" and a "rhetor" who calls forth all. Rhetorically considered, however, until He creates the first human, this God seems to be His own audience, and His inventive utterances and actions appear as self-reflexive, as His own uniquely articulated self-addressed *soliloquy*. There may be no real difference in these lines between His "word" and His acts, since the Hebrew word *dabhar*, and its root, *dbr*, mean both *to say* and *to do*.[55] If this is true, then it becomes possible to suggest that the initial *narratio* for the Eden story is the narrator's way to invent both God's own supreme ethos and the very rhetorical grounds necessary to meet and argue with His human likenesses in the chapters of the Bible to come.

Still, whether He orders Himself to perform these acts or simply announces them as He makes them, God's precise rhetorical motive remains elusive and difficult to describe with much certainty. This God cannot be shown to speak or act under any obvious necessity, since He would have to have invented that necessity. If this God's first act is to invent the world out of nothing, as many believe, His act contradicts King Lear's famous admonition to his most beloved daughter, "Nothing will come of nothing,"[56]

---

53. Burke, *Philosophy of Literary Form*, 4. Further citations are to the 1973 reprint.

54. Burke, *Grammar of Motives*, 80.

55. Lee, *Jesus and the Metaphors of God*, 111–12. Lee admits there is no consensus on what this Hebrew word means, but he does add that for the early Hebrews saying meant doing, or causing an "objective fact" to occur. Lee does not, however, see God's saying or doing as different "personifications" or "hypostases" of God, but different metaphors human beings have used to name "the modes of God's presence" in Hebrew life, 122. Like Lee, Bloom argues that this Hebrew word happens to refer simultaneously to "a word, a thing, and an act," *Jesus and Yahweh*, 155.

56. Shakespeare, *King Lear*, 1. i. 90.

Shakespeare's rendition of the Latin maxim, *ex nihilo nihil fit* ("from nothing, nothing is made").[57] The God in Genesis *seems* to do exactly that, make something out of nothing, even as the narrator's story asks a reader to ignore the darkness, the unformed earth, and the deep, roiling waters as "nothing." God's *ex nihilo* generation turns the Latin maxim on its head, so that it becomes a central paradox God proposes within His own earliest address, to Himself.

Biblical annotations to these lines try to provide some context for this paradox. The ancient Hebrews believed the world existed as a watery chaos prior to God's willing and speaking it into existence. The "deep" (Gen 1:2) may also be an elliptical way to refer to a mythic dragon with which God struggled and eventually defeated, referenced in the Book of Job (3:8) and in Isaiah (51:9). These annotations, helpful as they are, do not dim the puzzling effect of God's own self-announced, self-addressed generation of all out of nothing. Not only does the apparent practical reasoning of the original Latin phrase get turned upside down, so too does the entire idea of rhetorical invention, from Aristotle to the present.

In its most "traditional" sense, *ex nihilo* generation suggests that this God does not make anything in the way mere humans could understand. He does not start by re-shaping some primordial stuff separate from Himself, though this seems to be what He is doing. God simply says what He wants, and it *is*. Each part of the world simply arises out of nowhere with each divine thought uttered as a name, in His naming it. In such a case, God's rhetoric, unlike humans', is thought to be creative, *not* inventive—an idea that has led to a number of different explanations. Some suggest that, to our own limited human minds, God would first have to generate "nothingness" as Himself. In other words, before God establishes the difference between night and day, heaven and earth, He has to *find*—that is, as a rhetor, He has to invent—an opening in Himself (if He is indeed *all*), an empty space so He can generate all that He is or does.[58] Accordingly, He has to fall into the empty space He invents in Himself.

This explanation evokes God's omitted history prior to Genesis which has stirred many followers of Kabbalah to speculate about "the mythic act called *zimzum*—divine self-exile," wherein God contracts, inhales, and yet multiplies Himself. As Harold Bloom, following Isaac Luria, phrases it, "in order to create, God had to cut himself down."[59] Accordingly, God "has to

---

57. Mawson, *Dictionary of Foreign Terms*, 137.
58. Bloom, *Jesus and Yahweh*, 200–201.
59. Ibid., 204.

fall into himself (as it were) in order to get creation started."⁶⁰ To understand this idea, Bloom urges us "to imagine that every time [we] hold [our] breath, and then release it, [we] create and ruin another world."⁶¹ Bloom, following his Gnostic and Kabbalistic sources, thinks that a necessary "abyss" exists within God's will, because "without a negative moment in the act of creation, God and the cosmos would fuse as one."⁶²

Certainly, more traditional, Catholic interpretations of *ex nihilo* generation claim this is precisely the paradox of the biblical God, and an efficacious one. Accordingly, in defiance of both Kabbalistic or Hegelian explanations, God both *is and is not* the nothingness out of which He generates the reality humans experience as *being in the world*. His acts take place in the "realm of irreducible paradox" which we humans inhabit. In that realm, the solid world humans experience may persist (thanks to God as the infinite source of perpetual being) even as that world vanishes, changes, or becomes at times simply obscure.⁶³ Since God is "an infinite actuality," a constant being in the world's constant becoming, He can "radically originate the finite [world humans experience], without any preexisting finite principle, such as the Greek *hyle*, unformed matter."⁶⁴

The philosophical and theological complexities that this God's paradoxical opening speech poses are immense and perhaps beyond untangling. But, if we see this paradox from a rhetorical perspective ("paradox," like "oxymoron," being, it so happens, a figure of rhetoric), we can at least wonder whether God opens this "void" in Himself so that He can fall into it and thereby generate reality entire, or whether He finds or discovers the "void" from the very first moment He finds His voice and addresses Himself. This "negative moment" in God's self-addressed rhetoric might be phrased as an implied issue, "Am I all?" Or perhaps, "Should I be all there is?" This question would be God's primordial issue. In effect, He would not see His being All as "good," so He utters His commands and makes His All into everything else that can be which, then, becomes the "good" that the Genesis narrator has Him recognize and praise.

To become more than All would seem to suggest a simultaneous outflow and influx, whereby God would find the cosmos He generates in that part of Himself He opens. These speculations suggest that God had to become His own rhetor before the cosmic generation could occur, and to

60. Ibid., 206.
61. Ibid., 210.
62. Ibid., 211.
63. Milbank, "The Double Glory, or Paradox versus Dialectics," 136–39, 159.
64. Ibid., 149.

become a rhetor, God must at the very least acknowledge the issue of His own power to generate and invent.

In this light, it is perhaps intriguing to consider the poetic musings of Edmund Jabès: "God, before the Creation, is All." But "afterwards, ah, afterwards," Jabès asks, "is He nothing?" If His "All is invisible," then "[v]isibility is between the All and the Nothing, [and] everywhere torn up from the All." So, Jabès continues, "[t]o create, God placed Himself outside of Himself, in order to penetrate his Self and destroy Himself." Each generative act, then, diminishes His All. To create the "world," "the day and the night," "the animals and the plants," God must lose "the sky and the earth," "the stars," all "flora and fauna"—until He makes "man," after which He "was without a face . . ."[65] In Jabès' fascinating speculations, God lessens Himself with each generative word and deed. So, in sum, Jabès writes: "The creator is rejected from His creation. Splendor of the universe. Man destroys himself creating."[66]

These thoughts and their implications hover around God's rhetoric in the pages ahead. For now, it may be enough to surmise that God's own Allness could have prompted His internal, self-addressed rhetoric. His own solitary, all-powerful comprehensiveness generates His own internal will *not* to be all there is, or else why invent anything? Put another way, this God's being All is not enough for God *to be* God. All must be made into Many, each one of the Many different, separate, ordered in just the way God intended. As All, God is utterly alone, so His All has to be the raw material out of which the Many comes, to show to Himself the Many that His All, in fact, is. This sort of rhetorical inventiveness, in the end, seems far beyond any similar human effort.

Inventing Human Likenesses— God Finds Another Audience

The biblical God's initial rhetorical stance, however complex, changes from the moment the narrator presents His deciding to make a human being. Once again addressing Himself, this time in plural first person, the narrator has God say: "Let us make man in our own image, after our likeness; and let them have dominion over the fish of the sea, and over the birds of the air, and over the cattle, and over all the earth, and over every creeping thing that creeps the earth" (Gen 1:26). Here, too, many questions arise about

---

65. Jabès, *Book of Questions*, 224–25.
66. Ibid., 194.

why this God would make His first humans in His own image, and how His own image becomes "*our* own image, *our* own likeness," and how one "man" becomes "*them*"?

The troublesome shift to a plural first person pronouns may be the result of carelessly edited splicings of two very different stories. Biblical historians try to explain the plural, first-person pronouns of this speech by saying that the early Hebrew God, Yahweh, was one god to represent Israel among a clearly polytheistic "divine assembly" of other gods, ruled by the main god of Canaan, El, and "his consort Asherah," while Yahweh only later becomes the single God of Hebraic monotheism.[67] However all this may have occurred, the biblical God now commands His already made humans to be "fruitful and multiply" and has given them complete sovereignty over all that He has invented (Gen 1:28).

Yet the rhetorical implications of this command do not stop with biblical history. First, God *now* at least has invented an external audience for His rhetoric—an audience *other* than Himself, or an audience *other* than what He calls into being and names—time, space, light, matter. Second, this God has found—that is, invented—His human audience out of substances already invented. In inventing this all-too-human audience, and in granting His human likenesses authority over all the flora (with one crucial exception—the tree of the knowledge of good and evil, [Gen 1:29–30; 2:15–17])—and fauna of the earth, He is shown to be setting the scene for a narrative unfolding more explicitly rhetorical than anything that has happened so far.

As a story, a rhetorically motivated story, this God appears to want an *other-than-Himself* to hear Him and perhaps even argue with Him. This singular requirement may justify all of His rhetoric in the Bible's larger narrative to follow, all the way to the Jesus of the New Testament.

Even before He has made it rain, the narrator shows God shaping the man later called Adam from the mist-dampened dust and breathing into his nostrils what the narrator calls "the breath of life" (Gen 2:4–7). To make this human at all requires the dust and "mist" from the earth that God has previously invented. Moreover, He breathes into Adam not only "life," but the very power to name, a capacity for language, and for all future human rhetorical motives and efforts, inasmuch as humankind also "speaks, names and communicates" just as its inventor does, only now in a spirit of "mutuality and dialogue."[68]

God has, then, invented human likenesses who will likewise be inventors themselves. It may be that this God wants—maybe even needs—images

---

67. Armstrong, *Bible*, 16.
68. Wilder, *Language of the Gospel*, 14.

of Himself who make images as well. The human likenesses of man and woman, the latter made from the former, can obviously do this through reproducing, having children—hence God's command for humans to be "fruitful and multiply," for inasmuch as His humans produce offspring, the producing of these offspring mirrors God's own generative fiat. From this perspective, "the motive for all that precedes the creation of mankind is, ultimately, provision for that culminating act by which God creates another creator."[69]

Children, though, are by no means the *only* way God's humans can reproduce and invent as God seems to. God's own symbol-making capacities, to speak and understand language, would have to flow into His humans' nostrils as well. Those capacities extend and "multiply" the ways God's human inventions may be "fruitful," making Adam and Eve subject *to* and inventors *of* their own rhetorics. They are born rhetors, born hermeneuts (since they can interpret, misinterpret, and make symbols). A crucial distinction, however, between these human powers of symbolic reproduction and God's own power turns on humans' inability to make their verbalized thoughts or emotions into actual, physical realities. Human likenesses can make symbols of what they know, want, need, fear, or hope for. The God of Genesis—so it seems—can not only symbolize what He thinks or desires—light, say—His symbolizing actually reproduces whatever God thinks to want.

It seems, then, only half-true to infer that "God makes a world because he wants mankind, and he wants mankind because he wants an image."[70] God could have other motives for making humankind. But why precisely God "wants an image" of Himself remains an open question. Perhaps, contrary to what He later demands of His Israelites in Exodus, this God does want *image-makers*. He has invented *rhetors*, as He Himself is, with that one single proviso—human symbol-making has an inherent limitation which His own symboling does not. This proviso makes humans only "images" of His image-making, not identities, and *not gods themselves*. Thus this God requires His humans to follow that most troubling of all His early dicta: to be like, but not too much like, Him.[71]

At bottom, God's desire (or again is it His implicit need?) for images of Himself as a rhetor perhaps presumes an even more radical meaning. Some orthodox interpretations of God's motive for inventing a human likeness often stress the resemblance between the higher, god-like functions

---

69. Miles, *God*, 28.
70. Ibid.
71. Bloom, *Jesus and Yahweh*, 118.

of the human mind and God's own. This resemblance underlies "the well-known motifs of a human being as a deficient copy of divinity, of man's finite substance as a copy of the divine substance . . ."[72] This metaphor becomes even more complex if we consider a more fundamental link between God and human likenesses: "that God himself must also be not only an essential substance, but, as He is often imagined, also a person."[73] "Person," in this instance, does not necessarily refer to each individual's "personal idiosyncrasies, the quirks of [each human's] particular nature . . ." It refers, instead, to "the abyss of [each] personality." The darkest depths which humans can never really know—their own essence as a "person"—joins them to their divine inventor's own immense, inscrutable depths.

This shared abysmal personhood between God and His human likenesses may account for other resemblances between human "persons" and God as "a 'pure' person," except that, as Kenneth Burke sees it, a wholly "pure person" would, in effect, be "an 'im-person'" and, as a result, a "super person."[74] The "super," "im-person" of this God may explain why human likenesses, as has been suggested, often resort to "negative," rhetorical descriptions that emphasize both His "nothingness" (God is *no* thing like a book, a word, or a leaf, or even a "mind") and His association with the negative command of "No" as the "*principle*" behind His many acts.[75] These various links between person, super-person, and the impersonal may have arisen, Burke suggests, out of "[t]he Christian merging of Aristotle's self-enwrapt *eromenon* [the detached, unmoved Mover who created the universe and then withdrew from his creation] with the Creator Jehovah [Yahweh] (a tribal, tutelary deity made universal)."[76]

Even to say all this only brings us back to the biblical God's invention of human likenesses who, like Himself, flow back into language, and so back into rhetoric. Recall that God's verbal commands generate light, time, space—*almost* all that *is*. In that respect, His divine word has the same generative power as Babylonian, Egyptian, and Indian gods.[77] That verbal power appears in one of the names biblical authors use for Him, *Elohim*, "formed from *El* (meaning strength, or the strong one), and *alah* (to swear, to bind oneself by an oath) . . ."[78] It shows as well in the Sanskrit past participial form,

72. Žižek, "Fear of Four Words," 42–43.
73. Ibid., 50.
74. Burke, *Grammar of Motives*, 80.
75. Burke, *Rhetoric of Religion*, 22, 20.
76. Burke, *Grammar of Motives*, 68.
77. Burke, *Rhetoric of Religion*, 11.
78. Ibid., 12.

hūta, from which the English word "God" may have derived.[79] In this way, God invents images of Himself, as Burke suggests, because "the principle of personality implicit in the idea of first creative fiats, whereby all things are approached in terms of the word, applies also to the feel for symbol systems on the part of the human animal." God utters nature into existence. This is His first "act" as a "super-person," so it will become "a distinctive ingredient of 'personality,'" God's and the human likenesses He invents.[80]

It becomes almost impossible to portray this God except through this most basic metaphor for a divine ethos as fully verbal and inventive as the humans He has made. However embarrassingly anthropomorphic, this metaphor may have occurred to the Genesis writers because, as Lewis Mumford explains, spoken language remains from its inception "the most impalpable and evanescent of man's creations before writing was invented." "The mere breath of his [humankind's] mind," Mumford observes, "has turned out to be the most formative human achievement: every other subsequent advance in human culture, even tool-making, depended upon it."[81] This singularly empirical fact about our humanness, and the "personality" of that humanness, became humanity's "earliest model of the universe itself."[82] It is, then, hardly surprising that the biblical God should be represented as speech, as a speaker, a rhetor who invents other rhetors. The logo-centric bias, as Derrida and other post-modern thinkers have described it, may indeed be the almost inescapable root metaphor, however limiting and problematic, for the invention of human cultures.

Inventing Covenant Rhetoric

Even though the narrator presents God as judging each inventive act as "good," He makes no such judgment of His human likenesses.[83] This omission may already suggest God's own ambivalence about the very humans He has invented to be rhetors like Him. That ambivalence is soon confirmed in the covenant of Eden: God tells Adam he "may freely eat of every tree of the garden; but of the tree of the knowledge of good and evil [he] shall not eat, for in the day that [he eats] of it [he] shall die" (Gen 2:15–17). Oddly, God does not prohibit human likenesses from eating from "the tree of life"

---

79. Ibid.
80. Ibid., 202–3.
81. Mumford, *Myth of the Machine*, vol. 1, 74.
82. Ibid.
83. Miles, *God*, 30.

(Gen 2:9), from which He later fears they could eat and become, like God, immortal (Gen 4:22).

Burke would treat this first divine covenant as he treats all others, as God's "motives"—rhetorically charged reasons for what He says and does.[84] The Eden covenant grants Adam the freedom to eat from all the trees—even apparently the tree of life—*except one*. But this divine permission comes with a prohibitive condition and a result, apparently intended as a reason. If Adam violates the prohibition, he will die. As an argument, this brief speech resembles the enthymeme, as Aristotle describes it. The major premise allows Adam a large degree of freedom. Stephen Toulmin would call it a claim,[85] the content or data for which God draws from the very natural world He has made for humans. God's presumptive authority to grant this permission appears self-evident to His human inventions, presumably because of His ethos. His human likenesses seem to know and accept that ethos, which may be the only possible warrant authorizing God's claim about the data, since He has made Adam, the garden, and all that grows in it.

Yet this claim comes with a conditional premise from which is drawn a fateful warning. The conditional premise draws upon the same natural content as the claim, but adds to it a threat—death. Nothing this God has done or said so far suggests death or dying, and He has uttered no threat against His human inventions at all. Nor does God supply for Adam the middle premise, the warrant: the reason why Adam and Eve should not eat the fruit of this *one* tree? God seems to expect Adam to know *why* this tree is forbidden, and *why* God as God can forbid it. While Adam may accept God's authoritative ethos as the warrant for the initial claim, he may not understand or be able to supply the warrant for the conditional premise. It is certainly clear what the fatal outcome would be, so the death threat may be God's added warrant.

Yet, as the intended audience for this argument, Adam may be as confused as someone reading this story for the first time without the vast accretions of Christian theology. From Adam's perspective, this second warrant may imply that the fruit is poisonous. However, this inference would possibly raise the question for Adam of why God would have poisonous fruit in His garden. Further complicating this rhetorical moment for Adam would be his uncertainty about whether the fruit would kill him or whether God would. That uncertainty, from Adam's position, would be quite troubling. God has killed nothing in the Bible so far, and has made no threat of doing so. If a reader were to identify with God's audience in this scene, it is

---

84. Burke, *Rhetoric of Religion*, 174.
85. Toulmin, *Uses of Argument*, 1417–28.

by no means difficult to imagine that Adam is discovering for the very first time another side of God's ethos. Adam and his mate are living in an idyllic place made by an all-powerful being fully capable of murdering them both or capable of making food that would kill them if they eat it, deliberately or accidentally.

The biblical narrator, obviously, allows readers no direct access to Adam's perspective here, only God's. As the divine maker, God argues from His position as an absolute authority; and His covenant-argument is intended to be read as a benign warning to His human likenesses, even as a text about their capacity to remain persuaded by God's ethos. Yet this conditional premise is God's *second* "No," embedded in His covenant with Adam. The first, recall, lies in the "No" He speaks against Adam's own solitude. Yet this covenant-argument, invented as a way for God to control His human likenesses, precedes an earlier speech that God makes to Himself, as a judgment against Adam's solitude: "It is not good that the man should be alone" (Gen 2:18).

This aside seems significant, for several reasons. It, *not* the Eden covenant, is the first judgment the Genesis narrator attributes to God in His *own voice* about any of His own inventions. Further, it is a negative injunction on God's part, God's first criticism of all that He has invented. If that is true, then solitude, not sex, disobedience, or pride, is the first, most original sin, the only condition He has decided *not* to call "good." As a critical aside to Himself, this small moment of epideictic rhetoric may hint at another reason for God's invention of His human likenesses and all that preceded them: God, too, did not want to be alone with His infinite Allness. So, the narrator tells us, He invents animals and birds "out of the ground"—the same ground out of which He made Adam—and lets Adam use his God-given symbolic power to name them all (Gen 2:19).

Obviously, the invented animals, even if named, cannot help Adam reproduce and multiply. Nor, with one fateful exception (the serpent), do these animals share Adam's own divinely endowed power for symbol-making, for speech, for rhetoric. So God invents the woman Eve out of Adam's body, inspiring Adam's very first speech—his eloquent praise of Eve as "bone of [his] bones / and flesh of [his] flesh," whom he names "Woman" (Gen 2:23). Adam's name for his companion takes the form of a brief argument. The name he gives her serves as a claim about his new companion for a stated reason, "because she was taken out of Man" (Gen 3:23). Here, Adam seems to be addressing God as much as himself. In any event, this second human, invented by God from another already invented human, sets the stage for all that follows, and God's first rhetorical outbursts and curses—the longest speech He will have made so far.

These outbursts, obviously, presume God's own engendered image of Himself, His ethos as absolute "authority" as the world's "originator," its "designer," its "author."[86] This invented ethos is crucial to His super *impersonhood*, investing Him with the power to make more covenants with His human likenesses, and with "ownership" of all that He has invented so far. These covenants, once made, imply for Burke the quite rhetorical "possibility of [their] being violated." Hence, the "Fall" in the garden might not have happened had God not also made the prohibited tree and His first covenant with Adam. God's inventiveness here may hint, too, at His own Fall. If, to make the world, God had to divide Himself from the primordial material from which He invented, and divide again all that He invents into "different categories of things," these categories, Burke speculates, "could be variously at odds with one another" because they "accordingly lack the proto-Edenic simplicity of absolute unity" of their inventor. The narrative order established by these conditions seems "irreversible." Thus God's rhetorical starting point *after* the issue of whether He should make a world—perhaps His primal issue—is the Fall and subsequent punishment. Punishment depends on an error or violation without which punishment makes no logical or narrative sense. If we ask, as Burke does, what "conditions . . . make the infraction possible," those "conditions" would lead us back to God's invention of a world where "disobedience" of His covenant, defiance of His ethos, *can occur*, and God presumably knows as much.

Why, then, would God make such a world remains one of the most perplexing questions for this narrative and the entire Bible. Recall that among the animals God invented for Adam to name was the "serpent . . . more subtle than any other wild creature the LORD God had made" (Gen 3:1). Seldom do we run across talking animals in the Bible. Even though God later speaks to Balaam through a donkey (Num 23:28–29), the serpent is His one grandly famous exception. Made, presumably, from the same primordial dust and mist as Adam and the other animals, the serpent's special subtlety happens to include the same symbol-making capacity as God's human likenesses. No other animal mentioned in the Bible has this capacity. Balaam's donkey is not really an exception, since this animal's speech clearly comes from God Himself. Yet the serpent's ability to speak, to symbolize, its own rhetoric, must also inevitably derive from the same God who invents this creature, even though the Genesis narrator does not seem to want readers to believe that what the serpent says comes from God, as it did for Balaam's donkey. The serpent can speak as freely as God's humans.

---

86. Burke, *Rhetoric of Religion*, 174–75.

Why the biblical God would invent this exceptional creature and endow it with speech, with rhetorical ability, remains yet another perplexing question which has invited countless speculations and lots of one-liners from America's comedians. Even so, it may disturbingly suggest that this God is responsible for inventing disobedience, disorder, evil, and, yes, for some non-believers, Satan himself. These speculations underscore the simple fact that God's own rhetoric dialectically and narratively requires a counter-rhetoric—a counter-rhetoric that He, too, seems to have invented—to engender repeatedly the supreme conflict throughout the argument God makes in the Bible's many other covenant-making and covenant-breaking story cycles—all "proofs" to support God's own ethos as supreme authority. The serpent serves as a negative, since it can be seen in God's earlier "No's," His first arguments. In these initial, negative exhortations, God may recognize the "'evil' . . . implicit in the idea of 'Order'" that He enacts through generation because His ordering All into being suggests its dialectical opposite, "an idea of 'Disorder.'"[87] This implied "disorder" may arise out of the humans' incapacity to comply with all of God's verbal commands, or out of the humans' "deliberate allegiance to a Counter-Order."

This Counter-Order, or Disorder, to whom human likenesses might pledge their allegiance emerges in 1 Chronicles as "Satan," who opposes King David and Israel (21:1). Biblical annotations explain that, in the half century separating 1 Chronicles from 2 Samuel, the Old Testament authors had ceased to think of God's wrath as the source of evil and misfortunes and invented a word and the character of "Satan" (meaning simply "adversary") to be evil's source, a Counter-Order separate from God's own invented design. An earlier image of Satan as a "lying spirit" seated in God's celestial palace appears in 1 Kings (22:19–22). But Satan is also supposed to be one of God's "sons" in the opening of the Book of Job (1:7–9), before Judaism became ardently monotheistic and before Christianity demonizes this "son" in 1 Chronicles.[88]

Obviously, many devout Christians would reject the view that the source of evil is God Himself, just as they would reject God's having to fall into Himself to begin inventing the world. These unorthodox interpretations forget that God's generation *ex nihilo* is "pure gift," a gift God gives to Himself as His creatures come back to him.[89] Yet God's very own rhetorical prohibitions in Genesis, not to mention Judaism's own changing sense

---

87. Ibid., 195.

88. For an extended study of the social and political forces which impacted Satan in the Bible, see Pagels, *Origin of Satan*.

89. Milbank, "Double Glory, or Paradox Versus Dialectics," 195, 199–201.

of evil's source, make it nearly inevitable that almost anyone who seriously thinks about the Bible is likely to ask these kinds of questions, wrong-headed as they may seem to believers, whatever their denomination.

Rhetoric Out of Eden

In Genesis, the narrator has Eve confess that a serpent "beguile[d]" her just as Eve "beguile[d]" Adam (Gen 3:13). This rhetorically charged scene, and what follows from it, largely unfolds in a series of subtle interrogatives the Genesis narrator orchestrates before God delivers His longest and most sustained argument yet. Critic of biblical rhetoric Kenneth M. Craig Jr. offers a highly detailed, useful reading of these interrogatives. Craig thinks that the movement of this God's questioning "from opening to closure reveals that questions not only mean something; they *do* something."[90] Not only do Biblical figures ask questions to gain information, questions are posed to "remind us [readers] of the representational function of language, of persuasion, of the establishment of power and the exercise of authority—or, in a word, rhetoric."[91]

Craig reads the Eden narrative as "mediated discourse, filtered to us through the norms, intentions, and rhetoric of the narrator," woven together by "competing voices, an interaction of speakers and points of view . . ."[92] Obviously, my concern here is not with so much with narrators but with the rhetoric those narrators compose as God's speech. Even so, despite the one prohibition, Craig Jr. correctly observes that God directly addresses Adam with a rhetorical "command" that is notably "remarkable for the freedom it gives" His first human likeness.

God's explicit, if strange, covenant-command prompts several paraphrases later on, starting with the serpent's. Often described in Hebrew as more "clever" and "cunning" than other creatures, the actual Hebrew words for the serpent are difficult to translate; and, as Craig Jr. explains, they are not to be found anywhere else in Genesis, though they do appear in other parts of the Old Testament (Exodus, Job, Proverbs). In these other books, cleverness and guile are "ambivalent" terms, suggesting both "desirable" and "undesirable traits."

---

90. Craig, *Asking for Rhetoric*, 3. Drawing from his knowledge of the Hebrew texts, Craig offers a highly detailed rhetorical analysis of the Bible's many interrogatives.

91. Ibid., 9.

92. All subsequent citations of Craig are to 11–26, to which I am indebted in my comments on God's rhetoric in Eden.

Craig further points out that, when addressing Eve, the serpent distorts God's covenant-argument with Adam through paraphrase, embedding His earlier prohibition within a question: "Did God say 'you shall not eat of any tree in the garden?'" (Gen 3:1). The serpent's *aporia* softens God's verbal command to "say" and changes God's name, from the narrator's LORD God or "YHWH Elohim," to the simpler "God," or "Elohim," which Eve echoes throughout her conversation with the serpent. Both depend on plural pronouns in their exchanges, the serpent, the second person plural "you" and Eve, first person plural "we" when referring to herself and her mate.

The rhetoric of the serpent's paraphrase, Craig Jr. continues, distorts in still other ways. The serpent never refers to the specific tree prohibited and reverses God's command to make it sound more sweeping. Nor does the serpent mention God's otherwise carte blanche invitation to eat fruit from all the other trees. It is, then, not difficult to suppose that the serpent may be exploiting its suspicion that Eve may think that God was being a little too demanding. The serpent's rhetoric proves potent enough, even as paraphrase, to persuade Eve to doubt God's veracity as she yearns to eat the fruit and become God-like in knowledge. Both Eve's own paraphrase of God's command, while naming the wrong forbidden tree, along with the serpent's interrogative rephrasing, weaken the argument of divine prohibition.

This weakening continues in the serpent's quick challenge to Eve's paraphrase, countering God's threat, "You will not die. For God knows that when you eat of it [the tree of knowledge of good and evil] your eyes will be opened and you will be like God, knowing good and evil" (Gen 3:4). This maneuver would turn God's initial covenant-argument inside out, deriving a very different conclusion, and a very different warrant, to refute God's own. The serpent's rhetoric specifically focuses on God's ethos, His power, His apparent need to protect that power and keep it for Himself, and not the deathly consequences of violating His order. Yet this counter-argument presumes the serpent's own unexplained knowledge of God's true intent in inventing humans to be like Him, knowledge also exploited to persuade Eve. To Eve, it seems perfectly reasonable to believe that she and Adam would like to be more similar to their inventor than they already are. Eating the forbidden fruit, she may have hoped, could flatter God's own reason for making them.

Whatever Eve may have believed or hoped (the biblical narrator denies readers access to Eve's mind, like Adam's), once God arrives to ask Adam, "Where are you?" (Gen 3:9), Adam's first-person responses (four in total) not only suggest his shame but, as Craig suggests, his separation from his mate, whom he tries to blame for his mistake. No longer a "we," Adam's first-person rhetoric, Craig argues, now shows him to be isolated, alone—exactly what God first condemned as *not good*. Adam is now shown as afraid of his God for the first time, and fully aware he now lives in a world where the whole truth cannot always be told (Gen 3:10).

God's own cross-examination demonstrates full awareness of what His human likenesses have done, and He intends to force them to confess their errors (Gen 3:11). Adam, of course, shifts the blame to his mate and, then, partly to God, for inventing a mate who can mislead him (Gen 3:12). But God then turns to interrogate Eve, asking, "What is this that you have done?"(Gen 3:13). This question, of course, begs another—that she's committed a terrible mistake—and immediately implies her guilt. She, like Adam, tries to blame the serpent; but, contrary to Craig's inference, this effort seems to suggest that God Himself is to blame, since He made the serpent just as He made all the other creatures in Eden.[93] Eve's opening first-person statement, unlike Adam's, is a full admission of her own guilt, but not her mate's. Biblical annotations on this famous scene typically suggest that God's subtle serpent makes the child-like Adam and Eve question the motives of God's prohibition and seek their freedom from His rule. While that may be true, it may also be that they really hoped to please God by imitating His ability to divide up and categorize the world into the grand categories of good and evil, since God had made them as likenesses of Himself and He, not the serpent, wanted them to be "like" Him.

The God of this narrative now behaves as a "theomorphic human,"[94] "walking in the garden in the cool of the day" (Gen 3:8), a God who has now forced admissions of guilt from His humans (but, oddly, not from the rhetorically gifted serpent), so He is ready to pass judgment—in verse, as

---

93. Here, I depart from Craig's analysis and Trible's characterization of the differences between Adam's reply and Eve's (see Trible's *God and the Rhetoric of Sexuality*, 119–20). Craig, following Trible's analysis, fails to mention God's implicit responsibility in Eve's blaming the serpent. Trible herself argues that Eve "does not say . . . 'The serpent whom you made to dwell in the garden with me,'" 119. Obviously, Eve does not say these exact words, but it is safe to assume that whoever wrote this story would likely know readers might infer the implicit blaming of God for the serpent's being in the garden. God is the sole author of all living creatures in Eden. Further, since Eve seems to know about God's first covenant argument, why could she not also have learned of God's singular role as inventor of all other creatures? If Craig wishes to impute to Adam an implicit blaming of God for inventing his mate, I see no compelling reason why this same logic would not also apply to Eve. Trible's attempt to excuse Eve's admission of guilt strikes me as special pleading for this character because of her gender, though that is fully understandable, given the tendency to blame females for all the world's ills, with this one story often cited as evidence for such a ridiculous claim. But the Bible, at least here, more than a little resembles the Pandora myth in its casting of a woman as the cause of humanity's misfortunes.

94. Bloom, *Jesus and Yahweh*, 130.

a poem, His longest speech so far. What God argues in this inserted verse, however, can hardly be called "an explanation of the consequences of disobedience."[95] In this speech, God first reveals His "mercurial" ethos as an arguer[96]—an ethos He reveals on many other occasions—through His curses of the serpent, Eve and, finally, Adam. In one sense, these curses are largely pathos, emotional appeals, *aras* intended to amplify the guilt in His several audiences and to warn any reader who dares ignore His arguments in the future (Gen 3:15–19).

God's *aras* may baffle any attentive reader of Genesis, since, here, two creation stories appeared to have been fused together.[97] In the first, God's human likenesses are free to enjoy themselves in a "gigantic natural paradise" where they can be fruitful and multiply. Adam is denied nothing except the fruit from one tree. Still, God has not proclaimed Adam, unlike His other works, as "good." God knows Adam needs a companion, so He supplies him with one after His other living creatures, all now named, fail to suit Adam's reproductive needs. So in the "first account of creation," God's human likenesses never speak to their inventor, and God seems to expect little of them. This account hardly seems like a "story . . . of human transgression."

The second story, though, does dramatize human transgressions, which stir God's most violent, angry rhetoric thus far. In the second story, too, a whole host of interpretive problems arise. "[O]rganized around tightly woven dialogue" with at least five crucial interrogatives among the principal actors, the second Genesis story never explains why the serpent is so much more clever than other creatures.[98] Nor does the narrator explain why, among all of God's invented creatures, the serpent has the singular ability to make symbols and engage rhetorically with God's human likenesses (if not with its inventor), or how the serpent knows about God's first covenant-argument and its prohibition, or why the serpent selects Eve, not Adam, to "beguile" (Gen 2:9—3:1). Further, the serpent, for all its devious paraphrasing of God's covenant-argument, does tell Eve the *truth*: the couple does not die after they eat the forbidden fruit and violate God's order—at least not immediately—as God had warned (Gen 2:16). For some Christian theologians, God's first couple dies a "spiritual" death.[99] But the serpent seems honest enough to tell Eve that wisdom—knowing the difference between good and evil—is greatly valued, since it seems so in much of

---

95. Craig, *Asking for Rhetoric*, 24.
96. Bloom, *Jesus and Yahweh*, 176.
97. Miles, *God*, 30–31.
98. Craig, *Asking for Rhetoric*, 25.
99. Wilder, *Language of the Gospel*, 15.

the Bible.¹⁰⁰ While it may be understandable why Eve eats the fruit (the serpent's rhetoric has been very persuasive), it is less clear why Adam does.¹⁰¹ Thus it is quite hard to resist suspecting that the whole story is staged, with the serpent as God's own "secret or unwitting agent."

However these questions may be answered, if they ever are, no reader of the Bible can ignore God's angry curses at the end of the Eden narrative. While each *ara* consists of slightly different deformations of the accused, all three's guilt depends on the symmetry of a reciprocal argument whereby one shared feature among the accused—a challenge to God's covenant-argument—is seen as "essential" to the justice imposed.¹⁰² God's curse of the serpent makes it the most hated of all creatures, willing away its limbs so it must crawl upon its belly and eat "dust"—the same material, presumably, out of which it, all animals, and Adam have been made—"all the days of [its] life" (Gen 3:14). The serpent's persuasive counter-rhetoric incites God to deform the creature's physical form as much as its assumed status, lowering the serpent and forcing it to crawl wherever it goes while raising other animals and humans above its efforts. This subordination is also a subjugation, since human beings will forever tread on the serpent. God has invented a curse that robs the serpent of any stature in the animal world and makes the very humans it seduced its principal tormentors. Strangely, though, God's curse does not extend to the serpent's rhetorical capacity, a fully illogical omission inasmuch as this capacity was precisely the means used to tempt God's human likenesses.

God's curse against Eve "greatly multipl[ies]" her pain "in childbearing" and places her, like the serpent, in a subordinate position to the man whom she "desire[s]," the same one who "shall rule over [her]" (Gen 3:16). This *ara* consists of doubly punishing consequences for Eve and all her female progeny to come. For her role in doubting and defying God's rhetoric, all women must suffer intense pain in childbirth, a darkly ironic outcome of being "fruitful" and multiplying God's rhetorical image-makers after eating forbidden fruit. Perhaps worse, God condemns women to a masochistic desire for their own male subjugators. Like the serpent who tempted her, Eve loses whatever status she may have shared with Adam and now must remain an underling to the very one she tempted.

God's curse on Adam is slightly different. In fact, God curses the "ground" out of which Adam was made, not Adam per se. The couple's dual fate becomes God's second Eden covenant, for Adam and his progeny will

100. Miles, *God*, 30.
101. Craig, *Asking for Rhetoric*, 25.
102. Perelman and Olbrechts-Tyteca, *New Rhetoric*, 221.

have to make the earth yield food and not "just till it and keep it" (Gen 2:15). Directly addressing Adam as "you," God declares that "cursed is the ground because of you; / in toil you shall eat of it all the days of your life" (Gen 3:17). Adam and his progeny must now perform constant, grueling work just to survive. Similar to the serpent's having to eat dust for eternity, Adam's challenge to God's rhetoric results in his having to eat what is grown out of the ground. Even more damning perhaps, after a life of unceasing labor to make this ground yield food to live, Adam and his lot must "return to the ground, / for out of it you were taken; you are dust, / and to dust you shall return" (Gen 3:19). Pain, "enmity," physical deformation, perpetual toil, an accursed ground, subordination, and death—these *aras* spell out the awful, fateful consequences of defying God's initial covenant-argument. The willfulness of this violation may be one of many instances in the Bible's various narratives where we may find the theme of human likenesses' "forgetting" God,[103] or it may more likely be one of many instances where His human likenesses ignore God's arguments and defy His rhetorical authority.

The account offered here of this highly-charged rhetorical scene is not what many devout American Christians are likely to have heard. They are more likely to see this entire speech as the Bible's rather tidy explanation for a number of facts about the world human beings have to live in—a world of pain, suffering, and a constant struggle to survive in the face of certain death. But this explanation evades the rhetorical complexities of all-too-familiar story, missing or ignoring the important roles rhetoric and argument play in it.

God's "rhetorical explosion" in this narrative is, for some, "all too sudden, too massive, and too unopposed by the serpent, who never speaks or acts again, for the scene to function as a mythic battle."[104] For that reason, if not others, it seems possible to argue that this scene shows God, treated as a literary character, as the central "cause of both weal and woe in the lives of his creatures because good and evil impulses conflict within his [God's] character."[105] As the Bible's central rhetor, however, God's *aras* also reveal "the breakdown of communication and understanding" as "one of the deepest concerns in Eden."[106] In other words, it indicates a rupture in God's rhetorical persuasiveness, His own authoritative ethos. From the moment they became capable of rhetoric themselves, like their Inventor, God's human

---

103. Josipovici, *Book of God*, 136–52.
104. Miles, *God*, 34.
105. Ibid., 32.
106. Craig, *Asking for Rhetoric*, 26.

likenesses became capable of resisting God's arguments, His "orders," or of at least considering and succumbing to an alternative rhetoric. The serpent's rhetoric offers another way to understand God's command—as a harmless bluff to preserve God's ethos of authority and power.

God's expulsion of Adam and Eve from Eden after clothing them contains another crucial moment of self-addressed rhetoric, when God mutters to Himself perhaps His own deepest fears about the invented human likenesses: "Behold, the man [Adam] has become like one of us, knowing good and evil; and now, lest he put forth his hand and take also of the tree of life, and eat, and live forever . . ." (Gen 3:22). God breaks off and does not complete His thought, but this aposiopesis does not disguise how He would have finished it, since He expels Adam and Eve and appoints an angel (one of God's typical theophanies) to guard the tree of life in Eden (Gen 3.23–24). If Adam were to eat the fruit from the second tree, he would not only have God's ability to differentiate good from evil; he would be immortal as well, just as God is. Added together, that would make His invented humans *more than a likeness*. Mere likeness would become closer to identity. God's humans would possess not only His power to differentiate, to symbolize, to argue; they also would not die. This revealing admission may suggest that His own rhetorically endowed creatures could become *not* His likenesses, not just an audience for His rhetorical pleas, but rivals to His rhetorical power.

To the earth, the heavens, the light, the seasons, the many plants and animals, and the human image-makers this God has now added suffering, pain, toil, death, time, history, and exile—the end results of God's complex, exuberant acts of invention to generate a second covenant. He has already shaped a world of time, space, and causality which will require of Him many more rhetorical acts, performed, as they must be, to persuade His rapidly multiplying images of Himself to remain true to His changing covenants.

Without His inventions out of Himself, of dividing and reshaping the parts of Himself He seems to have generated, there would be no terrestrial and historical stage for all the rhetoric of God to come; no reasons for Him to invent any more rhetoric at all, or for His human likenesses' rhetoric either. No divine or human exhortations, no prayer, no rhetoric of petition, no songs, no prophecies. Without this Fall of His human likenesses—this perpetual Fall, repeated so often in the centuries and narratives to come— no issues for His rhetoric to address. Without modified images of His own symbol-making, His own rhetoric, no reluctant, resistant audience to appeal to.

But this God *does* appeal to them, many times over. In many instances, His rhetoric succeeds. In other instances, it does not. This perhaps explains why He has to keep changing the rhetoric of His covenant-arguments. His human likenesses keep changing as well, just as they kept changing the texts and narratives in which He plays His rhetorical parts. To these later covenant-arguments we must now turn.

3

Inventing and Arguing More Covenants

How Much Does God Directly Argue?

In my attempt to describe and assess the arguments God's invents in the opening chapters of Genesis, it could easily be said that "the Bible's peculiar rhetoric of sublimity"[1] posed several obstacles. Those obstacles, in part, turned upon God's verbal fiats, His invention of His own authorial-rhetorical ethos. Such an invention the Bible assumes to be a "unique, unrepeatable origin" wherein "word, intention and referent" fuse in "an original plenitude in which meaning is complete and self-sufficient."[2] That unifying plenitude, spoken freely and to God Himself, could have been a fall into or out of that All that God, in speaking, could no longer be. Yet, in making Himself the "author" (and rhetor) of that primordial unity, God's invented ethos "authorizes" all future "human authorship," even the idea of an author's "unified self" made manifest in a unified text—be it the Bible or any other secular work of Western culture. As a model for cosmic generation and textual interpretation, God's "authorship" rests on the ever-early metaphor of how a supreme imperson could call a world into being. God's plenitude, though, could not have been made, invented, except through His dividing His All into Many—hence the Bible's "sublime" weaves together in one singular act a rhetoric that unifies the Many into an order even as that rhetoric necessarily depends upon division and disorder once He invents human likenesses.

1. Poland, "Bible and the Rhetorical Sublime," 30.
2. Ibid., 34.

Once those initial "divining acts," mysterious and sublimely complex as they are, have taken place, it is at least possible to say that, whatever else He has done, and however He may have done it, God has invented a world in which He can now argue with His human likenesses, as He does through much of the Old Testament. No study—including this one—of what various narrators represent as His direct arguments can do justice to *all* of these arguments, even though many often repeat or elaborate on previous ones. This chapter, then, only focuses on a few specific scenes from the Old Testament where God makes His case to several important audiences. These scenes may be readily familiar to some readers, however much of the Bible they have read or resisted reading, because they have been part of the authorial shape this God has taken in many American imaginations.

Nevertheless, before describing and, where possible, assessing the arguments made in these scenes, a caveat is in order. If readers were to examine the entire Christian Bible, noting when, where, and to whom God speaks directly, excluding poetic reveries, prophetic mediation, or interpretation and exposition of His speeches, those readers will likely discover that among all His human likenesses, God argues most with Moses, His primary audience. Equally important, those same readers should notice that, over the course of the Bible, God is shown speaking *directly* to humans less and less. In the Book of Ruth, He does not speak at all. Nor does he address anyone in the Books of Ezra, Ecclesiastes, Esther, or in Psalms, Proverbs, or the Song of Solomon. The Prophets typically speak *for* God, to articulate His promises and warnings indirectly, often focused on Israel's need to follow His various covenants or else face disastrous consequences. Even in the New Testament, God speaks directly only on a few occasions (as we will see in chapter 4), since Jesus's rhetoric dominates that part of the Bible. The almost inescapable conclusion readers may draw, then, is that God's own *direct rhetoric* diminishes as the Bible's overall narrative unfolds. Why this should be so is a question perhaps no one can fully answer, though the final chapter of this book attempts one.

In the Hebrew Old Testament, Job is the audience for God's final words. There, too, God makes His last appearance as the "'Ancient of Days,' white-haired and silent, looking forward to the end of history from a remote, cloudy throne."[3] Of course, if treated as a literary character, as Jack Miles does, this God appears with different and varying parts of His invented ethos enhanced—as Warrior, Lawgiver, and so forth. These partial *ethoi* of the Hebrew Bible's God considerably overlaps the God of the Christian Old Testament. From a rhetorical perspective, these various *ethoi* show Him

3. Miles, *God*, 10–11.

to be "capricious," at times a "stern imp," or, like Plato's Demiurge in the *Timaeus*, "a mad moralist," and yet "the most formidable of ironists, ever."[4] Some may consider the God called Yahweh, and not God the Father (*Abba*, as Jesus calls Him) or the "Ancient of Days,"[5] "the best of rhetoricians."[6] Whatever name a narrator chooses (a point we shall return to in chapter 8), if this God is the "best of rhetoricians," that quality should most clearly emerge, not in the prophecies or poems *about* Him, visionary and rhetorically powerful as they are, but in His direct, rhetorical encounters with His human likenesses, individually and collectively, and in His arguments over what seems most precious to Him—His rhetorically motivated covenants. These covenant-arguments are on full display in several of the key narratives of the Pentateuch.

A Flood of Rhetoric

God's interrogatives—His questions—staged His furious *aras* against Adam, Eve, and the serpent, ending with another rhetorical moment of anxious, self-addressed soliloquy. Another crucial instance of His self-address appears at the start of the Noah story which, as it happens, leads to God's third covenant-argument. There, we may overhear God's own internal deliberations preface another powerful moment of anger as God vows to destroy all the living creatures He has invented—not a homicide but a *zoacide*. Adam's progeny, it seems, have done exactly what God invited them to do—reproduce themselves (Gen 6:1). In one of the most puzzling passages in the Old Testament, the narrator mentions not only humans multiplying their numbers, but the "sons of God," or "Nephilim," who became attracted to "the daughters of men . . . [and] took to wife such of them as they [the sons of God] chose" (Gen 6:1–2).

Who these "sons of God," the Nephilim, are has sparked considerable Internet speculation. Some think the Nephilim are God's fallen angels, since the Hebrew root means "fallen ones." Others consider the Nephilim a pre-Deluvian race of giants, similar to the mythic Greek Titans. Others believe they are earlier, taller, Middle Eastern tribes such as the Philistine's champion, Goliath. Still others see them as extra-terrestrial visitors. Biblical historians might hasten to remind us that the ancient Hebraic God, Yahweh, was once one god among a divine assembly ruled by El, the Canaanite god, before Yahweh routed the other gods and became the single deity of the

---

4. Bloom, *Jesus and Yahweh*, 8–9, 12.
5. Ibid., 13, 120.
6. Bloom, *Book of J*, 235.

Bible. Yet, whoever the Nephlim were, what matters is what God *says* about them, to Himself alone, and what He *does* about them.

Initially, God admits only to Himself that His "spirit will not abide in man forever" (Gen 6:3). This brief aside recalls the God who breathed life, and symbolic power, into His first human likeness, except now this life-force has a time limit. Without the temporal limitation, His humans could live on as if they had actually gotten to nibble from the tree of life in Eden. God's aside is a claim, another negation, another "No," apparently this time to His own power. Yet that is not the reason God offers to support this claim. Rather, the narrator has Him say this: "he [man] is flesh, but his days shall be a hundred and twenty years." What God is shown persuading Himself to think is that humans age and die because they have fleshly bodies, even though they have these bodies precisely because of what God made them from, and not just because His "spirit," His breath, has limited power to sustain those bodies. It is as though God must blame any defects His humans have on the terrestrial materials used to invent them, not on any contribution—His breath, His spirit, His handiwork—He contributed to their making.

If this reasoning seems fallacious and askew, that is precisely because it *is*: the narrator, obviously, will not or cannot—which, is impossible to say—allow God to assign any blame for this fleshly defect on Himself. God must remain blameless, even though it was His curses that forced Adam and Eden from Eden, and He who chose the materials from which they were invented. No omniscient narrator intrudes to explain why God cannot make humans as He made the cosmos and all other living species, fleshly and not, by calling them forth with His rhetorically generative words. The temporal limits of human flesh appear to reside solely within the temporal limits of dust and water out of which humans and, presumably, all other fleshly creatures are constituted. Rhetorically speaking, it is hard not to call this argument an obvious example of God's "blaming the victim(s)."

Set this speech, though, against God's next, destructive outburst and the rhetorical issue becomes clearer. Between these passages of God's self-addressed rhetoric, the narrator omnisciently reports that the Nephlim, "on the earth in those days, and also afterwards" (Gen 6:4), seemed to have so accelerated the population growth that all the entire human species—and, presumably, all fleshly creatures—can think about is copulation and reproduction. God sees "the wickedness" of His human likenesses, the narrator reports, and is now "sorry [H]e had made man on the earth, and it grieved [H]im to [H]is heart" (Gen 6:5–6).

This narrative thread also happens to be God's second overt sign of regret over inventing the human audience for His own rhetoric: the first being His fear of Adam's eating from the tree of life. What to do with this recalcitrant, disobedient, copulating audience He has invented seems precisely the issue God is debating with Himself about. The narrator does not say as much, probably for good reasons; but it certainly seems inferable from God's acts and speeches so far that He is unsure about how to respond to what the narrator describes Him as seeing, the flagrant wickedness in the audience He invented for His own rhetoric. They seem no longer mindful of His orders, His commands. This God's uncertainty, readers soon discover, is an *aporia*, feigned doubt, quite similar to the serpent's earlier interrogatives to Eve about what God had prohibited. Like the narrator, God already knows what He is going to do about it.

Had God's self-address been allowed to develop as a genuine *aporia*, similar to Augustine's soliloquies, He might have been shown considering other possibilities. He could ignore the copulation, its presumed wickedness. Or He could simply destroy the Nephilim or have intervened, to persuade His human likenesses and the Nephilum that overpopulating His world was not quite what He meant by being "fruitful" and multiplying. Or He could have simply stated His displeasure and ordered the copulation to stop, attaching to this command His favorite threat—death, or total, violent annihilation. God could have been allowed a soliloquy in which He debates these choices to show how He comes to the decision He makes.

Of course, that is not what happens and not what the narrator's portrayal of His self-address shows. Even though He has only provided His human inventions so much information, even though He has commanded them to be fruitful and multiply, and even though they have done precisely as ordered, and been cooperative, it seems, to a fault, God makes a murderous vow, initially only to Himself: "I will blot out man whom I have created from the face of the ground, man and beast and creeping things and birds of the air, for I am sorry that I made them" (Gen 6:7). This vow largely repeats the narrator's earlier report, now rendered as God's own self-address; but it is notable for God's rejection of all other options except one: force, violence. This vow certainly resembles God's covenant-rhetoric with Adam, which ends with the threat of death if His likenesses ignore His argument and eat the forbidden fruit. As arguments, though, both appeals are fallacious examples of *argumentum ad baculum*, threats of violence similar to ones human rhetors can and do make to audiences whom they have been unable to persuade through any other means, especially through reasons and evidence. Here, God does not consider any other means, even though His means would presumably be infinite.

These arguments are not only fallacious by mere human standards; based on Aristotle's definition, they are "inartistic." They do not depend on reasons and evidence God could surely invent and articulate. They depend on God's power to alter the natural order, a powerful proof to which He often resorts. Here, in the Noah narrative, God initially utters His violent plan to Himself alone, not to His human likenesses, as readers might expect. The narrator shows this God talking Himself into the threat and then openly declaring the violence He is about to perform. Because this God seems to have invented creatures whose actions He cannot fully control, despite His best rhetorical efforts, He abruptly decides to destroy them.

Once He has chosen Noah and his family as survivors, God reveals His plan to Noah in another, very brief argument. His initial vow of destruction, made to Himself with no reason other than His "regret," becomes a claim He makes to convince Noah, to which He appends a reason the narrator has already supplied: violence and corruption now cover the earth, so God will use divine violence to stop terrestrial violence (Gen 6:11-13). Readers, if not Noah, will have to look very hard in this story to find any decisive textual evidence for the human "violence" that provokes God's regret or justifies His own violent plan. Whoever the Nephilim were or became, the Bible does not mention any violent acts they or the humans (whose daughters the Nephilim chose as wives) committed. Perhaps these wives were *taken*, raped, ravished, and *not* chosen; for that could have been violence enough for God's ire. Oddly, even ironically, though, the narrator centers God's confessed regret over humans doing exactly what He wanted them to do—be fruitful and multiply—an exhortation that has been perhaps rather loosely interpreted by His human likenesses, the Nephilim, and all other species of organic life.

In the end, God persuades Himself that only *His* violence can stop the purported human violence, so He selects Noah and takes him aside to make His case. This argument will lead to another covenant, this time with Noah, as God selects a remnant from the world He has invented so that this remnant can replenish the world He is about to destroy. Why *all* living creatures, including Noah and his family, are not destroyed so that God can start over completely is an option neither He nor the narrator propose, though some readers certainly might wonder about it.

God's ethos quickly changes in this narrative. He soon becomes the Supreme Instructor and Architect, outlining in specific detail how Noah is to build the ark and which animals are to be saved (Gen 6:11-22; 7:1-5). God does not speak again until He tells Noah the flood is finished, the destruction complete, after which the narrator shows God speaking to Himself again. The narrator initially and omnisciently reports what is "in [God's] heart" before showing God speaking *from* His heart: "I will never again curse the ground because of man, for the imagination of man's heart is evil from his youth; neither will I ever again destroy every living creature as I have done. While the earth remains, seedtime and harvest, cold and heat, summer and winter, day and night, shall not cease"(Gen 8:21). Thus, the narrative doubles itself and the message, apparently to underscore God's post-violent regret as some strange form of divine mercy.

Merciful or not, God's promise to Himself is a crucial rehearsal for the covenant-argument that Noah will hear soon after God smells the "pleasing odor" of Noah's "burnt offerings" of "every clean animal and . . . every clean bird" (Gen 9:1–20). God's heart-felt rhetoric again consists of two pairs of arguments, with each reason signaled by "for." God's claim takes the form of a promise: never again to destroy "the ground because of man." His reasons are hardly surprising, since He has mentioned them already: human likenesses are corrupt from the start, in flesh and now in "the imagination of man's heart." It would be pointless for God to punish them again simply for what they are and cannot help but be. The narrator obviously omits from this soliloquy any responsibility God has for making them as they are; so, once again, it is difficult to avoid thinking that again God is fallaciously blaming the victims that He has invented to be like Him.

His second argument consists of a claim that vows never to destroy the earth again "while [it] remains" (Gen 8:22), since He would be destroying a great deal of what He had already invented. Neither the rhetoric of the soliloquy nor the narrator's reporting suggests God could generate the world and humans a second time, but why He could not would require more premises and reasons than the narrator or God provide. In His covenant with Noah, God is shown repeating the command He made to Adam—to reproduce (Gen 9:1–7). This time He adds another reason to His covenant with Himself. God will permit Noah and all future human likenesses to eat the plants *and* animals, but the animals cannot be eaten with the blood still in them. This conditional contract parallels the one God made with Adam, except God now adds "animals" to the plant life humans can eat. But this condition soon leads God to add another reason, and another threat. His human likenesses cannot kill or eat each other, presuming they had been doing *that* all along. Thus God has already started to outline His laws, the ones He writes for Moses. Humans may kill anyone who has killed another human being, since each one God "made in [H]is own image'"

God then expands His covenant with Noah when He addresses Noah's "sons" as well, paraphrasing what He has already vowed to Himself and, in effect, negating the very violence He has already enacted against his fleshly inventions (Gen 9:8–17). To these negations He adds what Aristotle would call His "sign" as an "infallible" proof,[7] the rainbow. God is shown as thinking this apparently new, natural sign will serve as a mnemonic device, a way to remind Himself of His own prohibitive covenant never to destroy "all that is flesh upon the earth" with another great flood. However, the rainbow also serves God's argument as naturally recurring evidence for claims He has made to and about Himself and now repeated to Noah and his family. This sign's mnemonic purpose will aid this God's own memory of this particular covenant, as if He is in danger of forgetting it—a curious point to which we will return in chapter 7.

God certainly has *not* excluded other ways of destroying all earthly flesh or the "ground" on which creatures live. He does not promise the earth will always exist, presumably because He knows it will not. God's arguments often leave out as much as they include. These omissions, all of them His own assumptions and characteristic of rhetorical enthymemes, provide this God with some argumentative space for the historical narratives to come. Noah, obedient audience as he is, does not seem to notice them. Or, if he does, he thinks better about asking God to supply the missing premises. If readers take Noah's perspective on all that has happened, and not the narrator's or the narrator's God, he would have valid reasons for his reluctance. Disagreeing with this God, or displeasing Him, he may have thought, might prompt other regrets, even more violence. Noah has already witnessed the catastrophic evidence of one regret God happen to have.

Like readers, Noah has also witnessed a God fully capable of and ready to call upon the natural world to do His bidding. The great flood is one of God's many theophanies, a manifestation of His divine regret that turns rain and time into weapons of violence against His fleshly inventions. The rainbow is His second theophany, a repeated reminder and sign, the narrator wants readers to believe, of God's merciful vow to Himself and all organic life that God regrets the violence of the first theophany. Here, in the most destructive narrative so far, God offers reasons for what he does. But the arguments He makes for His actions hardly seem sufficient for or proportionate to the actions He takes. Each speech leaves out what His human likenesses would most need to hear, as if those absences make His presence all the more powerfully felt in His inartistic proofs, the flood, the rainbow—ironic signs, extra-verbal arguments that make the absence of His

---

7. Aristotle, *Rhetoric* 1.ii.14–18. A "sign" in Aristotle's theory of rhetoric can be a "necessary" part or fact leading to a certain "universal" conclusion, while other signs may lead to more probable and, consequently, refutable conclusions. Aristotle offers two examples of the first type of sign—a fever signifying illness and lactation signifying pregnancy.

own rhetorical artistry violently present and to be remembered as such for future narratives.

Inventing Rhetorical Babel

The biblical God's propensity for self-addressed rhetoric, for soliloquy, appears again in the famous Tower of Babel narrative. In this story, the narrator suggests no other audience than God Himself for His longest soliloquy so far. When God sees the tower His human likenesses are building encroaching upon His heavenly space, He identifies at once the causes of their success: they are acting as *one* people, all speaking *one* language. "This tower," God warns Himself, "is only the beginning of what they will do; and nothing they propose to do will now be impossible for them" (Gen 11:1–9). This issue seems very similar to the one in Eden and the one the Nephilim raised: What should God do to keep human power limited and His human likenesses persuaded by His covenant-arguments? In the Babel story, some group of humans, it seems, have been able to exploit a limited but shared language to overcome both architectural and rhetorical problems. Having and speaking the same language empowers them to cooperate so fully with each other, they seem to have no need for rhetoric at all. The sheer absence of any verbal conflicts would offer these human likenesses unparalleled technological and social advantages. They not only share the same language; they act *as* one mind, *with* one mind.

Annotations for the Babel story point out that, historically considered, the tower suggests the culture of great Mesopotamian cities architecturally marked by a pyramidal ziggurat, at the top of which lay the way to heaven. It is precisely this sort of structure which archeologists and cultural historians have identified with the development of a centralized, hierarchical power-state, with a king or pharaoh who claims divine origin in solar-celestial metaphors to justify his rule and fortify his power to force other human beings to do this despot's bidding.[8] In such a socio-political configuration, rhetorical speech would not likely be necessary. Whatever a king or a pharaoh decreed was law, and not to be argued, only to be accomplished.

In this case, God does not destroy the Tower. Rather, He announces to Himself the obvious conclusion He has reached, given the causes identified. He decides to "confuse their language, that they may not understand one another's speech" (Gen 11:7). Once this God persuades Himself to accept such a conclusion—an easy task since God is seldom shown to second-guess His own decisions—one people, with one limited language, with no

---

8. Mumford, *Myth of the Machine*, vol. 1, 168–85.

apparent linguistic or rhetorical discord to impede them, becomes *many* people speaking *many* languages, with all the cognitive and rhetorical discord a plurality of languages ensures. It is no accident that Kenneth Burke should comment that "[r]hetoric is concerned with the state of Babel after the Fall,"[9] except that God's rhetoric—even His self-addressed rhetoric—*precedes* both Babel and the Fall and, in the case of Eden, *ensures* the Fall He curses.

Given Burke's later comments on the rhetorical motives of God's covenants, this one seems premature and a bit misleading. While "Babel" frequently appears as a metaphoric allusion to the confusing proliferations of ideologies, perspectives, and rhetorics within secular writers, typical American Christian renditions of this story, if mentioned at all, usually flog an audience with admonitory sermons about God's almost certain intent to punish human pride and arrogance. American Christians may have even heard the story as the Bible's ancient attempt to account for the singular fact of linguistic, cultural, and racial diversity across the globe. So Burke must be applauded, in part, for recognizing the role rhetoric plays in this tale even if, later, he must move rhetoric's temporal and logical origins to the opening chapters of Genesis.

Yet Burke fails to note the pre-rhetorical accomplishments the Tower assumes and represents. Linguistic uniformity would be a necessary but insufficient cause of the architectural splendor that apparently threatens God's ethos. Rhetorical uniformity demands more than the tower-builders' knowing what each other's words mean; it requires a uniform consensus on the purpose of the Tower and a collective willingness to construct it. Among other possibilities, "collective willingness" may be the consensual result of verbal persuasion; or it may be the result of authoritative coercion. Only in the first case would the builders benefit from linguistic uniformity, though it would be no guarantee that the builders, even if they understood each other perfectly, agreed on the Tower's purpose or their parts in realizing it. Authoritative coercion, to the extent that the builders surrender to it, requires neither linguistic nor rhetorical uniformity, only the instruments of violence to threaten harm if the builders hesitate or refuse to obey in the building of the Tower.

Here, too, God's self-persuasion seems to be the strangest of ironies and hardly based on sufficient reasoning as humans would expect it. Assuming He has accurately identified the causes of this insulting, architectural encroachment, why should this God be content with merely confusing this people's languages, since the gift of language came from His own generative

---

9. Burke, *Rhetoric of Motives*, 23.

word? Again, the biblical God is shown as refusing to consider other ways to punish the ostensible pride of these tower-builders. Why He did not simply remove their gift for language, for symboling, seems almost inexplicable. That choice would not have even necessarily meant He had to make the entire human race mute, only this one people. Why He did not simply level the Tower and destroy its builders, as He will Sodom and Gomorrah (Gen 19:1–38), remains just as inexplicable.

Perhaps this is the biblical God at one of His most ironic moments, given the punishment chosen. Instead of "blotting" out the source of the problem—a single tongue and mind—He multiplies both. The Babel story can certainly offer a celestial, divine rationale for linguistic and other forms of diversity. Yet such diversity, as we rhetorically clever human likenesses soon discover, can be overcome by learning each other's languages. The translatability of God's gift of symboling He must have recognized. Even so, rhetorical diversity, unlike linguistic diversity, is a far more harmful punishment for human pride and arrogance, as it centers issues not on simply coding and decoding verbal signs, but on human struggles to communicate their understandings and reach consensus on what to do, value, or believe. This God has, from the very start, confronted precisely this strife in persuading His human inventions to accept His own covenant-arguments.

Inventing the Covenant with Abraham

God soon turns His rhetorical attention to Abraham, the audience for His next covenant-argument. In this narrative, God, the narrator says, simply appears and orders Abraham to leave his family, his home country, though He makes a somewhat different promise, offering His favored audience land and a legacy, if Abraham obeys God's will (Gen 12:1–2). Intriguingly, God bases this claim on an "incentive," not a prohibition, as in the case of Adam, or on a prohibition against His own violence, as with Noah. The issue motivating this revised covenant-argument is not as explicit as it was for Adam and Noah. Here, God seems concerned about His own continuing power and authority over His human likenesses, not to mention His own divine legacy; concerned, that is, with how He can keep His followers persuaded as a people.

These largely implicit issues lead God to sweeten His covenant-argument for Abraham, in an effort to induce him to become the father of all those nations that God will rule over in the days to come. Even more, He claims He will protect Abraham: "I will bless those who bless you, and him whom curses you, I shall curse" (Gen 12:1–3). This part of the covenant-argument implies another threat of violence, but it is at least not directed at Abraham, His covenant-partner, but his enemies. God is shown as Abraham's protector when He punishes the Egyptian Pharaoh with plagues for taking Abraham's beautiful wife, Sarah (whom Abraham presents to Pharaoh as Abraham's sister to save himself), into his harem (Gen 12:10–17).

Later in the narrative, after Abraham has grown richer and much older, he remains without an heir, so God repeats His covenant-argument, this time appearing to Abraham "in a vision," proclaiming Himself to be Abraham's "shield" (Gen 15:1). This is another of God's many theophanies, to manifest Himself, His ethos, indirectly in a hallucination, a dream, or through an angel. These divine manifestations have a rhetorical goal, especially to those like Abraham, who already considered such visions and dreams to be sacred. They reinforce Abraham's beliefs and demonstrate God's power, His ethos as divine authority.

This dreamed speech is rhetorically significant because it is one of several dialogues within which human beings participate. Abraham, no longer the submissive devout, dares to question God's repeated covenant-argument: "O Lord GOD, what wilt thou give me, for I continue childless, and the heir of my house is Eliezer of Damascus . . . a slave born in my house shall be my heir" (Gen 15:2–4). In answering, God appears to Abraham, this time as His "word" (Gen 15:4)—a term more closely linked to *dabhar*, the Hebrew word for a co-occurring "word" and "deed."[10] God escorts Abraham under the night sky and commands him to look up at the countless stars and count them (Gen 15:5–6).

The stars are yet another natural sign, like the rainbow, to support God's covenant-argument. They constitute celestial evidence to Abraham that a slave will not be his heir (Gen 15:4), and a reminder to Abraham about God's power, what Abraham cannot do that God can—count those stars. In this speech, and in the covenant-argument, God invokes astral signs to convince Abraham that His covenant-claim is beyond doubt or dispute. Earlier, God had argued that Abraham's "descendants" would be invented, like Adam, out of "the dust of the earth; so that if one [a mere human] can count the dust of the earth," then Abraham would be able to count his future progeny (Gen 13:16). In both arguments, God draws upon rhetorically infallible signs from the natural world He has made to amplify the magnitude of Abraham's future as well as God's power over that future.

---

10. Lee, *Jesus and the Metaphors of God*, 112. Lee calculates that God as "word" appears in the Bible 240 times in singular form and twenty times in plural form, with nearly half of the singular pronoun references based on "the prophetic Word/Event formula, 'The word of God came to me,'" 113.

In both, too, God seems to draw arguments from three different "places" or *topoi*, as Aristotle called them, common to all kinds of arguments—the future, magnitude, and the possible vs. impossible.[11] As the origin of all history, God is shown to predict with unwavering certainty what Abraham's future will be. As the source of this history, God must appear to have impossibly accurate calibrating powers far in excess of Abraham and all other humans. To be able to count all the stars in the sky or all the specks of dust on the earth are direct challenges to Abraham's quiet doubts about his covenant-partner's abilities. The sheer enormity of these natural signs magnify God's power to do what no one else can, offered as irrefutable evidence for the truthfulness of His covenant to a listener even now not entirely sure of his promised legacy. Confronted by even a modicum of doubt, such as Abraham's, God invents and amplifies His rhetoric to overwhelm that doubt, a strategy He uses on many occasions, especially, as we will see in the next chapter, to refute Job.

To magnify His power even further, God draws an argument from another of Aristotle's common *topoi*—past facts[12]—to convince Abraham that He will honor the covenant: "I am the LORD who brought you from Ur of the Chaldeans, to give you this land to possess" (Gen 15:7). God, we must remember, has already invented an argument from past facts in the Noah story, when He recalls why His human likenesses will only live a certain amount of time, given how He made them. But Abraham's doubts persist, so God must now resort to an old ritual of moving between the parts of several sacrificed animals to show Abraham another infallible sign of how he shall know that he *has* the land God offers (Gen 15:7–11).

Abraham, however, remains a dubious audience, far more resistant than Adam or Noah. As a result, God comes to Abraham in the theophany of a dream of His voice and paints a bit darker future for His covenant-partner. Drawing from His unlimited knowledge of that future, God is shown to emphasize why it will take a long time for Abraham to see the land God promised. In that dream, God describes the Hebrew enslavement under the Amorites and the wanderings of the Hebrews for 400 years before they inherit the land He has promised Abraham (Gen 15:12–14). This fate He commands Abraham to "[k]now of a surety . . ." But Abraham himself "shall go to [his] fathers in peace . . . [and] shall be buried in a good old age" (Gen 16:15). Such assurance seems to be God's way of softening what is otherwise a quite nightmarish future for Abraham's progeny, one that prophesies what later happens to the Hebrews in the Book of Exodus.

11. Aristotle, *Rhetoric* 2.xxiii–xxv, 1.vii.3–4.
12. Aristotle, *Rhetoric* 2.xix.11–22.

This foretold delay does not stop God from again appearing to Abraham at the ripe old age of ninety-six, once again to argue for the covenant He has made with him and to change His covenant partner's earlier name of "Abram" to "Abraham," characteristic Hebrew word-play, annotators indicate, for "father of a multitude." Speaking behind Abraham's back, God asserts: "I am God Almighty . . . I will make my covenant between me and you, and will multiply you exceedingly" (Gen 17:1–3). Face down, Abraham hears his name changed so that God can repeat again the same reasons He has offered before: Abraham's new name signifies his future fecundity, a father out of whom God "will make" many "nations" and many "kings." God again promises to be the single deity of all of Abraham's descendants and to give them the land He has already promised.

The one new demand God argues for is "the sign of the covenant"—the circumcision of all Abraham's descendants, be they progeny or "bought" from foreigners (Gen 17:9–14). This demand is another of God's conditional claims. If any in Abraham's line is not circumcised, he violates God's covenant-argument and—the pun could hardly be accidental—"shall be cut off from his people . . ." In this same scene, God also changes Abraham's wife's name from Sar'ai to Sarah, since she shall bear Abraham a son and become "a mother of nations; kings of peoples shall come from her" (Gen 17:15–16).

God's renaming of Abram and Sar'ai has a clear rhetorical function in inventing this covenant-argument, as does His including the sign of circumcised males. God is shown to be reinforcing and further amplifying His promises of generational fecundity, fame, and land acquisition through the names He gives His audiences—one of the many ways Aristotle outlines for inventing arguments.[13] These new names enlarge and implicitly praise the very attributes God promises the name-bearers shall embody. The circumcision sign, Bible annotators explain, is "external," implying that Abraham and his descendants will represent members of an exclusive community bound to their one God. As a sign, it both *proves* that membership and *reminds* members of their obligations to God to uphold it, to stay persuaded by His covenant. In being so particular, it is markedly different from the rainbow, which represents a far broader covenant with Noah and all living creatures.

Readers should pay close attention to Abraham's quite unusual reaction to God's repeated covenant-argument. He laughs at it, as later does Sarah (Gen 17:17; 18:12). Laughter is a rare response to God's rhetoric, and

---

13. Aristotle, *Rhetoric* 2.xxiii.29. Aristotle explains that arguments drawn from names are "commonly employed in praising the gods." Here, God's name changes reinforce His covenant-argument as a way of praising Abraham and Sarah, not to mention God Himself.

so far as I can tell it is *the first and the last time* in the Bible anyone laughs at what God claims. Abraham and Sarah cannot quite believe they can have a child at their ages. However, God's rebuttals to Abraham's and Sarah's skeptical laughter differ. He counters Abraham's by simply reiterating His prediction: that Sarah will, indeed, give birth to a son, whom God, showing His penchant for ironic puns, names "Isaac," meaning "he laughs" (Gen 17:19–21). This act, too, illustrates God's inventing a name to make a self-reflexive comment on Abraham's unusual response. Abraham's other son, Ishmael, born of his wife's maid, Hagar, will also be fertile and prosperous; but God's covenant-argument is only relevant for Isaac.

Sarah, on the other hand, only "laughed to herself" about having sex and bearing a child. God's absolute power as a rhetor is shown to include mind-reading (Gen 18:13–14). He can hear her laugh and her doubt, though the narrator explains neither is audible, so God asks Abraham: "Why did Sarah laugh, and say, 'Shall I indeed bear a child, now that I am old?' Is anything too hard for the LORD? At the appointed time, I will return to you, in the spring, and Sarah shall have a son." Abraham says nothing in response to God's prediction: but, fearing what God may do, Sarah denies her skeptical laughter. God's retort to her denial is swift, corrective, and stern: "No, but you did laugh" (Gen 18:15).

All these interactions take place, recall, when God assumes human form one hot afternoon in front of Abraham's tent "at the oaks of Mamre" (Gen 18:1), long believed to be a sacred location to Hebron's north. It is there that Abraham invites into his tent three strangers passing by for food and drink, a common courtesy of the time and place. It is a matter of some theological debate, given the annotations to this scene, whether God appears as three men, two, or just one, or whether the three were all angels, theophanies of God, or God Himself. In any event, Abraham does not seem at first to recognize the strangers' divinity, though the narrator explains that God took human form to speak directly to Abraham. This, it seems, is God's first explicit human incarnation, well in advance of His supposed incarnation as Jesus in the New Testament. So God asks, as He did of Adam and Cain, where Sarah is, though He knows full well her location and what she thinks to herself.

God's later question about Sarah's internal laughter is fully rhetorical, since God paraphrases her thoughts *before* He makes a key argument nested inside another rhetorical interrogative. Strangely, God's paraphrase seems very loose, if not mistaken. After she laughs to herself, the narrator further reports that Sarah thought, "After I have grown old, and my husband is old, shall I have pleasure?" (Gen 18:12). Given their ages, she and Abraham have not been sexually active for some time, and this very fact prompts her silent laughter after she hears God promise Abraham heirs. Despite its interrogative form, Sarah silently scoffs at God's claim, doubtful she can still enjoy sex.

Yet the narrator's report is notably different from God's paraphrase of what she is thinking. God recasts her argument as a question about her reproductive capability: "Why did Sarah laugh, and say 'Shall I indeed bear a child, now that I am old?'" (Gen 18:13). God rephrases Sarah's thoughts to stress human reproduction, but Sarah's unspoken concern seems far more carnal. God's second rhetorical question exploits the earlier paraphrase. He counters Sarah's interrogative with one of His own, implying His rebuttal argument. God claims power to make the impossible possible, as He did with Abraham—Sarah's impregnation in her late 90s. God compares Sarah's doubts and human limitations to His own divine power and again answers His own ironic question as He asks it: "Is anything too hard for the LORD?" (Gen 18:14).

Bolder and more quarrelsome than either Adam or Noah, Abraham resists God's rhetoric in a later scene. On the verge of totally destroying Sodom and Gomorrah, God pauses in another moment of self-addressed rhetoric. Apparently, while still in human form, God and the other two "men" are being led to the fateful cities, when God wonders, "Shall I hide from Abraham what I am about to do, seeing that Abraham shall become a great and mighty nation, and all the nations of the earth shall bless themselves by him?"(Gen 18:17-19). The issue for God in this brief soliloquy appears twofold: whether He should reveal His plan of destruction, as He did to Noah, and whether He is close enough to Abraham to do that. On the first issue, God is shown to be ostensibly worried about what Abraham might think about what He is going to do to these cities. Abraham could think Him monstrous, even evil, and be afraid that God will do much the same to the many nations Abraham will sire. The second issue is more a matter of trust. God does not speak to just *anyone*, much less waste arguments on those He does not in some way know or want to use. He has, indeed, chosen Abraham as His new covenant-partner, His new audience, yet God still wonders if He can trust him.

God seldom soliloquizes very long before He quickly talks Himself out of any doubt or hesitation—"No, [that is, God shall not hide his plan from Abraham]." This is God's claim against His own uncertainty, followed by His reason, "for I have chosen him, that he may charge his children and his household after him to keep the way of the LORD by doing righteousness and justice; so that the LORD may bring to Abraham what he has promised" (Gen 18:19). God is shown to convince Himself to reveal His plan to Abraham, based largely on His own ethos as God, who makes no wrong choices, and not on any inherent traits Abraham may have as His trusted partner. Further, this God has heard "the outcry" against the cities' "sins" and "will go down" to find out if the indictments have any basis in fact (Gen 18:20–21).

The last time God went "down" to investigate a rumor, the world fell into a great confusion of tongues and into many contending rhetorics. God's decision to destroy the collective wickedness in these cities again shows His willingness to use Aristotle's inartificial proofs—in this case, violence—if artificial ones—arguments and signs—do not or will not work. Here, though, as with the Nephilum, God makes no verbal effort to persuade the wicked in these cities to stop their abominations, or even to command them to do so predicated on a threat of violence if they do not comply. His planned violence as well as His brief self-address may strike some readers as odd, even contradictory, since this God is presumably a mind-reading, all-knowing deity. He should be able to tell already what Abraham will think of what He is about to do, since He seems to know the inhabitants of these cities will simply ignore His appeals, even if they included a threat, just as He knew Sarah's thoughts.

God's rather thin justification prepares readers for the narrator's report of His argument with Abraham, His chosen one. Abraham, as it happens, tries to talk God out of His own self-appeal to violence against the wicked, trying to convince God *not* to destroy both the "righteous with the wicked" (Gen 18:23–32). To counter God's planned violence, Abraham proposes a series of hypothetical cases, each in interrogatives, each decreasing the number of righteous people, from fifty to ten. With each hypothetical, Abraham strives to overcome God's own *argumentum ad baculum*. More important, though, than the diminishing numbers in his hypotheticals are the arguments Abraham makes to elicit God's concessions.

First, Abraham appeals to God's ethos as a fair judge of people's sins: 'Far be it from thee to do such a thing, to slay the righteous with the wicked, so the righteous fare as the wicked" (Gen 18:25). Then he repeats the key phrase, "Far be that from thee!" and argues further by asking, "Shall not the Judge of all the earth do right?" This is an astonishing moment in the development of God's rhetoric so far. It is the first time any human being in the Old Testament tries to challenge, if only implicitly, God's own morality, His own invented and widely promulgated ethos as supremely good and just. Job, of course, does precisely that later on, but here God relents, or seems to. He appears momentarily convinced that He must maintain His ethos, or else some of His divine authority and rhetorical power may appear to others as fully compromised.

Abraham also helps his case when he belittles his own ethos, his right to argue with God, since he is, like Adam and all living creatures, "but dust and ashes" (Gen 18:27). God, however, grows quite impatient with these counter-arguments, since twice Abraham pleads, "Let not the Lord be angry" (Gen 18:30–32). Persuading this God not to be angry, not to engage in wholesale destruction, is no small task; and some readers may think Abraham is heroic for even trying. In the end, though, God will not be persuaded; and He largely dismisses Abraham's pleas, saving only Lot, Abraham's grandson, and Lot's two daughters. Resorting to another destructive theophany, as "brimstone and fire," this God destroys all the wickedness of the cities. Not since the flood has this God turned to a rhetoric of sweeping violence, manifested through nature's own forces—in this case, forces many Christians now typically associate with Hell, not God's persuasive theophanies. In a later scene, God only utters a *threat* of violence to accomplish His rhetorical goal, again exploiting *argumentum ad baculum* to persuade a king to give Sarah back to Abraham before the king, again thinking Sarah was Abraham's sister, has had a chance to sleep with her. Speaking through a dream theophany, God spares the king duped by Abraham's lie and lifts the curse of sterility He had imposed on the king's land (Gen 20:1–18).

A very different, far more submissive Abraham emerges when God demands that His covenant-partner sacrifice his son, Isaac. In this well-known narrative, God is shown as needing to test His servant once more, to verify his obedience (Gen 22:1–24). God's need for such verification could very easily be justified, since an earlier, even more humble Abraham had dared to argue with God and question His own ethos. The issue, in this case, seems much the same for God as the one in Eden: How loyal are His likenesses to His covenants? Put another way He is asking, "How fully persuaded and convinced are My human inventions that I am who I say I am?" Like some human rhetors, God appears as anxious about His own invented ethos of infallible power as He is about how effectively He is making His case.

Oddly, Abraham makes no counter-arguments in this story as he did in earlier ones (Gen 22:1–18). Nor does he laugh. Beyond His simple command, God does not even have to persuade Abraham to sacrifice his son. The very absence of any rhetorical exchange may be what makes this story so horrifying for some readers. God simply orders the man to whom He has promised a legitimate heir for building a vast nation to murder that very heir, his own son. Abraham dutifully obeys, though the narrator presents the entire scene as but a "test" as far as God is concerned. Why God should want to test Abraham's loyalty and faith is for merely quizzical readers far from clear, and neither God nor the narrator makes any effort to explain this test.

Yet God stops the sacrifice at the very last second, taking the theophany of an angel who explains that God now "know[s] that [Abraham] fear[s] God" (Gen 22:12). To be afraid of God's power and authority is one way—one very important way—His human likenesses can show they are fully compliant with His rhetorical demands. Abraham's reward for not just being afraid but *showing* this fear in what he is about to do is God's repeated covenant-argument: now God "will indeed bless" His servant and multiply his descendants (Gen 22:17). God later repeats much the same covenant-argument to Abraham's favored son, Isaac. There, He appeals to His authority and the tradition of covenant-making with Abraham, whose obedience to God's "voice" and "laws" is His reason for re-making the covenant with Isaac (Gen 26:1–5). God's appeal is, rhetorically, *argumentum ad verecundiam*, except that *He* is the authority of all the ancestry to which he appeals. This strategy of persuasion, it so happens, like the *argumentum ad bacculum*, ends up in human rhetorical traditions among other fallacious appeals that can and should be easily dismissed.

God adopts this strategy many times in the Bible, since He must often remind His different audiences that His covenants are based on a long, hallowed tradition that He must often invoke. He repeats the Abrahamic covenant to urge Isaac to build an altar at Beersheba (Gen 26:24). He repeats it to Jacob, who dreams of a ladder ascending to heaven, this time adding Isaac's name to the roll-call of God's covenant-partners (Gen 28:13–15). Each appeal underscores God's authority, and the tradition of covenant-arguments He has made with other audiences in the past. Yet each time this God must make the appeal suggests His own need to keep bolstering His invented ethos in the face of humans' quite predictable tendency not only to forget God, but to cease being persuaded by His covenant-arguments.

Inventing the Covenant-Argument for Moses

God's most profuse rhetorical performances appear in the Book of Exodus, with Moses as His primary audience. Crushed by their enslavement in Egypt, the biblical narrator explains, "Israel groaned under their [Egyptians'] bondage and cried out for help," until "God heard their groaning, and God remembered his covenant with Abraham, with Isaac, and with Jacob. And God saw the people of Israel, and God knew their condition" (Exod 2:23–25). On Mount Sinai (or Horeb), Moses confronts God's angel as a burning bush—a double theophany—who calls out to Moses, whose answer, "Here am I" (Exod 3:4), repeats Abraham's when God had called upon him to sacrifice his son (Gen 22:1). God warns Moses not to approach the burning bush, appealing to Moses as He appealed to Isaac, based on the same tradition and authority of His past covenant-making (Exod 3:5–6).

Thus begins God's debate with Moses, and His efforts to persuade Moses to free Israel. God clearly starts this debate by inducing fear in Moses, who must hide his face while God speaks through the burning bush. The mere fact that Moses sees a bush burning without being consumed is cause enough for fear, since it is a theophany that obviously violates Moses's and most humans' understanding of how the natural world works.

God, meanwhile, begins His argument through personally identifying with Israel's suffering (Exod 3:7–8). "Identification," Kenneth Burke explains, "is affirmed with earnestness precisely because there is division" so that "[i]dentification is compensatory to division."[14] God knows Israel's suffering and oppression and assumes His people's interests are His own, though He remains utterly separate from Israel itself. God attempts to become "consubstantial," as Burke would say, with the nation He has been trying to form insofar as He identifies with Israel's plight even if His "interests are not joined" to Israel's but only assumed to be, or if He's persuaded Himself that they are.[15] In fact, God's very identification with Israel's condition is the primary reason He offers Moses for coming "down to deliver them [Hebrews] out of the hand of the Egyptians, and to bring them up out of that land to a good and broad land, a land flowing with milk and honey . . ." (Exod 3:8). This, presumably, is the same land God had offered to Abraham to induce him to accept His covenant-argument. Moses must now become God's human agency to fulfill and support His earlier yet not kept covenant-claim.

Initially, Moses doubts whether he's the one to deliver an entire nation out of slavery. God tries to overcome those doubts, repeating part of the same covenant He had made with Abraham, Isaac, and Jacob: "But I will be with you; and this will be the sign for you, that I have sent you: when you have brought forth the people out of Egypt, you shall serve God upon this mountain [Horeb]" (Exod 3:11–12). This brief argument again shows God's identifying His power and authority with Moses himself, pointing to the evidentiary "sign" He will show Moses when he brings Israel to Horeb/Sinai to worship Him.

But Moses resists and, for all his fear and trembling, insists on knowing what he is to call this God when the people of Israel ask for His name. This question, not to mention Moses's resistance, prompts one of God's most powerful, memorable rhetorical inventions so far. We have already

---

14. Burke, *Rhetoric of Motives*, 22.
15. Ibid., 20.

remarked on the absolute inventive power of God's own words, His power to make what He names—a power partly transmitted to His human likenesses, or else human beings would lack the rhetorical capacity to name and argue with each other and with God Himself. In this instance, Moses calls upon God to name Himself, and God answers: "I AM WHO [THAT] I AM" (Exod 3:14). This is one translation of what is not so much a name as a full-blown rhetorical claim, a proposition. Biblical annotators observe that this line refers to the etymology of Israel's God's name, Yahweh, originally spelled without vowels as YHWH. However, this translation can be connected with another, I WILL BE WHAT I WILL BE, insofar as YHWH is linked to the Hebrew verb *havah*, "to be." The name itself suggests not the first-person pronoun "I" but the third person, making the literal translation, "He causes to be." This ancient, enigmatic name for God appears about six thousand times in the Hebrew Bible, each time an assertion of God's covenant-arguments with Israel.[16] Originating with the Israelites who lived in the small state of Judah in the south, "Yahweh" became God's name passed on through oral traditions, while the name "Elohim" was adopted by those living in the larger northern city of Israel.[17]

Certainly more must and will be said about these and other names for God in chapter 8; but this one line has been seen as a vivid instance of how God's "rhetoric overflows into sheer authority" when He confronts Moses.[18] To answer Moses, "Yahweh massively proclaims, *Ehyeh asher ehyeh*," which may be translated, not as tradition has it, "I Am Who/That I Am," but as "I will be present whenever and wherever I will be present."[19] This alternate translation can imply a darker sense, "And I will be absent whenever and wherever I will be absent," including God's absence at the destruction of His own temple, at the German death camps, [and] at Golgotha."[20] This single line can be seen as well to suggest God's ethos as a frightening ironist[21]—not irony in the sense of God's verbal style (I address that in chapter 6), but irony, as Kenneth Burke puts it, as a way of thinking, a way of arguing and dialectically proving and saying opposites—in this case by *being opposites*. Irony as a mode of thought, not simply a turn of phrase, is closely associated with issues of law, justice, and "matters of prophecy and prediction in

16. Bloom, *Jesus and Yahweh*, 127.
17. Armstrong, *Bible*, 14.
18. Bloom, *Book of J*, 245.
19. Bloom, *Jesus and Yahweh*, 27.
20. Ibid., 28.
21. Ibid., 133.

history," whereby what may cause a society to rise and succeed may also necessarily lead to its fall and decline.[22]

In deciphering the details of this line in ancient Hebrew, some have argued that God's claim lacks sufficient "context" to be translated with complete accuracy. Thus, "God could be saying, 'I am what I shall be'; in effect, the more threatening, 'You'll find out who I am.'"[23] The line could also mean "I am what I do," since "God is defined by what he does, [and] defined this way even for himself." It has also been suggested that, as a literary character in the Hebrew Bible, God's "actions precede his intentions, or at least they precede full consciousness about his intentions," leading readers to conclude that God does not really know Himself very well at all.

As a rhetor, though, this God is shown to know exactly what to say to amplify His authority before Moses, His chosen deliverer. In the traditional translation of the line in the Christian Bible, God's self-naming looks like a mere tautology, repeating the same idea—His "I am"—twice, with the tenuous, quasi-logical link of "who" or "that" between the two copulatives. A tautology like this, if said or written by one of God's human likenesses, could very likely be rejected by some listeners as wholly fallacious. Coming from God's reason-defying theophanies, the same utterance takes on qualities that both anticipate and defy any skeptical retort to the first assertion of "I am." God's claim seems very close to what one philosopher has called a "pragmatic tautology," wherein a given statement such as "I am awake" "is vindicated in [the] very act of asserting it." This kind of tautology recalls Descartes' famous formulation, "I think, therefore, I am," perhaps unconsciously derived from Saint Augustine's counter-arguments to academic skeptics.[24] It may even be the very sort of verbal act God performs in inventing the world.

The exact meaning or origins of God's own proper name may never be completely known or decided. What matters in His name-revelation to Moses is God's insistence that His name and His identity are at the core of this covenant-argument. To amplify His initial self-naming, God repeats it in the longest speech He has so far made. In that speech, He invents Moses's own rhetorical authority, instructing His messenger to repeat a shortened form of it: "Say this to the people of Israel, 'I AM,' has sent me to you" (Exod 3:14). This abbreviated form of God's initial tautology may explain why so many philosophers have tried to link God's proper name with existence itself, with the very cause of being. It may explain, too, why some postmodern

22. Burke, *Grammar of Motives*, 503, 516–17.
23. Miles, *God*, 99.
24. Sorensen, *Brief History of the Paradox*, 169–70.

thinkers have questioned whether these associations do not, in fact, turn the biblical God into an existential "idol," making God as Being the fundamental premise for all philosophical and scientific thought, without which both philosophic and scientific inquiry could never begin.[25]

None of these concerns, obviously, is on Moses's mind. Moses seeks very practical information, since most gods have names which, when used, invoke power and authority for the speaker using them. As He has with Abraham and others, God recalls for Moses His traditional covenant-making authority (Exod 3:15). Yet, as He does this, He teaches Moses the very same *argumentum ad verecundiam* that Moses will need to bolster his own authority as God's deliverer. God's speech, then, must emphasize His covenant-argument for Moses, an argument largely focused on His own name: "this is my name for ever, and thus I am to be remembered throughout all generations" (Exod 3:15). Further, this God of naming, this God who invents through names, this God as name, repeats all that Moses must say to convince "the elders of Israel." Moses must repeat what God has already said; but, in repeating it, God predicts the rhetorical outcomes of His name-argument (Exod 3:13–19): Israel's elders will believe Moses and accept his ethos as God's messenger, but the Pharaoh will not and will not free Israel "unless compelled by a mighty hand." This prediction precedes another of God's violent threats, one that He will eventually enact against Egypt, even as He commands Moses to allow Israel to loot Egypt's wealth (Exod 3:19–22).

In these respects, God's rhetorical address to Moses differs from previous arguments. God has never before promised *any other audience He would destroy any particular nation*, even though Abraham had to go to war against other nations without God's help (Gen 14). Prior to Exodus, some argue, God has not adopted a war-like ethos or urged any covenant-audience to conquer an enemy-nation and ransack its wealth. It is certainly true that God does destroy Sodom and Gomorrah, but He does not do it as part of any war but because the cities represented "a direct, sexual affront" to God on His visit as a human theophany.[26] If readers of the Christian Bible take a closer look, though, they will find that God *does* foreshadow His war-like ethos prior to Exodus. Jacob encounters God's angelic theophanies on his way back home, calling them "God's army" (Gen 32:2). In Jacob's journey back to Mamre, God creates "a terror ... upon the cities" surrounding Jacob and his sons to protect them in their travels (Gen 35:5).

Like Abraham, the quarrelsome Moses does not think the elders of Israel will accept his authority as God's messenger; and Moses's own

---

25. For this view, see Marion, *God without Being*, 3, 33–36.
26. Miles, *God*, 100–101.

skepticism here may very likely mirror Israel's. Moses does not believe he is "eloquent" enough to persuade anyone (Exod 4:1–10). To convince Moses, God orders him to perform two acts, both intended as rhetorical signs to support the authority of His claim, and advises Moses on other signs he will need to show to persuade Pharaoh (Exod 4:2–9). To quell Moses's worries about his lack of rhetorical abilities, God chastises Moses, much as He does Sarah, who doubts her capacity to have sex in old age, and later Job, in his moment of deepest spiritual despair. Here the narrator shows God's adopting the rhetorical mask of feigned doubt—an *aporia*—to ask questions to which He already knows the answers. God's *aporiae* have appeared before: in Eden, and later with Abraham. His questions suggest answers that chastise Moses for doubting His powers: "Who has made man's mouth? Who makes him dumb, or deaf, or seeing, or blind? Is it not I, the LORD?" God then promises Moses He will be his "mouth and teach [him] what [he] shall speak" (Exod 4:11–12).

Moses, however, continues to resist these arguments, pleading with God to send someone else (Exod 4:13), presumably someone with greater rhetorical ability than he has. This is the first but not the last time Moses will anger God. In fact, soon after God has called Moses to be in His service, He tries to kill him because, being Egyptian, he is uncircumcised, though his wife performs a symbolic circumcision to save him (Exod 4:24–26). Still, God placates Moses, appointing his brother, Aaron, "who can speak well . . . And you shall speak to him [Aaron] and put words in his mouth; and I will be with your mouth, and with his mouth, and will teach you what you shall do" (Exod 4:14–15). God seems to have a very specific rhetorical pedagogy of imitation in mind here: Aaron will be the rhetor for Israel, a "mouth" for Moses who, in turn, will be the "mouth" for God, who also happens to be Moses's mouth. Yet Moses shall show the signs of God's ethos, His power, with his rod and, in doing so, be "as God" to Aaron (Exod 4:16–17). A transmission of rhetorical power is described here, based on two intermediaries, Moses and Aaron. Moses will repeat what God commands, and Aaron will echo those commands to other audiences. Yet the source of Moses's power remains with his teacher, to be channeled through Moses's rod, not as just verbal arguments but as God's rhetorical theophanies.

Fully aware of how difficult Pharaoh will be to persuade, regardless of Aaron's rhetorical abilities and Moses's divinely empowered rod, God plans on making His Egyptian audience even more resistant to Moses's pleas and signs. In fact, He tells Moses as much:

'I will harden Pharaoh's heart, and though I multiply my signs and wonders in the land of Egypt, Pharaoh will not listen to you;

then I will lay my hand upon Egypt and bring forth my hosts, my people the sons of Israel, out of the land of Egypt by great acts of judgment. And the Egyptians shall know that I am the LORD, when I stretch forth my hand upon Egypt and bring out the people of Israel from among them.' (Exod 7:3–5).

From a strictly rhetorical perspective, this is an astonishing speech, perhaps as astonishing as God's uttering the world into existence. Instead of multiplying languages, as He did in the Babel story, this God plans to multiply the resistance of an already antagonistic audience to the persuasive effects of His own rhetoric, and His own divinely taught rhetors, Moses and Aaron. Even the intensified recalcitrance on Pharaoh's side is rhetorically motivated to provoke God to argue even more persuasively and, in the end, to provide justification for His use of violent force to end all Egyptian resistance.

Judged according to any practical criteria for mere human rhetoric, God's plan makes no sense. No human rhetor, Aaron lest of all, would deliberately want to make an audience more resistant to persuasion, much less perform a violent act against an already persuaded one. A human rhetor would very likely seek strategies to soften a resistant audience's heart, not harden it. Few human rhetors, at least until the invention of atomic weaponry, would have imagined they had the military capability to threaten instant destruction of an entire army once verbal, rational persuasion failed. Here, though, God maintains precisely all of this. Drawing again upon the common *topos* of the future He knows and makes, God predicts Moses's rhetorical failures through words or God's actions through Moses's rod. These foreseen failures of God's "signs," those wondrously unnatural theophanies that manifest His ethos of power, are fully intentional, deliberate and, finally, the rationalization for yet another *argumentum ad bacculum*, for the rhetoric of violence that often follows such violent rhetoric once rhetoric's rational means are exhausted. Yet this final resort seems to have an unspoken rhetorical goal for God: not just His way to persuade Pharaoh to liberate the people of Israel but also to show both Hebrews and Egyptians He is the one, true God, that He *is* what He calls Himself.

No other motive I can think of quite accounts for God's prophecy of His own or His intermediaries' rhetorical failures. It will not be Aaron's eloquence or even necessarily *all* of the signs and wonders that ultimately prove persuasive. As a divine rhetor, God does not *have to* persuade anyone simply with words or arguments. In fact, Aaron's and Moses's arguments end up being the same pleas to Pharaoh that God had taught them. They are repeated, indignant commands to let the Hebrews leave Egypt, each with an appended threat of dire consequences if Pharaoh refuses to obey, as God knows Pharaoh will (Exod 7—8).

The ten plagues God sends against Egypt, each stronger, more destructive than the next, are theophanies of divine power; but these theophanies also resemble Aristotle's "inartistic proofs." They are not reasons, enthymemes, examples, signs, and analogies a rhetor may invent, or appeals to a rhetor's own character and credibility and his audience's emotions and values.[27] Knowing how to invent artificial proofs, Aristotle declares, "make[s] a man a master of rhetorical argument."[28] "Inartificial" proofs, by contrast, include any evidence "which [has] not been furnished" by a rhetor's "own efforts . . . but were already in existence, such as witnesses, torture, contracts, and the like"—none of which a rhetor "must invent."[29] These inartificial proofs would presumably include violence or its threat, since this is the final, dark resort when all other arguments fail.

We should recall, too, that among Aristotle's various strategies for inventing an argument are those "signs" which necessarily prove a conclusion that a rhetor draws and wants others to accept. Clearly, as the biblical narrator presents them, these plagues are "signs" of God's power, His ethos, which he "multiplies" unto failure, failure that "multiplies" His power expressed in still more violent proportions. These "signs," not Aaron's verbal pleas, make the case which eventually persuades Pharaoh to release the people of Israel. God's final proof, opening the Sea of Reeds, destroys His Egyptian audience for the sake of persuading His own people that He is, indeed, who He says He is. As signs and wonders, then, God's theophany proofs depend on natural elements that *exist outside* of Him and are, as Aristotle says, "already in existence." In that sense, God's plagues could, like His other violent acts, fall under Aristotle's category of "inartificial" proofs.

Yet, in another sense, God's theophanies complicate Aristotle's distinction between these two kinds arguments. As theophanies, God's plagues are certainly not artistic in Aristotle's sense. Their forms are extra-verbal, even extra-rational. Yet many of them consist entirely of natural elements—serpents, frogs, gnats, flies, locusts, animal diseases, hailstorms. Only a few— the rain of fire, waters turned to blood, the angel of Death—seem obviously supernatural. Yet none of them lies outside of God and what He has already invented and fully controls, so they manifest and prove His own claim, His name and all that it implies. Those natural elements would, following Aristotle, have to be considered necessarily "true" signs. But what God does with

---

27. Aristotle, *Rhetoric* 1.ii.2.
28. Aristotle, *Rhetoric* 1.i.11.
29. Aristotle, *Rhetoric* 1.ii.2.

them—how He shows His power and authority *through* them, as arguments to persuade—clearly appear to violate many of the natural laws both Egyptians and Hebrews were familiar with and expected to apply. However, this God, as the narrator repeatedly demonstrates, controls these laws, having invented those just as much as He invented the elements. As His messenger, Moses can invoke the elements and revoke the laws governing them, using them as God's arguments against Pharaoh. This is not to say that the various plagues could not naturally occur; it means that God can make them occur whenever He wants, through Moses, as signs, as weapons to persuade and, finally, to subdue Pharaoh.

Some of God's plague-proofs Pharaoh's court sorcerers can mimic and, in other cases, He simply relents and stops the plagues (Exod 7—9). Not until the gnat plague do Pharaoh's magicians fail to reproduce God's; so Egypt's magicians, the narrator reports, are forced to admit the gnat plagues show "the finger of God" (Exod 8:18-19). The apparent weakness of some of these plague-proofs is intentional and permits God to keep hardening His audience's heart, even to the point that Pharaoh agrees to liberate Moses's people, only to renege, prompting even more plague-proofs (Exod 10—11). Only God's next-to-last proof finally persuades Pharaoh to release Moses's people—a proof inaugurating the festival of Passover, for which God instructs Moses in all the ritualistic details and their meanings (Exod 12—13). Here, as elsewhere, God's ethos shifts to that of Instructor, and His rhetorical goal becomes clearly didactic. Passover shall serve always as a reminder to Israel—again a necessary sign—of the night God passed over the homes of His people to kill the first-born of all Egyptian families. It will be a way for the people of Israel to remember the day of their liberation and recognize the truth of God's claim to absolute power as the one, true deity, His claim to the name He gives Himself. This is the lethal proof which finally breaks Pharaoh's will to resist, so God's rhetorical plague-proofs *do* finally succeed, temporarily (Exod 12:29-32).

Yet God's power to harden hearts against His own rhetoric soon compels Pharaoh to send his Egyptian armies after the liberated Hebrews. God's ethos cannot be fully persuasive until and unless His own people witness the utter destruction of Pharaoh's army. In another moment of self-addressed rhetoric, the narrator's omniscience permits our overhearing God's justification for leading Israel to the Sea of Reeds, and then into the wilderness, instead of directly taking them to the land of Canaan. God reasons that Israel may "repent when they see war, and return to Egypt" (Exod 13:17). This brief aside suggests that God believes His own people would choose continued slavery over war with the Egyptians if they believed they could escape both options and reach the promised land more quickly. Thus God redirects them, forcing them to prepare for battle (Exod 13:18). The implication is far from flattering to God's chosen people, but harsher criticisms from God await them.

Assuming the theophanies of fiery pillars for night travel and of cloud for day travel, God leads His people to camp by the Sea, prepared for battle, and once again hardens Pharaoh's heart. He justifies this strategy for Moses alone: to destroy the Egyptians allows God to "get glory over Pharaoh and all his host, and the Egyptians shall know that [He is] the LORD" (Exod 14:3-4). This sweeping destruction, in effect, serves as the lethal conclusion of God's rhetorical manipulation of Israel's enslavers, even though this miraculous sign has two audiences at once, Egyptians and Hebrews.

God repeatedly tries to persuade His people to accept the power and glory of His ethos as they wander in the wilderness. He makes bread from dew, forces water from rock—to bolster their faith and quell the murmurings against Himself and Moses (Exod 16-17). These, too, are rhetorical signs, intended to support God's claim to His name. But His people continue to balk at His commands, even after He helps Moses defeat the enemy, Am'alek. Finally, God offers a covenant to the people of Israel camping under Sinai: If they will heed His authority and commandments, He will make them "a kingdom of priests and a holy nation" (Exod 19:3-6).

To increase His persuasiveness, God assumes the form of fire and cloud, speaking to Moses "in thunder" (Exod 20:19). Through this theophany, God enumerates to Moses the Ten Commandments, the Decalogue.

Of all that God says in the Bible, the Decalogue perhaps remains His most well-known speech. Some would not would consider the Decalogue rhetorical at all, since they are God's "commandments," His divine rules to live by. Still, whatever else the Decalogue may be, it is, as Kenneth Burke remarks, an exemplar of hortatory language—language concerned not with what is or is not but language urging what human beings shall and shall not do.[30] The language of God's Decalogue, for Burke, depends on "the principle of negation" so characteristic of most laws.[31] In fact, the Decalogue's negations suggest that even a divine rhetor such as God realizes He must rely on such verbal forms to address His human likenesses who seem already predisposed to doubt and violate God's covenant-arguments.[32]

30. Burke, *Language as Symbolic Action*, 44.
31. Ibid., 421.
32. See Horn, *Natural History of Negation*, 92. In this massive linguistics study, Horn traces many kinds of negations, noting "the central role of negation" in the "negative theology" of Buddhism and Hinduism, not to mention its importance in Christianity. Horne even refers to studies of Christ's use of the repeated negative formulation, "not X but Y" found in the Sermon on the Mount. Citation is to the reprint.

However negatively framed the Decalogue rhetoric may be, God's exhortations are not without reasoning, since they consist not only of commands but arguments based on premises.[33] God begins, for instance, by declaring who He is, the sort of God He is, and cites the recent historical evidence of His liberating the people of Israel from Egyptian slavery to support the ethos He projects (Exod 20:2). He will not tolerate Israel's worship of any other gods or any "graven image, or any likeness of anything that is in heaven above, or that is in the earth beneath, or that is in the water under the earth" (Exod 20:4-5). He offers a reason for this command—He is "a jealous God," an admission that precedes another threat of violence, another *argumentatum ad baculum*, against future generations "of those who hate" Him, a threat immediately softened by His promises of "steadfast love to thousands of those who love [Him] and keep [his] commandments" (Exod 20:5-6).

God offers a different reason to support the claim that His name not be spoken in vain, since it was long believed that knowing God's name gave humans magical power and could be misused.[34] In the Decalogue, too, God recalls past facts—His own process in inventing the world—to justify His commandment to keep the Sabbath day "holy" (Exod 20:8-11). Other exhortations against killing, adultery, theft, lying, and envy of others, however, are not justified (Exod 20:13-17), as if these orders needed no further elaboration beyond His own ethos to issue them. God follows His Decalogue with a far lengthier, more elaborate list of "ordinances," called the "Covenant Code" (Exod 21—24.), in some instances providing reasons for the laws He had earlier imparted to Moses (Exod 23). However, in many cases He simply exhorts His people, providing a catalog of case-law that they must follow. Near the end of His ordinances, God promises an angelic theophany to guard and protect Moses and Israel. This theophany must be obeyed precisely because the angel "will not pardon your [Israel's] transgression; for

---

33. Kennedy, *New Testament Interpretation through Rhetorical Criticism*, 7. In claiming that the Bible contains arguments, Kennedy is trying to rebut Grassi's argument in *Rhetoric as Philosophy*, 103-104, that the Bible's rhetoric is more revelatory, absolutist, and metaphorical than either classical Greek rhetoric's or the more modernist language of science. Throughout my analysis of the rhetoric of the Decalogue, I am indebted to Kennedy's work.

34. Bloom, *Jesus and Yahweh*, 127-28. Bloom notes that God's name, "YHWH," is as ancient and "forbidden" as it is magical and that "Yahweh is never rueful in affirming his true name, almost as though he himself felt the charismatic force and magical suggestiveness of that opening 'Yah.'" Bloom claims that the name is mentioned in Syria as early as 1400 BCE, and that it appears in "Deborah's Great War song" in the fifth chapter of Judges, which dates back as far as "the eleventh century BCE and could be the oldest text in Hebrew."

[M]y name is in him" (Exod 23:20). If Israel obeys God's angel, if it remains persuaded by all that He has exhorted them to believe, value, and do, and for the reasons offered, Israel's enemies will be God's own, and He will destroy Israel's future opponents so long as Israel does not adopt their gods. This is God's conditional claim to be Israel's defender *if* His people keep His covenant and *if* they remain persuaded to follow His commands. This claim, needless to say, foreshadows a great deal of God's violence and the punishments He will impose when Israel no longer acts as if it is persuaded (Exod 23:23–33).

Moses repeats orally both the Decalogue and the many ordinances to the people of Israel before he writes them all down (Exod 24:3–4). Later, Moses enters God's dark cloud and stays forty days and nights as God orally recites the commandments and laws, adding lengthy, detailed instructions for how He wants the ark, table, lamp stand, tabernacle, curtains, altars, and priestly vestments constructed and designed. God's didactic rhetoric extends through chapters twenty five to thirty-one, ending when He gives Moses "the two tables of the testimony, written with the finger of God" (Exod 31:18)—the same "finger" that Egyptian priests believed produced those persuasive plagues.

However, as happens many times over, the people of Israel are not fully persuaded by God's exhortations and soon defy His covenant-rhetoric. They make false idols and begin to worship them, prompting God's anger and yet another threat of violence against "the stiff-necked people" whom He has saved (Exod 32:9). God seems ready to kill them all, until Moses seizes on this issue and, like Abraham before him, tries to calm God down, appealing to His vanity as much as to His reason. After more Abrahamic interrogatives, Moses finally makes an emotional appeal to God, questioning Him in order to reproach Him. This *epiplexis* is a risky rhetorical strategy for Moses. It begins with Moses asking why God's "wrath burns against [His] people"— the very people He has freed (Exod 32:11). Here, Moses slyly reproaches God for overreacting to what *some* of His people did, implicitly warning God against reaching a hasty, sweeping generalization based on limited evidence. However inept Moses had felt about his own rhetorical abilities before, he is shown in this scene to be acutely aware that God's anger is rhetorically disproportionate and rhetorically fallacious. Moses taunts God again, asking whether He wants surviving Egyptians to think His intention in saving Israel was "evil," since He only saved them to destroy them Himself (Exod 32:12). The implicit reproach in Moses's question implies that God will not tolerate being thought or called "evil" by His enemies and that He will not perform an act that contradicts His previous actions. God, in short, should not want His intention miscast or seen as contradictory, since either would compromise His ethos.

I dwell on Moses's rhetoric here because it *does* persuade God not to destroy *all* of His people at that precise moment. Instead, as the biblical narrator omnisciently reports, God "repented of the evil which he thought to do to his people" and reaffirmed His covenant with them (Exod 32:14, 33:1-2). That reaffirmation does not stop Him from sending another plague theophany against Israel for the golden idol it made. Nor does Moses's rhetoric change His judgment about the Hebrews' stubbornness, even admitting to Moses that He cannot lead them to the promised land because He will "consume" them if He does (Exod 33:3-5). Instead, He wants angelic theophanies to lead them. Apparently, Moses is not satisfied with this decision and again talks God into sending His "presence"—His "face"—with them. God and Moses, the biblical narrator assures readers, speak to each other as "friends" (Exod 33:11), and their rhetorical exchanges are supposed to reflect that. Yet it is not entirely clear if God ever speaks directly, face-to-face, with Moses later on. God *does* agree to go with His people, but His reasons for changing His mind remain largely personal: Moses has pleased Him and He knows Moses by name, just as Moses knows Him by name (Exod 33:17).

God will have to rewrite the Decalogue, with Moses serving as His amanuensis, and much else after Moses breaks the first set of tablets (Exod 34:1-28). Yet Moses is far more to God than His scrivener. Moses will build the altar and tabernacle, at God's direction. Along with Aaron, Moses remains God's primary audience through most of the detailed rituals and hygienic and horticultural advice of the Book of Leviticus. In the Book of Numbers, Moses takes a census of God's nations and divides them up. In this same book, God takes on many roles: He plots military strategy with Moses, directs rituals for burnt offerings, sends plagues against His people when they violate His covenant, drafts people to fight in wars, sets property boundaries for Israel, appoints Joshua as Moses's successor, divides up the land, and directs the building of cities. In Deuteronomy, Moses speaks *for* God far more than God speaks *to* Moses, except that God does dictate "The Song of Moses" to Moses himself, who then teaches it to all of Israel to sing so they may be consoled in times of trouble (Deut 32).

Prior to that dictation, God argues with Moses again, drawing His claims, as He has done on many other occasions, from the common *topos* of future facts. He already knows *why* Israel will need the "Song" He composes for Moses to copy. Here, as elsewhere, the often omniscient biblical narrator presents God as a fully omniscient rhetor Himself who knows Israel's future and is completely capable of foreseeing what Israel will do, no matter how eloquent God's arguments are. God knows that, after Moses's death, His people will abandon Him, embrace other gods, and violate His covenant-arguments (Deut 32). God knows He will become angry with them and abandon them as well. No human rhetor ever enjoys this degree of omniscience and could never invent an argument that forecasts future events with such sweeping, absolute certainty; and the narrator's frequent omniscience underscores God's own, His ethos as sole, unrepeatable Author of all authorship.

God, though, is not just predicting what will happen to Israel: He is inventing the argument from the future to persuade Moses to copy and teach the "Song" to Israel, because they are going to *need* it. The "Song" "shall confront them as a witness" for failing to remain His persuaded elect. God's song about Moses, then, is not only a comfort to Israel but further evidence to indict them when they cease being persuaded to act on His covenant-arguments.

Obviously, describing and assessing every speech that God makes in the first five Books of the Bible would be a mammoth and tedious task, since God is shown repeating Himself quite often, largely because He *has to*—His audience's stubbornness and resistance demand it. These early Books of the Bible often show God as an often frustrated, easy-to-anger rhetor struggling to maintain His credibility with a doubting, stubborn audience. Yet, based on the examples presented here, readers should appreciate the ways God's rhetoric resembles that of His human likenesses and how it sometimes radically departs from theirs. Much, if not all, of what God invents when He argues is covenant-based. Each covenant is an argument invented to persuade various figures in the Bible, often framed in conditional promises to His human likenesses. They sometimes take the Aristotelian form of enthymemes, with a claim, premise, or exhortation, followed by a reason or a conclusion, but they often must be described in different terms. In other cases, when invoking His authority, or threatening or using violence to persuade, what God argues, and how, would easily fall into the human category of fallacious reasoning, judged in human terms, and even when he does, He appears impatient with any human likeness who dares to challenge Him. His omniscience, like His theophanies, collude in surpassing any capability a human rhetor has ever had.

Since "theophany" is mentioned often in this chapter as a rhetorical strategy quite beyond a human rhetor's capacities, and since this strategy will be the focus of attention in the next chapter as well, it is important to understand that the rhetorical function of "theophany" is closely connected to Perelman and Olbretchts-Tyteca's concept of evoking "presence" in an argument.[35] In human rhetoric, "presence" "acts directly on [an audience's] sensibility" by confronting that audience with a rhetor's selected data or datum, making what is remote, absent, in the future, or merely probable more immediate and certain. While Perelman and Olbretchts-Tyteca do not think the strategy of inventing rhetorical presence requires a "philosophical formulation," based on "ontology" or "anthropology," it is useful to recall that such a "formulation" does exist and is closely linked to rhetoric in Martin Heidegger's comments on *logos*.

Heidegger observes that Plato and Aristotle seldom consistently attach the same meaning to *logos*.[36] If its primary sense is "speech," as it seems to have been for the sophists, then Heidegger believes we must ask what we mean by "speech." And if we ask that, Heidegger argues, we are led to such "translations"—that is, interpretations—of *logos* as "reason, judgment, concept, ground, relation," and, finally, to speech-as-*logos*: "'connecting two things' or 'taking a position' by either endorsing or rejecting" what a speech is about. Though Heidegger never mentions the word "rhetoric" per se in his comments on *logos*, this last sense—positioning for judgment on what *logos* speaks about—seems closest to the conventional history of rhetoric's meaning. For Heidegger, the primary meaning of *logos*-as-speech is to make manifest what a speech talks about. "Logos," he writes, "lets something be seen (*phainesthai*), namely what is being talked about" to whomever is addressed. What is talked about demands speech as words (there are, after all, other ways to speak than vocalized sounds), which can "let something be seen in its togetherness with something, to let something be seen *as* something." That "seen *as* something" can be "true or false." The "true" speech of *logos* "take[s] beings that are being talked about . . . out of their concealment; to let them be seen as something unconcealed . . . ; to *discover* them." *Logos*-as-"false" speech does the opposite. It conceals or covers up, places "something in front of something else (by way of letting it be seen) and thereby proffering it *as* something it is not."

God's theophanies, regardless of their form, do just that for the figures He addresses—they let God be seen as present, His logos-as-speech or as act are made manifest and immediate to His audiences. By the same token, His theophanies can cover or conceal His full presence through selecting and presenting only what He considers necessary to let be seen. In this manner, His logos will show and not show itself in any given theophany, just as His name suggests.

---

35. Perelman and Olbrechts-Tyteca, *New Rhetoric*, 116–19.
36. Heidegger, "Being and Time," 77–79.

From all this, it is hard to agree completely with those who claim *all* of God's rhetoric is purely revelatory or invented "outside time."[37] Quite the contrary. God's rhetoric vacillates from being hortatory to didactic, clearly intending to intervene in the history of Israel, even to make and invent that history. His rhetoric is not completely inscrutable, though it often relies on and amplifies the mystery and authority of His ethos. His ironic mode often proves dangerous for His human likenesses, and He often invents His arguments from the *topoi* Aristotle and others have long since recognized in human rhetoric. Like His human inventions, too, He is fully capable of rhetorical self-address, posing issues and arguing with Himself about what He should or should not do, though these asides and soliloquies seldom depict a selfhood as fractured, divided, or changeable as human soliloquies do. On significant occasions, it is certainly reasonable to expect or desire this God to show an even greater degree of reflection and self-awareness than the self-addressed rhetoric provides. God is even shown to be amenable to human rhetoric, sometimes relenting and allowing Himself to be persuaded.

The question, obviously, is whether or how He varies His inventive strategies to make the rest of his case in the remaining books of the Old Testament, culminating, it seems, in His address to Job. Addressing that question, however, leads to another, more intensely theological issue: whether Christ and his story are God's final covenant,[38] His final invention, the last attempt He makes to persuade His human likenesses. These two questions are central to my next, and final, chapter on God's rhetorical inventiveness.

---

37. Kennedy, *New Testament Interpretation through Rhetorical Criticism*, 7.
38. Sutherland, "History, Truth, and Narrative," 113.

4

Inventing Final Covenants?

God's Rhetoric after Moses

Except for the Book of Job, which I come to shortly, God's rhetoric, from the Book of Joshua, through the Book of Judges, Samuel 1 and 2, Kings 1 and 2, Chronicles 1 and 2, seems to diminish considerably—and then we reach Jesus Christ of the New Testament. There, we face two daunting questions that must be addressed, if not definitively answered. Whether Christ himself may be seen as God's final rhetorical invention, the last covenant-argument to persuade His human likenesses to heed His exhortations and remain persuaded of His laws and His supreme authority? Second, precisely what argument is God making that we are to infer from Jesus's story (or stories) and his teachings?

God, obviously, is shown to speak rhetorically in the other biblical books mentioned above, and a great deal of rhetoric *about* God or *on* God's behalf appears in the major and minor prophets, in Psalms and Proverbs. Again, if the entire Bible is seen as one vast, intricate rhetorical act, as a singularly unified "book" (and not all would agree that it should be seen this way), hundreds if not thousands of pages would be needed to examine fully every argument God invents or every argument invented *for* Him by prophets, or *about* Him by poets.

My interest in this book, though, is only in God's *direct* rhetoric, in what the all-too-human narrators represent Him as saying and arguing for specific audiences in specific situations. Each of the prophetic books, from Isaiah through Malachi, represents what God has presumably told the various prophets to argue before the different generations of the people of Israel. God, for instance, speaks through Isaiah (Isa 1:1–2), just as He speaks through Jeremiah (Jer 1:4). Ezekiel reports in a first-person narrative what God allowed him to see and what God told him. In fact, in a wonderfully poetic passage, Ezekiel confesses that God forced him to eat scrolls which God presumably wrote in order for Ezekiel to prophesy at all (2:8). In the major and minor prophets, then, God's rhetoric, His eloquence, is mediated, indirect, expressed *through* the prophets, but not directly *by* Him.

In other books of the Old Testament, God remains conspicuously silent. As previously mentioned, He does not speak in the Book of Ezra or Book of Nehemiah. He remains silent in the Book of Esther and Ruth, as well as in Ecclesiastes and in the Lamentations of Jeremiah. In the Book of Daniel, He addresses King Nebuchadnezzer through two theophanies, a dream and a cryptically inscribed message, both warning the King that Daniel's prophecies come from God Himself (5:5). But this is true of almost all of the prophetic books, since each prophet takes upon himself the rhetorical responsibilities that God otherwise directly assumes in other, earlier books. I omit these works not because they lack mystical and poetic exuberance or rhetorical power. I omit them because the focus of this book, and these chapters, is on what God is directly shown to be arguing.

Much of what readers will find in the prophetic works—predictions of doom and disaster if Israel continues to sin against God and promises of great blessings if Israel repents its sins and accepts and keeps God's laws—could be classified as what Aristotle called epideictic rhetoric, arguments which praise or blame. Epideictic rhetoric has often been described, following Aristotle's lead, as "ceremonial" speech or writing, meant to display a rhetor's verbal abilities for a audience of spectators to judge. The etymological root of the word "epideictic," in fact, refers to its *showing*. As Aristotle points out, rhetors primarily base this kind of rhetoric in the present moment, the here and now. But rhetors may also "avail themselves of other times, of the past by way of recalling it, or of the future by way of anticipating it."[1] Nor is there any reason why praise or blame may not be a part—a significant part in some cases—of forensic or deliberative rhetoric.

In more recent times, however, Aristotle's description of epideictic rhetoric has been rightly challenged and significantly expanded. Chaim Perelman has argued that Aristotle's treatment is, at best, "misleading." To Perelman, epideictic rhetoric "is not only important but essential" to educate an audience. In making epideictic arguments, rhetors try to get audiences

---

1. Aristotle, *Rhetoric* 1.iii.4.

or readers to agree with those "values" being celebrated or those being condemned.[2] Perelman's view of epideictic rhetoric, then, seems far more applicable to the biblical prophets than Aristotle's. The prophets' efforts are by no means meant as mere "show." Their goal is exactly to condemn God's human likenesses when they drift away from God's covenant-arguments and to praise them and articulate the blessings they will receive if and when they act persuaded. In each case, the prophets focus on the God-given values the Israelites are supposed to follow. Yet to say as much already oversimplifies a great deal of rhetoric in these books which other scholars have spent much more time analyzing in detail than my one chapter could accomplish.[3]

In other Old Testament books, beginning with Joshua and including Judges, 1 and 2 Samuel, and 1 and 2 Kings, God *does* speak and often intervenes in Israel's history and its many wars. For readers of the Hebrew version of the Old Testament, the central narrative issue would seem to be whether the people of Israel will remain convinced and persuaded by God, since we already know what happens if God's human likenesses awaken from His powerful spell or forget, in His absence, the powerful presence He shows when He punishes those who ignore His arguments.[4] This narrative issue is obviously raised and addressed as well in the Christian Old Testament. For a rhetorical critic, it remains a central issue for God as a rhetor, just as it is the central issue for the prophets who speak for Him. Framed in this way, the issue often becomes, how long will the people of Israel stay persuaded by God's arguments? How effective and lasting is the rhetoric God has invented so far? These questions implicitly raise another—one of evaluation: How persuasive a rhetor is this God to those human likenesses He addresses, a complex issue addressed more fully in chapter 8.

After Moses's death, God only directly speaks to Joshua, Moses's successor. In that book, too, God speaks and acts as Joshua's military advisor and general, bolstering Joshua's courage and calling upon His past history with Moses as evidence to support His claim to keep His early covenant with Abraham (Josh 1:1–9). He "exalts" Joshua as Israel's new leader and

2. Perelman, "New Rhetoric," 1388.

3. Aside from works already cited, for rhetorical approaches, variously defined and defended, to analyzing the prophets and other works in the Bible, readers may wish to consult some of these studies as a brief sampling of what is available: Gitay, *Prophecy and Persuasion*; Barton, "History and Rhetoric of the Prophets," 51–64; Duke, *The Persuasive Style of the Chronicler*; Zulick, "Prophecy and Providence," 195–207; Kinneavy, *The Greek Rhetorical Origins of Christian Faith*; Lundbom, *Jeremiah*; Boomershine, "The Structure of Narrative Rhetoric in Genesis 2–3," 113–29; Fox, "Rhetoric of Ezekiel's Vision of the Valley of Bones," 1–15; Sternberg, "Bible's Art of Persuasion," 234–71; Pernot, "Rhetoric of Religion," 235–54; Slater, "Imagining Arrival," 107–121.

4. Miles, *God*, 154.

orders him to have the twelve tribes of Israel build a stone memorial where they cross the river Jordan (Josh 3:7-8). He appears as an angelic theophany, armed for battle, to topple the city of Jericho (Josh 5:13-14). In another natural theophany, He appears as hailstones to destroy Israel's enemies and later suspends natural law by stopping the sun's course (Josh 10). Even as Joshua becomes too old to engage in war against Israel's enemies, God assumes command as a military general in taking yet more land for Israel (Josh 13).

At one point, God is shown addressing all His people, again as an angelic theophany. There, too, He invents an argument by drawing from the *topos* of past facts, to remind Israel of its history with Him and the covenant to be upheld. Then He condemns Israel for their covenant violations and withdraws His military support (Judg 2:1-3—2:20-22). He later speaks to Judah, Samuel, Saul, David, Solomon, and various prophets. In only one instance in these later Books does God return to the self-addressed rhetoric often found in the Pentateuch, when He justifies to Himself cutting off Judah from Israel (2 Kgs 23:27).

All told, then, God variously commands, predicts, strategizes, and condemns in His various speeches, often through angelic and natural theophanies, as He has previously done—all to persuade His people to remain faithful to His covenant-arguments. No matter how forceful His ethos, or how authoritative His commands, or how miraculous His theophanies, His various audiences do not *stay* convinced or persuaded. If they did, God would no longer need to intervene, to invent appeals, or to threaten His human likenesses' very existence. In inventing those human likenesses, and in giving them the very verbal and rhetorical capacities He, too, displays, God seems also to have invented a very tough audience for Himself.

God's Rhetorical Whirlwind in Job

Certainly, Job is one of the toughest audiences God addresses, since Job provokes the longest, most magnificent instance of God's mercurial eloquence since the Pentateuch. This may be why the Book of Job generates so much controversy.[5] Biblical annotators characterize Job as a very old folktale orally circulated during the second millennium BCE, and likely written in Hebrew

---

5. The Book of Job has been a favorite text for rhetorical analysis. See Miles' interpretation, *God*, 308–33; and Greenstein's "In Job's Face/Facing Job," 301–317, setting two parallel and contrasting reviews of different interpretations of the Job story, side-by-side in opposing columns of text; and Steiner's comments on the story, *Grammars of Creation*, 44–50.

during the reigns of King David or King Solomon a hundred years later (1000—800 BCE). However readers may interpret this tale, it is impossible to ignore God's *enargia* in this speech, His vivid depictions of all that He has done, and His powerful ethos as divine authority. Likewise, it is hard to ignore parallels between the tormented, afflicted Job and the scourges and suffering that befall Jesus in the New Testament.

Given how the Book of Job ends, its beginning does not cast God in a very flattering light. After all, God lavishes ample praise on His servant's faith; but this praise prompts Satan (in Job still one of "the sons of God") to urge God to take away all He has given Job (Job 1:6). Satan quietly challenges God's praise of Job, again through interrogatives: "Does Job fear God for nought? Hast thou not put a hedge about him and his house and all that he has, on every side? Thou hast blessed the work of his hands, and his possessions have increased in the land." Then comes Satan's dare: "But put forth thy hand now, and touch all that he has, and he will curse thee to thy face" (Job 1:9–11). Strangely, perhaps for some readers even perversely, God takes Satan's dare, but with a condition: "Behold, all that he [Job] has is in your [Satan's] power; only upon himself do not put your hand" (Job 1:12).

This opening seems to be another of God's seemingly ironic "tests" of His most fervent believers and devoted servants, a way for Him to see how persuaded they really are. Yet, in his deconstructive reading of the Job story, biblical rhetorical critic David Clines argues that, for God, testing Job is more of "an experiment in causality," since "Satan has nothing to win or lose" in the "wager" with God.[6] Rather, the entire point of what happens to Job is for God to find out—to discover, or invent—whether "[Job's] piety hangs on [his] prosperity." For Clines, God must experiment with Job "not only for the sake of the truth, but even more for the sake of God's well-being." Otherwise, Clines reasons, God's own ethos would be greatly diminished, if not destroyed, "if it were to turn out that none of his [God's] creatures, not even the most godfearing man of all, loves [H]im for [H]is own sake but only for what they [His creatures] can get out of [H]im." Contra Clines, I would suggest that this is quite a lot for God to lose to Satan, since it would amount to God's loss of one of the most persuasive strategies He has, His ethos.

As an "experiment," however, the issue God seeks to address in the Job narrative seems quite different from His nearly incomprehensible testing of Abraham's belief when He orders the sacrifice of Isaac. Here, as with Abraham, God addresses an audience apparently already fully persuaded of His power and goodness. Yet Job's being and acting persuaded is not enough to

---

6. Clines, "Deconstructing the Book of Job," 74.

resolve the question of "moral retribution, the doctrine that one is rewarded or punished in strict conformity with the moral quality of one's deeds."[7] Clines's deconstruction of the Job story, a story to which over a "1,000 books and articles" have been devoted to display "the unequivocal answers of Job" about human suffering, highlights the many difficulties God's own experiment raises,[8] including God's and Job's motives.

God's own motives may outrage some readers, perhaps as they should. Why God, who can apparently read minds, should order Abraham, His trusted covenant-partner, to kill Isaac, Abraham's God-promised heir, to test Abraham's faith may seem incongruous and incomprehensible. Why God should agree to let one of His putative "sons"—Satan—punish and torment the devout, prosperous servant Job for the sake of testing a moral doctrine seems no less mysterious. In both cases, God's own omniscient ethos has to be set aside or ignored for the sake of each narrative's plausibility. Whether these narratives consist of tests or experiments does not appear to matter so much as whether God Himself is satisfied that His rhetoric remains persuasive.

Like the Abraham narrative, Job's story poses many questions this chapter can never satisfactorily answer. As one biblical scholar observes, being persuaded of God's rhetoric may not depend on intellectual assent at all. For ancient Hebrew writings, God's most devout must be persuaded in their "hearts," not just in their heads, that God's covenant-arguments are true, lasting, and just.[9] Of the eighty parts of the human body mentioned in the early books of the Bible, "brain" or its synonym is never mentioned, while *"leb"* and *"kardia"*—Hebrew words for "heart," for who a person really is, his or her internal, individual values—appear many more times and multiply in the prophetic books. The heart is an important metaphor for the location of the truth of God's arguments. The many words for that "truth" suggest God's arguments are appeals to His ethos as much as to His audiences' pathos, the innermost regions of their emotions and values. Yet, even in this sense, it is possible to wonder again why God's omniscient ethos does not extend to Abraham's or Job's hearts, why such cruel tests or, if you prefer, "experiments," are necessary at all.

Satan, of course, brings Job to utter ruin and Job's reactions to each loss, and his friends' reactions to Job's, make up the bulk of this narrative, until the very end, when God answers Job's most profound complaints "out of the whirlwind" (Job 38:1). Through this famous theophany, perhaps

---

7. Ibid., 66.
8. Ibid., 65.
9. Lee, *Jesus and the Metaphors of God*, 59, 66–67, 69–73.

rivalled only by the burning bush in Exodus, God's questions as well as His answers are reproaches of Job, apparently God's emotional appeals to Job's own heart. They form another, and more extensive, *epiplexis* such as Moses made in his debate with God. God's rhetorical stratagem is to put His questions to Job to rebuke and upbraid him while, at the same time, amplifying His argument by reminding Job, as He often does, of His ethos and all He has done to invent that ethos.

God's whirlwind rhetoric is complexly layered. In its broadest sense, God's entire speech, while in poetic form just as His *aras* are in Genesis, can be described as forensic or legal rhetoric, since God puts Job's complaints on trial and, as He does, again draws His arguments and appeals from two of Aristotle's common *topoi*—past facts and magnitude. Here, God begins his rebuke with more feigned doubt, another *aporia*, pretending not to know *who* Job is: "Who is this that darkens counsel / by words without knowledge?"(Job 38:2). God knows very well *who* Job is, so this question, like many others, does not seek information. God's question intends to ask *what* Job is, in his heart; thereby shrinking any authority Job may think he has to question God or to complain about what has happened to him. Then He demands that Job brace himself "like a man"; for God's role is to "question" Job and demand answers from him (Job 38:3).

The interrogation is ruthless, by any human standard, with each interrogative challenge aimed at belittling the already ruined Job, since he certainly cannot tell God where he was when God "laid the foundation of the earth," created day and night, the stars, and separated the land from the sea (Job 38:4–11). Here, and elsewhere, God invokes a knowledge of the past Job could not possibly have and flogs him with his ignorance. Job may have heard about God's generative fiats, but God continues to mock and taunt him by answering His own questions, since "surely [Job] know[s]" who determined the earth's measurements (Job 38:5). The interrogative bombardment continues, as God asks Job if he can control the movement of time, if he has "walked in the recesses of the deep," if he has confronted "the gates of death / . . . the gates of deep / darkness," and if he knows how large the earth is (Job 38:16–18). Here, and later, God pauses to command Job to answer His questions: "Declare, if you know all this" (Job 38:18), fully aware that Job cannot "declare" because he cannot know.

In the course of this mocking, ironic interrogation, God's questions emerge from what's happened in the past, so it seems understandable why some readers might want to leap to Job's defense and object that God's trying to badger His witness into a confession. Neither Job, nor his so-called friends, is eager to try that courtroom tactic with this prosecutor who also happens to be the judge as well. Given God's double role, Job has no audience for any objections he might raise. Job, of course, cannot possibly answer any of God's relentless questions. And that is their entire point: each one is an ironic reminder to Job of God's ultimate power over and knowledge of all natural forces and processes in the heavens and on the earth, so God pauses to ask again, "Shall a faultfinder contend with the Almighty? / He who argues with God, let him answer it" (Job 40:2).

At long last, Job does answer, only to admit his smallness, his inability to respond to God's questions, after which he falls silent and becomes a clearly reluctant witness (Job 40:3-5). Still, neither his admission nor his silence satisfies God, so He continues to challenge Job's power and knowledge. Only when Job can show "splendor" and sublime "anger" and destroy the prideful and the wicked will God "also acknowledge" that Job has any right to question Him (Job 40:10-14). Here, God pretends to concede Job some authority, but it remains an ironic concession God uses to wound Job yet again. This time, God recalls for Job the making of the great "Be'hemoth," the "Levi'athan," out of the same dust and clay used to invent Job and all earthly creatures. God vividly describes the Leviathan's power, size, and strength, then challenges Job again, "let him who made him [Levi'athan] bring near his sword" (Job 40:15-19). Following this challenge, God questions Job again—all to show that this servant, like His other human likenesses, cannot control or defeat the monstrous strength and power of God's Levi'athan, so Job should never presume he has the strength to challenge the Leviathan's own inventor (Job 40:19-24, 41:1--34). This elaborate example of God's past feats is but one of many He uses to support His case against Job. In the end, Job surrenders, repents his ignorance and weakness, and even quotes God's initial challenge to him. Now, though, Job has *seen* God's power, instead of just hearing about it (Job 42:1-6). So God restores to Job what Satan had taken from him and condemns Job's friends for their poor counsel and advice. Now reconciled to his God, Job "die[s], an old man, and full of days" (Job 42:7-17).

God's *epiplexis* against Job's presumptions is but one strategy of forensic rhetoric. Through His questions, God calls upon His own history for the evidence He rains down on Job. The evidence, obviously, enlarges God's own ethos at the expense of Job's as a mere human "faultfinder." Yet, if readers ask whether God really addresses Job's many laments, his spiritual sorrows, and the wretchedness that can befall even the most faithful and devoted of God's servants, the Job narrative remains an open, troubling question. Not all are likely to agree that God's blend of emotional appeals and past facts, His sarcastic taunts and ironic ridicule, really speak to Job's woes and complaints. The rhetorical strategies God invents may look like one grandiose digression from the painfully real suffering Job must endure to pass this divine test or survive this experiment. These questions still vibrate in any reader who pauses to consider seriously the issues the Book of Job raises about the human condition long after God's *epiplexis* concludes.

If we were focused on the Hebrew version of the Old Testament, not the Christian Bible's, the *epiplexis* would be the last speech God makes to His human likenesses, and it would be possible to conclude, perhaps provocatively, that Job has in effect silenced God.[10] But the Christian version of the Old Testament ends, not with Job, or God's *epiplexis*, but with the Book of Malachi, another prophetic work, written as a dialogue, to warn Israel to keep God's covenant with Moses and Abraham. The prophetic Malachi hints at a "messenger to prepare the way" before God sits in judgment on His human likenesses (Mal 3:1). This future messenger, at first ambiguous, becomes "Elijah" by the Book's end (Mal 4:6); yet Malachi's prophecy may further serve as a tenuous link between the rhetorical inducements of God's earlier covenants and the dominant figure of Jesus Christ in the New Testament.

Beyond that link, tenuous as it is, lies the more revealing parallel between Job, the last human being with whom God directly argues in the Hebrew Old Testament, and the figure of Jesus Christ suggested in Malachi's prophecy which ends the Christian Old Testament. Perhaps no other figure *before* Job suffers so much from God's pre-arranged punishments, be they test or experiment. God almost allows Satan to destroy Job and all that he possesses. Awaiting on the other side of the Old Testament Job's incredible suffering, however, is the figure of Jesus, whom God allows to be ridiculed, scourged, and humiliatingly crucified. Job is the nearly faultless human analogue to Christ's own sufferings, except that Jesus is supposed to be God's own "son," a perfect incarnation of God's own perfections. The theophany of God as a whirlwind of belittling, scourging rhetoric for Job ultimately leads to another divine incarnation, another theophany who will be as belittled and scourged as Job, and even killed for his uprightness.

Jesus Christ as the Final Covenant-Argument Theophany?

The contentious question, however, is the extent to which readers may consider Jesus as God's last theophany, the final covenant-argument God invents. This is a quite different question from whether Jesus *uses rhetoric* in the New Testament Gospels. Few scholars of rhetoric have doubts about this. One has examined in great detail what Aristotle called "deliberative

10. Miles, *God*, 329.

rhetoric"—arguments that Jesus made focused on what should or should not be done about any given issue, often political ones. This kind of rhetoric appears in Jesus's Sermons on the Mount and on the Plain.[11] Yet the more complicated interpretive problem, given this book's focus on God's eloquence, His rhetoric, is what Jesus's own life and ministry represent if he is God's own concluding attempt to invent a covenant-argument to persuade His human likenesses for good and for all.

Many readers may abandon my exploration here simply because the word "invention" is coupled to a divine personage who, it is widely believed, *actually* lived and died for human sinfulness. Again, the word "invention" as used throughout this book does not necessarily mean Jesus is a "fiction," "unreal," or "false." What I am suggesting is this: since much of God's rhetoric so far has been driven by His ethos and His rationales, such as they are, for His covenants; and since God often must find ways to convince and persuade His various audiences to accept and keep the covenants He offers, He has to keep finding ways to achieve this rhetorical goal. Finding these "ways" to argue and persuade audiences is what invention means for any rhetor, human or divine. It is in this sense that I speak of Jesus as the last argument God "invents." As a concluding theophany of God's ethos, Jesus dominates the four Gospels and much of what follows, so his persuasiveness cannot and should not be ignored.

As I have already said, the Gospel narrators do not often show God speaking directly in the New Testament. In the Gospel of Matthew, He appears to Joseph, Jesus's human father, in a double theophany, as an angel in a dream who assures Joseph, addressed as the "son of David," that he need not be afraid to marry Mary, whom Joseph was thinking of divorcing "quietly," because she was already pregnant (1:18–21). God's angelic theophany follows this claim with a reason: "for that which is conceived in her is of the Holy Spirit." The angel then issues an order, telling Joseph what to name the child and why: "she will bear a son, and you shall call his name Jesus, for he will save his people from their sins." This brief argument, like others, starts with an exhortation, an imperative claim, supported with a reason why such an exhortation is being made for the listener. In this case, God's angel draws one claim from the *topos* of past facts—Mary's conception with the Holy Spirit has already occurred. To speak of this divine "conception" as a "past fact," of course, already blurs any sharp line a rhetorical critic might hope to draw between this *topos* and Aristotle's *topos* for inventing arguments based on what is possible and impossible, since the angel's claim appears to violate all known "facts" about human births, then as now. The

---

11. Kennedy, *New Testament Interpretation through Rhetorical Criticism*, 42–72.

narrator, in this instance, reports the angel's speech as if those facts would not matter to Joseph or any reader. The holy conception is presented as a fait accompli whose impossibility is made overwhelmingly persuasive through the rhetorical presence of God's ethos as the angel.

The angel's second claim comes from the *topos* of future facts—why the child should be named "Jesus" and what he will do. Obviously, this exhortation, as narrated, can only be believed if the narrator already accepts the impossible facts of the first claim and knows God's intended meaning for the name and what Jesus will do in life. Divine foreknowledge is here, as elsewhere, asserted as an unarguable trait of God's ethos and a warrant for the truthfulness of the prophecy itself. Yet, as a prediction of what will happen, the angel's argument certainly resembles the claims made in the deliberative rhetoric human beings have long practiced. Joseph, confronted with God's truth-bearing theophany, is clearly in no position to question or reject either the argument or the prediction, though his acceptance of both seems fully necessary if he is to marry an already impregnated Mary and thus participate in verifying the angelic prediction.

Later, God briefly addresses all those who witness John's baptism of Jesus (Matt 3:16–17). In this scene, as soon as the baptism is complete, the gospel narrator claims that "the heavens were opened," and Jesus sees "the Spirit of God descending like a dove," and hears "a voice from heaven, saying, 'This is my beloved Son, with whom I am well pleased.'" Thus one theophany addresses and declares to listeners another theophany, Jesus himself. This particular identification of Jesus as God's "son" has generated any number of controversies, some of which are addressed below. Yet this brief speech seems, at the very least, to praise Jesus—another instance of God's recurring epideictic rhetoric, which began as far back as His genesis of all that is "good" in the world. God repeats the same praise to Jesus's disciples, Peter, James, and John, when Jesus is transfigured on top of a mountain and converses with Moses and Elijah. In this praise, God's audible theophany adds another exhortation, commanding the assembly to "listen to him [Jesus]" (Matt 17:1–5). These speeches and theophanies in the Matthew gospel appear again in the Mark Gospel (Mark 1:10–11—9:7), widely considered the earliest account of Jesus's life and teachings even though it has always been placed *after* Matthew's, in direct violation of any strict historical chronology.[12]

---

12. Ehrman, *Jesus, Interrupted*, 25, 64. Ehrman explains that, since the nineteenth century, most biblical scholars have agreed that Mark was likely the earliest of the Gospels, written between 65–70 CE, several decades after Jesus's death, because Matthew and Luke both draw from it in writing their own, later gospels.

In the first chapter of Luke's Gospel, God's angelic theophany has the name of Gabriel, who addresses John the Baptist's father and the priest, Zechari'ah. Again, God's angel appeals to the future, predicting what would seem to most a blatant impossibility: a child's birth to a barren wife and praise for John the Baptist's later importance as a prophet (Luke 1:8-23). When the old priest asks God's angel how he'll know this has happened, the angel, the narrator reports, strikes the priest "dumb" until the birth occurs because of his presumptuous doubts—an overreaction an earlier theophany did not have when God overheard Sarah's doubts. Gabriel also appears to Mary in Nazareth, praising her as the "favored one" and commanding her to name her son "Jesus." Through Gabriel, God sings of "the Son of the Most High" and predicts Jesus shall inherit King David's former throne and "will reign over the house of Jacob for ever; / and of his kingdom there will be no end" (Luke 1:26-33).

Troubled by this unexpected theophany of praise, Mary cannot quite understand how she will become pregnant, since, in this version of Jesus's story, she has not yet married Joseph. But God's angel reassures Mary with more claims, again drawn from the *topos* of the future. She will conceive with the "Holy Spirit" and give birth to "the Son of God," just as Zechari'ah's barren wife, Elizabeth, will give birth to John the Baptist, because "with God nothing will be impossible" (Luke 1:34-37). These birth announcements certainly recall God's earlier predictions for Abraham and Sarah, all the way down to the doubts each one has about these predictions, and God's obvious appeal to His ethos as the divine authority to justify His seemingly impossible claims and to praise those figures, including Jesus, who will confirm His predictions.

God addresses shepherds on the eve of Jesus's birth through another angelic theophany. Here, God's angel must calm the fearful shepherds before announcing this birth, to be made identifiable through another of God's rhetorical, predictive "sign[s]" to persuade them: the infant Jesus will be "wrapped in swaddling clothes and lying in a manger" (Luke 2:10-13). With this birth announcement, the voices of God's countless angelic theophanies sing out praises of His work. God further praises Jesus's baptism to those who witness it, this time through a dove theophany (Luke 3:21-22). God even speaks to Jesus's disciples as a cloud theophany, and the disciples hear more praise of Jesus and more urging to listen to his teachings (Luke 9:35-36). In the Gospel of John, God speaks only once, as a thunder theophany, saying "I have glorified it [Jesus's name], and I will glorify it again" (12:28). Finally, God speaks the Revelation of the Apocalypse to Jesus, who then shows it to "[Christ's] servant John," who repeats it again as the visionary closing text of the Bible (Rev 1:1).

Compared to how much Jesus says in the four Gospels, then, God's direct rhetoric is minimal, mediated by various, confirming theophanies of His ethos who blend epideictic with deliberative assertions, all to suggest that Jesus may well be speaking *for* God, much as the Old Testament prophets did. If this inference is drawn, though, the question would become, Why should Jesus's ethos be accorded any more status than, say, Elijah, Isaiah, or Jeremiah? Why should Jesus be seen as God's last theophany, His effort to invent a covenant-argument that will finally keep His human likenesses convinced and persuaded?

Jesus as God's Logos

These questions hint at the controversies that have been stirred among many careful readers' comments on the Bible, theologians' as much as historians'. That Jesus should be seen as God's invention, a newly revised covenant, significantly rests on the Gospel of John, especially its opening. The annotations to this Gospel explain that, unlike the three preceding Synoptic Gospels, John's tries to explain and provide a pre-history for the mysterious person called Jesus. This Gospel, unlike the others, places Jesus *with* God at the initial point of the generation of the universe, an explanation largely supported by the very famous first verse in John:

> In the beginning was the WORD, and the Word was with God, and the Word was God; all things were made through him, and without him was not anything made. In him was life, and the life was the light of men ... And the Word became flesh and dwelt among us, full of grace and truth; we have beheld his glory, glory as of the only Son from the Father ... For the law was given through Moses; grace and truth came through Jesus Christ. No one has ever seen God; the only Son, who is in the bosom of the Father, he has made him known. (John 1:1–18)

This conspicuously poetic prologue has led many to believe and accept that Jesus *is* God incarnate, that Jesus was present at God's invention of all that is, and that Jesus *is* God's Word, His *logos*.

Controversial, and variously interpreted, this prologue invokes God's rhetorical generation in the opening chapters of the Book of Genesis as an argument from the *topos* of past fact.[13] Some will argue that God's *logos* was within His mind *before* it was uttered. Once uttered, God's *logos* turns into and becomes incarnated as Jesus Christ. As God-man, man-God—each

---

13. Ibid., 75.

variant may have slight or significantly different implications for readers—Christ as God's *logos* has been a crucial analogy in the formulation of and arguments for the Catholic idea of a Triune God—one God manifesting Himself in three different ways, as Father, Son, and Holy Spirit.[14] Explained in this way, Jesus Christ transcends his mere historical reality as "Yeshua of Nazareth" and as the historical "descendent of King David" so that he becomes God's "last word."[15] Theologians and historians of religion have argued for centuries over the exact meaning of John's prologue, over the Trinity as a defense against the charge that Christianity is not really as monotheistic as it appears, and even over whether the Gospel of John, so different from the other Synoptic Gospels, is authentic.[16]

I lack the space or the expertise to do justice to these various theological and philological arguments. What often seems missing in these disputes, though, is a fuller consideration of Jesus Christ as God's "last word," His final invented argument, His closing rhetorical appeal to His always backsliding, wayward human likenesses. Christ's rhetorical dominance as God's *logos* can hardly be neglected, and we should at least acknowledge that, *as* God's *logos*, the anonymous author who wrote John's Gospel adopts a term with a specific history in rhetoric that even extends into Heidegger's expositions on the term.

Scholars of rhetoric have long been aware that the Greek word *logos* has many meanings, referring to an entire verbal system, an idea or thought, or the more orderly, rational parts of the world expressed through language.[17] Italian professor of rhetoric Giambattista Vico adds another meaning to consider in his *The New Science* (1744): "'Logic' comes from *logos*, whose first and proper meaning was *fabula*, fable, carried over into Italian as *favella*, speech," but "in Greek the fable was also called *mythos*,

---

14. The concept of the Holy Trinity or "Triune God" is one of the most complicated concepts in Christianity. For historical background, discussions, and various interpretations, see Erhman, *Jesus, Interrupted*, 254–60; Bloom, *Jesus and Yahweh*, 96–109; Armstrong, *History of God*, 107–131 and *Case for God*, 114–19; Burke, *Rhetoric of Religion*, 133–38; Smith, *Quest for Charisma*, 69–73; Lee, *Jesus and the Metaphors of God*, 145–71; Vattimo, *After Christianity*, 67; Žižek, "Fear of Four Words," 253–54; and Milbank, "Double Glory, or Paradox vs. Dialectics," 184–86.

15. Bloom, *Jesus and Yahweh*, 97, 100.

16. Smith addresses the question of the authenticity of the Gospel of John in *Quest for Charisma*, 70, 69, 73. Acknowledging that biblical scholars have long believed that John's Gospel is the "least reliable" account of Jesus's life and ministry, in part because it is historically later than Mark's, Matthew's, and Luke's and so different from the earlier Gospel accounts, Smith nevertheless argues that John's Gospel, while not synoptic, is "Gnostic in nature," and so different from the other Gospels that some scholars now claim that its very differences "*argue for its authenticity rather than for its inaccuracy.*"

17. Lanham, *Handlist*, 96.

myth, whence comes the Latin *mutus*, mute."[18] As Vico understood it, *logos* emerged *before* human beings could speak, "in mute times as mental [or sign] language, which Strabo in a golden passage says existed before vocal or articulate [language]; whence *logos* means both word and idea."

This conflation of *logos* and *mythos*, word and idea, sign and sense, however, would likely confound rhetorical critic Roger Trigg's efforts to argue for their separation in biblical narratives. Trigg contends that the central difference lies in the ancient Greeks' gradual realization that any asserted *logos* was a claim to "truth" and subject to "challenge" and criticism, as in a court of law, while a myth or fable could "please" or "bore" an audience but would never be taken so seriously as to invite rational challenge.[19] Consequently, for Trigg, as *logos*, God's words, or the Gospel story-tellers' words about Jesus, were not myths or fables but were offered so they could "be rationally assessed and criticized."[20]

Unlike Trigg, Vico fuses the meanings of *logos* with human beings' use of sign language and images to tell stories, construct narratives, even before they could tell them orally or write them down. But to Vico's suggestion we must add another: Plato's possibly coining the term "rhetoric" to name disparagingly what others before him—the sophists especially—had taught and called the "art of the logos," the art of making an argument.[21] When the word *logos* enters Aristotle's *Rhetoric*, it will refer to a rhetor's own invention of "artificial" or "artistic" proofs (enthymemes, examples, maxims, and so forth) from various *topoi*, general and specific. From these *topoi* a rhetor may construct and defend "true or apparently true" assertions about an issue in dispute. These logical proofs assume both rhetor and audience are "capable of logical reasoning."[22] Appeals to an audience's logical abilities, their ability to reason and draw inferences, became what most scholars of rhetoric mean when they refer to *logos*.[23]

Yet Vico's point should not be forgotten: narratives can certainly make arguments while those who invent such narratives, such as the author of John's Gospel, try to present a narrator who is as persuasive as possible in trying to get readers to accept this Gospel's view of Jesus.[24] Whoever argues

18. Vico, *New Science*, trans. Bergin and Fisch, 85. Further references are to this translation and edition.
19. Trigg, "Tales Artfully Spun," 129.
20. Ibid., 127.
21. Schiappa, "Did Plato Coin RHĒTORIKĒ?" 457–70.
22. Aristotle, *Rhetoric* 1.ii.6–7.
23. Lanham, *Handlist of Rhetorical Terms*, 96.
24. Culpepper, *Anatomy of the Fourth Gospel*, 16. Culpepper's efforts to analyze the Gospel of John is considered by many critics of biblical narrative to have begun a

through narrative, through the various forms of story-telling, must at least try to make the narrative logically consistent and plausible to an audience, just as a courtroom witness might need to be, because we often accept or reject stories, fictional or non-fictional, not just because they please or bore us but because they seem plausible or implausible on their face.

The anonymous authors of the Synoptic Gospels, we must remember, were probably well-educated Christians who, living just outside Palestine, spoke, read, and wrote in the Greek language of the Gospels themselves.[25] Recall, too, that these authors were probably *not* trying to write Jesus's biography. Rather, they may have been trying to write "conversionary inspiration[s]."[26] So it is by no means a mere accident that Christ would be seen as God's *logos* or that the writer of John's Gospel would identify Jesus with the term. Further, as one biblical scholar has argued, *logos* can be seen as one of many metaphors human beings use to speak and write about God's otherwise unknowable, ineffable reality.[27] To say God begins His inventions by speaking, by uttering the Word that, in John's Gospel, *is* Jesus Christ, may be trying to imply a link between this metaphor and the *dabhar* metaphor and the Sophia/Wisdom metaphor found in Jewish texts of the Old Testament.

Philo of Alexandria (30 BCE—45 CE), a Jewish Platonist and inventor of allegorical interpretation of the Bible, is often credited with making the *logos* metaphor of God so central to Christianity. Philo distinguishes God's mind, or *nous*, from His being, or *ousia*, which humans can never come to know.[28] This distinction leaves only His *logos*, or thoughts, as they co-occur with His spoken and unspoken words. So Philo sees a major difference between *logos endiathetos*, God's unspoken Word, and His *logos prophorikos*, His spoken words. Philo makes *logos* "a strange sort of hybrid," since *logos* does not *cause* God to invent the world or Jesus. Yet for Philo, as for others, *logos* is God's "first born son . . ."[29] *Logos*, to the Platonic Philo, is God's inventive force, bringing rational order and pattern out of a chaotic muddle, and seems closer in meaning to the Greek term for Wisdom (*sophia*). The

---

major break from biblical historians' long-standing tendency to focus on extra-biblical sources to the neglect of the actual texts of John's Gospel and other biblical narratives. For Culpepper's importance and his influence, see Thatcher's "Anatomies of the Fourth Gospel," 1–24.

25. Ehrman, *Jesus, Interrupted*, 106.
26. Bloom, *Jesus and Yahweh*, 12.
27. Lee, *Jesus and the Metaphors of God*, 145.
28. Ibid., 157–58.
29. Ibid.

Jewish word *dabhar* is God's active *logos*, words that have practical and immediate effects.[30]

The Rhetorics of Jesus

All this, complex as it is, seems to radiate from the *logos*-prologue of John's Gospel. So, if Jesus Christ is God's *logos* (word/idea/act, all somehow combined) uttered and incarnated in human form (and, again, not the first time God's taken the human form as a theophany), it appears reasonable to ask what sort of *logos* Jesus asserts as God's last argument, His final appeal. This question is no easier to answer than previous ones, for the simple reason that what Jesus says and does is by no means identical *across* the four Gospels.

Many American Christians would very likely say that Jesus's death and resurrection mean exactly what Jesus says they mean. Jesus was born to die for human sins, starting with Adam's; and those who believe this *logos* of Jesus, who accept him as their personal savior, accept Jesus's covenant-argument. Their belief in him will save them from God's final judgment and reward them with eternal life in heaven. There is quite a lot of John's Gospel in this interpretation of Jesus as the final covenant-argument. Yet, as an argument drawn from the *topos* of the future, it does resemble those made by God's angelic theophanies. Of course, what Jesus argues *for* and what he argues *against*, what he does and what he does not do, what he praises and what he condemns, generate a wide variety of interpretations. Still, as a narrative, what kind of argument does Jesus's *entire story* advance? If Jesus *is* God, His *logos*, His last invention, what case does God want to make to His human likenesses through the narrative *mythos* that unfolds Jesus as *logos*?

If this God incarnates Himself or His Word as separate from Himself, as Jesus, as His "son," then it follows that God permits precisely what He stopped Abraham from doing—killing his only son. More, God seems to have deliberately intended for His son to be killed. This view of Jesus would certainly make him the sacrificial *logos* many Christians believe he is, but it would also make God complicit in the murder of His own, and only, offspring. If, however, God and Jesus are one and the same *logos*, and Jesus is another theophany of God's *logos*, then God kills Himself, or allows Himself to be crucified. But, if God and Jesus are the same, who is Jesus praying to and calling *Abba*, his Father in heaven, in the New Testament?

Obviously, Jesus is fairly consistently seen as a *logos* of promise, representing what human beings can become if they believe in him and accept his sacrifice and its meaning. In that sense, he resembles other

30. Ibid.

covenant-arguments God makes in the Old Testament. The rewards God offers and argues from for each covenant always lie in the *topos* of future facts, a time to-come that, in the Jesus-*logos*, is present and has always been present and with God Himself, as central to His ethos. Abraham was promised an heir, generations of descendants, and vast tracts of land and prosperity for his generations, even though Abraham waits a long time for an heir and never makes it to the promised land. Moses gets to see this land, works diligently to keep God's people in line with His covenant as they travel toward it, but he does not make it to the promised land either.

As covenant-rhetoric, Jesus's promise seems even more remotely projected into the future, and is far less specific than land and prosperity or generations of descendants. In at least some of what Jesus argues, keeping faith with him as a sacrificial *logos* seems to require human beings to invert their entire system of values—to abandon hopes for prosperity and longevity, family ties, lands, titles, wealth, and power as the earthly evils they are, and to prepare themselves for an eternal life without desire and need. Jesus's covenant-argument would further require humans to love their enemies, to treat the unfortunate, the poor, the sick, and the elderly with love and respect, to love the least loveable human beings on the planet. That is the way human beings will get to God, to live with Him in His realm.

But the covenant-argument just described does not quite do justice to various teachings of Jesus as the various narrators present him in the Gospels. In fact, the *logos* presented above is derived from selectively reading the Gospels, as have many ministers and commentators have done, partly to suggest how easy it is to infer one, *final* covenant-argument from Jesus's many words and deeds. It is one thing to argue, as scholars have, that certain speeches Jesus makes in certain Gospels (the Sermon on the Mount, say) cohere as rhetorical arguments. It is quite another to infer from *all* the Gospels a coherent argument that Jesus makes to various audiences at various times. The apocalyptic rhetoric of Jesus in the Gospel of Mark is not quite the same as the *logos*-centered rhetoric in the Gospel of John.

New Testament historian Bart D. Ehrman, himself a former evangelical Christian, makes this precise point in some detail in his account of the matter.[31] In Mark, Jesus's argument emerges almost "immediately"—a repeated refrain in Mark's Gospel—as apocalyptic: "The time is fulfilled, and the kingdom of God is at hand; repent, and believe in the gospel [or good news]" (Mark 1:15). Ehrman reminds us that *apocalyptic* assertions—the Greek term for "revealing" or "unveiling"—were part of the Judaic tradition

---

31. I rely here on Ehrman's useful comparison of the Jesus in Mark's Gospel with the Jesus in John's Gospel, *Jesus, Interrupted*, 77–82; Ehrman's comparison finds support in Bloom's account in *Jesus and Yahweh*, 58–88.

long before the historical Jesus was supposedly born. Readers may see similar assertions in the major and minor prophetic books, which culminate in the Revelation of Saint John in the New Testament. The "rhetoric"—my term, not Ehrman's—of apocalypse argues that all the evil and suffering in a world which God has somehow allowed Satan to control are about to end and presage the coming kingdom of God *on earth*, when God will return and end all the evil and suffering and punish the wicked. So Jesus's rhetoric urges his audiences to get ready for this new age promised in his disciples' lifetime, when "the son of Man" will come back from the dead and establish God's perfect kingdom *on earth* (Mark 8:31). All that Jesus does in his ministry—healing the sick, raising the dead—anticipate what God's renewed earth will be like once it is purged of sickness, death, aging, and corrupt, human rule.

Through all this, Ehrman observes, Jesus seldom refers to himself in Mark's Gospel. Instead, he focuses on God, His coming Kingdom, and has to be forced into admitting he is a "son of God," like so many others mentioned in the Old Testament, including the mysterious Nephilim and Satan himself in the Job narrative. Yet, Ehrman concludes, Mark's Jesus does not call himself divine or suggest he was with God at the beginning of the world, as John's Gospel asserts. John's Jesus-as-*logos*, Ehrman notes, talks largely about himself, not God's coming kingdom. He seems pre-occupied by four issues: "who he is, where he has come from, where he is going, and how he is the one who can provide eternal life." Jesus's frequent assertions, starting with "I am" in John's Gospel, underline Jesus's own personal identity—even to the point of asserting his equality with God: "I and the father are one" (10:30). John's Jesus, Ehrman adds, even claims the name of God for himself, asserting "Before Abraham was, I am" (8:58).

This "I am" assertion happens to lead this Jesus's Jewish listeners in the temple to throw stones at him, largely because it echoes God's own mysterious self-naming before Moses in the Old Testament. Jesus's Jewish audience would have likely heard this assertion as blasphemy. John's Jesus makes no covenant-promise of God's kingdom being established *on* earth. John's Jesus, Ehrman explains, promises "eternal life in heaven above, by achieving a heavenly birth" in believing in Jesus's divinity (John 3:36). Unlike Mark's Jesus, the Jesus of John's Gospel, Ehrman argues, "rotates the horizontal dualism of apocalyptic thinking [in Mark's Gospel]"—God's heaven on earth temporally follows and reveals the corrupt, unjust wicked world—"so that it becomes a vertical dualism . . . a dualism of life down here and the life above."

Deeply influenced by previous biblical scholars, Ehrman thinks there is an historical and social explanation for these quite different versions of

Jesus's rhetoric. The Jesus of Mark's Gospel—apparently the earliest telling of Jesus's story—had to be reinterpreted by the later author of John's Gospel, probably written sometime between 90 to 95 CE, though some scholars think it was much earlier, while Mark's Gospel was probably written around 70 CE., before Jerusalem fell, and almost a full generation before John's Gospel. Jesus's life and message, Ehrman reasons, would have had to have been greatly revised, since the apocalypse that Mark's Jesus preached failed to occur, and since most of the disciples had already died, as well as the generation to whom they had preached.

If nothing else, Ehrman's detailed comparison of just these two Gospel accounts point to the immense difficulties of trying to glean from all *four* Gospels a consistent and coherent covenant-argument which God invented for His Jesus-logos-theophany to persuade various audiences to accept and live by. Yet it is also fair to say the Jesus-as-*logos* whom so many Christians believe in and accept and whom non-believers attack or challenge seems more to resemble the Jesus of John's Gospel. For better *and* perhaps for worse, this Jesus, claiming to be God, claiming belief in him and his sacrifice is the only way to gain eternal life above with God, is God's "last word," His final effort to induce those who have not yet accepted God's previous arguments and have not been persuaded that they can reach this heavenly future.

The prologue to John's Gospel has had a tremendous impact on Christianity since its composition, even though it is apparently a later and, some scholars think, *inauthentic* Gospel.[32] John's Jesus has mastered the "authentic charisma" which augments his rhetorical appeals. He fuses within his own individual persona the humanity of his listeners, their emotions and experiences, to which he can appeal (arguments invented as pathos), the mysterious teacher and rabbi (arguments from ethos) who uses his knowledge of the Old Testament and his parable-making abilities and enthymemes to draw many followers to accept his teachings (arguments from logos) and his divinity as God's "son" (again, an argument from ethos). This divinity-claim, like his other arguments, would likely threaten those in power, be they Jews or Romans.

Still, the Jesus of Mark, and to some extent of Matthew and Luke, is a rhetor whose arguments not only sometimes fail to convince but, like his actions, are often misunderstood or not understood at all.[33] Jesus often appears to nurture this misunderstanding. Following the seed parable, Jesus tells both his disciples and presumably those "who were about him" why he

32. Smith, *Quest for Charisma*, viii, 20.
33. Bloom, *Jesus and Yahweh*, 2.

uses parables to argue his points: "To you has been given the secret of the kingdom of God, but for those outside everything is in parables; so that they may indeed see but not perceive, and may indeed hear but not understand; lest they should turn again, and be forgiven" (Mark 4:11–12).

But his disciple-students still do not understand, so Jesus asks them: "Do you not understand this parable? How then will you understand all the parables?" (Mark 4:13). After this rebuke, Jesus has to explain the parable (Mark 4:14–20). Matthew's Jesus offers a softer rebuke, though at last the disciples do come to understand the parable (Matt 13). So does Luke's Jesus, though the disciples seem much less puzzled than in the other Gospels (Luke 8:9–18). A similar theme appears as well in John's Gospel, since Jesus's riddles and ironies sometimes escape his auditors, even if the narrator describes such misunderstandings from a more distant, post-Resurrection perspective.[34] The point here is that if Jesus's rhetoric is supposed to persuade his various audiences—starting with his own apostles—to accept his arguments, this rhetoric's effectiveness is, at best, uneven and, at worst, a less than impressive rendering of God's *logos* if judged simply on the grounds of how the various narrators represent Jesus's meaning from their omniscient, post-Resurrection perspectives. Not only does Jesus have to invent parables, the narrator frequently has to show him inventing the interpretation he wants listeners to infer from them. His parable rhetoric seems to attract attention, if not satisfy the understanding, of his many different audiences; yet their appeal may lie precisely in Jesus's apparent obscurity, if not the parables' novelty—perhaps a deliberate obscurity in the case of Mark's Jesus. The parables themselves, like the hypothetical examples and analogies classical rhetors invented, implicitly and indirectly argue the claims Jesus expects some listeners to infer for themselves, if they are capable.

Yet the Jesus many Christians—especially many American Protestant Christians—believe in seems to be the Jesus of John's unusual Gospel. This is the Jesus of the Yahweh-like "I am," the Jesus who claims to be God, and was *in* or *with* God as God's *logos* from a time before time had meaning. This Jesus is not so much Yeshua of Nazareth, whose actual existence historians have tried, without much success, to document. This Jesus is "a theological God presented by rival traditions," from Catholics to Protestants, and the center of many "sects old and new, many of them American originals."[35] This Jesus, as God's *logos*, along with the Holy Spirit and the Virgin Mary, Harold Bloom sadly concedes, has displaced Yahweh's "I am" with "a remote

---

34. See Leroy's early, important analysis of the misunderstood, riddling nature of Jesus's preachings, from the folklorist perspective in *Rätsel und Missverständnis;* and Wead, *The Literary Devices in John's Gospel.*

35. Bloom, *Jesus and Yahweh,* 6.

God the Father," who too quickly "blends into the identity of Jesus Christ" himself.

As a literary critic and self-identified Jewish Gnostic, Bloom spends some pages showing how Yeshua of Nazareth turns into this "theological God."[36] Here, I highlight just one of Bloom's observations about Jesus as God's final rhetorical invention, His last covenant-argument, if for no other reason than Bloom himself personally resists interpreting Jesus "as a dying and reviving God." If read this way, Jesus's *logos* ends up being about God's suicide through Jesus's crucifixion—an act Bloom believes the Old Testament literary character of Yahweh would never have performed. Not until the Gospel of John, Bloom adds, is Jesus's Incarnation a pivotal part of his appeal as a final and lasting covenant. The Incarnation depends on Jesus's divine pre-existence with his *Abba*, God the Father, and not the mercurial Yahweh whose rhetoric dominates so much of the Old Testament.

Many American Christians—Protestant Christians at least—would, I suspect, avoid, ignore, or reject the suicidal implications raised by John's Jesus. Yet in most other respects these same Christians might very likely accept the message of John's Jesus as God's central, divine exhortation. Unfamiliar or uncomfortable with the Catholic Trinity, they may prefer to think of Jesus as God's "son," though that preference implies God deliberately accomplishes what He stopped Abraham from doing. Such Christians may not wonder whether the term "son" had any other than a literal, familial meaning in the context of the New Testament or the Old. If these speculations have any validity, they lead to the potential conclusion that many of America's Christians would be more willing to accept and worship a God who kills His own son than a God who kills Himself to save His deeply flawed human likenesses. In short, they may be more comfortable with God's final *logos* as a story of homicide rather than a story of suicide (or, what is better, *theocide*).

Kenneth Burke rightly urges us to pay close attention to the rhetorical motives underlying all images of homicide or suicide (including *theocide*). Framed as narratives or no, these images of killing imply contrasting *logoi* and, "from the 'neutral' point of view," indicate a rhetor's "concern with terms for transformation in general."[37] While it may seem rather naïve to think the issue of God's homicide or suicide can be addressed from a "neutral" viewpoint, Burke nevertheless urges readers to consider a rhetorical motive, a cause which "ambiguously contain[s]" and so "transcends" the clash of these discordant images and the opposing narratives they support.

---

36. Ibid., 55.
37. Burke, *Rhetoric of Motives*, 10–11.

In either case, Burke suggests, a rhetor would be asserting and defending a claim which, though grounded in images of killing, calls for and urges a transformation.

Killing someone or some thing or killing one's self in a narrative would be a way for a rhetor to destroy *implicitly* a principle or idea that the victim represents. Death is perhaps the most radical way to show how a human being, or the *principle* a specific human being represents, can be transformed. It fittingly and perfectly sums up a person's or an idea's promised end. As a result, Burke adds, "the Christian injunction to lead the 'dying life' [just as Jesus does] is itself a formula" for "death *as* transfiguration."[38] The rhetorical motive underlying Jesus as God's closing argument would, then, turn upon "the imagery of slaying" as "a special case of transformation" largely because "the *killing* of something is the *changing* of it," whereby we can "identify" what that something was "before and after the change" shown through the killing imagery.[39]

What Burke goes on to say about the story of Abraham's near sacrifice of his son, as revised by Sorën Kierkegaard in his book, *Fear and Trembling*, offers an even richer understanding of the rhetoric of transformation underlying the homicidal and suicidal narratives of Jesus's *logos*. God, Burke explains, only demands that Abraham be *willing* to sacrifice his son.[40] God, in this case, does not require a killing so much as He requires a "sign" from Abraham that he is *willing* to slay Isaac *for* God. God, as we have seen, often resorts to signs to argue for His covenants. Here, God draws upon a pre-existing "opinion" or "topic" (place) that Aristotle mentions in his *Rhetoric*. The ancient Greek lists the happiness and pleasure children represent for their parents as a source from which to draw arguments.[41] So "God," Burke explains, "not absurdly, but like a good Aristotelian," invokes the value of the eldest son as part of the *"tribal morality"* of a religion that "demands of the devout the willingness to sacrifice even the most precious thing."[42] God's test of Abraham, Burke concludes, is less about murder than it is about strengthening Abraham's own ethos as God's elect. He must be willing to sacrifice his most precious son to "signify" to God his own faith and resolve. Abraham's willingness, then, is his own rhetorical "sign" to persuade God that he is His most worthy servant.

38. Ibid., 14.
39. Ibid., 20.
40. Ibid., 252–53.
41. Aristotle, *Rhetoric* 1.xi.26.
42. Burke, *Rhetoric of Motives*, 253.

The suicidal implications of Jesus's crucifixion are, for Burke, more troublesome, given Christianity's resoluteness as a monotheistic religion. A polytheistic religion would have "no problem in accounting for such sacrifices as God the Father's surrender of Christ the Son."[43] In other cosmic battles between deities both good and evil, the "good" god(s) might have to sacrifice his, her (their) son(s) to save the world. But, "under monotheism, the cosmological import of Jesus's sacrifice is far more difficult to rationalize than under polytheism," since monotheism by definition lacks *other* gods. Even so, Burke cautions, no rhetorical analysis of Jesus's crucifixion should "isolate the killing itself," in which all humanity's involved, "as the essence of the [New Testament's] exaltation."[44] Even if we think of suicide as a "variant of dying," it remains a "sacrifice" and is thus the "essence of religion" itself.[45] That "essence" in the case of the Bible's rhetoric depends upon "the mystery of Christ as sacrificial king," to Burke a brilliant "oxymoron" in that Christ plays the "double role as victimized and victorious."[46]

Inventing Jesus's Utopian Rhetoric

What Burke's typically useful insights do not help us understand here is what the precise "essence" of the "exaltation" would be. That "essence" would be the central, governing claim God invents and represents through Jesus as His theophany-*logos*. Granted, homicide and suicide are both rhetorical "variants," images of death as transformation. If Jesus's death, imaged in either story's ending, homicidal or suicidal, represents the rhetorical goal of transformation, exactly what does God want His human likenesses to change about themselves? However we understand or answer this question, Jesus's *logos* and his story cannot and should not be reduced to the rhetorical imagery of either homicide or suicide without also exaggerating the "killing" or "slaying" dimension of sacrifice. That means that God's final argument, invented for the New Testament, would contend that we humans be willing to transform ourselves. Here, God would be stressing the *logos* and argument of Jesus's resurrection, *not* his crucifixion.

Perhaps this emphasis is as close we can get to what God's last covenant-argument means: Jesus's resurrection, *not his crucifixion*, would implicitly argue the change God pleads for. If God's last invented *logos* is Christ, then Christ can only be "victorious" insofar as Christ-as-God transforms himself

43. Ibid., 255–56.
44. Ibid., 265.
45. Ibid., 266.
46. Ibid., 328.

by defeating the one natural force in God's invented world that no one—not even the Old Testament prophets—had yet conquered: Death. This conquest, far more than opening up seas or destroying whole cities and armies, surpasses and transcends all accepted natural laws that every human rhetor has to recognize, regardless of the argument made or the issue addressed. It surpasses and transcends even God's own imposed time limitation on the "flesh" of His human likenesses and all other living creatures.

In every narrative Gospel account, however various in details of plot or characters or in portraying Jesus, his resurrection "slays" death. This willingness to be sacrificed to that end is an attempt to destroy the violence of death with and through divine violence, much as God hoped to do in flooding the violence-ridden, over-copulating earth in the Old Testament. Sacrifice in all religions, as Rene Girard has argued, "is primarily an act of violence without risk of vengeance" performed in response to communal crises.[47] So "[v]iolence and the sacred," Girard insists, "are inseparable" because religion attempts to quell vengeance-driven violence through ritualized violence, through sacrificing surrogate victims such as Jesus.[48] In its broadest sense, then, religion for Girard "must be another term for that obscurity that surrounds man's efforts to defend himself by curative and preventative means against his own violence."[49] Far from being "useless," as its many atheistic and scientific critics contend, religion "humanizes violence" and "protects" human beings from endless cycles of revenge by projecting and controlling violence through sacred rituals. Religion takes violence out of human hands and makes it "divine." Only when this divinization of violence occurs as "the last word" and is "accepted as divine" can the cycles of human violence cease.[50] Jesus's resurrection following a violent death, seen as God's last invented argument, would then be a triumph not only over death but over violence itself and the seemingly endless cycles of violence rehearsed in the Old Testament as well as in other sacred works.

"Resurrection," from the Latin infinitive *resurgere*, means to "to rise up" and "to appear again." Latin dictionaries point to the contexts of vegetation, of arising from bed each morning. These contexts, ordinary as they are, refer to cyclical acts in both the vegetative and human worlds. But God did not invent His human likenesses in the image of plants, and a moment will come when none of us shall rise out of bed again. Thus God's final

---

47. Girard, *Violence and the Sacred*, trans. Gregory, 13, 18. Further references are to this reprinted translation.

48. Ibid., 19, 20.

49. Ibid., 23.

50. Ibid., 134.

covenant-argument would offer His human inventions the chance to eat from the fruit of the tree of life He had earlier feared Adam and Eve might sample if they had remained in Eden, presuming, of course, they had not eaten from it already. That tree returns, is incarnated and resurrected in the theophany of a human form, in Jesus's *logos*, his promise to those who will believe in his rhetoric, who will stay persuaded or allow themselves to be persuaded by the eternal life Jesus and the tree represent.

If this is the argument God makes through Jesus, His final invented *logos*, it radically changes Isaiah's beautifully dark, metaphorical maxim, "All flesh is grass" (Isa 40:6). There, God's prophet seems to isolate only the mutable quality of grass: it withers and dies, as does the flesh God invented from the dampened dust and earth. But grass, trees, and many plant species, unlike the flesh of most creatures, return, alive and green in the spring. The prophet's metaphor ignores or slights this cyclic quality of grass and much of the vegetative world. That quality becomes absorbed and amplified in the rhetorical appeal of resurrection and eternal life, if humans believe and accept Jesus's sacrificed flesh as their own. Their flesh, saved through belief in Jesus's *logos*, becomes the grass that returns in the next life, in God's kingdom, the proverbial "grass" growing on the "other side" of time, and of fallen human history.

Resurrection and eternal life, the defeat of death and the cessation of endless violence through one divine, violent act, the escape from time, and time's decay—all are invoked in Jesus's appeal as God's last invented argument. But it is by no means entirely clear what "eternal life" means in the future to-come for the persuaded. God's argument to accept eternal life already assumes its dialectically necessary opposite, eternal torment and suffering (and a dialectically and rhetroically opposite *place* for this torment in "hell") if His human likenesses cease believing or refuse to be convinced by His closing argument, Jesus's story, his *logos-as-mythos*. In both cases, God would expand the temporal world and His humans' post-death experience. The symmetry of the first promise—eternal life—requires the symmetry of the threat that underlies it—not death per se but eternal suffering. To live again, as grass and trees do, and never to wither, as grass, trees, and flesh must, is God's last best offer. To walk away from His argument is to suffer *always* what the grass and trees only suffer *sometimes*—perpetual withering and decay.

Certainly, it is possible to argue over whether the eternal life a persuaded Christian audience will gain or the eternal torment the non-persuaded will suffer is physical or spiritual, and there is no shortage of religious and theological works which struggle with this problem. Yet, for all that, if this is the argument Jesus's resurrection makes for God, it lacks, as I have said before, the concreteness and palpability of the covenant-arguments He makes to Abraham and Moses. The rhetorical appeal of transformation through belief in Christ's death and resurrection is for many hard to resist, even if a person realizes that God's underlying motive is rhetorical. To accept Jesus as God's final invention may be to accept that human likenesses can once again become like their immortal inventor. It is to accept the premise that God's human likenesses can only share in His love and mind and Being if they change. They, too, must die and return from this death. That is what this rhetoric requires—the ceasing to be just human and to become more like the God who made humans in His own image.

So what might we conclude from considering Jesus Christ as God's final invention, His last argument in the Bible as so many Christians know or assume it to be? Simply asking the question in this way hints at other assumptions. First, that Jesus is God's own offspring or, as in the Gospel of John, that Jesus is actually the Incarnation (theophany) of the same God who invented the world by just thinking and saying what He wanted to invent, the same God who argued through covenants, from Adam through Jacob unto all the generations of Israel, who negotiated with Abraham and Moses, and who blasts out of the whirlwind to "pull rank," as we might say, on Job's despair. Neither assumption, so far as I can tell, can be safely made and absolutely confirmed based on the Christian Bible as it has come down to us.

We would further assume—perhaps even expect—that there's *only one Jesus Christ* who emerges out of the New Testament, and that what this Jesus argues, and how he argues, are uniform and coherent across the four Gospels. For how could it be otherwise, since God's divine mastery of rhetoric should permit no self-contradictions? Again, we have seen that neither of these assumptions can be vigorously maintained without selectively reading the Gospels and thereby, as readers, inventing our own version of a singular, unified interpretation of Jesus. Some Christian sects and denominations seem to have done exactly that. Yet Jesus's rhetoric, the ethos he invents for himself, the arguments he invents for different audiences, appears at once too variable for any plausible, sustained argument to emerge by the end of the last Gospel.

To the extent that Christian believers and non-believers alike may seize upon an "essential" rhetoric that Jesus argued across the four Gospels—one not filled in, colored, or otherwise bent by Paul's and others' interpretations—that rhetoric appears to belong to the resurrected Jesus of John's Gospel. John's Jesus, however unlike Mark's or Matthew's or Luke's, remains the Jesus who says he *is* God, who dies and rises again to prove it, and who insists that only belief in what amounts to his own dramatically staged passion, death, and resurrection will allow others to transform themselves and survive his return to judge the living and the dead and ascend with him into a heavenly afterlife. This Jesus, so it seems, is the one many Christians identify with ultimate love and forgiveness, with moral perfection, with a future always to-come where they can live without pain, injustice, disease, suffering, death, or endless violence. This, for lack of a better word, is utopian rhetoric, appealing to a time that is always but never quite arriving, for a world we have never had and may never have.

Jesus's individual arguments, parables, and dialogical exchanges in the four Gospels all show him to be a master rhetor whose very mastery, it seems, leads him to Golgotha, to the tomb he will escape, to the heavenly ascension he performs. His is the "good death" that for believers destroys the inevitability of age, decay, and carnal death—all that God's invention of human likenesses out of the earth's dust and mist entailed. Jesus is the premise in John's Gospel of that underlying, certain conclusion that there is another life beyond this fallen one. This afterlife God's earlier human inventions ensured would be made necessary by intermittently questioning God's rhetoric, His authority to make and condition promises His human likenesses, rhetors themselves, by virtue of God's own breath, and His own rhetorical abilities, sought to imitate but failed to master fully.

Perhaps Jesus's utopian rhetoric persuades many far more readily than God's own Old Testament covenant-arguments. Perhaps it keeps on persuading those who want very much to believe there is something more than this world's ceaseless violence and certain corruption. This is a rhetoric that appeals to the human desire for the unseen, the ahistorical, the seemingly impossible possibilities only a God, or a man-God, can ensure and metaphorically, if not literally, embody. It offers neither a wholly tragic nor wholly comic narrative to resolve the riddles of human existence epitomized in Job's complaints. Rather, it may come closer to tragic-comedy. Jesus's crucifixion and resurrection may be utterly unpersuasive to those who will not indulge any utopian desires. Skeptics will fear the ravages of blasted hopes more than they fear the endless hopelessness of this our all-too-contingent, imperfect world. But these remain the final acts of Jesus's story in all four Gospels, however variously Jesus and his arguments are portrayed within each account. As such, they seem to be the final invention God makes in the Bible that is His argument, His incarnated *logos*.

Whether these acts are theological concepts or one final metaphor for the nature of a God who is beyond all metaphor and so beyond any merely human rhetoric to describe or explain, the crucified and resurrected Jesus whom a great many Christians believe in may be best summed by the prayer of John's Jesus, during the Last Supper, just before Jesus's arrest.

Jesus addresses his "Father," his *Abba,* but clearly the prayer is for his anxious disciples and any other reader who happens upon them. For Jesus "the hour has come" for reciprocal glorification, of both his and God's "power over all flesh, to give eternal life to all whom thou hast given him," so Jesus may receive further glory in returning to be with God as His *logos* "before the world was made" (John 17:1–5). This covenant-argument begins with two conditional premises—belief in Jesus's godhood and emulation of his values—and concludes with a promise of a perfect future as reward for allowing one's self to be persuaded to believe in transformation in the present.

In some ways, this argument's enthymemic structure greatly resembles others God makes in the Old Testament. Yet it is hard to ignore a certain scaling down here. God's earlier covenant-arguments often depended on premises and conclusions, too. But, in that earlier rhetoric, God seems anxious that His listeners may decide to believe in *other* gods than He, rather than being anxious that they believe in *any* god at all. Both God and Jesus insist that their followers conduct their lives according to a moral code (though Jesus's code isn't quite identical to God's Decalogue or its elaborations). Still, Jesus's promise has less to do with acquiring real estate or generational fecundity and more to do with the "vertical dualism" that Ehrman refers to—a promise of eternal life in paradise: no death, no suffering, no sickness, no wars.

If Jesus is the last argument and theophany God invents, a case made through Jesus-as-*logos*, as reason *and* fable, or through Jesus as God's sacrificed offspring, its implications may be disturbing for some non-believers and some Christians as well. It seems to recommend passive acceptance of all that's wrong, sinful, and destructive in this world while we all wait for a perfect future that is always about to but never arrives. In the meantime, we believe and wait. We wait to arrive in a place so unlike our own world, it must remain a series of vague negations of our ordinary, all-too-human existence and the few pleasures to which we have become accustomed.

If we accept—and many have—the covenant-argument of John's Jesus, what are we to *do* while we wait? Do we all become later-day Job's, tabulating the cruelties, mayhem, and corpses, all the while asking why—please, why—does not God stay Satan's hand, unless of course Satan's hand is the dialectical other side of God's own? Is a whirlwind of historical boasts and sarcastic jibes enough of an answer? Is Jesus's own promise of eternal life through belief in him any better as an answer? Can we, as latter-day Job's, do nothing to make the world a better place while we wait for the next one, up there?

Believe now and wait for the perfect life to come seems a very different kind of argument than the one a more apocalyptic Jesus makes in Mark's

Gospel. It suggests an even more radical change in God's Old Testament rhetoric. Old Testament authors, whoever they may have been, often invoke God as a metaphor for "justice," though the "justice" God is supposed to administer is, to say the least, ambivalently imagined and often deferred. This justice that God presumably argues for, observes one biblical scholar, has less to do with law and more to do with God's own ethos, His own intrinsic "goodness" as expressed through justice, the key to Israel's "salvation history."[51] Yet God's justice, metaphorical or no, could be interpreted by those in power, those possessed of "royal consciousness" and charged to administer justice and enforce existing laws, as a rationale for creating and maintaining order—God's order—since God invented that order which the powerful think they embody and must protect. Those without power, dispossessed, and speaking or writing through "prophetic consciousness," would see God as a divine force to avenge the many injustices the powerful commit against the powerless in the name of God's order. The net result, rhetorically speaking, of these two quite different interpretations is a God whose "own polarity translates into a continuous dialectic [in the Bible] between the songs of majesty [as in Psalms] and the chants of mercy" and the prophets' "primal scream" against any and all dominion.[52] Perhaps Jesus-as-God's *logos* must be thought to sing and scream at once to persuade us.

In these several chapters, I have tried to explore God's inventiveness as a rhetor, including Jesus as His closing argument. I have tried to highlight through various examples the way God argues, how He tries to convince and persuade various audiences, even Himself. I have also mentioned some of the types of rhetoric God depends on, and the strategies He uses to persuade—covenant-arguments, signs, curses, and blessings, violence, and threats of violence, and predictions of trials and sufferings, as well as God's various theophanies—only the last of which seems wholly impossible for human rhetors. I have mentioned, too, but did not dwell on God's didactic speeches, some of His detailed instructions and orders.

As we have seen in this and previous chapters, it is certainly possible to examine how God invents the arguments He makes, though we also saw that God can easily and radically deviate from what mere human rhetors do to invent their cases. The challenge God's inventiveness poses for a rhetorical critic begins from the very beginning, in His "genesis" of the world and of Himself. God's rhetoric, as we saw, can be addressed to specific audiences, including Himself, or to other audiences, including the entire nation of Israel and beyond, to readers across nations and centuries. The persuasive

---

51. Lee, *Jesus and the Metaphors of God*, 75.
52. Ibid., 77.

strategies He adopts, as we also saw, often but do not always resemble those of human rhetors. God certainly seems ready to threaten His human likenesses with violence if and when the effects of His arguments wear off, and He will resort to violence if He cannot persuade in any other way. God's violence, then, does not lack a rhetorical motive. As we have seen, it most certainly does—to compel and coerce agreement and belief when His covenant-arguments are ignored.

No human rhetor, however gifted, can by definition exploit theophanies as God does, or predict the future, or read minds. But we all know that human rhetors have, like God, appealed to ancestry and past authority *(argumentum ad vericundiam)* and used threats of violence and actual violence *(argumentum ad baculum)* to persuade—so much so that both strategies have come to be classified as fallacious arguments.[53] It is all too obvious that human beings, like God, will sometimes wield and employ actual weapons of violence against those whom they have been unable to persuade by other means. It is probably no stretch to say that God had a monopoly on "shock and awe" strategies long before any human, secular leader adopted them. Once humans invented their own technological likenesses, these images of our own violent impulses are, as we fondly say, fully intended to "put the fear of God" into audiences, including entire nations, when their leaders appear impervious to other modes of persuasion. Whatever we might *wish* were the case, rhetoric, in its fullest sense, whether human or divine, cannot exclude violence from strategies of persuasion, any more than it can exclude character assassination, smear tactics, and outright lies and deceptions. Rhetoric, though, always has stressed its other means of invention as an "art," including the means to identify, analyze, defend against, and even resist its own "art."

To understand or appreciate fully the arguments God invents, however persuasive we find them, we must account, too, for *how* He makes His case, how He arranges and organizes His arguments. The Bible, if it is to be read as God's rhetoric, must have a shape and a form. As any merely human rhetor must take care to organize her argument so that it will persuade as many as possible, so we would expect that of God. How, then, does God do this, if He indeed does? That is the next question I will explore and, as we will soon see, it is no easier to address than God's powers of rhetorical invention.

---

53. See Hamblin, *Fallacies*, 154–76.

5

The Shape of God's Rhetoric

Preliminary Problems

The mere title of this chapter begs at least two important questions. Biblical historians and textual critics might wonder if there can ever be any identifiable "shape" to God's rhetoric, since the Bible itself is far from a singularly unified text, just as the "God" of the Christian Bible, as well as the speeches He makes and the acts He performs, appears to be a series of different authorial perspectives on such a "God" formed and composed for various readerships at different historical periods. Rhetorical critics of the Bible may also wonder whether the "shape" being referred to applies to the different genres assembled within the Bible, or to the genres within any single book of the Bible, or to the various shapes God imposes on individual speeches, or to the Bible as God's "rhetoric" entire. We have, after all, noted that this God's *aras* against His human likenesses took poetic form in Genesis, as did His whirlwind theophany in the Book of Job, and we have repeatedly referred to "stories" and "narratives" in the chapters exploring God's rhetorical inventiveness. We have noted as well this God's use of verbal asides and brief soliloquies, instances of His epideictic, forensic, and deliberative rhetoric, not to mention didactic rhetoric to instruct His audiences.

These are by no means frivolous questions, simply because the terms "shape," "form," "organization," or "arrangement" already imply the issue of how much analytical scope any one of them presupposes about "God's" rhetoric. If our goal is to examine how this God tries to organize the various, invented arguments, verbal and extra-verbal, in the hope that describing that organization will shed more—and a different—light on the eloquent pleadings He makes and develops; and if, to do so, we seek guidance from rhetorical theories, past and present, we are likely to find that this canon of *human* rhetoric, like invention, contains within itself a host of other issues yet to be fully resolved. As a result, before we can even begin to explore the scope and circumference of God's attempts to shape His rhetoric, we must first briefly re-visit what has been written about *dispositio* to show how and why it, too, is a contested concept for human rhetoric. Only then will we be in a better position to explore the other questions the title of this chapter clearly begs.

Problems of Rhetorical Order

Most classical theories of rhetoric agreed that arrangement was important to successful persuasion. The Roman teacher of rhetoric Quintilian offered two analogies to emphasize that importance. In the first, he warns that it is "not sufficient" simply "to collect stone and timber and other building materials [the invention phase]" to construct a dwelling, for "skilled masons" would still be needed "to arrange and place" these materials. Likewise, in composing an argument: "however abundant" our inventions, they would still have to be ordered and arranged to ensure "firmness of structure."[1] This analogy, while reasonable enough, unfortunately slights the architect or building planner who must first design the structure before anyone starts looking for stones to lay.

Quintilian's second analogy, however, seems closer to the mark. There, students of rhetoric are reminded that even though a sculptor may have separately cast "all the limbs of a statue," *that* "does not make it a statue."[2] The sculptor must assemble the limbs so the statue resembles what it is supposed to, since the parts are not *necessarily* interchangeable. If a sculptor places casts of bird's wings where human arms need to be, that sculptor, Quintilian warns, may end up producing "a monster." To Quintilian, a careful ordering of appropriate parts comes down to a law of "nature" itself. "Without order in the world," he warns, "everything would go to wrack and ruin." This is why organizing the arguments a rhetor invents is the second of the five departments of oratory, since "without it [order] the first [invention] would be useless."

---

1. Quintilian, *Institutio Oratoria*, vol. 3, 7. Pr. 1-3.
2. Ibid.

Even at this early date, Quintilian underscores a salient point about arrangement: no one can really establish "general rules" for organizing *all* the arguments a rhetor invents.³ These rules "would [not] fit all subjects." Even in making legal arguments, whose shape would need to be sensitive to the ritualistic formalities of courtrooms, no two cases are "exactly alike." Nevertheless, Quintilian tries to outline "some points" about organization he believes rhetors must consider. We will come back to those points below, but why Quintilian believes it is next to impossible to set forth prescriptive rules for arranging all arguments invented hints at some long-standing quarrels over *dispositio* that necessarily complicate any effort to examine how God shapes His own rhetoric.

These quarrels may lie in the very Greek and Latin terms for this stage of rhetoric, *taxis* and *dispositio*, since they point in two, somewhat different directions: to name the rhetor's acts of deciding what invented material to include and in what order; or to name the assembled whole, its overall form or structure once completed. Even less clear is what that structure should be, how many parts it should have and, most importantly, whether any rhetor can predict the exact order of those parts for each specific audience and each situation that permits or invites persuasion.

While scholars typically credit Aristotle as the first to address these questions, his teacher, Plato, had commented on *dispositio*'s second sense and, even before Plato, the sophists seems to have taken an apparently different view of ordering an argument. While scholars cannot be overly confident about what these sophists did or did not think or teach, or whether their thinking and teaching was so uniform that it constituted an actual school or movement beyond historians' efforts to imagine such a movement,⁴ they, too, were apparently concerned about organizing *logos*, their Pre-Platonic word for "rhetoric." These concerns seem implicit in an incomplete, anonymous work called the *Dissoi Logoi*, probably written by one sophistic instructor between 403 and 395 BCE.⁵ The Greek title of this fragmentary work, "double arguments," suggests the author advocated that students learn to compose what has been described as "two-sided argument[s]."⁶ "The essential feature" of *dissoi logoi*, one scholar explains, "was not simply the occurrence of opposing arguments [on any issue of debate] but the fact that both opposing arguments could be expressed by a single speaker [or

---

3. Ibid., 3.

4. See Schiappa's intriguing argument on this point in "Sophistic Rhetoric," 5–18.

5. Anonymous, "*Dissoi Logoi*," trans. Robinson, 47–55. Further citations are to this translation.

6. Lanham, *Handlist of Rhetorical Terms*, 57.

writer]," though not at the same time, "*within* a single complex argument."⁷ Two-sided arguments in the *Dissoi Logoi* move from one side to the other, in linear order. For example, "food, drink, and sex," generally considered valuable essentials to a human being, may be "bad for those who are sick, but good for the person who is healthy and needs them."⁸ The structure of *dissoi logoi* is, in fact, still preserved within the "antithetical structure" of courtroom trials in the West,⁹ with a judge and jury hearing arguments from the prosecution and the defense before rendering a verdict. This structure may even recall Plato's dialogic,¹⁰ except that a rhetor who shapes arguments as *dissoi logoi* might genuinely start out by believing that "truth" in every real instance of debate, legal or otherwise, would consist of at least two sides, one emerging from and responding to the other, with the *logos* ending in an *aporia*, in this case genuine—*not feigned*—doubt over which side possessed the "truth" about an issue.¹¹ Arguments shaped as *dissoi logoi*, argues one scholar, were not necessarily intended to persuade but, as in Antiphon's *Tetralogies*, rather to make rhetors aware of opposing interpretations of a set of facts or events without being concerned about which one was really true.¹²

Plato, of course, while more interested in the dialectical method of invention to find the True, does mockingly describe what has come to be called "the classical" order of an argument in his *Phaedrus*.¹³ That order, Plato's Socrates reminds his young student, includes "such niceties of the art" found in "rhetorical manuals" or *technai*, compiled and circulated by Corax and Tisias, advising rhetors to begin with a "preamble," followed by "exposition, accompanied by direct evidence; thirdly, indirect evidence; fourthly, probabilities; besides which there are proof and supplementary proof," after which comes "refutation" and, finally, "recapitulation," the summary of an argument's main points. Here, Plato's Socrates says nothing about the *dissoi*

---

7. Kerford, *Sophistic Movement*, 84. The surviving text of the *dissoi logoi* has been a complex document to translate and understand. Many of those complexities are addressed in Robinson's "Introduction" to his translation of the full text in *Contrasting Arguments*, 1–81. Robinson speculates that the work was written by a sophist for instructional purposes, though he remains cautious about this inference. A more recent study by Tindale places the *dissoi logoi* among a number of argument strategies used by the sophists. See Tindale's *Reason's Dark Champions*, 99–112. For an analysis of Hamlet's famous "To Be . . ." soliloquy as *dissoi logoi*, see Arrington's "Feigned Soliloquy, Feigned Argument," 101–118.

8. Anonymous, "*Dissoi Logoi*," 48.

9. Chaim Perelman, "New Rhetoric,"1404.

10. Arrington, *Rhetoric's Agons*, 72.

11. Lanham, *Handlist of Rhetorical Terms*, 57-58.

12. Tindale, *Reason's Dark Champions*, 100, 111.

13. Plato, *Phaedru*s, 266d-e, 267a-b.

logoi order;¹⁴ instead, Plato's Socrates advises his young charge to follow a "cogent principle of composition" by shaping his entire discourse "like a living creature, with its own body," a "head" and "feet" and a "middle" with "extremities" or limbs.¹⁵

Plato's metaphor famously anticipates those Romantic critics and poets who emphasized the "organic form" of literature and art centuries later,¹⁶ even though his comparison between the order of a rhetorical speech and actual "living creatures" seems crudely schematic, almost cartoonish. Organic life is highly complex, and immensely various in form, appearance, and function—especially human organisms.¹⁷ Plato's metaphor, in its plainness and over-simplification, may be a satirical jab at the quite ornate rhetorical form of the *technai* that Plato has Socrates later recite to the young Phaedrus. By the same token, this metaphor would not offer much guidance to a young rhetor who must try to solve the ongoing problem of giving shape and form to arguments made under various, and fluid, circumstances.

Certainly, Aristotle himself understood organic form;¹⁸ and, like his teacher, shows disdain for any complicated order for an argument. Ignoring Plato's metaphor, Aristotle takes an even more practical view of *dispositio*. Appearing alongside his remarks on style and delivery, Aristotle insists that any argument has only two essential parts—stating the case and proving it.¹⁹ This may seem even more simplistic than Plato's metaphor, except Plato seems to be merely pointing to the most basic parts of any speech or text *after* it is composed, while Aristotle appears to be thinking here of what a rhetor must *do* when he argues, since that determines what should constitute rhetorical order. Yet, not far into his elaboration, Aristotle also begins to describe what seems to be the actual structure of a finished product, admitting that this product can have up to four parts, starting with "exordium [the beginning, what Plato called the "head"], statement [of the facts of any given case], proof [making up Plato's middle torso and limbs], and "an epilogue" [Plato's "feet," or the closing]. All the other parts—refutation, comparison, amplification, etc.—Aristotle, like his teacher, dismisses as

---

14. On Plato's relationship to his rivals and precursors, see Arrington, *Rhetoric's Agons*, 67–94.

15. Plato, *Phaedrus*, 264c. Plato's silence on *dissoi logoi*'s arrangement may be attributed to his appropriation of this strategy to construct his dialectical method. On this point, see Arrington, *Rhetoric's Agons*, 72.

16. Abrams, *Mirror and the Lamp*, 184–85.

17. Mumford, *Myth of the Machine*, vol. 1, 35–37.

18. Hughes, "Contemporaneity of Classical Rhetoric," 157–59.

19. Aristotle, *Rhetoric* 3.xiii.3.

needless additions swallowed up under "proving the case" a rhetor has to invent and make.

The exordium and epilogue, meanwhile, "are merely aids to memory." In the first, a rhetor states what he is going to argue; in the second, he sums up what he has argued.[20] Yet Aristotle did not believe every argument needed these aids. Depending on *when* a rhetor speaks and the *kind* of case it is, the exordium and epilogue could be completely omitted. Aristotle further explains "the sources" for each part of each sub-type of rhetoric—forensic, deliberative, or epideictic—advising rhetors on how to invent ideas to expand the different parts of each type of speech,[21] as if to demonstrate how closely connected form and invention are often thought to be.

By the time the anonymous author writes the *Rhetorica ad Herennium* (ca. 84 BCE), considered the oldest, most complete Latin manual on rhetoric to include advice on invention, arrangement, style, memory, and delivery,[22] *dispositio*'s parts had increased from Aristotle's begrudging four to six. Like Aristotle, the *ad Herennium* advises rhetors to start with the exordium and follow that with the narration, stating the facts of the case, typically in chronological order, and then dividing up the facts or points upon which a rhetor and his opponent agree and the ones they dispute, the division or partition. Afterwards, rhetors should offer proofs for their sides of the argument and then refute the arguments of their opponents. Finally, rhetors sum up the arguments made and try to sway the audience to their side of the issue in what is variously called the *peroratio, epilogus,* or *conclusio*.[23]

These six parts may have come to represent the "classical model" of rhetorical arrangement, but that honorific status certainly did not stop others from adding more parts or sub-dividing the parts added. The number and order of the parts varied according to the type of rhetoric the situation called for—forensic, deliberative, or epideictic—and the vagaries of the situations themselves. Yet, despite these variables, and Aristotle's practical advice, many Roman rhetorics agreed that openings (*exordia*) and closings (*peroratia*) were basic to rhetorical order. Once emotional appeals were included, rhetors were then advised to alternate between appealing to emotions and stating facts.[24]

20. Aristotle, *Rhetoric* 3.xiii.4–5.
21. Aristot*le, Rhetoric* 3.xiv—xvi.1–11.
22. Caplan, "Introduction," vii, xxxiv.
23. Cicero, *Rhetorica ad Herennium*, trans. Caplan, vol. 1, 3.viii–xi, 16–19. Further references are to this translation.
24. Lanham, *Handlist of Rhetorical Terms*, 172.

Quintilian, with whom we began, is largely faithful to this model, but he exhorts would-be rhetors to follow his own strategy for organizing.[25] He starts his organizing process by dividing (*divisio*) an entire case into its various parts, separating each individual part "into its elements" and placing the various elements into "the correct disposition" or "order" (*ordo*) so that "what follows coheres with what precedes." Arranging all the parts and elements into a coherent argument, however, depends not on any esthetic or epistemological criteria but on "expediency," what will work *best* for each case given his opponent's arguments and the specifics of the case itself. This, in broad outline, is Quintilian's method. He illustrates it more specifically with "instruction received from others" supplemented by his "own reasoning"[26] which had taught him to be careful to familiarize himself with "with every circumstance connected with the case" and then to review these circumstances from the "opponent's point of view" as well as his own. The main goal he sets for himself is simple enough, and is a well-established practice even before Quintilian embraces it—to find out precisely *where* the issues in the case are, and *where* and *how* he and his opponent agree and disagree. Still, the precise order of arguments to be made must depend, for Quintilian, on whether any rhetor is arguing for the defendant or the plaintiff, when he argues (first or second), and what has already been argued or conceded.

Like Aristotle, Quintilian spends considerable pages showing how a rhetor can find different issues in cases—issues of fact or "conjecture," of definition, and so forth, illustrating his method along the way to show how expediency, the effects he wants to have on the judge, and what the opponent argues, can shape and affect his organization. In fact, he devotes all of book seven of his twelve book work, *Institutio Oratoria*, "the largest rhetorical treatise which survives from antiquity"[27] and the one which has had the greatest "impact" on "literacy" and "education" in Western culture,[28] entirely to *dispositio*.

Yet to review these different stances on how human rhetoric should be ordered is certainly to wonder if any of these ideas can be usefully applied to the Christian Bible, or God's rhetoric in that Bible. These ancient thinkers, however much they disagreed about *dispositio*, were certainly not describing the order and shape of an *entire book*, whether that book is seen

25. Quintilian, *Institutio Oratoria*, vol. 3, 7. i. 1–8.

26. Quintilian, *Institutio Oratoria*, vol. 3, 7. i. 1–8.

27. Kennedy, *Classical Rhetoric and Its Christian and Secular Tradition from Ancient to Modern Times*, 100.

28. Murphy, "Rhetorical History as a Guide to the Salvation of Reading and Writing," 5.

as a unified work, or a motley of genres loosely assembled. Their focus, at best, was on organizing a single speech or text; but, even within so narrow a scope as that, they could not arrive at any real consensus, save on the importance of organization and the array of factors that could affect that organization. The question, then, becomes whether post-classical ideas on *dispositio* will prove any more useful.

Post-Classical Views of Rhetorical Structure

Quintilian's ideas about rhetorical order, like his hero and mentor, Cicero's, are obviously shaped by the Roman world's interest in law and empire. Even so, for eighteenth century rhetorical handbooks like Scotsman Hugh Blair's *Lectures on Rhetoric and Belles Lettres* (1783), the Roman model of organization remained dominant, though with some minor variations, depending on the kind of speech—legal, political, or religious (a new kind of rhetoric)—to be delivered.[29] In the century after Blair's popular handbook appeared, rhetorical form was reconsidered. For the American Congregationalist minister and teacher of rhetoric, Henry A. Day, the form that rhetoric (and by this time primarily *written* rhetoric) should take was largely a matter of esthetics, of beauty and taste. An argument's shape arises from a rhetor's imaginative capacity, so that, in *The Art of Discourse* (1867), Day reasons that because "discourse is, in its proper, essential nature, a communication to other minds," a rhetor must look to his "imagination" as "the more essential faculty" so he might "form the thought in such verbal body that shall be received by the mind addressed."[30] For Day, "the construction of discourse" is "the proper work of the imagination as the [rhetor's] faculty of form," now dictated by "the laws of the imagination."

Exactly what those "laws of imagination" were, and how they affected a rhetor's choices in shaping his arguments, shows up, at least in part, in Alexander Bain's popular textbook, *English Composition and Rhetoric* (1866), widely used in teaching composition to the many students from middle and upper-middle class backgrounds then flooding Scotland's schools and colleges.[31] Author of two important books on the links between psychology and physiology, the more scientific Bain, following his fellow Scotsman George Campbell's *The Philosophy of Rhetoric* (1776), took a psychological approach to rhetoric and writing. He grounded what he considered to be its basic ordering "principles" on the underlying laws of mental

29. Blair, *Lectures on Rhetoric and Belles Lettres*, 106–128.
30. Day, *Art of Discourse*, 868.
31. See Bizzell and Herzberg, "Alexander Bain and Adams Sherman Hill," 1141–43.

association—resemblance, contrast, and discrimination.[32] (More recent efforts, of course, ground the principles of language itself on the findings of cognitive neuroscience.[33]) Bain identifies "five kinds of Composition" students must learn, "Description, Narration, Exposition, Oratory, and Poetry." Only the fourth one—Oratory—is directly connected to rhetoric as Quintilian or Aristotle would have understood the term. Yet Bain further attempts to show how the mental laws of association correspond to and govern each kind of composition and the different figures of speech—metaphor, metonymy, and so forth—appropriate to each kind.

Bain's taxonomy of "kinds" of writing looks severely limited by today's standards. In fact, it hardly suffices as a taxonomy of writing genres at all. "Description," "narration," and "exposition," in fact, were derived from rhetoric or "Oratory" itself. "Narration" and "exposition" show up as overlapping terms among the various parts of rhetoric's *dispositio* while "description" or *descriptio* derives from the overlapping rhetorical categories of *energia* and *enargia*, complimentary terms for a speaker's or writer's vivid, active style. In this sense, then, Bain's taxonomy consists of only two genres, oratory and poetry, both of which pre-existed his textbook and were often in classical times placed alongside such other genres as history, tragedy, comedy, and so forth.

A more nuanced approach than Bain's to the psychology of rhetorical order appears in Kenneth Burke's early book *Counterstatement* (1931).[34] Though Burke focuses on *literary* "forms," he defines *any* verbal form, spoken or written, literary or non-literary, as the "arousing and fulfillment of [readers'] desires" and, to the extent that "one part of" of a speech or a text "anticipate[s] another part," a reader's desire "to be gratified" is met through a writer's selection of formal ordering principles. Long before any explicit formulations of reader-response theories, or before reader-response theories became entangled and absorbed into the various types of narrative criticism of biblical texts,[35] Burke grounds his idea of *dispositio* on how a text impacts readers' affective states, outlining five different but overlapping types of form rhetors may exploit. These forms are *not*, for Burke, *types* of writing or literary genres, but structural patterns rhetors may adopt in the hope of their having their due effects on readers' expectations. "Progressive" form, the first, follows a "syllogistic progression," like "the form of a perfectly conducted argument, advancing step by step, from point A to point

---

32. Bain, *English Composition and Rhetoric*, 1146–47.
33. See Pinker, *Stuff of Thought*.
34. Burke, *Counterstatement*, 124–27. Further references are to the 1968 reprint.
35. Moore, "Afterwords," 255.

THE SHAPE OF GOD'S RHETORIC   139

B." But there is no reason why a rhetor may not also exploit "qualitative progression," where a quality (goodness or badness) of one element of a case prepares an audience for a shift to another, opposing quality. A writer may require, too, "repetitive form," to recast a point or points in different ways throughout an argument. Likewise, rhetoric as such has conventional forms, such as the *exordia*, which have "the appeal of form *as form*." Finally, though usually identified with style, the focus of the next chapter, Burke lists such *"minor or incidental forms"* as "metaphor, paradox, disclosure, reversal [as in irony], contraction, expansion, bathos, apostrophe, series, chiasmus—which can be discussed as formal events themselves."[36] Because the first three formal patterns have a wider scope than the last one, they can recur at different places within an entire speech, text, or even a book as long and complexly layered as the Bible, irrespective of a writer's purposes or genres.

Like Burke, in addressing the delicate, even tenuous bond between rhetorical order and audience psychology, Chaim Perelman has argued that classical models of form simply fail to solve a rhetor's problem of how to arrange arguments. To be advised to place strong arguments at the beginning and at the end, leaving weaker arguments for the middle, "presumes that an argument's forcefulness is constant, regardless of the circumstances in which an argument is presented."[37] Further, since a rhetor can never be certain in advance whether any given order will be effective for any given audience, "the effort of adaptation must always be taken up anew." For Perelman, there is no "natural or rational order," much less a pleasing, esthetic one, for any given audience;[38] "[r]educing the problems of order to a scientific or aesthetic methodology," he admonishes, "separates questions of content from questions of form and discards the problematic proper to rhetoric: the adaptation of discourse to the audience." This reduction, he fears, leads to "rhetoric's degeneration."[39]

Perelman does, however, think that "practical" or "[n]onformal argument [the kinds of arguments most people, not scientists or logicians, make] consists, not of a *chain* of ideas [such as Burke's "progressive," syllogistic form] of which some [arguments] are derived from others according to the accepted [that is, scientific-logical] rules of inference . . ."[40] Instead, nonformal arguments are more like "web[s] formed from all the arguments

36. Burke, *Counterstatement*, 127.
37. Perelman, *Realm of Rhetoric*, 148–49. Further references are to this translation.
38. Ibid., 149–51.
39. Ibid., 152.
40. Perelman, "New Rhetoric," 1396.

and all the reasons that combine to achieve the desired result . . . to bring the audience to the conclusions offered by the orator, starting from the premises they already accept . . ." In the end, how many arguments a rhetor should include and how to assess the strength, weakness, or relevance of each, are questions Perelman does not answer and ones he believes need much more study.[41]

Those who study writing and teaching others to write have tried to fill this gap in knowledge. Like their classical ancestors, some have suggested that form or structure is, in fact, a critical part of reading and inventing certain types of writing.[42] Others have offered an array of different schemes to help young writers organize written texts, all departures from the classical model.[43] More recently, one scholar, recalling Burke's definition of form, has argued that young writers and their teachers have been far too concerned about organization and form as a spatial phenomenon.[44] Readers experience texts in time, not just space. It takes time to read a text, just as it takes time to write one; so a rhetor producing a written document might do better to understand form on the analogy with music, not painting or other visual media. Musical form, at its simplest and most complex, depends, as Burke saw, upon arousing a listener's expectations and then trying to satisfy them. To form effective rhetoric, then, is not about shaping particular *blocks* of verbal material in space, as Quintilian imagined, but about "the binding of time" so the rhetoric gains "the music of form," from the rhythms of individual sentences to entire paragraphs and entire texts,[45] such as can be found in the Bible itself.

This all-too-brief, overly simplified sketch of theoretical ideas about *dispositio* available to human rhetors and writers shows that, while organization is widely considered important and the classical model is sometimes embraced, no *real* consensus has emerged over the centuries on the *best way* to organize *every* speech or *every* text. In fact, arranging arguments, much like inventing the arguments arranged, seems as much a name for an unresolved theoretical issue as it is a step or stage that every theorist agrees rhetors must perform. Even if a rhetor follows the classical model, that rhetor would still face all sorts of unpredictable constraints that can affect or even demand departures from the model. Further, what sort of form

---

41. Ibid., 1400.

42. See Coe, "Apology for Form," 13–28.

43. See Podis and Podis, "Identifying and Teaching Rhetorical Plans for Arrangement," 430–442.

44. See Elbow, "Music of Form," 620–66.

45. Ibid., 623.

or shape may arouse and satisfy some readers' expectations may not arouse or satisfy expectations for other readers. The alleged "music of form" can be heard in a simple commercial jingle or in the complex thematic variations of a Shubert piano sonata, though the satisfactions offered in the first may not at all be qualitatively the same in the second. Readers of generic texts—romances, westerns, spy novels, or even academic articles and books—may not react positively at all to a text that too openly and too frequently violates or frustrates expectations aroused by and embedded in a given genre.

God's Rhetorical Order vs. the Bible's Order?

So the question remains: do these contentious ideas about *dispositio* have any analytical relevance to God's rhetoric in the Bible? After all, some may say, He *organized* the entire universe, so it would hardly be a problem for Him to establish an effective order for the arguments He makes. Certainly, for many devout Christians, God's capacity to organize goes without saying.

The trouble is, the Bible through which God makes His case to persuade His human likenesses, as many historical critics would remind us, was arranged and re-arranged by many human hands over a long stretch of time. This is not, obviously, how earlier readers saw the Bible. They would have read it as "all one book, with Psalms calling out to Genesis and Job to the Gospels, Paul to Leviticus and Ecclesiastes to Kings."[46] In this so-called "pre-critical' period," Bible readers from the Middle Ages through the Reformation saw each "individual narrative ... as a chapter in the larger story arc of salvation history, an epic that extended beyond the pages of the Bible and into the life of every subsequent reader."[47] But now, in the wake of more recent historical criticism, the question is whether the Bible is "a whole, perhaps a narrative and poetic whole ... book or a ragbag."[48] This may seem far too stark a choice, a surrender to a falsifying either/or rather than a full consideration of both/and, however difficult it may be to see the Bible as both "book" and "ragbag." If the Bible is, indeed, but a "ragbag," a miscellany of different texts, edited and redacted over time, and not a single book, to think of it as God's "rhetoric," and to wonder whether His *dispositio*, however theoretically contested, contributes to His book's persuasiveness may seem grossly misguided, if not utterly foolish.

An effort to examine God's *dispositio* may seem even more foolish when confronting the glaring fact that the Bible, be it book or ragbag, is not

---

46. Josipovici, *Book of God*, xii.
47. Thatcher, "Anatomies of the Fourth Gospel," 4–5.
48. Josipovici, *Book of God*, 9.

explicitly written as an argument. The physical artifact most call the "Bible" may, as Plato argued, have a beginning, middle, and an end; but that tells readers very little about what is in those parts. Neither does the whole text conform to the classical model of rhetoric, oral or written, or completely serve the singular purposes of Aristotle's taxonomy of forensic, deliberative, or epideictic rhetoric. Its very title comes from the Greek, *ta biblia*, or "little books," which were, in ancient times, "separate scrolls" and far more "diverse" than Shakespeare's or any other secular writer's works.[49]

Some argue that, whatever else the Bible may be, it should first and foremost be read and heard and received as "literature," as it is in countless English departments, if not seminaries.[50] Its status as a "literary" text, as "imaginative literature," rests in no small part on the Old Testament's being mainly comprised of stories and poetry, with only "minor" parts of the text devoted to "straight-forward 'referential' or 'non-literary' . . ." discourse.[51] A literary approach to the Bible's narratives and poetry allows readers to appreciate and interpret the Bible's complex of meanings; whereas, read as "Scripture" rather than "story," readers must be more concerned with its historical veracity and truthfulness, with what the Bible "say[s], teach[es], affirm[s], assert[s, and], den[ies]."[52] Yet taking a literary approach to the Bible's stories and poetry does not help a critic who wants to examine *what* this Bible's God affirms, asserts, and denies—and *argues*—truthfully or no, through the Bible as "story." Nor does it solve the problem of whether the Bible's overall story-arc, as God propels it, is a more or less unified whole or a disparate collection of parts, with "laws and religious instruction" the province of "theologians and scholars" and the stories and poetry the province of "students of literature" and their instructors.[53] If the Bible's story is also, as widely believed, God's story, this story still consists of many other stories. Yet, even in this case, the various narratives unfold to include the poetry of the Psalms, an outline of Israel's history, its genealogies, prophecies, and so on. Further, the larger narrative and the smaller ones both contain and make different types of arguments, all variously shaped.

If a critic of rhetoric seeks to examine how God shapes His rhetoric as "story," that critic must start with the larger, framing narrative, since God's case starts at the very beginning, with Genesis. In fact, God's rhetoric starts before "beginning" has any really human narrative sense whatsoever. God

49. Ibid., 28.
50. Clines, "Story and Poem," 26–27.
51. Ibid., 28.
52. Ibid., 29.
53. Josipovici, *Book of God*, xi.–xii.

can make no opening statement of His case because He *is* the statement that opens up the possibilities of all other statements. Once opened, His narrative and other narratives may begin.

Narrative, or *narratio*, we need to remember, has long had a home in classical rhetoric's *dispositio*, as part of the exordium. In a rhetorical *narratio*, if one is needed, speakers and writers state whatever facts a given case turns upon on, often chronologically. In the classical *dispositio*, the chronological unfolding of these facts, if they were so narrated, or could be, their not having been narrated already, was entirely subordinate to a rhetor's persuasive intent. Whatever "facts" there were to narrate, of course, did not and could not match the "facts" as modern science or historiography understands "fact." Though both Aristotle and Cicero certainly can distinguish "fact" from "fable," neither's "facts" would exactly conform to scientific expectations. Even though Thomas Kuhn's "science" seems more provocatively moved to newer and higher discoveries by shifts in "paradigms" than "facts,"[54] it remains the case that many human beings now want more than easily refutable eye-witness accounts, the circumstantial props of a crime scene, or the dubious evidence wrenched from tortured bodies before they assent to believe in a rhetor's factual narrative.

In the classical model, too, a rhetor's *narratio* depended on such facts as could be accepted and believed in a lawcourt or public assembly, so if a rhetorical critic were to agree simply that the Bible's *dispositio* and God's were identical and consisted largely of a "factual" narrative in a scientific sense, that critic must soon confront historical critics' and modern science's own skepticism about what would constitute a narrative statement of "facts" in the Bible. In other words, if a critic identifies the Bible's and God's *dispositio* with rhetoric's *narratio*, this critic at the same time would appear to be assuming that the Bible's narratives are a "factual" chronology of how the world came to be and how it will end. The result of that equation would be a regression to and re-adoption of the "pre-critical" view of the Bible, and the God of that Bible, that historical critics have generously labored to dislodge and replace with the truer, more documentable biblical ragbag composed by hypothetical authors, editors, and redactors working from putative sources to compose and assemble the Bible so many assume to be a single, sacred book written and arranged in a particularly irrevocable way. It would, in effect, be a return to and an endorsement of what biblical scholar Hans Frei, much to some theologians' dismay, favors: a "realistic" view of biblical

---

54. This is the provocative argument Kuhn made in *Structure of Scientific Revolutions*.

narratives, stories whose "literal" meanings cannot be really separated from their "literary" forms.[55]

Yet, if the Bible is largely shaped after a rhetorical *narratio*, in whole and in its various parts, and not as a "literary" narrative, the "facts" upon which it relies need not conform to the standards historical critics or scientists assume. "Facts" in classical rhetoric were often, in the end, matters of "conjecture," a person's best guess about what happened, where, and when. That these "facts" could be disputed; that witnesses could be cross-examined and shown to be mistaken or lying; that the language of laws could be variously interpreted; and that torture evidence was as subject to refutation as any other kind of evidence—all this must be assumed, too, about whatever factual narratives may be needed for different kinds of rhetoric. That a "fact" was always already "conjectural" the moment it slides into the matrices of any given rhetorical event should remind us that neither Aristotle nor Cicero necessarily believed a factual narrative serving a rhetor's argument was simply to be accepted as "truth," even in an historical period without our more modern scientific prejudices about what a "fact" or the "truth" must be.[56]

Yet, even if a critic accepts the Bible's overall narrative arc as God's own rhetorical, if not strictly "literary" or even strictly "historical," design, a critic must still decide if he is to describe this design at the macro-or micro-level.

Before addressing this question, it must again be stressed that some Christians now, as in the past, read the Bible quite literally as God's word, not humankind's. Nor are they necessarily aberrant in this respect, since "rabbis who pored over the [biblical] text in the early centuries . . . and whose writings are enshrined in the Talmud and various midrashes," not to mention the early Church Fathers and most readers during the Middle Ages, all assumed the Bible "was written by God and so must be significant."[57] The content, the arguments, the stories, *belong to Him*, as supreme and sovereign Author, the ethos He invented in Genesis. In Exodus, God supposedly wrote a great deal on the stone tablets Moses carries back to his people—a great deal at least compared to Jesus, who only writes once, in the Gospel of John (8:6), prompting some scholars to argue over Jesus's own limited "literacy" as a rabbi.[58] Yet other Christians, like the "pre-critical" rabbis, Church Fa-

55. See Thatcher, "Anatomies of the Fourth Gospel," 2-3; Frei, *Eclipse of Biblical Narrative*, 3, 13-14, 324.

56. See Triggs, "Tales Artfully Spun," 124-31. Triggs neglects to acknowledge the "conjectural" status of rhetorical "facts."

57. Josipovici, *Book of God*, 19.

58. For an examination of this issue, see Evans, "Jewish Scripture and the Literacy of Jesus," 41-54. For a more recent, fuller analysis of this single incident in which Jesus

thers, and medieval readers, are reluctant to think that God wrote every word of the Bible, or resistant to taking every utterance God makes literally. For these Christians, God is thought to have inspired the Bible and those many authors who wrote it and attributed speeches to Him, to Jesus, and to all the other figures in this singular book.

Historical critics of the Bible, obviously, have known for some time that the Bible as we now have it did not come about by divine fiat at all. German biblical scholars, using the "historical-critical method,"[59] uncovered at least "four different sources" that anonymous authors relied on to invent the content and the shape of the first five books of the Old Testament (the Pentateuch), from Genesis through Deuteronomy, which were then combined in the fifth century BCE.[60] Further, and more important for God's *dispositio,* while the Hebrew Bible's Torah follows the exact order of the first five books of the Old Testament, the human effort to collate separate sources from different authors may explain why there are two different accounts of God's generation of the world, two different accounts of the Flood, and other strange, even contradictory sections in those first five books. Given the different sources, and the editorial efforts to unify them as one singular, "holy" text, it is not always clear if the volatile God called "Yahweh," who invents Adam out of dust and mist and confronts Moses, is the *only* God or the *same God* as the one called "Elohim" by a different source, or "El Shaddai" or just "El," the last of which forms part of the Hebrew name, "Isra-el or Ishma-El," by another source.[61]

These difficulties will reappear in chapter 8, on evaluating God's rhetoric. For now, though, a critic seeking to describe God's *dispositio* rhetorically must confront the simple, obvious fact that the arrangement of the *entire* Hebrew Bible, the Tanakh, differs quite a bit from the Bible's Old Testament. The Tanakh, as we know, is a "postbiblical acronym" in which the letter *T* stands for the Torah or the "teachings" of the first five books, while the letter *N* or *nebiʾ im* stands for the prophetic writings, and the letter *K* stands for *ketubim* or "other writings."[62] In the Tanakh, God's final direct speech is to Job, and God is spoken about less and less, and sometimes not at all.[63] So the Hebrew Bible follows an order in which God speaks, acts, and then falls

---

writes, especially as it pertains to rhetoric, see Deans, "The Rhetoric of Jesus Writing in the Story of the Woman Accused of Adultery," 406–29.

59. Ehrman, *Jesus, Interrupted,* 4.
60. Armstrong, *History of God,* 12.
61. Ibid.
62. Miles, *God,* 18.
63. Ibid. 11.

silent. In the Old Testament, the major and minor prophets which make up the middle of the Hebrew Bible have been moved to the end, while other books, including Job, which end the Tanakh, shift to the middle.[64] Whatever a reader's beliefs may or may not be, re-ordering the canon of Hebrew texts so the Old Testament ends with prophetic announcements may have served the Christian editors' rhetorical purpose—to stage the "New" Testament and the final covenant-argument represented as Jesus Christ.[65]

I say "may" because it is difficult to be certain that this was the exact purpose of the reordering. Some critics suspect that "[t]he central procedure of the New Testament is the conversion of the Hebrew Bible into the Old Testament, so as to abrogate any stigma of belatedness that might be assigned to the New Covenant [Jesus], when contrasted with the 'Old' Covenant."[66] Christian editors, then, may have re-arranged the sequence of books in the Hebrew Bible to lay claim to an inheritance and a tradition that the New Testament of Christians took for their very own.[67] In this way, when the Old Testament ends with the minor prophet, Malachi, meaning "messengers," that ending prepares the way for John the Baptist and the New Covenant of Jesus the Christ—an ending decidedly different from the Tanakh's closing with 2 Chronicles, "and a final 'let us go up' to the rebuilding of Jerusalem and the restoration of Yahweh's temple."[68]

If the added New Testament is, indeed, an attempt to revise and co-opt the Tanakh, the Christian Bible's ordering is, indeed, more rhetorical than coincidental. Further, if the various efforts to represent Jesus's story were arranged in strict chronological order, as a rhetorical *narratio* often demands, based on our best guesses—"conjectures"—about the dates of their composition, the New Testament would begin with Paul's letters, followed by Mark, Matthew, Luke, and Acts, after which would come James, John, and the Apocalypse.[69] Yet the current order and inclusion of the twenty-seven sections of the New Testament was not established until 367 CE, almost three centuries after these added sections may have been written.[70] During this period, historical records indicate intense, sometimes vitriolic debate over which texts to include and in what order. Many available gospels, of course, did not make it into the New Testament canon. These, in fact, have

64. Ibid., 16.
65. Ibid., 18.
66. Bloom, *Jesus and Yahweh*, 44.
67. Ibid., 45.
68. Ibid., 52.
69. Ibid., 37.
70. Ehrman, *Jesus, Interrupted*, 36.

been collected, edited, and gathered into an anthology that serves as an alternative to the Bible most people know.[71]

Certainly, some devout Christians may insist that God's will was working throughout the long historical process that finally produced *both* the Old and the New Testaments, all edited and arranged just as God wanted. Such a claim, of course, collides with the voluminous historical evidence that shows a number of very strong-willed human beings who played major parts in this process as well. Yet, for all this debate over the centuries, we do have a more or less received canon of books and gospels that most accept as the Christian Bible we now read, if and when we read it. So the next question is what that accepted arrangement—the Bible's current *dispositio*—may suggest to us, if anything, about God's own rhetorical ordering.

Early on, biblical scholars were preoccupied with questions about the history of biblical texts and the study of its ancient languages and sources. Less attention was paid to the Bible's rhetorical and poetic qualities. Even when attention *was* paid, critics of the Bible's rhetoric tended to focus on matters of style and such formal genres as the parable, comedy, and tragedy.[72] In his 1968 Presidential Address at the yearly gathering of the Society of Biblical Studies, later originally published in the *Journal of Biblical Literature*, scholar James Muilenburg outlined many of the contributions made by those critics and acknowledged their importance to Israel and other Middle Eastern countries.[73] But Muilenburg challenged Old Testament scholars to go "beyond" identifying literary forms and types. What lay "beyond" this kind of study, for Muilenberg, was "rhetorical criticism"—detailed attention to how the various units of the Old Testament were formed, why, and who or what the various Old Testament authors may have been imitating.[74]

At the time, Muilenburg believed rhetorical criticism could aid in understanding various formal features of the Old Testament, and his call for more study of Old Testament rhetoric inspired many to take this approach, with varying degrees of success.[75] Reading the Bible as "literature" rather than "scripture," as is so often done in seminaries, leads to the indisputable fact that, however diverse the literary forms and types of the Bible are, some literary scholars grappling with the Bible's rhetoric came to believe that each story, poem, or prophecy had to be read within its "communicative

71. See the excerpts compiled as *The Other Bible*.
72. See Howard Jr., "Rhetorical Criticism in Old Testament Studies," 87–89.
73. Muilenburg, "Form Criticism and Beyond," 49–52.
74. Ibid., 57–69.
75. Howard J., "Rhetorical Criticism in Old Testament Studies," 90. Howard argues that, despite Muilenburg's call for rhetorical approaches to the Bible, especially the Old Testament, the results have led to a great deal of attention to "surface structures."

context."[76] That means scholars would have to ask and answer this basic question: "what... does the biblical narrator want to accomplish, and under what conditions does he operate."

This question clearly underscores the simple fact that, quite apart from *who* actually wrote these narratives, when, and for whom, "the biblical storyteller is a persuader," in part because "he wields discourse to shape [a reader's] response and attitude."[77] At the same time, each narrator should be seen as "an ideological persuader" who struggles within the "tension" between a "commitment to the divine system of norms, absolute and demanding and in application often ruthless," and an "awareness of the necessity and difficulty" of how to persuade readers "to adopt a world-picture that both transcends and threatens" human beings. The biblical storyteller must decide "how to win the audience over to the side of God rather than ... [to] fellow-mortals"—"the task of persuasion"—"without dwarfing, betraying or compromising the object of persuasion [God]."[78]

Given this "ideological commitment," any biblical narrator, whether of Genesis or the Jonah story, seems unlike any other narrator in secular literary works. Secular narrators try to shape responses and attitudes toward each story,[79] and this fact leads us to the trickiest part of what this chapter is about. How should anyone interested in exploring God's rhetoric, and *not* the rhetorical motives of all those specific narrators who attribute speeches to God; or the authors, implied or real, behind those invented narrators, approach the question of how this God arranges His rhetoric? Do we go small, dealing with the arrangement of each narrative, each poem, each prophecy? Or do we widen our lens, to take in the arrangement and shape of the *entire* Christian Bible as it has been shaped by the many human hands that invented the single text with which most are familiar?

Some biblical rhetorical critics have taken the first approach, offering highly detailed analyses of different chapters, sections, or stories in the Bible.[80] Despite one scholar's justifiable cautions,[81] I am inclined toward

---

76. Sternberg, "Bible's Art of Persuasion," 235.

77. Ibid.

78. Ibid.

79. Ibid., 236.

80. Howard, "Rhetorical Criticism in Old Testament Studies" lists a number of such works, 101, n58: Boomershine, "Structure of Narrative Rhetoric in Genesis 2-3," 113-29; Fox, "Rhetoric of Ezekiel's Vision," 1-15; Gitay's "A Study of Amos' Art of Speech," 293-309, and his *Prophecy and Persuasion*.

81. See Bar-Efrat's "Some Observations on the Analysis of Structure in Biblical Narrative," 186-205. Bar-Efrat cautions that those analyzing the structures of biblical narratives must be clear about the size and scope of the narrative "unit" they are analyzing

the second approach—to explore God's *dispositio* across both Old and New Testaments. To my mind, the Bible invites both approaches and the either/or dilemma, posed above, seems as unsatisfactory as the earlier view of the Bible as a book or a ragbag. Consequently, it is largely accurate to argue "that the Bible's main form of exposition" is "narrative" whose main goal is "to persuade its audience."[82] It also seems correct to say that it does not really matter whether the authors of the Old Testament or the New "had access to the Greek concept of rhetoric as the art of persuasion."[83] While the Greeks self-consciously developed rhetoric as a system of concepts applicable to secular forms of rhetoric, there is no compelling reason to think that the ancient Hebrews did not understand that the narratives they wrote should try to be as effective and persuasive as possible, whether they developed a self-conscious theory for them or not.[84]

Narratio in the classical rhetorical model had, to be sure, a fairly restricted scope, to the exordium, and a fairly restricted role, to state the conjectural facts of a case in such a way as to serve a rhetor's persuasive intent. Yet, within the Old Testament certainly, the human authors of the texts themselves, whoever they were, seem to realize that God acts in the world and that these acts were rhetorical in nature, intended to persuade His various audiences and all audiences to come.[85] *Narratio*, then, can advance God's rhetorical intent, so long as it is recognized that its initially narrow scope has been greatly extended to encompass the Bible entire. Biblical authors may very well have thought their narratives mirrors of God's own. This God, after all, sees Himself as *Author* of the world, and in control of the history of that world as it unfolds after He invents His human likenesses, or at least that is how many of the biblical authors' narrators present Him.

Like any attentive rhetor, this God acts and speaks in response to what His human inventions, His primary audience, do and do not do. His acts and speeches try to address rhetorical situations where conflicts, flaws, and

---

and warns against pre-mature judgments about the narrative levels a critic focuses on, and against describing plots in "in too abstract and general terms" as Kenneth Burke does in *Rhetoric of Religion*. Bar-Efrat accepts the view that many but not all biblical narratives follow a "successive order" in which "time flows in one direction only"; however, he also observes that some biblical narratives, such as David's war with the Amalekites, do have flashbacks and flash forwards in time, while others move in space, from earth to heaven, use dates for temporal sequencing, or use other parallel forms.

82. Patrick and Scult, *Rhetoric and Biblical Interpretation*, 29.

83. Ibid., 31. Kennedy also makes this argument in *New Testament Interpretation through Rhetorical Criticism*, 8–12. For further analysis of the link between narrative and exposition, see Arrington's "Reflections on the Expository Principle," 314–32.

84. Patrick and Scult, *Rhetoric and Biblical Interpretation*, 31.

85. Ibid.

problems arise, so He seeks to persuade and correct those conflicts. As a result, it seems, "[t]he Bible's narrative discourse unfolds as the story of" such conflicts as God "attempts to 'correct' . . . through interventions," thereby giving His words and acts "rhetorical meaning."[86] His interventions make up many of the "narratives" which "serve as a guide to making the realization of his [God's] vision a continual possibility in [human] history."[87]

Why biblical authors chose narrative as one of their primary methods of arrangement, and why editors and redactors sought to arrange the entire Bible as a narrative, is a difficult question to answer with certainty. Some biblical scholars point to evidence which indicates that these authors may have invented this "innovative form of prose art" simply because earlier narrative forms—the chronicle and the epic—did not allow authors to point out the "moral significance to events in the very act of telling a story about them."[88] Beyond that, the gaps, sparse style, and even contradictions within biblical narratives, as, say, opposed to the more elaborate details of the Homeric epics, may even account for the Bible's continuing influence today and the many interpretive efforts it invites.[89] It may further suggest the "rhetoric of sublimity" in these narratives that Lynn Poland explores, insofar as the narrative gaps, complex figuration, and the breaking of storytelling conventions is evidence, as Augustine long ago recognized, of "spiritual eloquence . . . divine rhetoric" that breaks through mere human language.[90] For Augustine, that which is figuratively obscure in the Bible shows that its language was "not devised by human industry, but [was] poured forth from the divine mind both wisely and eloquently."[91]

What all this suggests is that the kind of "history" the biblical narratives present is "rhetorical," and not "realistic," as histories are supposed to be, or even necessarily "literary," where readers are expected to find in the narrative a plausible, as-if situation that might or could happen to someone someday.[92] In one very real sense, biblical narratives are "rhetorical" to the extent that they remind and re-enforce for their authors and especially their Jewish auditors and readers a sense of communal identity as a people, their past, present, and future. These narratives can be read as responses to moments in Israel's communal life when its own sense of identity as a people

86. Ibid., 34.
87. Ibid.
88. Ibid., 36–38.
89. Ibid., 39–40.
90. Poland, "Bible and the Rhetorical Sublime," 37.
91. Augustine, *On Christian Doctrine*, 4. vii. 21.
92. Patrick and Scult, *Rhetoric and Biblical Interpretation*, 40–43, 58–60.

deviated from what God demanded, so the narratives' rhetorical goal was to persuade and lead them, to get Israel "back on track," or to warn Israel of what would—and often *did*—happen to them if they did not get back on track.

Certainly, some of the biblical narratives resemble those in "forensic" rhetoric, apparently intended to condemn or "exonerate" the principal actors in the stories and serve the purpose of confronting the Bible's auditors and readers with some unflattering traits that the people of Israel would just as soon ignore or forget.[93] Many forensic narratives may be found in the Book of Deuteronomy, where God explains to Moses how different sorts of disputes should be handled, and God's legal and moral reasoning for handling these cases under His covenant-arguments. In other narratives, such as David's ascent to power, recounted in 1 Samuel 16—24, and the revolt of Jehu in 2 Kings 9—10, God defends "the usurpers' legitimacy" by describing their acts as "either innocent or justified."[94] Other forensic narratives focus on the offenses of a guilty party and prophesy God's judgment against them, as in the story of Naboth, Ahab, and Jezebel, and the prophet Elijah (1 Kings 21). In these narratives, the biblical narrator often tries "to 'defend' the God of the prophets."[95]

The Structure of God's Covenant-Rhetoric

A useful way to think of these many, and various, narratives is to recognize the overarching function of God's many, and various, covenant-arguments. Kenneth Burke's observation here is again useful: from the Book of Genesis all the way through to the New Testament, covenants are "motives," rhetorical motives on God's part and specific to God's human likenesses. Only His humans can violate them. Inanimate objects—stones and trees, say—cannot possibly break covenants because they cannot understand "agreements or commands."[96] These covenants make up what one biblical scholar calls the "deep story" underlying all the various, shorter rhetorical narratives.[97] After all, in most of the specific narratives, and in the Bible's larger narrative, "time flows in one direction only," from past to the future or end-time.[98] The Bible does have stories with flashbacks and flash forwards, but

93. Ibid., 60.
94. Ibid., 61, 63.
95. Ibid., 72.
96. Burke, *Rhetoric of Religion*, 174.
97. Lee, *Jesus and the Metaphors*, 29
98. Bar-Efrat, "Some Observations on the Analysis of Structure in Biblical

the overall arrangement of God's rhetoric remains primarily linear.[99] God's covenants organize that deep story that links the many different narratives to Jesus Christ, and his link to "God and the world," since Jesus, as Yeshua of Nazareth, was Jewish—a fact that can sometimes block or complicate some Christians' understanding of his significance.

Covenants, then, and covenant-arguments, can unify the largest segments of the Bible, its Old and New Testaments.[100] Since the religious beliefs of ancient Hebrews seem to have developed in stages, moving from polytheism to "henotheism"—the concession that only one God *matters* among many other gods—and, finally, to monotheism,[101] early Hebrews experienced covenants as the history through which God reveals Himself in the flow of time. As "treaties" between various parties, covenants end up reflecting the national and social lives of the early Hebrews. Adopted among different tribes and villages, covenants were also "basic political acts" which Hebrews "stretched to name the Jewish experience of Ultimacy."[102] As Hebrew society assumed a "lord/vassal" model, wherein God becomes Lord and then Father, the Hebrew understanding of covenant changes as well.[103]

Covenant treaties, it turns out, have their own particular *dispositio*.[104] A preamble identifies parties to the covenant, followed next by a historical prologue (the past histories of the parties enjoined in the covenant), then with instructions on where the covenant-treaty was to be stored. Ritual readings of the covenant-treaty served to remind the parties of the covenant's terms, and gods were called upon as witnesses to its agreement. Covenants also listed the blessings for those who followed and kept to the covenant terms and the curses against a party who violated them.

God's covenants with Noah and Abraham place all the obligations on God Himself—quite unusual for the Middle East.[105] God's covenant not to destroy His living creatures by water is eternally binding on Him alone, but not on Noah or his progeny. In the covenant with Abraham, circumcision is a binding ritual, but God seems to threaten no one who violates it, except, grimly and ironically, Moses. Nor are there any ritualized readings required to recall either covenant—only the rainbow and circumcision serve as re-

---

Narrative," 192.

99. Ibid., 192–93.
100. Lee, *Jesus and the Metaphors of God*, 29-30, 35.
101. Ibid., 32-33.
102. Ibid., 36-37.
103. Ibid., 38-39.
104. Ibid., 39.
105. Ibid., 40–41.

minders, rhetorical "signs" invented to reiterate the covenant-arguments. God's covenant with Moses, though, is "the most fully elaborated" and follows the lord/vassal model.[106] God makes no promises to any individuals in the Mosaic covenant, as He had with Adam, Noah, and Abraham. When Israel changes from being a theocracy of priests to a monarchy, beginning with Saul and extending through David, each king becomes a "son of God."[107] Later on, Hebrews became more self-conscious about their own individual responsibilities to God, so that, by the time of Jeremiah's prophecies, the covenant with God shifts to each human heart and away from exclusive identification with the nation of Israel.[108] So the covenant becomes the "root metaphor" of the entire Hebrew deep story.[109]

This emphasis on covenant as a "root metaphor" may be misleading, unless readers understand that a *root metaphor* is not just stylistic decoration, a mere verbal flourish, or a phrase to suggest that God's covenants are made-up, false, and not worthy of God's or anyone's serious attention. Metaphors are, rhetorically speaking, one of many figures of speech, usually classified, following Aristotle, as one stylistic device among many others—the focus of the next chapter.

As it happens, the idea of a "root metaphor" comes from philosopher Stephen C. Pepper, who derives a set of "world theories" based on the premise that human beings, when trying to understand a new or strange phenomenon, often invent an analogy between what they already understand and what they are trying to grasp.[110] The analogies invented are usually grounded in common-sense experiences of seeing a possible resemblance between the known and some unknown, from which human beings tease out from each analogy a number of concepts and categories that help them explain the unknown or less known. So a "root metaphor," far from being a merely clever turn of a word or phrase, is a fundamental way human beings try to discover and think about a problem, puzzle, or mystery. In short, a root metaphor is Pepper's name for analogical thinking on a grand, cosmological scale.

The choice of "covenant" as the root metaphor for the Hebrews' deep story across both Testaments is based on the simple recognition that no biblical author and no story narrator can "know" God; and, even if s/he could, s/he would still have to express what s/he knew in language, and no

---

106. Ibid., 41, 44.
107. Ibid., 45.
108. Ibid., 46–48.
109. Ibid., 49.
110. Pepper, *World Hypotheses*, 84–92. References are to the reprint.

language, no single word or phrase, can possibly describe God or His acts.[111] The best humans can do is to invent analogies or root metaphors for what is ultimately unknowable and inexpressible. That is why root metaphors are helpful to examine, reminding us of "the epistemological function of metaphor, the role it plays in the origination of knowing."[112] Root metaphors are a key part of our "thought process," both in the "invention of an idea" and that idea's elaboration.

The root metaphor of covenant can perhaps increase our understanding of God's *dispositio*, so that the *entire* Bible becomes His *entire* argument. God's *narratio* starts with cosmic generation and then the invention of the first covenant-argument with Adam. Other covenants follow, in a roughly chronological sequence: the covenant with Noah, with Abraham, with Moses, and many more after that. God seems to vary and revise, in small or significant ways, each previous covenant. The "history" of God's covenants continues to unfold through the narratives that follow Moses, through Israel's lineage of ruling priests, its kings, and the prophetic works, where the major and minor prophets speak *about* God's covenants, and *for* God as the inventor of such covenants.

Since covenants, by definition, can be violated and can only be violated by God's own invented human likenesses, rhetors themselves, like their inventor, Adam's Fall propels a narrative sequence of Falls throughout the Old Testament.[113] In both the Exodus narrative and narratives following God's invention and elaboration of the Decalogue and the Covenant Code that Moses receives, the Fall narrative shows up repeatedly, typically in the form of violating God's laws and contradicting His expectations. In this sense, the Fall narrative appears and reappears in different guises, becoming what Burke called a "repetitive" form across the many narratives, with each Fall narrative focused on a person or group who, for different reasons, will no longer remain persuaded by God's covenant-arguments.

Closely connected to these Fall narratives are other structural traits of the covenant-treaty. The biblical God frequently promises great blessings and rewards if His human likenesses are persuaded to follow His covenant terms. The major and minor prophets often repeat these blessings and rewards. Likewise, and conversely, God warns and threatens punishments and curses if His human likenesses fall out of their persuaded state and violate the covenant terms.

---

111. Lee, *Jesus and the Metaphors of God*, 14–16, 18–21.
112. Ibid., 14, 16.
113. Burke, *Rhetoric of Religion*, 176.

So it would then be possible to trace "qualitative progression," as Burke calls it, in the case God makes in the Bible, from the uplifting tone of promised rewards and blessings for keeping God's covenants, for staying convinced of and persuaded by them, to the fiery, angry, denunciations and curses that God Himself utters or that His prophets, speaking for God, foretell.

Burke's comments on the rhetoric of covenants further suggest that acts of punishment—"'payment' for wrong[s]" done[114]—are implicit in the violation of God's covenants. Likewise, implicit in God's punishment of covenant-violators is the idea of being able "to 'redeem' oneself, to cancel one's debt, to ransom or 'buy back'" the wrongs committed. Since God's human likenesses act as agents, as "persons," it is possible to infer "that in the idea of redemption there is implicit the idea of a personal redeemer." If one of God's human likenesses finds him/herself in a situation where God exacts payment for a covenant violation, that human likeness, as individual or as representative of humanity as a whole, may think of the personal redeemer as a means, "as an instrument, or agency," to achieve redemption. This instrumental redeemer may, then, "substitute" for the human likeness who violated the covenant, so s/he becomes a "sacrificial substitute" to redeem and pay God back for the covenant-violation. Burke's schematic for the narrative case God makes throughout the Old and New Testaments recognizes "the important role played by the sacrificial principle in the cycle of terms that cluster about the idea of a Covenant."[115]

Burke will abandon "covenant" for a more useful synonym, "order" and its opposite term, "disorder," to track the dialectical unfolding of the first three chapters of Genesis.[116] To describe the large narrative arc of the Bible, not just Genesis, requires Burke's discarded term.

God starts His rhetorical narrative by inventing the cosmic scene, including His own audience—human likenesses—followed by the invention of the first and subsequent covenant-arguments, which lead to violations, disobedience, and the Fall, punishment, and atonement and redemption through a sacrificial figure, Jesus Christ, the final covenant-argument God seems to offer to His human likenesses. Obviously, along the way, the violations of God's covenant-arguments may be more or less severe and offensive to God, and require more or less substantial payments to achieve redemption through various sacrificial offerings. The Bible, as it has been organized and received, however, emphasizes one grand payment and sacrificial substitute

---

114. Ibid.
115. Ibid., 178.
116. Ibid., 181–83.

for both Adam's "original sin" in violating God's first covenant and for all human likenesses' subsequent violations of all later, revised covenants. This, at least, is how many Christians appear to understand Jesus Christ as God's last covenant, His "last word."

According to the common and religiously articulated synopsis of God's narrative, God sacrifices His own son to pay for and atone for all human sins past and future. In rhetorical terms, God offers His son as the final argument which He surely knows and expects His human likenesses to reject. But the covenant He offers is conditioned, finally, by belief. If His human likenesses believe in what Jesus Christ argues, and further believe Jesus is God's own son, begotten without any sexual act save God's verbal fiat, then they will be rewarded with eternal life with God for their belief. Hence Jesus's death, his sacrifice, substitutes for God's punishing and destroying *all* of His human likenesses for failing to remain persuaded by His previous covenant-arguments.

This description of God's *dispositio* for the Bible, though, evades problems already addressed in the previous chapter—that is, *which* Jesus Christ represents God's final covenant-argument and whether readers are to understand Jesus as God's son, as God's own incarnated self, or God's *logos*. Beyond even that is the more salient question, the precise sense of what the resurrection means as an argument. Yet, for all those evasions, this overall structure, based on covenant-arguments, does seem to capture God's *dispositio* across both Testaments.

A Revealing End for God's Argument

One simple fact about the shape of God's argument *in* and *as* the Bible remains: while Jesus may be God's closing argument, his resurrection and all that it may claim or imply does not *literally* constitute the end of the Bible. The Bible ends with the Revelation to John, subtitled "The Apocalypse." Thus God has arranged His rhetoric so that an Absolute Beginning precedes an Absolute End. These antithetical, narrative poles are as evenly extreme as any story could be, or any argument a story or many stories might develop and support. Cosmic invention, the given, is God's prologue to cosmic destruction and cosmic resurrection.

It seems a strange understatement to say that John's Revelation is well-suited end for the scriptural narrative. Given the divine sanctions of the Bible's opening, it would seem to be *the only conceivable* kind of ending any reader could expect. So ordered, it is, in all its deceptive clarity and simplicity, the narrative paradigm for almost all story-telling structures, however complexly unfolded, revised, and elaborated. No secular story-teller escapes this quotidian order, however subtly or radically evaded. Narratives must, by definition, start and end. So, too, must arguments arranged as an encompassing narrative of various covenants.

Some would seem anxious to surround John's Revelation with the barbed-wire of caveats, warning readers that while this book's mysterious symbols are subject to many different readings, the truer significance of its mystical, poetic obscurity arises from being read within the contexts of the Book of Daniel and Ezekiel and other Old Testament prophecies. There is little question that John's Revelation belongs to and extends those Old Testament prophets, though one rhetorical critic argues that, like all poetry, and all visionary language, "it is futile and fatuous" to try to insist "the language of ecstasy" in this book can reasonably be translated into specific meanings or doctrines, however based, like all human language, on "sensory terms."[117]

It is by no means certain if an ending such as Revelation offers can ever be tamed or safely interpreted, or even whether its ecstatic language does not precisely invite readers to interpret it as they will. But it is certainly easier to see that, unlike Daniel's or Ezekiel's prophetic outbursts, John's Revelation is far more mediated and indirect in its divine source.

In the opening verse, the unknown author/narrator named "John" tells us that the Revelation he is about to offer comes from Jesus Christ. Jesus has been given the apocalyptic vision of the end-to-come from God, perhaps implying God and Jesus are *not* fused or *reunited* as one deity even after the resurrection. John, however, does not receive the vision from Jesus but through another angelic theophany (Rev 2:1). So, whoever John may have been, and whenever this Apocalypse may have been written, before Jerusalem's fall in 70 CE, or near the end of Emperor Domitian's reign (81–96 CE), and whether the author was writing in exile on the island of Patmos or somewhere else, the author/narrator bears "witness" to a prophecy thrice-removed from its ultimate source, God. Jesus seems to be the caretaker of the prophecy that God gave him, but Revelation's author/narrator hears it through an angelic messenger. Daniel, we are told, received his prophecy from a dream-theophany and, like King Solomon, his wisdom and interpretive acumen from God Himself (Dan 2:17). Ezekiel must eat a scroll God wrote so he can utter God's prophecies (Ezek 2:8). John's Apocalypse must have the double imprimatur of God and Jesus Christ, though neither speaks to John except through a theophany.

Jesus, as we have seen, was fully capable of apocalyptic rhetoric of his own. As a Jewish rabbi, he continued this rhetoric from the Old Testament

---

117. Barrett, "Language of Ecstasy and the Ecstasy of Language," 218.

prophets. Mark's Jesus believes apocalypse to be his central message, and Jesus's predictions of the end of days also appear in Matthew's (24. 1:3), Luke's (21:5-7), and John's Gospels (8:24)—predictions which not only supply Revelation with some of its poetic symbols but perhaps also explain why this work includes Jesus as one of its mediating sources.

Revelation has been called "a toxic book," wracked with the Christian church's fears of Rome's imperial power, other, competing versions of Christianity, not to mention the threat of those Jews still faithful to the Torah.[118] Its deliberate, obscure symbolism might not have been easily understood by outsiders, even by other Christian sects; and this fact may explain why some did not think it belonged in the New Testament with which most Christians are familiar. Revelation is still unacceptable to Greek Christian orthodoxy, "perhaps because of learned mistrust of over-literal interpretation" of its many symbols.[119] In fact, the very first mention of the twenty-seven books of the New Testament as an *official canon*, including Revelation, did not occur until Athanasius, the Bishop of Alexandria, mentions them in his annual letter to Egyptian churches in 367 CE.[120] When editors finally did place Revelation at the end of the Bible, it "transformed the historical story of the rise of Christianity into a future-oriented apocalypse" and replaced "Judaism and its most sacred symbols" with what one historian calls "a victorious, militant Christianity."[121]

Toxic and militant or no, once Revelation became the last book in the New Testament canon, the book came to enjoy, as Frank Kermode explains, "a vitality and resource that suggest its consonance with our more naïve requirements of fiction."[122] While Kermode's study is of "fictions of the End . . . ways in which, under varying existential pressure, we have imagined the ends of the world,"[123] certainly some Christian readers may object to Kermode's labeling Revelation a "fiction." Yet Kermode's purpose in starting his study with the Apocalypse is to remind students of literature that "[t]he Bible is a familiar model of history" and that the "Apocalypse is a radical instance of such fictions and a source for others." "Familiar" seems an unintentional understatement here, since the historical model the Bible "conjectures" may very be the most basic *dispositio* imaginable.

---

118. Armstrong, *Bible*, 76.
119. Kermode, *Sense of an Ending*, 7.
120. Ehrman, *Misquoting Jesus*, 36.
121. Armstrong, *Bible*, 76.
122. Kermode, *Sense of an Ending*, 7.
123. Ibid., 5–6.

The Bible starts with Genesis and concludes with Apocalypse, so the Bible, Kermode finally admits, is "[i]deally . . . a wholly concordant structure" because "the end is in harmony with the beginning, the middle with the beginning and the end."[124] Meanwhile, the end "is traditionally held to resume the whole structure" which the Apocalypse can only do "by figures predictive of that part of it which has not been historically revealed." To this Kermode adds the more significant point: that the Apocalypse of Revelation "can be disconfirmed [as has happened many times over] without being discredited," since this is part of its "extraordinary resilience."[125] The Bible's concluding Apocalypse can "absorb changing interests, rival apocalypses," adapting and surviving all the while and into our own time and beyond. This may be "why the image of the end can never be *permanently* falsified," and why human beings keep altering their interpretations of Revelation's symbols.[126] Changes in how to make sense of the Apocalypse can even be justified by Mark's Jesus, who warns his disciples: "But of that day or that hour no one knows, not even the angels in heaven, nor the Son, but only the Father. Take heed, watch; for you do not know when the time will come" (14:32–33). As an ominous as this deliberative argument sounds, it defies human reasoning to believe anyone can be careful and watchful for "signs" of an ending no one can possibly know or predict except God Himself, for what could anyone "watch" for?

Despite this problem, Kermode would remind us that the "apocalyptic thought" of Revelation "belongs to rectilinear rather than cyclical views of the world," though the difference between such views is hardly rigid.[127] What does remain rigid in Revelation is "the strict concordance between the [quite Platonic] beginning, middle, and the end."[128] That strictness belongs to God's rhetoric in the Bible, His ethos as supreme authority and the absolute beginning of cosmic and human history, of *history* as such. To the extent that the Bible's overall narrative shape represents to any degree God's shaping of it, He presents His human likenesses with the Story of all other stories, within the Bible and without. Yet, to the extent that God's devout, Jews and Christians alike, "were the first to experience the disconfirmation of literal predictions" of an end-time,[129] we return to the crucial but oddly illogical warning of Mark's Jesus: many will predict God's and Jesus's return and the

---

124. Ibid., 6–7.
125. Ibid., 8.
126. Ibid., 16.
127. Ibid., 5.
128. Ibid., 30.
129. Ibid., 9.

signs, great and terrible, of His coming; but none knows save God Himself precisely when the culminating concordance between His beginning and His final word will occur. This vertiginous closing of God's case may leave any reader of it now or in the future placed squarely in the middle, between the need for a belief in a concordant ending and an uncertainty about who or what may be trusted as the "sign" of that ending.

If the Bible is to be read and understood as *one* text, *one* work (and, despite the knowledgeable pleas of historical critics, many still read it that way), and if that one work presents God's Word (as many also believe), then any effort to describe the shape of God's rhetoric must acknowledge how He starts His argument and how He ends it. Obviously, the narrative that God adopts to frame the many other, shorter narratives (and the many other genres the Bible contains to amplify and develop God's major covenant-arguments) does not stop with the Old Testament. God Himself, to recall, falls silent in many books of the Old Testament as the prophets take center-stage, serving as His key witnesses on the importance of the covenant-arguments He invents and revises as He intervenes in the history of His human likenesses.

God's rhetoric in the Old Testament, of course, does *not* disappear or become simply displaced by the New Testament. As a Jewish rabbi, Jesus often mentions or quotes previous covenants, while the prophets' various rhetorics become co-extensive arguments anticipating God's final covenant-argument in the New Testament. But only rarely does God speak directly to audiences in the New Testament, and even the vision of Revelation does not come directly from Him or Jesus but through another theophany. That may be because God seems to have passed the rhetorical burdens to Jesus, the God-man, man-God, the one God, or the Son of God, God's *logos*, as story, as Word, as Reason to believe the story.

Kermode refers to the ancient physician Alkmeon, who, "with Aristotle's approval," believed "that men die because they cannot join the beginning and the end."[130] Sacred, if not all secular, books which strive not to "die" also seek to join beginnings and endings. The Bible, and its central rhetor, God, cannot be said to have made a very successful argument if He cannot join the beginning of His case with its end. Yet, as we have seen, all-too-human hands and minds helped to shape the case He makes in the Bible. Certainly, devout Christians can argue that God's divine hand guided each and every decision in this Bible's organization and arrangement. That argument, though, is no less applicable to the Hebrew Bible, except the Tanakh has a quite different arrangement for God's case and does not include the

---

130. Ibid. 4.

New Testament. So, if God, and not human beings, is ultimately responsible for the shape His case takes, we are left to wonder why He is not also responsible for the shape of His case in the Tanakh. If Jesus, or at least the Jesus of John's Gospel, is God's peroration, His closing covenant-argument, He ends His case with yet another beginning. Jesus's death entails his resurrection as God's final covenant-argument. The concluding Apocalypse of the New Testament may prophesy a gruesome, if ambiguous, end for God's human likenesses, just as Jesus does in the various Gospels. But even this last word is not, in fact, God's *last* word. God's apocalyptic ending comes to the author /narrator of Revelation at several removes from its divine source and remains, like earlier Hebrew prophecies and Jesus's prophecies of an end-time, an indirect, mediated image of God's last word.

The only appropriate ending that God, proclaimed inventor of any ending, offers His human likenesses is the next beginning to-come, the future that is always but never arriving. In the end, the New Testament's covenant-argument, represented in Jesus's *logos-as-mythos*, does not end as a story of homicide or suicide. Resurrection, however imagined, waits at the end of either ending—that future which recedes and rushes past human likenesses from the very moment they become aware enough to say, "soon, but not yet, not yet—the promised end." So they wait, and watch, interpreting and revising their efforts to read the signs of the ending no one knows, the images of its horror and its promise.

The biblical God's *dispositio* of what He invents, obviously, demands He use words, language, to persuade His human likenesses. Such a God would, then, like any human rhetor, presumably seek a style or manner of expressing His arguments to achieve His persuasive goal. The question, though, would and must be whether God's rhetorical style or styles can be analyzed and described as human rhetors' can be; and whether this God must concern Himself with how He sounds when He speaks, or what gestures He should make, or how He should remember what He wants to argue. Style, delivery, and memory have for human rhetors been the important final stages of preparing to make a case. But whether or how this is true for the God of the Bible is the central question examined in the next two chapters.

6

Style–How God Puts His Case

Biblical Style and God's Styles

For both Christian and Jewish traditions, Lynn Poland observes, the study of the Bible's style has long rested on the "distinction between divine and human speech."[1] This "distinction," as James Kugel explains, depends on the recognition that what seems obviously "rhetorical" or "poetic" to human interpreters at any given historical moment could be "attributed to the notion that the Divine Word was accommodated to human capacities, or to the fact that human beings were the vehicle for God's word."[2] Whatever seemed difficult, "awkward, unrhetorical, and even incomprehensible" or "lawless" about the Bible's style, Kugel adds, was wholly attributable to God Himself, since His wholly mysterious speech could break any or all of the rules and conventions of human language or its discursive forms. It is in such rule-breaking moments that Poland believes readers confront what she calls the Bible's "rhetorical sublimity."[3] Like Augustine, who early on noticed these stylistic ruptures as evidence of God's own speech and intent, Poland would call attention to those passages in the Bible where "[h]uman language is . . . discontinuous with divine rhetoric, even as, in its failure, it provides a place" for interpretive, often allegorical, work, Augustine's or any other reader's.[4]

1. Poland, "Bible and the Rhetorical Sublime," 36.
2. Kugel, *Idea of Biblical Poetry*, 205–206.
3. Poland, "Bible and the Rhetorical Sublime," 30.
4. Ibid., 37.

Such divinely intended discontinuity places a heavy burden on a chapter that seeks precisely to examine the style of this "divine rhetoric." Despite complaints that rhetorical critics have focused far too much attention "upon the stylistic devices and mechanics" of the Bible's style,[5] and despite the "contradictory procedures" of past biblical exegetes who labored "to identify the metres, tropes and figures of 'pagan' literature" in the Bible while at the same time arguing that the Bible's departures from these stylistic devices were the certain signs of God's own "special divine eloquence,"[6] it would be a serious mistake to ignore God's eloquent style and, as this chapter argues, an even more serious mistake to think that this style is always as discontinuous, obscure, and resistant to rhetorical description as some have supposed. God's manner of expression would likely affect those He sought to persuade, and how He hoped to affect them would depend on how He articulates His arguments when addressing His human likenesses. Clearly, though, this chapter may be begging the question of whether God has *a* style, or just *one* style, for His pleadings as well as whether His style(s) are so obscure and discontinuous that they cannot be analyzed and described much as the styles of human rhetors are.

These questions should not suggest this chapter focuses on the style or styles making up the *entire* Bible, or the many genres it represents. The primary focus here is to examine, if possible, the style or styles God adopts when He directly argues in the Bible; or, as some historical critics may insist, the style or styles that all-too-human translators and editors adopt for Him when He argues. Even within this narrower focus, I cannot address *all* that God says in the Bible, since He says quite a bit—especially in the Old Testament—before Jesus's rhetoric largely displaces His own. So this chapter must consider only a few examples of the styles of God's and, later, for comparison, Jesus's speeches. For convenience, some of these speeches will be the same as those analyzed in previous chapters on God's inventive strategies, but this time we will be concerned with these speeches' stylistic qualities.

Certainly, no one who seeks to analyze the Bible's style, or even parts of it, should pretend to be breaking new ground. Augustine was likely the first to attempt such an analysis in 396 CE, when he began *On Christian Doctrine* (*De doctrina Christiana*), finishing it over three decades later, in 427 CE, and just three years before his death.[7] Augustine hoped to provide

---

5. Clines, "Story and Poem," 25–26; see also Howard Jr., "Rhetorical Criticism in Old Testament Studies," 89–90.

6. Poland, "Bible and the Rhetorical Sublime," 37.

7. Robertson, "Introduction," ix.

those teaching the scriptures a method to interpret and explain the Bible's many difficult passages for largely illiterate congregations. Fully aware that the Bible's style was a challenge for the most learned of readers, Augustine tried to establish rules for interpreting the many obscure, figurative parts of the Scriptures. "[B]y following certain traces," he wrote, "he [the reader-expositor] may come to the hidden sense without any error, or at least . . . will not fall into the absurdity of wicked meanings."[8] In many instances, those "traces" lay in the Bible's densely figured style, which the exegete, in explaining, had to avoid adopting himself, lest he lose his audience.[9]

Augustine devotes most of Book IV of *On Christian Doctrine* to showing the Scriptures are as eloquent as the ancient rhetors he had read and studied in his pagan youth, before his conversion to Christianity. He wanted to demonstrate that the Bible contained abundant examples of the grand, middle, and plain styles that pagan rhetoricians had described and was especially intent to defend the figural obscurities of the scriptures, since these "poured forth" from God's own mind, and were not the result of "human industry."[10] Augustine realized any explanation of these divinely scripted passages demanded a great deal of linguistic and historical knowledge on the expositor's part—knowledge often "pagan" in origins, and knowledge he would not sacrifice or surrender to those claiming "revealed" knowledge of God's Word.

Since the Bible comes to us as written text, *not speech*, when God or Jesus verbally argue, they do what any human rhetor *must*—use words, phrases, sentences to try to achieve their persuasive goals. That means God's speech, like His written words, should, from a rhetorical perspective, adopt some type of style suited for His immediate purposes, the situations, and the audiences He addresses. Even so, this immediacy does not limit—and clearly *has not* limited—the appeal of God's style. It has had incalculable influence on the styles of poets, novelists, and orators over the centuries. So, however embedded in specific contexts His styles may be, God's eloquence, like the Bible's, continues to shape the styles of many authors hoping to share in that style's grandeur.

Despite this acknowledged grandeur, since James Muilenberg's call for more "rhetorical criticism" of the Bible, especially of the Old Testament, some have objected to those (including Muilenberg himself) who understood this call to mean rhetoric was nothing more than a collection

---

8. Augustine, *On Christian Doctrine*, trans. D. W. Robertson Jr., Pro. 9. Further references are to this translation.

9. Augustine, *On Christian Doctrine*, 4. viii–ix, 22–23.

10. Augustine, *On Christian Doctrine*, 4. vii. 21; Pro. 4.

of tropes, figures, and schemes to be analyzed as if divorced from their persuasive aim.[11] It is beyond the scope of this chapter to rehearse the various reactions to Muilenberg's proposal, but the primary objection raised here against too much attention to the Bible's style can, in fact, be found within the tradition of rhetoric itself. "Style" is no less a contested term in rhetorical study than is *dispositio* or *inventio*; so, before making any attempt to analyze God's and, later, Jesus's styles, it seems important to examine, if only briefly, style's contentious place among some of the most important rhetorical theorists who have addressed it.

Style and Rhetoric—A Troubled Couple

From its beginnings in ancient Greece and Rome, the art of rhetoric has typically placed style, delivery, and memory as the final parts or stages of preparing to persuade an audience—at least for *oral* rhetoric. For the ancient Greeks, style was called *lexis* or *phrasis*, words Latin theorists of rhetoric translated as *elocutio*. If we ask why style should be one of the "final" stages or parts of rhetoric, the implicit answer for ancient rhetoric seems reasonable enough: once a rhetor has invented, selected, and organized the best arguments, that rhetor must then decide how to articulate these arguments—what words, phrases, and so forth would work best for this or that audience in this or that circumstance. Nor was *lexis* or *elocutio* limited to words or phrases. Both terms encompassed *cola*, clauses of varying lengths and forms, in addition to such tropes as metaphor, metonymy, irony—those "incidental forms" that Burke included in his psychological treatment of *dispositio*.

The English synonym for *lexis* and *elocutio*—"style"—has almost no explicit connection to the Greek and Latin terms, being a name for a *literal* stylus attached to the end of pen or quill to vary the look of script on paper and, before paper, on waxen tablets or other malleable surfaces. Still, even in the script culture of ancient times, before a stylus was pressed into wax or parchment, rhetors had probably already expressed themselves to some extent, even *while* inventing arguments. Those arguments could have been written down, sketched out, or simply thought about long before a rhetor felt it necessary to worry about making the "style" as effective and persuasive as possible for a given audience. So even in the earliest stage—invention—a rhetor must have been looking for words and phrases for the arguments to be made.

11. For a summary of some of the challenges to Mulienberg's proposals, see Trible, *Rhetorical Criticism*, 48–51.

The "styling" phase, as it might be more accurately called, was more deliberate. A rhetor then sought the most effective, memorable verbal patterns to represent the arguments found and shaped. This phase would assume, of course, a draft of a speech already or soon to be delivered. True, some rhetors did argue extemporaneously, as they still do, without cue-cards or prompters or any written text. Some, too, were very fluent and eloquent, without any extensive preparation. Others, it seems, had to be more deliberate, had to work on their styles.

With style, though, a problem arises similar to the one with *dispositio*. The very idea of a "style" points in two different directions: toward a deliberate, purposeful stage in a rhetor's development of a speech or text; and, conversely, toward those traits or qualities of an already scripted artifact. Whether a rhetor's "art" *should* include style at all, or delivery for that matter, has been a point of contention for many centuries. One historian points out that rhetoric's very meaning as an "art" was soon stretched to encompass all facets of a physically present speaker.[12] The root of the word, *rhe*, refers to the act of saying, of using discourse, or *logos*. But this discourse was by no means an ordinary manner of speaking. Its artistry depended on deliberate, skillful orchestration *en toto*: on reasons, arguments, as well as language, voice, and gesture. *All* of these dimensions of oral speech can affect an audience, then as now. Artfully handled, they could make one rhetor's speech more believable and persuasive than another's; mishandled or neglected entirely, they could repel that same audience and ruin a rhetor's chance to achieve persuasion.

The problem, of course, is that rhetoric's art was, like poetry's and drama's, a visceral experience for an audience. Rhetors were often judged the best and most persuasive based not on *what* they argued, but on *how* they argued, their style, their "showmanship," as it might be described today.[13] This visceral appeal is one reason why rhetoric, from its inception, has been so controversial an art to study, practice, or teach. For centuries, the central issue has been whether it is really fair for a rhetor to take advantage of an audience's susceptibility to such visceral appeals of rhetoric as style or delivery if that meant sacrificing facts, reasons, and thus "truth." By the same token, the question might be altered in this way: Why should a rhetor have to make such a choice? Why could not facts, reasons, and truth be melded with a memorable, effective style for oral presentations? Why, in short, should a rhetor not exploit whatever means were available to persuade an audience?

---

12. Barilli, *Rhetoric*, trans. Menozzi, vii. Further references are to this translation.
13. Ibid.

Obviously, not all these "means" are available to the rhetoric of the written or printed page. Historians think that, over time, the emphasis on oral speech-making so important to ancient Greece and Rome weakened as writing becomes more important, so important some scholars insist on the distinction between what is called "primary" rhetoric—the art of *oral* persuasion in civic and legal settings—and "secondary" rhetoric—the persuasive art adapted for the written medium, a process known as *letteraturizzazione*.[14] Once this process begins, rhetoric as a distinctly situated, historically specific oral/aural art blends into and becomes transformed into the written artistry of essays, books, treatises—what the eighteenth century eventually called *belles lettres*.

It is not entirely surprising that once the dominant rhetorical medium becomes script and, later, print, style eventually overshadows, if it does not quite completely displace, the entire art of rhetoric. Since the fifteenth century, the emphasis on print certainly would have hastened this transformation. Whatever may have happened, one part of rhetoric's art—style—came to define the whole; so much so that one critic believes, once oral arguments take more permanent, written form, stylistic power, not coherence, or even content, is what accounts for that speech's continuing fame and importance beyond the immediate circumstances that prompted the speaking.[15]

The preoccupation with trivial stylistic analyses of the Bible certainly finds its analogue in the dissatisfactions of some theorists of rhetoric with the art itself. Once rhetoric became just a collection of stylistic devices pored over in European classrooms, Chaim Perelman complains, it lost its intellectual integrity as a verbal art, so its study became reduced to the superficial conventions of figurative language, of "ornamentation."[16] The more "literary" rhetoric became, the more it was identified with empty, florid verbiage that students were forced to study in the schools and universities in the early decades of the last century. Yet, almost thirty years after rhetoric had become almost *nothing but style*,[17] another scholar begins an article, conspicuously entitled "Revitalizing Style," by lamenting that teachers no longer seem interested in helping students how to write with *any style at all*.[18]

14. Kennedy, *Classical Rhetoric and Its Christian and Secular Tradition from Ancient to Modern Times*, 4–5.

15. See Black, *Rhetorical Criticism*, 174–75. This transcendent feature of argument, Black adds, makes a rhetor's concerns about style akin to the poet's. References are to the reprint.

16. Perelman, "New Rhetoric," 1384–85.

17. Ibid., 1385.

18. Rankin, "Revitalizing Style," 8.

It is beyond the scope of this chapter—and this book—to account for all that has happened to rhetoric and style within its lengthy time span. Over a generation of thinking and teaching separates the two very different complaints mentioned above. Certainly, since the emergence of "written" rhetoric and the invention of printing, style, far more than delivery or memory, became a synonym for "rhetoric," blurring further the already less than distinct line separating rhetoric from literature. Some theorists of rhetoric surely deserve credit for forcing those who came after them to broaden and even to recover rhetoric's larger "art." Others deserve equal credit for reminding teachers that, in the heady atmosphere of reforming and revising writing pedagogies during the 60s and 70s, style appears to have gotten lost.[19]

Much of the earliest thinking about rhetoric, certainly, took the issue of style very seriously and seldom lost sight of its importance. Gorgias, the ancient Sicilian sophist and former student of the shaman-philosopher-poet Empedocles, believed a rhetor's style was essential to successful persuasion. Gorgias recognized early on the power language has to console or arouse an audience, to make listeners feel pleasure or pain.[20] For Gorgias, a rhetor's style can—and *should*—deeply move listeners, its effects being likened to the power of drugs on the body.[21] Plato will later mock Gorgias's views in the dialogue that bears the sophist's name;[22] but Gorgias, like Empedocles, believed a rhetor had to enchant an audience. To do that required a style perhaps more closely modeled on lyrical or religious poetry than, say, legal or political speeches.[23] Known himself for his own flamboyant, poetic style, Gorgias celebrated the rhetor whose style could charm the divided soul by turning one truth, or argument, against another rather than simply enshrining an absolute, transcendent truth as Plato usually preferred.[24] Gorgias's putative student, Isocrates, credited with making rhetoric the cornerstone of a liberal arts education in ancient Greece and, later, Rome,[25] did not overlook the importance of style either, praising that rhetor in "Against the Sophists" (composed around 390 BCE) who could argue a point others had

19. Ibid., 8–9.
20. Gorgias, *Encomium of Helen*, 45.
21. Ibid.
22. Plato, *Gorgias*, 447a–465e.
23. Bloom, *Wallace Stevens*, 390. De Romilly makes a similar argument in *Magic and Rhetoric in Ancient Greece*, v.
24. Bloom, *Wallace Stevens*, 390.
25. Kennedy, *Classical Rhetoric and Its Christian and Secular Tradition from Ancient to Modern Times*, 31.

failed to make while clothing his argument in a melodic style suited to the opportune moment (known as *kairos*) and the audience addressed.²⁶

Aristotle, like his teacher, was not so enchanted by the allurements of style as Gorgias or Isocrates, only begrudgingly including it in the third book of his *Rhetoric*. Aristotle apparently feared some audiences would be more impressed with stylistic performance than with what a rhetor actually tried to persuade an audience to believe,²⁷ so he concentrates on what kinds of words to use and the persuasive value of metaphors. Clearly, though, granting these exceptions, Aristotle strongly objected to rhetors' adopting the poetically enhanced style for which Gorgias's arguments were famous.²⁸

Not perhaps until Cicero does another classical thinker appear so enamored with style's importance as Gorgias. In his mature work, *De Oratore*, Cicero, speaking through Crassus, seems eager to admit that "the poet is a very near kinsman of the orator."²⁹ Cicero's ideal orator must have "the subtlety of the logician, the thoughts of a philosopher, a diction almost poetic, a lawyer's memory, a tragedian's voice, and the bearing almost of the consummate actor." These expectations do not, of course, depend entirely upon a rhetor's style; but they remain as ideals for Cicero's great admirer, Quintilian, who later insists, as had Cicero, that rhetors must know what sort of style to use for the purpose at hand, be it instruction, amusement, or persuading.³⁰

Certainly, the most complete and detailed ancient work on style, and on delivery and memory, is the *Rhetorica ad Herennium*. Written around 84 BCE, and long believed to be Cicero's work, the *ad Herennium* is the most ancient, *complete* treatment of rhetoric that has survived from antiquity. According to its translator, the anonymous *ad Herennium* provides the most ancient treatment of style written in Latin and represents the first effort to divide rhetorical styles into three types—grand, middle, and plain.³¹ Rhetors were to adopt the grand style, often rich in passionate, figurative language, when persuading, but use the plain style when informing or instructing an audience, and the middle style when they wish to amuse and delight an audience, a taxonomy Cicero and, later, Augustine, repeats.³² The *ad Heren-*

26. Isocrates, "Against the Sophists," trans. Nolin, par. 16–17.
27. Aristotle, *Rhetoric* 3.i.5–6.
28. Aristotle, *Rhetoric* 3.i.8–9.
29. Cicero, *De Oratore*, vol. 3, 1.xvi.70, xxviii.128–129. Here, we find another classical source anticipating Black's own high estimate of a rhetor's style as a transcendent quality.
30. Quintilian, *Institutio Oratoria*, vol. 4, 12.x.69–72.
31. Caplan, "Introduction," vii, xx.
32. Cicero, *De Optimo Genere Oratorum*, trans. Hubbell, vol. 2, 1.3; Augustine, *On*

nium includes as well the oldest cataloguing of different types of figurative language a rhetor may use to color or embellish his arguments.³³ In book four, the *ad Herennium* lists thirty five figures of diction—unusual forms or uses of words—and ten tropes, ways to turn words or phrases from a direct or literal to more indirect meanings—and nineteen figures of thought, usually considered to be more verbally expansive than tropes in making meaning more indirect. Many of these tropes and figures are further sub-divided. Metonymy, a way to re-name an object by substituting another word associated with it, takes nine different forms.³⁴

Quintilian, like other classical thinkers, often fretted over the distinctions between tropes as simple wordplay or more complex, figurative turns in thought and meaning such as irony.³⁵ And, over time, the number of tropes and figurative devices multiplied, as did the number of exotic names for some of the same devices. In the case of tropes, the *ad Herrennium*'s ten increases to a dozen in Quintilian's *Institutio Oratoria*. During the Middle Ages, the Venerable Bede increases the total to forty one.³⁶ Later, though, in his eighteenth century work, *The New Science*, Giambattista Vico reverses this proliferating trend and reduces *all* tropes and figures to the four, most important ones—metaphor, metonymy, synecdoche, and irony³⁷—a reduction that parallels in name and number, if not function, Kenneth Burke's later analysis of what he calls the "four master tropes."³⁸

Not only have the number and names of stylistic devices varied over time, so have the types and qualities of style human rhetors strive for. Unlike

---

Christian Doctrine, 4. xii. 27.

33. Caplan, "Introduction," xx.

34. Cicero, *Rhetorica ad Herennium*, trans. Caplan, 4. vol. 43. xxxii. Further references are to this translation.

35. Arrington, "Content(ious) Forms," 151–54.

36. Ibid., 151. See also Curtius's detailed and valuable study, *European Literature and the Latin Middle Ages*, in which Curtius argues that Bede, like many others before him, including Augustine, believed the Bible embodied all the various types of figurative language identified by pagan rhetoric and that understanding the Bible depended on a knowledge of the pagan rhetorical figures, 47–48. References to Curtius are to the reprint.

37. See Vico, *New Science*, 87–91.

38. Burke, *Grammar of Motives*, 503–517. In this appended essay, Burke argues that his four master tropes—metaphor, metonymy, synecdoche, and irony—are not simply turns of a word's or phrase's meaning but are crucial in the inventing and representing of an author's ideas and content. Vico's, Burke's, and others' re-thinking on tropes has been the focus of several scholarly studies: Kellner, "Inflatable Trope as Narrative Theory," 14–28; Martin, "Floating an Issue of Tropes," 75–83; Quinn, "The Four Master Tropes as Informing Principles," 242–52; D'Angelo, "Prolegomena to a Rhetoric of Tropes," 32–40.

Gorgias, who urged rhetors to embellish arguments with poetic devices, the more practical Aristotle insisted a rhetor only needed a clear, appropriate prose style suitable for the subject argued, the situation, and the intended audience. Rhetors, he advised, should depend on the accepted vocabulary of the time, even though they could also exploit the advantages of vivid metaphors and analogies to infuse their arguments with life and energy—especially metaphors whose imagery can adorn or disparage whatever a rhetor refers to.[39] Cicero, too, insisted a rhetor's style be clear, appropriate, grammatically correct; but, like Aristotle, he urges rhetors to enliven their arguments with vivid figures of speech.[40]

These broad generalizations about style certainly do not attend to the many nuances and complexities of the subject both Aristotle and Cicero address at far greater length. Still, what seems to emerge among classical thinkers is perhaps an even more sweeping theme—that style follows function: a rhetor's chosen words, sentence patterns, and figures of speech all seem governed by that rhetor's purposes, be it instruction, entertainment, or persuasion, as well as the type of rhetoric being used (legal, say, or political), the issue argued, and the audience to be persuaded. These constraints, it so happens, are largely the same ones that confounded a rhetor trying to arrange invented arguments.

While some have treated rhetoric as *nothing but style* since Shakespeare's time, this trend certainly did not stop debate on the subject. In 1690, John Locke will insist that writers abandon the easy, seductive pleasures of rhetorical ornamentation, and write in a clear, forceful style suited to "real knowledge" and "information,"[41] while Cicero's countryman, Vico, later tries to refute Locke in his 1709 address at the University of Naples, arguing that students needed to learn how to be eloquent speakers and imaginative thinkers. "What is eloquence, in effect," Vico asks, "but wisdom ornately and copiously delivered in words appropriate to the common opinion of mankind?"[42] Certainly, for Vico, a rhetor's "wisdom," the invented ideas and arguments, would be largely worthless if they lacked an ornate, eloquent style for their articulation.

Much later, in 1941, Kenneth Burke reinvigorates this classical wisdom about style, from Aristotle forward, claiming that both "[c]ritical and

---

39. Aristotle, *Rhetoric* 3.i–iii.2–14. Aristotle's sage advice to rhetors is to draw images for their metaphors from either objects or events that are "better" if praise is intended or "from the worse" if blame and criticism is the goal, *Rhetoric* 3.ii.10.

40. For the most concise statement of Cicero's ideal rhetorical style, see *De Optimo Genere Oratorum*, trans. Hubbell, vol. 2. Further references are to this translation.

41. Locke, *Essay Concerning Human Understanding*, 452.

42. Vico, *Study Methods of Our Time*, 877.

imaginative works are answers to questions posed by the situation in which they arose," but "not merely answers": they are "*strategic* answers, *stylized* answers" which try to "size up" and "encompass" real situations.[43] A few years later, Burke proposes that these stylized answers are important to the rhetorical principle of identification. "You persuade a man," he explains, "only insofar as you can talk his language by speech, gesture, tonality, order, image, attitude, idea, by identifying your ways with his."[44]

Burke's "identification" is not simply or only about adopting a style to flatter an audience but a way to bridge the distance between two separate individuals, to make them, in Burke's view, "consubstantial" enough for identification and persuasion to take place.[45] Such a style, then, becomes a case of trying to get two separate individuals to go beyond their obvious differences—social, political, even ontological, in the case of styles for prayers and invocations addressed to supernatural beings—so that they may discover what interests they share and so that they may identify with each other and act together in common cause.

Since Burke, some have tried to classify at least three different theories of style.[46] The first theory (and apparently the most useful for teaching) comes from many of the classical theorists already mentioned, all of whom appear to assume that verbal form can be separated from content and variously re-shaped to affect different audiences in different ways. The second assumes style depends on and naturally extends a writer's "personality," while a third rejects rhetoric's separation of form from content because both are organically connected. This classification scheme, however, has been largely superseded by those who have come to believe a rhetor's style depends on many other, and very different, constraints—genre, gender, ethnicity, social class, and sexual orientation.[47]

So, except for a moderately firm consensus about figurative language reached among classical thinkers, style remains, much like arrangement and invention, a complex and continuing issue even now. Certainly, not all classical thinkers agreed on every point about style, just as they did not always agree about how many styles a rhetor could adopt, or what the most important constraint on a rhetor's chosen style was. A great deal of debate, in fact, took place over what kind of style a rhetor *should* adopt. Not all theorists

43. Burke, *Philosophy of Literary Form*, 1.
44. Burke, *Rhetoric of Motives*, 55.
45. Ibid., 20–21.
46. See Milac, "Theories of Style and Their Implications for the Teaching of Composition," 66-69, 126.
47. See the various arguments for style's connections to some of these different constraints in Butler, ed. *Style in Rhetoric and Composition*, 279–336.

endorsed the complex, ornate style of a Cicero. Some argued, like Locke, for a more modest, plain style, especially as the sciences became more important. But the standards for what makes a rhetor's style more "clear" or appropriate, or what exemplars should serve as a standard for an acceptable or normative style, varied, as they will, over the centuries. These variations, and the debates that follow them, are likely to continue. Judging from one recent book, some now seem to be returning to and trying to rehabilitate interest in classical rhetoric's many stylistic devices and patterns.[48] Many of those devices will be described below, in the "divine rhetoric" that Poland has referred to, devices that may be at least as responsible for God's sublime style as those parts of it that are obscure and disruptive.

Accursed Style in the Garden of Eden

Complaints and arguments about the Bible's style often refer to Erich Auerbach's famous comparison between the luxuriant stylistic detail of Homer's *The Odyssey* and the sparse, largely implicit style of the story of Abraham's near sacrifice of his son, Isaac.[49] From this comparison Auerbach concludes that "[t]he Scripture stories do not, like Homer's, court our favor, they do not flatter us that they may please and enchant us—they seek to subject us, and if we refuse to be subjected we [as readers] are rebels."[50] Because the biblical stories carry within them "doctrine and promise," they are "fraught with background" and often "mysterious, containing a second, concealed meaning."[51] Further, Auerbach adds, the Bible's difficult style reinforces its "tyrannical" "claim to truth" insofar as it "excludes" any other truth in the name of the biblical author's (and narrators') belief in the God responsible for and shaping all human history.[52]

Auerbach, it would appear, has little patience for Meir Sternberg's "ideological persuader[s]" who narrate the Bible's various stories.[53] Yet, perhaps apart from the ideologically driven narrators, God's own direct rhetorical

---

48. As one example of this interest, see Farnsworth, *Farnsworth's Classical English Rhetoric*. Farnsworth restricts himself to a handful of rhetorical devices found in classical sources but provides plentiful examples and explanations of those he does include. See also Quinn's *Figures of Speech*; and Anderson's *Glossary of Greek Rhetorical Terms*.

49. Auerbach, *Mimesis*, trans. Trask, 1–11. References are to the reprinted translation.

50. Ibid., 12.

51. Ibid, 10.

52. Ibid., 12.

53. Sternberg, "Bible's Art of Persuasion," 235.

style cannot be so easily faulted simply because Auerbach thinks the God of the Bible "leaves his motives and purpose unexpressed."[54]

God conceals very little about his motives and purposes in His first long speech in the Old Testament, the *aras*, or cursings, of the serpent, Eve, and Adam. This speech shows God's ready use of a grand style fully suited for the divine judgments that He so memorably and clearly delivers (Gen 4:14–19). God's curses, recall, take poetic form and follow a very brief cross-examination of Adam and Eve about what has happened in the Garden, though God certainly knows (Gen 3:8–13). In pronouncing judgment, God starts with the serpent—the apparent source of Adam and Eve's temptation—and then addresses Eve, the second tempter, and finally Adam, His first invented human likeness.

Yet, despite its verse form, God's style for each audience is unmistakably direct and fairly uniform, addressing each auditor as "you," starting with the inexplicably persuasive serpent: "Because you have done this, / cursed are you above all cattle, / and above all wild animals; / upon your belly you shall go / and dust you shall eat / all the days of your life" (Gen 3:8–14). God immediately identifies the most remarkable of His invented creatures as the "cause" of His humans' failures to remain persuaded. Even a cursory reading of this first curse will show that God repeats certain words and phrases, just as He sometimes deviates from the sentence structure of most English sentences, and depends on fairly simple, plain diction.

These initial reactions are, of course, not surprising. God's curses are *stylized* for the situation and His auditors, calling attention to His utterances through stylistic devices well-known to the study of human rhetoric. Here, it is not enough to observe God's eloquent repetition, an often noted feature of Hebrew poetry, since patterns of repetition, like deviations from normal syntactic order, will and must vary. Further, despite the plain diction, God's words often vibrate with figurative implications, though these implications are hardly obscure or divorced from the persuasive aim of the *aras*.

God's stylized curse of the serpent starts with *anastrophe*, reversing "you are cursed" to "cursed are you," followed by the stylized repetition of *conduplicatio*, mentioning "above all" twice, but not consecutively. Like *epizeuxis* (consecutive repetition), *conduplicatio* repeats to emphasize and link phrases and statements conjoined by God's most conspicuously repeated coordinator, "and," suggesting God's reliance on *polysyndeton* to pile the curses and consequences upon the serpent. The sentence structure of the next two parts of this curse parallel the first as *isocolons*, while God's main predicates—"upon your belly you shall go" and "dust you shall eat"—repeat

---

54. Auerbach, *Mimesis*, 8.

the initial *anastrophic* inversions. *Conduplicatio*'s repetition of "you shall" and "above all" continues in these inversions. Infused within both is God's damning verbal irony, placing the cursed serpent "above" all other animals for its offense—an elevation that results in utter degradation, condemning the serpent to move "below" all these same animals, including human beings, crawling on its belly. For the serpent, these antithetical prepositions underline God's declared, ironic outcomes for the serpent.

God's diction remains simple—at least in this part of the curses—but figurative implications reinforce the rhetoric of God's judgment. The "dust" churned up by human feet metaphorically becomes the degraded serpent's food, as well as a reminder of the base matter out of which all life, including human life, has been invented. This initial metaphor will twist again into a *metalepsis*, reversing the temporal and causal order, since "dust" is God's primal substance for inventing life as well as life's final quintessence. The end lives in its origin, the effect, in the cause.

God, though, curses the serpent twice more: "I will put enmity between you and the woman, / and between your seed and her seed; / he shall bruise your head, / and you shall bruise his heel" (Gen 3:15). These additional curses follow familiar syntactic order and are framed as *isocolons,* one parallel to the other. But God's damning emphasis continues through more *conduplacatio*, of "between," "shall," "you," and "your" at different points while indirectly referring to His human likenesses in third person nouns and pronouns, as "the woman," "her," "he," and "his." Again, these emphatic repetitions are infused with God's dark irony. The results of the "enmity" that God invents rebound in the human couple's future children and the serpent's struggle to survive being crushed underfoot. God's *litote*, "bruise," quietly understates His eternal decree that the now crawling serpent will be stomped, stepped on, and crushed even as humans will often feel its bite. These reciprocal punishments are implied through synecdoches, the serpent's "head" and the human's "heel," for whole bodies now assured of the unending "enmity" between humanity's and the serpent's struggles to survive each other. God's repeated "he," like the repeated "seed," are added synecdoches to represent all future human generations affected by this curse.

God's punishment of Eve is no less infused with irony: "I will greatly multiply your pain in / childbearing; / in pain you shall bring forth / children, / yet your desire shall be for your / husband, / and he shall rule over you'" (Gen 3:16). Eve suffers two consequences in God's curse, each phrased much like the consequences the serpent must suffer. But, when God repeats the first one, He returns to *anastrophic* inversion ("in pain you shall bring forth . . .") just as He had earlier in the serpent's curse, and continues the emphasis through *conduplicatio* ("pain," "you," "your," "shall").

Unlike His preferred connector, "and," God's "yet" signals not just another result of painful childbearing, but a contrasting—and more ironic—cause: Eve's "desire" for her male companion. As the first and only female so far invented, Eve serves as God's synecdoche for all females who must suffer even more pain in childbirth than, presumably, they would have if Eve had not surrendered to the serpent's rhetoric. A more deeply humiliating irony of the intensified birthing pain is that all future females will "desire" their "husband[s]" who "shall rule" them. Women, like the serpent, are cursed to sink in status and power, with Eve's generations further cursed to yearn for the male oppressors who impregnate them.

Lastly, God curses Adam in a similar style as the one He adopted for the previous two audiences:

> Because you have listened to the voice of your wife,
>   and have eaten of the tree
> of which I commanded you,
>   "You shall not eat of it,"
> cursed is the ground because of you;
>   in toil you shall eat of it all the days of your life;
> thorns and thistles it shall bring / forth to you;
>   and you shall eat the plants of the field.
> In the sweat of your face,
>   you shall eat bread
> till you return to the ground
>   for out of it you were taken;
> you are dust,
>   and to dust you shall return. (Gen 3:17–19)

God's cursing of Adam starts with the same word used for the serpent's curse, "because." This repeated pattern, coupled with God's "you shall," followed by different verbs in Eve's curse, completes the anaphoric structure of the entire *aras*.

Yet God's curse of Adam is the longest of the three, although why the extra expansion may be almost impossible to say with any certainty. Perhaps it is because Adam was invented first and had existed longer with God than Eve, even though he presumably had not been alive as long as the serpent. Perhaps it is because Adam deserves more of the blame, since God offers *two* reasons why Adam is the "cause" of what he must suffer, compared to *one* for the serpent and, oddly, *none* for Eve. Both causes are phrased in *isocolons*, parallel verb clauses starting with "because," just as God adopted when He cursed the serpent. Adam had apparently *obeyed* his wife, not *ruled* over her. Second, he did exactly what God told him not to do—eat the fruit from the forbidden tree. God even quotes—actually *misquotes*—Himself in the *oraculum* of what He commanded Adam *not* to do (Gen 2:15).

In each predictive *isocolon*, God embeds repeated *anastrophic* inversion just as He had done when cursing the serpent: "cursed is the ground because of you; / in toil you shall eat of it all the / days of your life . . ." (Gen 3:17). In each *isocolon*, God names the effect *before* the cause, repeating "Because you" at the start of this curse, only to vary it slightly as "because of you," when He describes Adam's punishment. God even repeats verbatim an entire phrase from the serpent-curse, "all the days of your life," an *epimone* which predicts an inescapable future for both humankind and serpents, since those futures turn upon another of God's seemingly simple yet ironic tropes, "ground." In fact, of the three curses, Adam's seems the most eloquent and emphatic, again combining *anastrophes* with *conduplacatio*, through "Cursed," "ground," "you / your," "shall," "eat," "return," and "dust"—both devices driving home Adam's fate through the musical refrains of the curse.

God's irony wraps around more synecdoches; for, like Eve, Adam stands for all male generations who must now work and till the "ground" to raise food and stay alive. This is the very same ground or "dust" the serpent is cursed to crawl on and swallow, the very same substance from which both the serpent and God's first human likeness were made. The agricultural labor suggests any and all grueling work human males must do. God's word for this endless drudgery—"toil"—is another *litote*, as understated as the verb "bruise" in the serpent's curse. The often unproductive results and strain of this "toil" God represents with "thorns and thistles" and "sweat" on human faces, metonyms for all that is associated with hard labor to make "Bread," another synecdoche for any and all sustenance humans produce from the "ground" and the "plants in the field."

Similar to the serpent, Adam must work slavishly "till [he] returns to the ground'" out of which God invented him. "Ground" and "dust" are perhaps God's most complex tropes in these *aras*. As metonyms for each other, they both recall God's earlier *metalepsis*, His reversal of the literal meanings of *dust* and *ground* as mere terrestrial matter so they become words whose meanings now point toward future decay and death. Thus God's ironic *metalepsis* may be perhaps His darkest trope—organic life's material origins now become their repository after death. God ends His curse on Adam's descendants in some of His most famous lines, often repeated in priests' and pastors' eulogies for the dead. This fame comes from its being phrased as a *chiasmus* whose flipped word order reinforces the time reversal of *metalepsis*. The dust and ground of the past are now an inescapable future.

God's first long speech, then, is a highly stylized, rhetorical performance, uttered in an elevated, grand style suited to the dramatic significance of His judgments of both human and non-human fates. Within a single speech, God is shown to pronounce devastating fates to His audiences. Drawing upon syntactic variation carefully blended with emphatic repetitions, God unfolds the ironic, *metaleptic* outcomes of His likenesses failure to remain persuaded by previous covenant-arguments—outcomes described in synecdoches that expand the effects of the specific offenders' errors for generations to come. This speech is no mere catalogue of human transgressions, as many American Christians may have been taught in Sunday school or church. Nor is it some fatuous "historical" chronicle to explain why snakes have no legs, why women suffer in childbirth or lack the status of males, or why human beings—especially men—must work to live. It is, rather, an eloquent condemnation of God's no longer persuaded creatures, rich with echoes and, though plain in its diction, thickened with ominously vivid tropes.

God's Didactic Style for Noah

God's second lengthy speech addresses Noah just before He floods the corrupted world, this time speaking in prose to proclaim what He is about to do and to instruct Noah on how to prepare for the catastrophe. This speech seems to be the first appearance of God's more didactic style, one adopted in even longer speeches when He directs Moses on the ordinances of His laws (Exod 21—23) and explains to Moses how to construct and use His sanctuary (Exod 25—31). Instruction, or *docere*, was for Cicero,[55] Augustine,[56] and many later thinkers, one of the three "duties" or "offices" of rhetoric, often the duty of a classical rhetor's exordium which, when necessary, lays out the factual conjectures in a law court. For Augustine in particular it was the most important "duty" or "office" for those who tried to teach scripture for their congregations, central to explaining the Bible's many obscure, complex figurations. For Cicero and Augustine, rhetorical instruction depends on a clear, plain, style, not the lofty, more impassioned style of God's *aras*.

Yet God's instructions for Noah do not begin plainly at all. They start with God's proclaimed intent to commit His first violent act, an intent He shares with Noah. There, the lofty, grand style adopted before, in the *aras*, reappears: "I have determined to make an end of all flesh; for the earth is filled with violence through them; behold, I will destroy them with the

---

55. Cicero, *Optimo Genere Oratorum*, vol. 2, 1. 3–4.
56. Augustine, *On Christian Doctrine*, 4. xii.27–28.

earth" (Gen 6:13). This darkly ironic utterance, both verbal and dramatic, describes God's intent to use the earth itself to destroy its own fleshly violence, just as He had used dust to make fleshly bodies subject to time's decay and eventual return to their earthly source. With His favorite, dramatic imperative, God commands Noah to "[b]ehold" His plan—a plan made all the more emphatic by the *anaphoric* repetition of "I," and by repeated, *isocolonic* phrases, "with violence" and "with the earth." God adds even more force to His intent through *disjuntio* or *palilogia*, repeating in slightly different words the same meanings, "to end," and "destroy."

Only after stating this intent does God command Noah to build an ark, directing him to cover the ark with pitch and specifying the ark's size (Gen 6:14–16), but withholding the reason for the ark and who or what will be on it. God does not justify Himself until after He proclaims His destructive intent for a second time. Even here, uttered in the same lofty style with which He began His speech, the second proclamation does not fully match the first; for it adds *how* God will destroy the fleshly parts of earth *with* the earth: "For behold, I will bring a flood of waters upon the earth, to destroy all flesh in which is the breath of life from under heaven; everything on the earth shall die" (Gen 6:17). The imperial, and now *anaphoric*, "Behold," would draw Noah's attention to "flesh," another of God's plain but resonant synecdoches for almost all the organic life about to be destroyed. God wants to make certain that Noah understands that the "breath of life" given to all fleshly creatures lies "under heaven," so, as its inventor, it apparently remains His to "destroy."

God's style shifts once He begins to teach Noah how to make the ark and replenish the earth, instructions driven by such imperative verbs as "make." Throughout the instruction, God addresses Noah directly, just as He had done with Adam and Eve and the serpent—at least until He tells Noah who will be saved and what animals are to be brought on the ark. This is the initial part of God's covenant-argument adapted specifically for Noah so that he knows who and what will survive as remnants of God's original inventions. Yet even these simple directions are eloquently phrased to combine *anaphora* with *epistrophe*, to form a *symploce*, each command beginning and ending with the same words or phrases, until the pattern is broken at the very end of the order (the prose divided and re-lined below shows this pattern's eloquent repetitions):

of every living thing . . .
Of the birds
according to their kinds,
and
of the animals

according to their kinds,
of every creeping thing of the ground,
according to its kind,
two of every sort shall come in to you,
to keep them alive. (Gen 6:19-20)

God twice states His reason for bringing the animals onto the ark—"to keep them alive"—before He returns to a more plain style of command, directing Noah to stock up on all edible foods for his family and the animals. Yet God offers a slightly different set of instructions in the very next speech. This time, Noah's to bring "seven pairs," one male and one female, from both "clean" and "unclean" animals—a distinction God does not fully explain until Moses leads the Hebrews to Mount Sinai and elaborates on this difference in the eleventh chapter of Leviticus. Nor is it until God's second speech that Noah finds out he will only have a week to prepare before God "send[s] rain upon the earth *for forty days and forty nights*" (Gen 7:1-4, emphasis added), an alliterative pair of *isocolonic*, antithetical phrases that have made this an almost unforgettable prediction even for non-readers of the Bible.

God's Style in Calling Abraham

Just as any human rhetor tends to do, God adopts a style for those selected to hear His covenant-arguments. In the case of Abraham, God simply appears and begins with another imperial command, ordering Abraham to "[g]o from [his] country and [his] kindred and [his] father's house to the land that [He] will show [him]" (Gen 12:1). Even here, the force of God's command emerges in the repetition of His favorite connector, "and," that joins one demand to another demand, piling on directives, the effect often sought through *polysendeton*. Then, to mark His eloquent closing, God switches to *isocolon*ic nouns, of "country," "kindred," and "father's house," framing these words and phrases between two opposed prepositional phrases, "from" and "to the land that [God] will show . . ." Finally, God adds His crucial covenant-promise: "And I will make of you [Abram] a great nation, and I will bless you, and make your name great so that you will be a blessing. I will bless those who bless you; and him who curses you I will curse; and by you all the families of the earth shall bless themselves" (Gen 12:2-3).

God's covenant-promise directly addresses His auditor as "you," just as He has done before, drawing upon *conduplacatio* and *polysendeton* to make the promise forceful, clear, and cohesive. This covenant-argument further highlights a crucial but consequential antithesis between those God will "bless" and those He will "curse," before turning to the *anastrophe* that differentiates who and who will *not* feel His curses and blessings on Abram's behalf. The key part of this promise is that God "will make" one man, Abram, into "a great nation" and into a "blessing," with Abram as God's own instrument, His own agency, a way "all the families of the earth shall bless themselves." As with Adam and Eve earlier, Abram is as much person as synecdoche, representing an entire, future nation—presumably God's own future as this nation's central deity. God's selection of Abram allows other human likenesses to "bless themselves" so long as the Hebrews and others who consider themselves part of that blessing do not "curse" him. That would be the same as cursing what God has made of Abram, one man standing for one nation and the many populations of God's invented world, and thereby cursing God Himself. In this speech, then, God elevates universal, binding promises to His auditor in a style that is as lofty as it is directive, as personally invested as it is predictive of what is to come for Abram and his progeny.

God's Style for Persuading Moses

God varies His covenant with Abraham several times over, but His style changes when He calls Moses into His service. As an angelic theophany who burns in a bush on Mount Sinai, "the mountain of God," as the narrator omnisciently calls it (Exod 3. 1–5), God calls Moses by name but does not change this auditor's name, as He did with Abram (Gen 17:5). In a similarly direct, imperial style adopted for Abraham, God warns Moses to stay back and remove his shoes because he walks on "holy ground" (Exod 3:5). At this point in the Bible's narrative, God more fully introduces Himself, invoking a past full of the fierce authority of a tradition Moses, raised as an Egyptian, cannot possibly know: "I am the God of your father, the God of Abraham, the God of Isaac, and the God of Jacob" (Exod 3:6). Each person in this roll-call has been previously persuaded to accept God's covenant-argument, however modified, but the repetition permits God to name Himself. It is to Moses, *not* Abraham, that God first addresses the issue of His name, what Moses shall call Him, so the Hebrews will believe in Moses's mission and be persuaded by his authority. God answers Moses's question in a style which shows once more His preference for powerful ironies: "I AM WHO [THAT] I AM" (Exod 4:13).

The irony, of course, lies in God's naming Himself by refusing to name Himself or, what is perhaps better, by claiming Himself to be the principle of all names, its divine *logos*. This ironic name/utterance has prompted speculation that the ancient Hebrew language could mean, "I am what I do," or even more simply, "I Will Act."[57] As "I am," God asserts that He has always been the God of Israel's fathers and founders, including Abraham, who never asks His name at all but obeys Him in almost every command. It has even been suggested that in this line God puns on His own dreaded name, suggesting He clearly understood its "charismatic force and magical suggestiveness."[58] Pun or no, God certainly adds to the name's irony by phrasing it as an *epanalepsis*, with the opening clause, "I am," identical with the closing clause, and only a single word, "who," "that," or "because," linking both clauses of equal length. This stylized name tightly knots God to an apparent reason which is perhaps not a reason at all—hence, the irony of the name becomes a closed or an infinite circle, since, given His ethos, He has and needs no reason for His presence, since any reason would simply repeat His name as a reason for all naming and a reason for all reasoning, a riddling style perfectly fit for an ethos that mixes playfulness with terrible seriousness.

This newly-named God becomes more serious when He answers a reluctant Moses, who admits his own poor rhetorical abilities. That admission prompts the sort of stylized, interrogative reply God made to Sarah, when she doubted she could have a child with Abraham, and anticipates the style of His response to Job's complaints. God rebuts Moses's objection, first by posing rhetorical questions which He answers with yet another rhetorical question, before He repeats His command: "Who has made man's mouth? Who makes him dumb, or deaf, or seeing, or blind? Is it not I, the LORD? Now therefore go, and I will be with your mouth, and teach you what you shall speak" (Exod 4:11–12).

God's questions are styled for maximum persuasive effect on Moses, since they answer themselves and remind Moses of God's overwhelmingly powerful ethos. The first two questions are linked by the *anaphoric* "who" and variations of the verb "make," while the second question serializes the alternatives, all connected with the conjunctive "or" instead of God's favorite connector, "and." It is certainly no accident either that God's questions and answers draw on other stylistic devices previously adopted. "Mouth," twice used, is another resonant synecdoche for the eloquence (rhetoric) Moses claims to lack. But this image also anticipates the other synecdoches for His human likenesses—the tongue ("dumb"), the ears ("deaf"), and the eyes ("seeing," or "blind"). Taken together, these synecdoches represent almost the entire human perceptual capacities that God first invented while simultaneously emphasizing His divine power to invent them.

57. Miles, *God*, 99.
58. Bloom, *Jesus and Yahweh*, 128.

God's Commanding Style in the Decalogue

God's full hortatory style emerges perhaps most famously in the Decalogue delivered before Moses on Mount Sinai (Exod 20:1–17). Of all the direct speeches God makes in the Bible, this one is the most familiar to Americans, believers and non-believers alike, however much of the Bible they have read. Explicitly dramatic, this speech directly addresses a "You" that includes Moses, the people of Israel, all blessed through Abraham's election and, ultimately, all human likenesses. It remains the core covenant-argument later elaborated as the laws, ordinances, rules, and customs in Leviticus and Deuteronomy. God begins most of the Decalogue exhortations—eight of them, in fact—with the *anaphoric phrase*, "You shall not"—utterances suffused with what Kenneth Burke has called that "distinctive marvel" of language, the particularly "admonitory," and "rhetorical quality" of "the negative," what God's human likenesses should and should not do for Him and because of Him, the supreme boundary of transgressions.[59]

God initially identifies Himself in first-person, but His self-references include not only "I" and "me"; but, later on, also third person, as "the LORD your God," when He demands that Israel not take His name in vain, "for the LORD will not hold him guiltless . . ." He refers to Himself again in the third person when He declares the Sabbath day as "holy" and when He recalls the six days He worked to invent the universe. However, God deviates from the *anaphoric* pattern in some of the other commandments. Despite the quite different context and audiences, His Sabbath command—"Remember the sabbath day . . ."—takes the same imperative form as His didactic style to instruct Noah and appears again later, when addressing Moses on the ordinances and the building of the Tabernacle. The imperatives continue in His command to honor parents.

But, as the Sabbath commandment unfolds, God returns to the loftier style in His *aras. Anastrophes*—"[s]ix days you shall labor," "in [the Sabbath] you shall not do any work," "for in six days the LORD made . . ."—combine with the reiterative force of *conduplicatio* in single words and phrases—"day," "you," "your," "shall," "six days," "work." Who must *not* work on the Sabbath, "you, or your son, or your daughter, your manservant or your maidservant, or your cattle, or the sojourner who is within your gates; . . .," rolls forward in balanced *isocolons*. God's reiteration intensifies as He links equally prohibited alternatives with "or," all shaping an eloquent arc that ends with two reasons for this command, introduced, as His reasons often are, with "for" or "therefore." God's exhortation to honor parents has a similar style to His

---

59. Burke, *Language as Symbolic Action*, 419, 421–22.

Sabbath command, except here God's imperative verb prefaces the honorable result of following this command—to live long in the land promised to Abraham.

God's longer commandments depend on elegant *isocolons*, each almost equal in length and structure, as He forbids the Hebrews to make "a graven image" or any "likeness" of Him or His inventions. Each alternative is introduced by an *anaphoric* phrase, linked with "or," not "and":

> *that is* (anaphora) in heaven above (isocolon # 1)
>
> or
>
> *that is* (anaphora) in the earth beneath (isocolon # 2)
>
> or
>
> *that is* (anaphora) in the water under the earth (isocolon # 3).

The prohibited sources for imagery move vertically in space, from top to bottom, foreclosing all celestial, terrestrial, and aquatic possibilities. God then closes this commandment with a dramatic antithesis (italicized) that sets "*visiting the iniquity* of the fathers upon the children to the third and the fourth generation *of those who hate [him]*," against those "*showing steadfast love* to thousands *of those who love [him] and keep [his] commandments.*"

What can be seen in these several speeches is not a divine style obscured by gaps and difficult tropes and figurations whose mysteries interpreters and theologians must ponder and gloss. Rather, their eloquence arises precisely from being directly addressed to audiences and drawing upon various rhetorical devices well-known to human rhetors who used, noticed, and eventually codified them in ancient Greece and Rome. Some of these devices clearly intend to reiterate what God wants His audiences to remember just as they serve to make His commands and instructions more emphatic. Some are elegant variations from normal grammatical patterns while others depend on plain, simple words whose metonymic and synecdochal functions and ironic intentions reach beyond the specifics of ordinary diction, but not beyond God's immediate and hortatory intentions. In these speeches at least, including His most famous one, God argues in a manner that seems both understandable and persuasive enough for almost any audience, and certainly the audiences most directly affected.

God's Hyperbolic Style in the Book of Job

With the obvious exception of the Decalogue, perhaps nowhere in the Bible is God's rhetorical style more vehement and lofty than in the famously controversial Book of Job. God, as we have seen, often poses threatening, ironic questions, curses those who cease to accept His covenant-arguments, and exhorts His likenesses to act as He prescribes, even though those same likenesses know all too well that He may strike out against them at any moment. As the theophany of a voice out of the whirlwind, God seeks to overwhelm the wretched Job's complaints, so much so that, as one commentator remarks, "[a]fter Job, God knows his own ambiguity as he has never known it before," Job having reduced Him "to silence," never to speak again in the Tanakh.[60]

The God of the Christian Bible, obviously, lets Jesus have the last words, and more traditional interpretations of the Job narrative often take God's side in this debate. However this magnificent story is interpreted, it is impossible to ignore the rhetorical lengths to which God goes to silence an auditor who desperately wants to "lay [his] case" before Him and argue with His reputed justice and goodness (Job 23:4). Job expects God to give him a fair hearing, to reason with him, and he does get to confront God (Job 23:7). Yet the whirlwind rhetoric answers Job in God's most hyperbolic mode. The whirlwind theophany seems especially suited to God's style here—not in the typical sense of mere exaggeration—but in the sense of rhetorically excessive language. Human hyperbole cannot be taken literally, no matter how extravagant or self-conscious a rhetor may be. Divine hyperbole can—and often *must*—be taken this way insofar as God, "though a frightening ironist, particularly in his rhetorical questions, is even more frequently given to hyperbole, the figure of excess or overthrow."[61]

In Job, God opens his speech with precisely one of those frightening rhetorical questions to overthrow His audience: "Who is this that darkens counsel / by words without knowledge?" (Job 38:2). Readers would know, quite as Job does, the answer to this question; for God fully intends to overthrow Job's complaints and laments, demanding he "[g]ird up [his] loins like a man," since God's intent is to "question [Job]," and force him to "declare to [God Himself]" (Job 38:3). What follows is one of the most stunning cross-examinations imaginable. God's reproach of Job goes on for several pages—too long for a detailed analysis of all its stylistic exuberance—so one passage must suffice.

In chapter 40, after Job admits his smallness and silently withdraws, God does not relent, scalding Job with more questions, as if His audience remains wholly unconvinced and stubbornly resistant: "Will you even put me in the wrong? / Will you condemn me that you / may be justified? / Have you an arm like God, and can you thunder with a voice like this?"

60. Miles, *God*, 328.
61. Bloom, *Jesus and Yahweh*, 133.

The anaphoric interrogatives that Job cannot possibly answer become more specific through synecdoches for God's size and power—His "arm" and His "voice," further described through the simile of "thunder." Bent on overwhelming any doubt Job may still have, God turns to an *exemplum*:

> Behold, Be'hemoth,
>> which I made as I made you;
>> he eats grass like an ox.
> Behold, his strength in his loins,
>> and his power in the muscles of his belly . . .
> He is the first of the works of God;
>> let him who made him bring near his sword! . . .
> Can one take him with hooks,
>> or pierce his nose with a snare? (Job 40:15–24)

God challenges Job to capture and kill the Levi'athan that He has invented, knowing full well that no human can contend with this primal monster, much less its inventor. God even asks Job if the Levi'athan

> [w]ill make a covenant with [him]
>> to take him for [his] servant for ever?
> Will you play with him as with a bird,
>> or will you put him on leash for your maidens?
> (Job 41:4–5)

God amplifies this hyperbolic irony with both simile and metaphor, before turning to the preemptory challenge:

> Can you fill his [Levi'athan's] skin with harpoons,
>> or his head with fishing spears?
> Lay hands on him;
>> think of the battle; you will not do it again!
> (Job 41:7–8)

Obviously, Job can do nothing to harm or tame the Levi'athan, and this leads God toward His swelling conclusion:

> No one is so fierce that he dares to stir him up.
>> Who then is he that can stand before me?
> Who has given to me, that I should repay him?
>> Whatever is under the whole heaven is mine.
> (Job 41:10–11)

God's own invented ethos, it seems, has been challenged, so the hyperbolic irony of these questions is meant to diminish any pretense Job may still have of thinking he has either the right or the capacity to question His maker.

The style here lifts God up even as it tears Job down—how much farther down it would be hard to say, since Job has lost all that he ever had, even his health. Yet Job's closing lines parallel God's own. At last convinced that nothing can stop God and no one can question His "purpose," Job will dare to ask, imitating God's style, "[w]ho is this that hides counsel without knowledge?" (Job 42:1–3). Job's question is not quite the same as God's asking who "darkens counsel by words without knowledge." In fact, here, it is not entirely clear what Job is asking, though he does presume to "question" God and demands God to "declare" Himself to Job (Job 42:4). If the answer to his question is God Himself, then the question may imply that God has hidden from Job who He really is. Had he understood better, Job might never have complained, since Job had "heard of" God but not seen Him in action (Job 42:5). Seeing God in this whirlwind of verbal action, and not simply hearing *of* Him, has the greater rhetorical force, so forceful that Job now "despise[s]" himself and "repent[s] in dust and ashes" (Job 42:6)—"dust and ashes" being two of God's favorite synecdoches for His human likenesses even as they recall God's curse in Eden.

In the end, God addresses Job's friends—Eliphaz, Bildad, and Zophar—only to condemn their actions, since their arguments and "counsel" to Job have "kindled [God's] wrath." They have entirely misrepresented God while, apparently, Job's questions and complaints have not (Job 42:7–8). God's verb metaphorically transmutes His "wrath" into fire, and the arguments of Job's friends into wood feeding that fire. However, after God threatens Job's friends, His style quickly turns directorial, and hortatory, ordering each of Job's companions to bring "seven bulls and seven rams" and make a "burnt offering" to Job for his prayers to save them from God's fiery anger. God, of course, predicts the acceptance of Job's prayers, repeating at the end of His orders the same reason with which He began: Job's friends "have not spoken of [God] what is right, as servant Job has" (Job 42:8).

Certainly, God's fondness for irony—especially ironic questions—and hyperbolic language mark the style of this argument. So does God's fondness for predictions, clear, specific instructions and direct, imperial exhortations. These stylistic traits reinforce different sides of God's ethos: the ironies, His unpredictability, the hyperbole, His power and authority, the predictions, His capacity to know and control time and history, the hortatory instructions, His didactic authority.

The Styles of Jesus

The question that arises from these stylistic preferences is whether they are at all similar to those of Jesus, if Jesus can be understood as God's final, invented argument, be he God's "son" or the incarnation of God's *Logos*, or Word, or both. Part of the answer, of course, depends on which Jesus in which Gospel a critic of rhetoric chooses. However, it is certainly not difficult to notice that Jesus's style can be just as ironic as God's. Nor is it difficult to find in Jesus's style the excesses of hyperbole, or predictions, instructions, and commands.

Jesus's style often depends on enigmas, riddles, and parables. An enigmatic style, in its Greek sense, usually suggests "dark sayings," riddles, and obscurities. People, as much as what they say or do, can be enigmatic riddles themselves. In that respect, Jesus's image of himself, who he is, to himself and others, ends up being an enigma, a riddle which certainly might enhance his charisma as a teacher and rabbi. This riddling, enigmatic style, the parable-making—these are thought perhaps to belong more to Jesus than to God. Yet God seldom speaks to His "son" in the New Testament, and when He does it is usually through a theophany.

What this means for Jesus's enigmatic, parabolic style an agnostic critic of rhetoric may only guess. It could certainly be cited as evidence that God and Jesus are not one and the same. However, it may also mean that Jesus and God are so much alike, as Father to son or as Father *and* Son, that no direct communication is necessary, or that Jesus communicates with God through silent prayer alone.

However this odd omission may be interpreted, the very first words of Mark's Jesus proclaim the apocalyptic revelation that John the Baptist had already been preaching: "The time is fulfilled, and the kingdom of God is at hand; repent, and believe in the gospel" (Mark 1:14). This proclamation is filled with as much urgency as mystery, since Jesus does not say exactly how the "time is fulfilled" or how long it will be before God's kingdom arrives. God's "gospel," His "good news," is what Jesus commands his listeners to believe, and not necessarily the Torah or God's earlier covenant-arguments. Jesus's final words in Mark's Gospel are also famous, and equally enigmatic when translated as "My God, my God, why hast thou forsaken me?" (15:34). The line, repeated in Matthew (27:46), is a direct quote from Psalms 22:1, and coming from the very same Jesus who already knows he will be betrayed and crucified (Mark 14:21–25). Job, of course, in his most miserable afflictions, might have asked the very same question. Presumably, here, it is an *erotema*, a rhetorical question, called out after Jesus's emphatically repeated *epinome*, "My God," a question wrenched from Jesus's own pathos. Even hanging in agony on the cross, Jesus stylizes the very manner and nature of the question that he recalls and quotes.

In between these two enigmatic proclamations are other riddling answers and parables that Mark's Jesus offers to various auditors. To the Pharisees' scribes who demand to know why Jesus eats with sinners and tax collectors, Jesus answers in an antithetical metaphor: "Those who are well have no need of a physician, but those who are sick [do]; I came not to call the righteous, but sinners" (Mark 2:17). The metaphor fuses for Jesus both spiritual and physical health at the same that it contrasts the sickness of the sinner whom he has come to help with the health of the "righteous" who do not need his help. In another instance, the Pharisees challenge his disciples' gathering grain on the Sabbath, so Jesus revises God's commandment, citing the authority of 2 Samuel so he may conclude that "[t]he sabbath was made for man, not man for the sabbath, so the Son of man is lord even of the sabbath" (Mark 2:25-27). This chiastic phrasing seems to reverse the traditional interpretation of God's commandment, with Jesus giving it a negative twist with the *litote* "not" so he can offer a more benign interpretation of the commandment before repeating it in almost exactly the same words. Jesus will deny, too, a visit from his own mother and brothers, posing another ironic question: "Who are my mother and my brothers?"—a question that would certainly strike Jesus's listeners as strange before his answer—"Whoever does the will of God is my brother, and sister, and mother" (Mark 3:31-35)—quickly reverses what his listeners likely thought of as the blood-bonds of family before they are re-grounded in faith. Mark's Jesus often weaves parables to persuade those outside his following, even though he often has to explain them for his disciples (Mark 4:10-34). As scholars often remark, Jesus usually draws the imagery and situations for his parables from the natural, everyday world. The parable of the sower and the mustard seed seems simple enough (Mark 4:2-8—30-32), yet Jesus seems to hint that there is some riddle in the story saying, "He who has ears to hear, let him hear" (Mark 4:9).[62]

The first major rhetorical address of Matthew's Jesus is the famous Sermon on the Mount (Matt 5—8). Like God in the Old Testament, Jesus speaks from the top of a high place, but he sits down when he begins teaching, though it is difficult to tell who Jesus's audience is for this sermon, the "crowds," "the disciples," or both, or whether Jesus switches from one audience to another (Matt 5:1). In one sense, this sermon revises God's

---

62. For fuller commentary on some of the enigmatic narratives of Jesus, see Kermode's *The Genesis of Secrecy*, 23-47. Kermode argues that Jesus's parables remain paradoxical narratives which both "proclaim a truth as a herald does" as well as "conceal truth like an oracle," a "double function."

Decalogue. The Beatitudes echo the language and ideas from some Old Testament works, the Psalms, Isaiah, and Chronicles, and anticipate themes extended in later New Testament works. But, whoever Jesus is addressing, it is important to appreciate how Jesus deftly blends into this sermon the musical refrain of "Blessed are . . ."—a famous *anaphora* introducing the first nine Beatitudes, each often followed by rather abstract diction.

At the close of each blessing, too, Jesus seems to anticipate an audience's objection. When he blesses "the poor in spirit," a phrase he draws from Isaiah (66:2), it seems a very vague way to appeal to those in the crowd who might be economically as well as spiritually impoverished or to those who may have wealth but no faith. In fact, Jesus's word, "poor," may have surprised some listeners, since "poor" usually refers to a person's material condition, though Jesus's metaphor identifies this poverty with the spirit. Then, as if anticipating a listener's objection about how blessed the spiritually poor could possibly be, Jesus concludes with a paradox, predicting that the spiritually destitute, like those persecuted for their "righteousness" (Matt 5:10), will receive "the kingdom of heaven" (Matt 5:1). Jesus uses the same paradoxical style when he blesses the "meek." That this group should expect to "inherit the earth" would likely puzzle, if not surprise, any listener who might assume that only the powerful would be earth's beneficiaries (Matt 5:5).

Jesus alters the pattern of *anaphora* after the ninth blessing, perhaps a change that signals he is now addressing his disciples. Twice, he directly addresses his listeners, whoever they are, as "you," just as God has previously done, while some of his metaphorical descriptions are now so familiar they have sadly become mere clichés to many. In the first, Jesus calls his audience "the salt of the earth," and warns they will be "trodden under foot" if they lose their salty taste (Matt 5:13). In the second, he calls his listeners "the light of the world" and, like a lighted "city set on a hill," they "cannot be hid" (Matt 5:14). He embellishes these metaphors with another—"Nor do men light a lamp and put it under a bushel, but on a stand, and gives light to all in the house" (Matt 5:15)—only to draw from the metaphor a direct exhortation: "Let your light so shine before men, that they may see your good works and give glory to your Father who is in heaven" (Matt 5:16).

Jesus's direct address to his auditors continues when he announces his purpose—to fulfill "the law and the prophets" of the Old Testament, not to destroy them (Matt 5:17–20). Here, though, he softens this quasi-defensive utterance with another *litote*, perhaps anticipating some will believe his teaching threatens Torah law: "Think not that I have come to abolish the law and the prophets; I have come not to abolish but to fulfill them"(Matt 5:17). "Think not" and "come not" understate the more confrontational, imperial phrasing, "Do not think." Jesus's crucial proclamation is made even more emphatic with the strategic repetition of *anadiplosis*, reiterating the end of one clause, "Think not that *I have come to* abolish the law and the prophets," to start the next clause, "*I have come* not to abolish but to fulfill them" (emphasis added). Jesus's *conduplicatio* repeats "abolish" and the *litote*, "not," in two different clauses, only to end his daring proclamation with the infinitive phrase "to fulfill" as the direct antithesis of "to abolish." This antithesis leads to another *isocolon* fully parallel to the first: "Whoever then *relaxes* one of the least of these commandments [God's Mosaic laws] and teaches men so, *shall be called least in the kingdom of heaven*; but he *who does them and teaches* them *shall be called great in the kingdom of heaven*"(Matt 5:19, emphasis added). This utterance, like the one above (Matt 5:17), is very similar to God's style at its loftiest; the syntax neatly divides and balances against each other two types of auditors—the blessed who follow Moses's law and who instruct others how to do the same, and the cursed who do not follow this law and teach otherwise.

In several arguments, the "hyperbolical demands" of Jesus's teachings emulate God's hyperbolic ironies, especially where Jesus insists on "perfections that mere humans scarcely can achieve."[63] Jesus demands that his followers not only avoid killing each other; they must also not be angry with each other or their accusers (Matt 5:21-25). Jesus further exhorts his followers to refrain from adulterous acts, actual as well as imaginary (Matt 5:27-30). Similar to God's, Jesus's synecdoches depend on specific body parts to substitute for and imply whole human beings. Like God, too, especially in His speech to Moses on the Covenant Code in Exodus (21—23), Jesus phrases arguments as hypothetical "if" statements, exhibiting Burke's "progressive" or nearly syllogistic form, ending with an imperial command. Each hypothetical parallels another through *isocolons* that syntactically reinforce the words Jesus repeats and emphasizes: "*If* your *eye* causes you to sin, pluck it out and throw it away ... *And if* your *hand* causes you to sin, cut it off and throw it away ..." (emphasis added). Jesus offers the same reason for each hypothetical injunction, in almost the exact form, before concluding that "it is better that you lose one of your members than that your whole body be thrown into hell."

Perhaps Jesus's rhetorical style reaches its most hyperbolic pitch when he exhorts his auditors to love their enemies and pray for their persecutors (Matt 5:43-47). Jesus begins this counter-argument with a direct reference to the Torah law of the Old Testament: "an eye for an eye and a tooth for a tooth." Jesus's counter-claim once again flies in the face of what Jesus's

---

63. Bloom, *Jesus and Yahweh*, 133.

disciples have "heard": "But I say to you, Do not resist one who is evil." If that were not shocking enough, Jesus adds other, apparently contrary admonitions:

> But if any one strikes you on the right cheek, turn to him the other also; and if any one would sue you and take your coat, let him have your cloak as well; and if any one forces you to go one mile, go with him two miles. Give to him who begs from you, and do not refuse him who would borrow from you.

Quite similar to God, Jesus joins his excessive hypotheticals with "and," while each hypothetical begins with *anaphora* and ends with a balanced, symmetrical *isocolon*, following this basic scheme, "if any one does x, do y." Still, as logically and syntactically parallel as these arguments are, they demand of their auditors reactions that defy common sense and seem contradictory to God's own Decalogue.

Jesus inverts another Torah law which demands that the Israelites love their neighbors and hate their enemies, arguing quite the outrageous opposite: "But I say to you, Love your enemies and pray for those who persecute you . . ." (Matt 5:44). Jesus's "But I say to you," is another of his *anaphoric* refrains, perhaps a quieter paraphrase of God's more commanding *anaphoric* imperative, "Behold." His disciples may have thought, but did not ask, the obviously implied question, "To what end should this be done?" Again, Jesus's reply is rhetorically *proleptic*, as he anticipates or implies questions neither he nor his audience have explicitly raised and then answers them in startling ways, as when he exhorts his disciples to follow his highly unorthodox injunction: "so that [they] may be sons of [their] Father who is in heaven . . ." (Matt 5:45). To amplify this premise, Jesus offers a pair of antithetical premises framed as perfectly balanced *isocolons*: "for he [the Father] makes his sun rise on the evil and on the good, and sends rain on the just and the unjust."

Like his "Father," too, some of Jesus's rhetorical questions (*erotema*) invite his listeners to answer as Jesus wishes: "For if you love those who love you, what reward have you? Do not even the tax collectors do the same? And if you salute only your brethren, what more are you doing than others? Do not even Gentiles do the same?" (Matt 5:46). Jesus, of course, will infer from these questions and their expected answers what his auditors may think is an utterly impossible, and certainly illogical, conclusion: "You, therefore, *must be perfect, as your heavenly Father is perfect*" (Matt 5.48, emphasis added). This injunction sets a standard most human beings would never presume for themselves: Jesus would have his auditors be as God, to act as God. This recommendation would likely strike many listeners, then as now, to be far beyond their capacities. To urge God's human likenesses to be as "perfect" as their divine inventor is a hortatory metaphor the likes of which even God Himself had not dared suggest, however much His covenant-arguments may have assumed it.

Of the many riddles, paradoxes, and parables that mark Jesus's style, perhaps the most startling emerges in his debate with the doubtful "Jews," as the omniscient gospel narrator of John refers to them (8:48–59). In chapter 4, I enumerated several of the key differences Bart D. Erhman observed between John's Jesus and other gospel accounts of him. John's Jesus is God's *logos*; he was *with* God, always. The Jews in John's account, however, interrogate Jesus, suggesting he is possessed by a demon. In the course of their debate, Jesus boldly asserts, "Truly, truly, I say to you, before Abraham *was, I am*" (John 8. 58, emphasis added). Preceded by the emphatic *epizeuxis*, "truly," this paradox captures much of the style of John's Jesus. Indeed, following the *epizeusis*, Jesus's *enallage* confounds two different verb tenses, shifting from the past "was" to the present "I am." Classical rhetoric would catalogue this tense shift as a fault, yet John's Jesus does more than make an intentional grammatical error for effect. Jesus's tense shift to "I am" also happens to be another *oraculum*, a direct quotation of God's mysteriously powerful name in Exodus. The paradox, of course, derives from Jesus's combining the *oraculum* with "before Abraham was."

Jesus's Jewish interrogators have just finished offering Abraham's death and the death of the prophets as examples to refute Jesus's assertion that anyone who accepts him and "keeps [Jesus's] word . . . will never see death" (John 8:51). To meet this counter-argument, Jesus dismisses his own "glory" as "nothing," since God glorifies him and is the same God that the Jews claim to "know" but do not. Jesus claims *he* does know God, and that "Abraham rejoiced that he was to see [Jesus's] day" and *did see it* and "was glad" (John 8:55–56). This claim would amount to blasphemy to his Jewish interlocutors, since he is willfully reversing the entire Jewish tradition, its patrimony, in asserting Abraham came *after* Jesus, rather than *before* him. Like God's trope of "dust" in His curse against Adam, Jesus's *enallage* ends up as *metalepsis*, with Jesus reversing mere chronology and denying himself any temporal limitation, hence the continuing present tense of "I am." *Metalepsis* can enact such a radical meaning, coming as close as any assertion that Jesus makes in the Gospels to claiming to be God Himself, far closer than the more ambiguous phrasings as "son of Man" or "son of God."

While these passages from God and Jesus may, indeed, represent what Auerbach saw as "tyrannical" claims on "truth" to the exclusion of any other truth, they show as well striking similarities in rhetorical aims and styles. While Jesus's style seems more enigmatic at times than God's, it is hardly an accident that his style, as God's final covenant-argument, should share much with the style of God's rhetoric in the Old Testament and that these styles can be described based on the nomenclature of classical rhetoric. The ancient Greek and Roman rhetoricians *did not invent* the stylistic patterns, tropes, or figures of speech they identified, classified, and often argued about; they only invented the *names* for these devices and tried to explain their various forms and effects. The eloquence attributed to God and to His final covenant spokesperson, as Augustine understood long ago, can certainly match the eloquence of many pagan rhetors. So there is very little in either God's or Jesus's *styles* of arguing that human rhetors have not tried to adopt themselves. Because God and Jesus largely depend on language to persuade, both of them word and phrase their arguments to achieve their intended purposes; and, because both address human likenesses as their audiences, they seek a stylistic virtuosity that will make what they argue as powerful, memorable, and "truthful" as possible to human ears.

Obviously, some may think it absurd that anyone should believe that God's or Jesus's styles in these or any other passages can be described and analyzed. Those influenced by modern historical criticism of the Bible may object that all that has been shown above are the eloquent styles of all-too-human *translators*, or the translators of translations, or editors and redactors, *not the styles these divine beings actually used*. Those more devout may object that a rhetorical description of God's and Jesus's styles is hardly surprising insofar as the Bible is God's "book," and that God invented rhetoric and the very rhetorical devices identified, just as He invented everything else, so it stands to reason that He and His "son" would adopt such devices. Those who read these and other passages as "scripture" may object that analyzing these passages as mere "rhetorical style" belies the many deeper, and more inscrutable, meanings theologians have debated for centuries. Those who read them as "literature" may object that treating the styles of these speeches as "rhetorical" too easily dismisses their "poetic" qualities and must subordinate this poetry to the religious ideology of those who, identifiable or no, wrote them.

These are, to be sure, reasonable objections, as far as they go. But, again, an agnostic critic of rhetoric cannot be certain about the actual "truth" of how God or Jesus may have spoken or *know* if what the unknown authors, translators, and editors attribute to God or Jesus was actually *what* these figures said or *how* they said it. It may, in the end, hardly matter. The Christian Bible that has come down to us shows God and Jesus speaking in certain ways. God and Jesus are *directly quoted* as saying what they said and how they said it as an empirical and cultural given of this one text, however many extra-biblical sources may lie beneath it. Translations of the Bible, of course, vary—some greatly. Here, the stylistic patterns and devices in what God and Jesus are quoted to have said come from the Standard Revised translation of the Bible, itself based on many other, older translations, and taken by many biblical rhetorical critics as sufficiently authoritative to cite. Still, even the handful of speeches highlighted in this chapter show stylistic patterns and figurative expressions that rhetoricians have also noticed, codified, and adopted themselves. If they are read as rhetoric, not just as "literature" or "scripture," the stylistic devices can be treated as ways to make God's and Jesus's arguments as persuasive and memorable as possible, however any one may assess the "truth" these arguments assume or claim.

At least since Aristotle, a human rhetor's styling of the arguments invented and arranged typically preceded memory and delivery, the final parts or canons of rhetoric. Yet these canons appear the least applicable to God's eloquent, stylized pleas. To speak of God's having to memorize what He was going to argue, or of having to consider how He was going to sound when He did argue, may be the two most question-begging considerations so far proposed. What exactly do classical thinkers believe memory and delivery entailed? And what relevance does either have to God's rhetoric in the Bible? These questions call for the next chapter.

7

Memory's Divine Delivery

Reminders of Voices Divine

The last two canons or stages in the traditional "art" of rhetoric, I must repeat, have no obvious application to God's biblical eloquence. Given the ethos He invents for Himself, this God has no apparent limits on His memory. Nor, it seems, would He need to modulate His voice or consider what gestures to make at any given moment when He speaks directly to His human likenesses. These long-accepted traits about the God who speaks and acts in the Bible certainly may account for why some critics of rhetoric would argue that it is pointless to deal with either God's *ars memoria* or His modes of delivery. No one can possibly recover the way God, Jesus, or anyone in the Bible sounded as they spoke.[1] All we are left with is the written text itself—a record of what God said, to whom, and when, but very little about *how* He sounded when He said it.

The same point can be made about Jesus, whichever version of him is selected from the four gospels. However Jesus sounded when he spoke, readers may largely have to be content with one gospel narrator's claim that what he said was uttered "as one who had authority" (Matt 7:29). That "as" might trouble devout readers, since it quietly suggests Jesus may not have had the "authority" he seemed to, or that the "authority" was a pose. Yet Jesus argues, commands, instructs, and preaches, just as God does. But the

---

1. Howard, "Rhetorical Criticism in Old Testament Studies," 96; Kennedy, *New Testament Interpretation through Rhetorical Criticism*, 13–14.

sound and tone of his voice when he performed these rhetorical acts remain largely hidden within the vague, innocuous, and endlessly repeated verbs of "said," "saying," and "says." In fact, these same verbs appear in most cases when *any* biblical figure, not just God or Jesus, speaks. Such verbs appear to invite readers to imagine for themselves exactly how God, Jesus, or anyone sounded, assuming of course these divine beings sounded differently from other biblical figures.

By the same token, these editorially "neutral" verbs may strive to have a rhetorical effect on those who read them. They could make the speeches they introduce sound as if they are being reported by first hand witnesses to events, as if the narrators were reporters on the scene, even if these narrators typically enjoy an omniscience that reporters surely lack and an ideological confidence in not only what the conjectured facts are, but what these facts portend, their meanings, the presumptive "truth" that today's reporters are in most cases ethically and professionally denied to signal. These neutral reporting verbs may imbue the narratives with an authenticity, even a "historical" veracity and "authority" that many "pre-critical" readers in the past and even now grant to and assume for the entire Bible, as the recorded or recording-inspired language of God and Jesus—perhaps a veracity that, as Auerbach complained, makes the Bible "tyrannical" in its "truthfulness." These divine speeches might not otherwise have this apparent veracity, this tyrannical truthfulness, had those who invented these biblical narrators allowed such narrators to qualify these simple, mundane verbs with adverbs to indicate *how* God or Jesus sounded when they spoke, as secular narrators often do in works of fiction. The saying *how* would appear to weaken the hoped for verisimilitude of the stories told in the saying.

Even if some critics of rhetoric think memory and delivery are wholly irrelevant to anything anyone says in the Bible, much less God or Jesus, these canons or stages at least deserve to be considered for whatever they can illuminate about the "divine eloquence" that is this book's subject. Memory and delivery may very well prove to be the most paradoxical dimensions of traditional rhetoric, initially cast off as intriguing historical curiosities with the arrival of print culture yet returning as victorious usurpers once digital culture arrived to swallow up and transform print culture. Before anyone can confidently assert that memory and delivery are wholly irrelevant and inapplicable to the written/printed Bible or to the two central rhetors of that Bible, God and Jesus, perhaps it is important to recall, however schematically, what these terms meant as theoretical concepts within the "art" of rhetoric itself and how their importance was justified over the centuries, since these centuries both witness their eclipse and their new-found resurgence.

Only then, it seems, can these rhetorical canons be usefully examined as they apply to God's and Jesus's rhetoric.

Recalling Memory's Rhetorical Purposes

The Greeks referred to "memory" as *mneme*, translated into Latin as *memoria*, and to "delivery" as *hypocrisis*, which for the Romans became *actio*. In her classic study on the subject, Frances A. Yates contends that much of what we know about the early history of memory comes from one, previously mentioned Latin source, the anonymously composed *Rhetorica ad Herenniuum*. For many years, the *ad Herenniuum* was thought to be based on a number of Greek works now lost to us.[2] One of these Greek authors, Yates speculates, could have been Simonides. Several Latin authors, Cicero and Quintilian among them, credit Simonides of Ceos (born around 556 BCE and dying in 468 BCE) as the inventor of the "art" of memory. Apparently, too, Yates adds, he was the first Greek thinker who equated poetry with painting and emphasized the visual over all other senses.[3] Simonides's influence may perhaps account for the importance attributed to the persuasive power of visual images by the Greek sophist Gorgias in his *Encomium of Helen*.[4]

Yates quotes a short passage on memory from an unfinished, anonymous Greek work called *Dialexis*. There, another unknown author advises those training to become rhetors to use repetition to enhance their natural memories and to associate words or names with images of objects—two key techniques later recalled and elaborated in the *ad Herennium*.[5] Of course, for Plato, declared enemy of the sophists, memory was crucial if a rhetor hoped to find true knowledge about a subject before trying to persuade others. Long before mechanical printing became widespread across Europe, Plato had famously worried about the effects of alphabetic writing on human memory and knowledge. In the frequently quoted passage from the *Phaedrus*, Plato's Socrates voices the fear that written words will "implant forgetfulness" in human beings, end up in the wrong hands, and lead to confusions and misunderstandings.[6] All that written words could do, Plato concedes, is "remind" the one who "knows" of what has been written.

---

2. Yates, *Art of Memory*, 5. Further citations are to the reprint.
3. Ibid., 28.
4. Gorgias, *Encomium of Helen*, 46.
5. Yates, *Art of Memory*, 29–30.
6. Plato, *Phaedrus*, 275a–b.

In the *Phaedrus*, too, Plato's Socrates extols the value of seeing *through* deceptive sensory images to the underlying, true forms human beings once beheld when their souls existed with the gods.[7] Plato even condemns alphabetic writing as an inferior image of this pre-exiting, divine truth—a truth best found through face-to-face conversations between human beings devoted to philosophy, not rhetoric or writing. Ironically, Plato presents these conversations as written dialogues, many showing the dialectical process Socrates presumably conducted in conversations. The intense, question-answer sessions of dialectic could nourish the seeds of truth in another listener. Written words, meanwhile, could only serve as a reminder of those truths that a person had already discovered.[8] Plato's student, Aristotle, says nothing about memory in his lectures on rhetoric. Yet Aristotle does, Yates notes, link memory to the *topoi* or "places" so important for rhetorical invention while, in other works, Aristotle considers the imagination—the part of the mind which turns sensory information into images—the crucial gateway to thought itself.[9]

Writing's threat to memory, seemingly a dangerous trait to Plato, is no threat for Roman rhetoricians. Cicero calls writing with "the pen . . . the best and most eminent author and teacher of eloquence."[10] Rhetors who wrote out their speeches, Cicero observed, won over more audiences than those who did not. The practice of writing speeches before they were delivered could help rhetors sound more like "the written word" even when they were speaking extemporaneously. Like Cicero, Quintilian endorses writing as an expedient way to become an excellent rhetor since he, too, thought of writing as a mnemonic device. "In writing," he explains, "are the roots, in writing are the foundations of eloquence; by writing resources are stored up, as it were, in a sacred repository, when they may be drawn forth for sudden emergencies, or as circumstances require."[11]

Even Francis Bacon, centuries later, couples writing and memorization as the best ways to gather and retain knowledge. This writing of memory often took the form of "commonplace books," where rhetors could store ideas and quotations for later use in speaking or writing itself. Yet Bacon laments how little memory had been studied in his day.[12] The few direct comments

---

7. Plato, *Phaedrus*, 249a–b, 250a–c.

8. Plato, *Phaedrus*, 275a–e, 276a–e.

9. Yates, *Art of Memory*, 31–32; on Aristotle and the "imagination," see also Burke, *Rhetoric of Motives*, 78.

10. Cicero, *De Oratore*, vol. 3, I. xxxii. 150.

11. Quintilian, *Institutio Oratoria*, vol. 4, 10. iii. 3.

12. Bacon, *Advancement of Learning*, 229.

Bacon makes about memory, it turns out, come from the section of the *ad Herennium* devoted to it. Despite Yates' reference to the Greek work, *Dialexis*, the *ad Herennium*'s translator attests that this section remains the "oldest surviving treatment of the subject."[13]

Although the *ad Herennium* author does refer to other Greek works on memory, none are named. Instead, the *ad Herennium* presents a practical way for rhetors to enhance their natural memories by using hand-made backgrounds, with various images drawn or painted on these backgrounds, which can be shifted and rearranged, perhaps similar to "storyboarding" done prior to movie productions. In this way, a rhetor learns to associate a particular argument he wishes to make with a particular scene—say, where a crime occurred—and images attached to it, the alleged criminal or murder weapon. This ancient system may be a precursor to what psychologists today call a "visuospatial sketchpad" for images in our minds that we wish to recall.[14] Words themselves, their very sounds, could also be mnemonic, forming a "phonological loop." So could some songs and rhythmic verbal patterns, such as "'i' before 'e' except after 'c,'" or the song children learn when memorizing the alphabet.

Today, technologies appear to have supplanted human beings' need to memorize as much as they used to. Most of us no longer deliberately memorize what has been written; we can read what we write aloud anytime, to anyone who will listen. Books and other written documents have replaced ancient scrolls and scripts, just as "Google" appears to be replacing libraries and archives of the recent past. People now have electronic storage and the means for almost instant retrieval of any "fact" or idea sought that no ancient Greek or Roman would have ever been able to find without a lot of time and a lot of searching, assuming these materials could be found at all—all now readily accessible through mobile phones, tablets, surfaces.

For all that, though, Yates thinks it would be a serious mistake to ignore the rhetorical origins of the art of memory. That art was passed down through the Middle Ages and into the Renaissance and beyond.[15] Cicero does not need to repeat the theory and instructions of the *ad Herennium* in his remarks on memory in *De Oratore* because his readers would have already been quite familiar with them. But Cicero does adopt a largely Platonic view of the power of human memory. This power, for Cicero, is central

---

13. Caplan, "Introduction," xix–xx.
14. Pinker, *Stuff of Thought*, 129.
15. This transmission process, and the complex transformations of the *ars memoriae*, is the focus of Yates' book, to which I am indebted here.

to invention itself and, ultimately, to the human soul's divine source.[16] This divine linkage may explain why the rhetorical art of memory did not simply die of neglect once the Renaissance world of printed books forever changed how human beings would record, store, retrieve, and communicate ideas and information. Instead, interest in human memory melded with the mystical, Neo-platonic mind-set of many sixteenth century intellectuals.[17] Eventually, this mystical approach to memory did provoke attacks and criticisms that led to more abstract, but far less occult, methods of memorizing. Still, as Yates admits, much still remains to be understood about how closely linked the rhetorical art of memory is to theology, philosophy, psychology, ethics, art, science, and literature.[18]

Rhetorical Voices, Persuasive Gestures

Ancient ideas about rhetorical delivery, like memory, became another widely-acknowledged casualty of the shift from oral to written rhetoric, from script to print culture. In Book III of his *Rhetoric*, Aristotle conveniently by-passes the art of memory to explain that after invention, arrangement, and style, a rhetor must consider delivery. To Aristotle, this step is "of the greatest importance," though it had been largely neglected by thinkers in his own day.[19] Aristotle blames this neglect on the simple fact that the authors of tragic plays in ancient Greece had also performed as actors, speaking their own lines and playing the parts of characters they imagined; so, for a long time, there was no real need to instruct others in how to deliver speeches in plays.[20] Even so, Aristotle was the first, so far as scholars can tell, to emphasize rhetorical delivery as the way a rhetor was to speak to affect listeners' emotions. Delivery included not only how loudly a rhetor should speak, but how the voice and tone were to be modulated to achieve the most persuasive effects.

Aristotle, it turns out, spends more time complaining about the importance of delivery than he does offering advice about it, presumably thinking delivery was simply another, visceral part of style and only important because of the corrupt politics of his own time and an audience's weakness for well-spoken, dramatic speakers.[21] Worrying about either style or delivery

16. Yates, *Art of Memory*, 44–45.
17. Ibid., 127–28.
18. Ibid., 389.
19. Aristotle, *Rhetoric* 3.i.2.
20. Aristotle, *Rhetoric* 3.i.2–3.
21. Ibid.

seemed to him "vulgar," even unethical. Of course, this ancient judgment may also explain why both subjects had been largely ignored by those previously occupied with rhetoric's art. Still, it was a "necessary" subject for Aristotle to cover, because all rhetors sought to shape and affect listeners' beliefs and opinions. However, a truly moral rhetor, Aristotle believed, "should aim at nothing more in a speech than how to avoid exciting pain or pleasure."[22] In his view, "justice should consist in fighting the case with the facts alone, so that everything else that is beside demonstration is superfluous." But that seldom happened in a world dominated by the power of the spoken; so delivery, like style, Aristotle concludes, "does make a difference," though both "are more outward show for pleasing the hearer."

"Outward show" or not, delivery was very likely a part of rhetoric long before Aristotle's brief comments on it, but the most elaborate account of it again appears in the *ad Herennium*. There, the author outlines fairly rigid rules about how a rhetor must modulate his voice, control his volume, and orchestrate gestures.[23] For this "body rhetoric," as it might be called, a rhetor was advised not to scream and shout throughout a speech, since that sort of delivery would damage the vocal chords. The *ad Herennium* further instructs rhetors on how and when to pause, what tone of voice to use in stating facts or arguing against an opponent, doing much the same with bodily movements, suiting different actions to the different parts and purposes of an argument. Contrary to Cicero's preference,[24] though, the *ad Herennium* warns rhetors not to imitate the way actors speak.

From the *ad Herennium*'s list of rules for voice, tone, and gesture emerged an entire movement in the eighteenth century—the so-called "elocutionary movement," zealously promoting correct pronunciation and precise, dramatic gestures, whose continuing preoccupations can be seen in George Bernard Shaw's classic, nineteenth century play, *Pygmalion* and its popularized version on the stage and in film adaptations, retitled *My Fair Lady*. Shaw's Professor Henry Higgins instructs Liza Doolittle in the elocutionary arts of proper speech and socially acceptable gestures, all that was left of *actio* by this time. Long before Shaw's satirical play, though, Thomas Sheridan had already seriously explored the rhetorical and communicative importance of body language and vocal tones in his 1762 work, *Lectures on Elocution*. Following Sheridan, Gilbert Austin produced an elaborately

---

22. Aristotle, *Rhetoric* 3.i.3–6.
23. Cicero, *Rhetorica ad Herennium*, vol. 1, 3.xi–xv, 20–28.
24. Cicero, *De Oratore*, vol. 3, 1.xxviii.129–30.

illustrated notational system in his *Chironomia* (1806) so that rhetors could choreograph their hand gestures and movements with their oral delivery.²⁵

Once written rhetoric seemingly overwhelms its oral counterpart, delivery, like memory, should have disappeared as a logical and practical concern for those interested in the study of rhetoric. But that is not exactly what happened. The development and emergence of electronic communications, multi-media, and the increasing importance of the image, the icon—all have led a number of scholars to re-think the importance of rhetorical delivery as it impacts any communicative effort, all the way down from the icons themselves to graphics and typography.²⁶ Before his death, Derrida felt compelled to call attention to "the medium of the media themselves (news, the press, tele-communications, techno-tele-discursivity, techno-tele-iconicity, that which in general assures and determines the spacing of public space..."²⁷

This "spacing of public space," it so happens, recalls one of Foucault's early observations. "[I]n the modern epoch," he writes, the ancient notion of theatrical "spectacle and inspection of a small number of objects" by those "gathered in a circle" to observe humans and animals in bloody conflict at the center, suffered an "inversion" to become the "surveillance" characteristic of prisons and hospitals.²⁸ The very same "techno-tele-iconicity" that floats along the Internet ether to deliver countless human messages and images so rapidly and easily—speed, ease, and massive distribution being the operant, built-in valences of such communication technologies—makes a "spectacle," if not a "carnival," of all manner of human endeavors and attitudes for anyone to see and hear, and imposes further surveillance demands on those charged to watch and be watchful of any dangers or threats those very same messages and images may present or suggest. Now, in the midst of wide-spread government and corporate surveillance, the means of delivering any persuasive message, and the formal and not-so-formal elements of its design and distribution, have expanded well beyond what anyone could have imagined even a decade ago. Rhetorical delivery encompasses e-mails, blogs, and tweets to engage audiences through mixing words with sounds and images to distribute their persuasive messages almost instantaneously world-wide, to any number of audiences. The rhetorical implications and

25. See Sheridan, *A Course of Lectures on Elocution*, Lecture VI; and Austin, *Chironomia*, in *Rhetorical Tradition*, 2nd. ed., 879–97.

26. The available literature on rhetoric's becoming an increasingly "visual" medium is immense, see Handa's edited collection, *Visual Rhetoric in a Digital Age*, 133–221, 225–302, 305–373.

27. Derrida, *Specters of Marx*, 63. Reference is to the reprint.

28. Foucault, *Punitive Society*, 22–23.

cultural impact of these tele-discursive, tele-iconic messages are still being explored and more fully considered as they intersect with the now digitalized cultural memory. Those so-called "memes"—that provocative cultural analogue to the biological gene—now spread through public, digital space at a rate and to an extent no experts can readily or accurately calculate.

Thus the paradox mentioned earlier: rhetoric's most cognitive and oral/aural dimensions—memory and delivery—once displaced and almost forgotten by print culture regain their importance within an increasingly visual, auditory, and multimodal digital culture absorbing print and script culture. Virtual *fora* beckon to virtual Cicero's around the globe. Those speaking from or on screens must now worry far more about how they sound and look as well as what they say and do as part of the rhetorical spectacle being both casually viewed and often surveilled. Failed and failing memories need only "google" to find out when Cicero died and how. Those who are younger may even wonder why any instructor would ask them to memorize a short poem or a proverb, much less a longer stretch of text or a set of "facts"—unless their career plans would place them on stage or before a camera. Cultural critics, meanwhile, predictably worry over whether digital memory and virtual iconicity portend variously imagined collapses of Western culture's values and institutions while other cultural critics approvingly applaud the sweep and reach of these technological supplements and their potential to "democratize" and improve all human lives.

This chapter is not the place for examining these broad, rhetorically-charged reactions from cultural critics. What remains before us here is whether, and to what extent, delivery or memory has any relevance to God's or Jesus's speeches in the Bible and, if they do, *how* they do. No one can plausibly deny that these speeches are *written* into the Bible or that, given God's invented ethos and the various portrayals of Jesus in the four Gospels, these canons of rhetoric seem far more tangential than invention, arrangement, and style. Yet sometimes tangents and exceptions may reveal more than may be anticipated.

Divine Deliveries, Remembered Covenants

God's initial speeches in the Bible—at least those attributed directly to Him by various narrators—seem to have been invented and spoken in a style intended only for Himself or, more speculatively, for the sparse materials from which He may have invented the universe, or for other gods that ancient Hebrew authors inherited from earlier traditions. When God later curses the serpent, Adam, and Eve, there are no overt textual clues about how

His curses may have sounded to His first human inventions or the serpent, though it is certainly clear that He remembered the covenant-argument that His human likenesses no longer found so persuasive. When God poses what have been described as *ironic* questions, the irony of those questions, even to be recognized as such, often presupposes the "truth" that biblical narrators seem already to know and accept as central to God's ethos. An omniscient, all-powerful God often quoted by apparently omniscient, ideologically-driven narrators, in addition to what God is quoted to have said before and after any given speech, are perhaps the best internal, textual evidence any critic can cite to support a claim about God's ironic style in the absence of being told by a narrator whether or how God's tone of voice changes when He speaks in this fashion. As a written rendering of the oral medium through which God chooses to deliver most of His rhetoric, whether "truly" recorded or imaginatively inspired, the most reasonable way a critic has to determine God's ironic tone depends on other, contextual evidence and the narrators' assumptions about the divine speaker they quote.

The biblical God's direct mode of oral delivery, however, will sometimes be a theophany—in many cases, an angelic theophany. We see this mode when God speaks to Hagar, Sarah's Egyptian maid who, with Abraham's child, Ishmael, in her womb, flees Sarah's harsh treatment (Gen 16:7-9). Yet, even as an angel, God speaks to Hagar in the same sort of ironic interrogatives that God had used with Adam, Eve, and other biblical figures. God speaks to Moses as well through a double theophany, an angel in a bush that burns but is "not consumed" (Exod 3:2). Later, God speaks to the Pharaoh through the natural theophanies of plagues and pestilence, even death itself, and through the suspension of natural laws governing natural bodies of water. Later still, God even sends an angel to speak through a donkey—another double theophany—to stop Balaam, a sorcerer, from laying a curse against Moses and the Hebrews invading Moab (Num 23:28). In fact, it is not until Moses and the Hebrews reach Mount Sinai that God's voice is described by the narrator as "thunder" (Exod 20:19)—the same thunderous voice God later raises against the Philistines to save His people (1 Sam 7:10), the same voice imagined as the whirlwind theophany Job encounters (40:9).

God's thunderous voice, of course, may be considered a predictable metaphor to enhance His invented ethos and His more hyperbolic style. As such, it may recall for secular readers the kind of imagery long associated with pagan gods—especially Zeus of Greek mythology. Without any modern, "scientific" understanding of the natural world, ancient peoples may have personified phenomena that they simply could not explain in any other way except as "gods" or theophanies, "super-natural" agents and agencies.

This is certainly one theory—in fact, a rather common one—of why rain, thunder, or lightning show up in myths and legends *as* gods and goddesses or as natural phenomena closely linked to their appearances. Unfortunately, this theory fails to account for why "pre-scientific" peoples could imagine super-beings—gods and goddesses—yet not have the intellectual capacity to consider other explanations for natural events. After all, widespread belief in *a* or in *many* gods is no meager mental act, but an "idea" or thought that human language, with its genius for the negative, the "No," invites us to articulate in an abstraction not so easily reducible to the conditioned nature of images perceived in our natural, day-to-day quotidian.[29] That this "No" should be abstracted as one or many gods, as "unconditioned" agents who act freely in an "unconditioned" realm, beyond the naturally constraining one humans inhabit—this shows, in a very basic sense, that what Vico called "imaginative metaphysics"[30] has often found its fulfillment in bringing the abstracted agents of verbal negations (gods), back to earth in images, personifications, and metaphors. Human language invites such figuration in being grounded in the conditioned world of nature that the very verbal idea of the "divine" would transcend and thus negate.

It would seem a grossly "scientistic" prejudice to suppose that ancient peoples, or peoples still largely insulated from science's influence, who thought a thunderstorm was an act of an angry god were or are more intellectually bereft than those who know the natural, "scientific" reasons for a storm. Both science and religion, and their respective rhetorics, recognize a *hidden causality* behind the storm's disruptive appearance and attempt to abstract from those conditions an "idea" of their origins. Nor is the banal fact that many scientists, now as in the past, acknowledge belief in supernatural powers, not to mention the biblical God and His reputed son, Jesus, to be simply dismissed in an effort to protect the interests and prejudices of science against the much maligned interests and prejudices of religion. Descartes himself, one of the major thinkers in the early emergence of scientific thought, finally had to ground his *ergo cogito sum* on God's existence.

The God of the Christian Bible, though, exists to do more than deliver His arguments in a thunderous voice—apparently the only way He is described as sounding. God wrote down His exhortations and arguments as well. At first, Moses takes dictation while God orally delivers the Decalogue and the Covenant Code (Exod 20—22). But God also delivers them in His own handwriting (Exod 32:18). Later, after breaking the original

---

29. Here, I extrapolate from Burke's "dramatistic" translation of Kantian ethics, *Language as Symbolic Action*, 436–38.

30. Vico, *New Science*, 88.

stone tablets, God dictates another set of laws and rituals to Moses (Exod 34:10–28), and dictates as well the "Song of Moses," which Moses copies and recites (Deut 31–32). Throughout the Old Testament, in addition to His writings, God variously delivers His commands and arguments through dreams, visions, His "word," and through the words assigned to or uttered by His own prophets. His is the voice of thunder, yes, and He can become persuasive pillars of fire and cloud. He manifests Himself as angels who sometimes take human form to deliver His message and enact His plans. He may have come as angelic strangers to the cities of Sodom and Gomorrah to warn Lot of the city's impending destruction (Gen 18–19). Taking human form, of course, to deliver the arguments He makes is, for many Christians, exactly what God does through Jesus in the New Testament.

All of these invented theophanies are also God's modes of delivery, and quite beyond any human rhetor. Still, however miraculous, astounding, and even violent they are for those who may have directly heard or witnessed them, God's modes of delivery remain primarily oral and, secondarily, written. These modes, like the rhetoric of violence, are completely compatible with human rhetoric as it has existed and still exists. God's voice is meant to be *heard*, not read, by those He selects. He *does* write, far more than Jesus does in the New Testament. But God and Jesus, like any human rhetor, typically rely on oral rhetoric to convince and persuade. The Apostle Paul emphasizes this point in the New Testament, concluding that "faith comes from what is heard" when Jesus's gospel is preached (Rom 10:17).

Intriguingly, narrative portrayals of Jesus's speeches include some notable exceptions to his otherwise neutralized "sayings," attempts to signal how Jesus may have sounded when he spoke. Matthew's Jesus cries out "in a loud voice" (27:50) just as Mark's Jesus does (15:34), as he somewhat mysteriously asks God why he has been forsaken, quoting Psalms 22:1 in the very clutch of his death throes (Matt 7:46). The volume and tenor of his voice is the same at the end of Luke's Gospel, though there Jesus does not cry out with a Psalms quotation (23:46). Jesus's tormented death-cry entirely disappears in John's Gospel, replaced simply by Jesus's flat declaration, "It is finished" (19:30), delivered, apparently, as much to himself as to anyone around him, except, of course, God, who already knew Jesus would be crucified and had sent him into the world for that purpose. The indefinite "it" in that declaration can refer as much to to Jesus's mission as it does to his own human life.

In another rare instance of a narrator's editorial commentary, Mark's Jesus "sternly charge[s]" the leper he heals not to tell others that Jesus has performed this act: "See that you say nothing to any one; but go, show yourself to a priest, and offer for your cleansing what Moses commanded, for a proof to the people" (Mark 1:43–44). In fact, the Jesus of Mark's Gospel repeatedly charges those he helps to keep his actions secret. This Jesus may have spoken in an anger that matched the way "he looked" and "grieved at ... the hardness of heart" of those in the synagogue when he heals a man's withered hand on the Sabbath (Mark 3:5). Mark's Jesus even becomes "indignant" when his disciples "rebuked" those who brought their children to "touch" Jesus: "Let the children come to me, do not hinder them; for to such [children] belongs the kingdom of God. Truly, I say to you, whoever does not receive the kingdom of God like a child shall not enter it" (10:14–15).

These apparent modifications, whoever made them, to signal how Jesus's speech sounds are rare. Jesus's manner of delivery and gestures, perhaps more than God's, usually remains left to a reader's own imagination. These narrative "blanks," of course, can make the styles Jesus or God adopt all the more important to their rhetorical impact, forcing readers to infer a great deal about how they "voiced" the styles they adopted for their speeches. The sparse, laconic style Auerbach mentions, and upon which the Bible's narrators depend, seems to leave readers with little choice but to infer, guess, interpret. It is even tempting to suggest that the very absence of much detail about how God's or Jesus's rhetoric sounded perhaps reinforces God's early dictum prohibiting the making of graven images.

Still, that dictum cannot be pressed too hard. The Bible remains lush in imagery, metaphors, parables, and paradoxes. So, too, do the speaking styles that God and Jesus adopt. These styles, however delivered, have so shaped the contours and products of the Western imagination that anyone would have a difficult time arguing that God's rhetoric is so thinly delivered that it had no impact on the numerous artists, poets, and thinkers who write under its large and lengthening shadow. It may very well be that the lacunae in God's and Jesus's manners of delivery and gestures made their rhetoric even more authoritative, more like "witnessed" events, at the same time that these blanks invited human beings to fill them with a wide variety of interpretations.

From the historical perspective of the current day, these lacunae are reminders that there has never been a *shortage* of ways humans *themselves* could *deliver* God's Word, however that Word has been understood. What may have begun as a limited circulation of hand-written scrolls and codices, or narratives embedded in stained-glass cathedral windows, soon became a printing industry all to itself that extended far beyond mere copies of the Bible. After that came all kinds of technological modes of delivering and distributing what God is thought to have said—through loudspeakers, pamphlets and fliers of biblical commentaries, radio, televised evangelists, and films, to the countless proliferation of religious websites that can be easily visited and that betoken the future delivery and distribution of what human beings of different Christian denominations think that God said and meant. Yet, as the Bible's central rhetors, God and Jesus themselves typically relied on the two technologies still central to the delivery of communications even in our own, more technologized lives today—the spoken and written word.

By the same token, the art of memory human rhetors have relied on and transformed over the centuries has little apparent relevance for God's rhetoric. In Homer's and Hesiod's times, no one had yet likened memory to any written record.[31] Even if we parse the concept as Plato did, wherein to *re-member* was to rejoin and participate once again in the divine realm of the human soul before it lost its wings and fell into time, history, and the corporeal body,[32] that parsing did not alleviate Plato's suspicions of the written word and did not make memory one of the biblical God's own concerns. Given His portrayal in the Bible as a rhetor, God would have no need to memorize any argument, prediction, or instruction He offers to His human inventions. He would need no artificial system like the famous one outlined for rhetors in the *ad Herrennium*. No critic of His rhetoric can even speak of what God remembers from His past, since the past did not exist until He invented it *for* and *with* His human likenesses.

Still, any careful study of God's rhetoric will notice what seem like intriguing lapses in God's memory. It seems that God forgot to make the serpent non-verbal like all the other animals in Eden, or to tell His human likenesses about that omission. Certainly, He would have known what the serpent could do with the rhetorical capacity it possessed. Yet God seems utterly unsurprised when He learns how Eve was persuaded to eat from the forbidden tree. This response may, of course, be another of God's many dark ironies; for it has catastrophic consequences for His human likenesses. So, too, does God's apparent forgetfulness about the obvious flaws and limitations in His human inventions. He mentions them later, before the flood He decrees. Yet, given His assumed omniscience, God must have known His own breath would not keep His fleshly creatures alive forever. That same omniscience collides with His apparent forgetting that the humans were *not* fully persuadable; that they would forget His exhortations and covenants; that they were made to possess in some degree His own symbolic-rhetorical abilities and would use these abilities to argue with and resist Him. Again, neither God's direct speeches nor the narrators' accounts can resolve the question of whether this was divine amnesia or further instances of God's own delight in irony, wherein He could continue to speak and act as if He

---

31. Curtius, *European Literature and the Latin Middle Ages*, 304.
32. Plato, *Phaedrus*, 246a–249b.

did not know any of this about His likenesses, or "be" present and then "absent," as He willed.

The biblical narrators do, however, show that God sometimes needs reminders, tokens or signs which He Himself makes. The rainbow sign after the great deluge serves as a covenant-argument to Noah and to all future human and animal life of God's promise that "the waters shall never again become a flood to destroy all flesh" (Gen 9:15). But the rainbow as a rhetorical sign also seems necessary to remind God of His promise not to perform this same destructive act: "When the bow is in the clouds, I will look upon it and remember the everlasting covenant between God and every living creature of all flesh that is upon the earth" (Gen 9:16). Why, it may be asked, would God *need* to remind Himself of His own covenant-argument with Noah unless He can forget it? For many Christian believers, certainly, the rainbow is not a rhetorical sign to support God's covenant-argument with humankind; it is rather a sign to remind human beings, *not* God, of the promise made. That interpretation, however justified when this passage is read as scripture, not as rhetoric, depends upon glossing over what God is shown to say about this sign. God will see the rainbow and, seeing it, will be reminded of His covenant-argument with Noah. So, if the speech is to be trusted, which goes directly to God's invented ethos, God has a memory that sometimes needs a supplement.

God seems to forget His covenant-argument with Abraham, too. God's promise that Abraham shall have an heir by his wife, Sarah, has not yet been kept by the time Abraham turns ninety-nine and is ordered to circumcise all his descendants as a sign of God's covenant. Abraham even complains about his predicament (Gen 17:1–9). Another year passes before Sarah gives birth to Isaac, Abraham's heir from Sarah (Gen 21:5).

In many respects, perhaps the most cruel instance of God's apparent amnesia is the long delay in delivering His people from their bondage in Egypt. Four centuries had passed since Joseph's death in Egypt, while Israel's population had greatly multiplied—so much that the Hebrews posed a security threat to Egypt's imperial ambitions, so God's chosen people become enslaved and suffer greatly (Exod 1). Only as Israel "groaned under their [Egyptians'] bondage and cried out for help" does God hear them and, the narrator relents, remember "his covenant with Abraham, with Isaac, and with Jacob" (Exod 2:23–25). It is certainly strange that this God, who has lavished so much attention on Abraham's descendants, only recalls His covenant-argument with them during Israel's enslavement. Strange, too, is how God forgets that Moses, whom He calls to deliver Israel out of slavery, was not raised as one of Abraham's descendants and is not circumcised, a glaring detail that almost leads God to kill Moses (Exod 5:24).

Moments of God's forgetfulness can be seen in the New Testament as well. There, Jesus's plaintive cry from the cross in Mark's Gospel reappears in Matthew's (27:46), "My God, my God, why hast thou forsaken me?" The cry would suggest that God has forgotten that He has left His own "son" to suffer for nine hours and die in a most humiliating way. True, God's forsaking His chosen people, individually and collectively, is a common theme in the Old Testament. It may very well be that His apparent lapses in memory, His forgetting of His people, of those individuals He calls, and even His own reputed "son," is part of His mysterious ethos as a divine rhetor. Perhaps, too, these strange lapses are clearly signaled in the mysterious meanings of the name, "Yahweh," first justified to Moses to suggest that God's time, and God's memory, is not the same as His human likenesses'. The human audiences for His rhetoric can never be certain if or when He will carry out what He predicts, or when or whether He will make good on His threats or promises, or if He will manifest Himself and intervene *at all*.

If we again step back from God's rhetoric, as the Bible narrators represent it, we may certainly see that in many undeniable ways the entire Bible *is* God's memory, His remembering, and reminding of those human likenesses He makes as His own. This view depends on our seeing God's rhetoric as primarily narrative in form, but not as "history" in the strictly naïve sense we think of it today—as just reported facts. God's rhetoric, developed significantly as narrative, as some scholars argue, is His attempt to invest an entire community with a sense of itself and its past, a collective memory intended to be projected into the future.[33] In other words, "[t]he purpose of Biblical narratives was to remember the national history and through memory to know YHWH the God of Israel." "The verb *zakhar*, 'remember,'" as one scholar notes, appears 169 times in the Bible, "nearly always with Israel or God as the subject."[34] While this God, as shown in both Christian and Hebrew Bibles, may not harken back to any knowable past for Himself, once human likenesses are invented, so is the history into which He often penetrates, so that "[m]emory and repetition make the past live again."[35] That may very well be the case for the biblical God as much as it is for Israel, who repeatedly forgets what God has tried to persuade them to do and believe, and God, who must repeat and remind Israel of what His covenant-arguments should and must mean to them.

---

33. Patrick and Scult, *Rhetoric and Biblical Interpretation*, 59. In these closing comments, I am particularly indebted to Patrick and Scult's excellent analyses of the Bible as rhetorical and forensic narrative, 29–67.

34. Josipovici, *Book of God*, 140.

35. Ibid., 150.

This rhetorical purpose may help all readers understand why the Bible's narratives retell Israel's forsaking God's laws and resisting His rhetoric, some showing Israel in most unflattering ways. Certain figures ceased to be persuaded by God's arguments or forgot about them and are put on trial for their failings and judged accordingly. God's rhetorical aim in such "forensic narratives" is to remind His human likenesses of what can happen when they ignore His exhortations or forget or doubt them. To the extent that Israel's God has become, along with Jesus, the popular composite God of so many American Christians, His narratives serve as well to help readers remember human history and, through memory, come to understand once again, and always, that God is the God of all, and not simply of Israel.

This view, though, may not help believers or non-believers make sense of God's apparent memory lapses. For modern historical critics, these lapses may arise because of how the Bible was spliced together from copies made and redacted by various, error-prone, ideologically motivated human hands. Maybe God, in all His omniscience, planned these lapses and incongruities in the whole story the Bible tells. That we must continue to interpret and re-interpret God's speeches in each generation, that we must hear so many re-claim so often God's words and their meanings, that we must be exhorted to remember again and again what God argues—these outcomes raise the final, and most difficult, question to be addressed: Can humans *dare* to evaluate God's rhetoric? Is or was His rhetoric ever *that* persuasive, since the Bible's narratives keep showing us how hard is was for Israel to believe the very God who made them a people, and how hard it is for other peoples to remain persuaded since? This is the final, albeit complicated, question to be explored.

8

Can God's Rhetoric Be Judged?

The Dilemmas of Criteria

To ask if the biblical God's rhetoric can be judged as human beings judge each other's rhetoric—a daring act already made in previous chapters—is not quite the same as asking whether the Bible itself, taken as a single, "sacred" book, can be judged as rhetoric. Even if we suppose that the entire Bible's *narratio* is God's remembering of His history with human likenesses, including His efforts to exhort and persuade them (a point made in the last chapter), that supposition does not necessarily entail a judgment about the effectiveness of God's rhetoric as directly presented within the narratives and other discourses that make up that history. While the veracity and factuality of biblical "history" has been an issue addressed for a very long time, and even within rhetorical criticism of the Bible,[1] this is not the question this chapter attempts to address.

In previous chapters on God's rhetorical inventiveness, how He argues and develops His arguments, including Jesus as His final covenant-argument, we have seen how He attempts to reason with His likenesses, making and supporting claims, and the frequent assertion of His own invented ethos as sufficient grounds for what He exhorts His various audiences to do and believe. Previous chapters have treated God's theophanies as rhetorical

---

1. On this point, for example, see Sutherland, "History, Truth, and Narrative," 105–11; Trigg, "Tales Artfully Spun," 117–32; and Kennedy, "'Truth' and 'Rhetoric' in the Pauline *Epistles*," 195–202.

strategies, even when the clear purpose of some of these theophanies is to threaten violence or enact it against His likenesses when they fail to stay convinced or persuaded. I have also noted some of the less than reasonable assumptions upon which some of these arguments rest. There, too, we noted that some of God's rhetorical tactics have, since Aristotle, come to be classified as fallacies in logic textbook after logic textbook. These were already judgments to be sure, made in advance of this chapter, and based on admittedly logical criteria long adopted to assess human arguments.

Yet, even as I made these judgments, I clearly begged the question of whether God's rhetoric, including His arguments—since "rhetoric" has a wider scope than "argumentation" per se—can be judged at all, as if to presume some *grand consensus* on the actual criteria any human argument, oral or written, must meet to be considered "good" has been achieved. But, admittedly, no such consensus exists among critics and scholars of rhetoric or argumentation. So we must then ask, why not?

Before his death in 2005, Wayne C. Booth pointedly acknowledged that sifting "good rhetoric from bad" is far "more complicated" than anyone supposes.[2] The complications, doubtless, turn upon shifting definitions of what "rhetoric" and "argument" mean, whether in isolation or conflated, whether as "process" or "product," and what criteria should be applied for judging either of them. For what is a critic of rhetoric to judge? Whether the rhetoric is fallacy-free, lathered in evidence, and tightly bound to the canons of logic, inference, and coherence, the traditional criteria for my own, earlier assessments? Whether the rhetor has been inventive, taking a fresh approach to an old issue, or discovering new arguments and evidence, even a new issue? Whether a rhetor's ethos is to be trusted? Or is the rhetoric to be judged by its structure, its style, or how well it achieves its desired effects? Or by whom is to be affected? What type of auditors or readers? A specific group all captive to a particular ideology, a motley of persons pulled in unpredictable ways by passions and prejudices and intellectual vagaries, or those reasonable, competent human beings who, in any age or place, make up what's been controversially called the "universal audience."[3]

---

2. Booth, *Rhetoric of Rhetoric*, 39. In his chapter on judging rhetoric, Booth bases his own judgments on largely ethical criteria, leading him to categorize rhetorical acts as "win rhetoric," "bargain rhetoric," and "listening rhetoric," and different sub-types of each, 39–54.

3. Perelman and Olbrechts-Tyteca, *New Rhetoric*, 30–35. For further commentary on the concept of "universal audience," see Crosswhite, "Universality in Rhetoric," 157–73; Gross, "Theory of Rhetorical Audience," 203–11; Jorgenson, "Interpreting Perelman's Universal Audience," 11–19.

All of these competing dimensions, vying for a critic's attention and evaluation, might explain why a full, consensus-making *"theory of argument"* or rhetoric has yet to be formulated. Some scholars and critics are unsure about whether such a consensus is even necessary, much less desirable.[4] Some solely devoted to the study of argumentation have been insisting that the part of rhetoric known since Aristotle as *logos*, as reasoning—that part which encompasses argumentation per se—has for too long been described and judged by the canons of formal, deductive, even syllogistic "structure," rather than by its practical purpose, "rational persuasion," persuasion without recourse to "force, flattery, or trickery . . ."[5] Taking a more practical, less logic-dominated approach, these scholars may claim that an argument not only *be* rational but *look* rational as well, though this apparent rationality is more likely to be "informal" than formal, presenting premises that are relatively acceptable and true, reasonably sufficient and relevant, all within a "dialectical" framework that acknowledges and tries to address the most standard objections opponents might bring against the arguments made.[6]

This purpose-driven, "pragmatic" view of the informal arguments humans *actually* make, a view that erroneously separates argumentation from rhetoric,[7] has emerged in part as a reaction to and a replacement of logical, objective criteria apparently adopted for centuries to assess human efforts to persuade each other, efforts shaped by an increasingly mathematical view of logic and the overwhelming prestige enjoyed at least since Descartes by

---

4. Boger, "Subordinating Truth,"188.
5. Johnson, *Manifest Rationality*, 152–54, 150.
6. Ibid., 164, 180–216.
7. Ibid., 163. Johnson's separation of argumentation from rhetoric rests on his view that a rhetorical text, while every bit as manifestly rational as a written argument, does not obligate a rhetor to have a dialectical tier wherein opposing arguments are addressed and so a rhetor may suppress these arguments. Yet the clear link between rhetoric and dialectic arises on the opening page of Aristotle's *Rhetoric*, where rhetoric becomes dialectic's ambiguous "counterpart" or "double," since they both address "matters that are in a manner within the cognizance of all men and not confined to any special science" (1.i). The necessity of a rhetor's ability in "proving opposites, as in logical arguments" arises from a rhetor's attempt to discover "the real state of the case" so that it "may not escape" a rhetor's attention and "to counteract false arguments, if *another* [rhetor] makes an unfair use of them" (1.i.12, emphasis added). This rhetorical preparation may very likely have originated with the sophists' use of *dissoi logoi*, known in Shakespeare's day under the Latin phrase, *disputatio in utramque partem*—arguing opposite sides of a question. It is a strategy Cicero's Crassus praises in his *De Oratore* as a crucial part of a rhetor's inventing arguments (vol. 3, 1.36.158–59). Tindale has provided a fairly detailed description of this sophistic practice in *Reason's Dark Champions*, 99–112. In any event, classical theorists of rhetoric did not ignore the impact of opponents on any rhetor's argument. Johnson's severance ignores, if it does not altogether dismiss, the long history of rhetoric in which theorists suggest otherwise.

scientific reasoning and demonstration.[8] Yet informal logicians' ideas have provoked some traditional philosophers to ask how such arguments may be judged as a contribution to human well-being and democratic values if traditional standards of logical validity and objective truth are abandoned for a more historically, socially sensitive criteria that only demands an argument be acceptable and well-suited to the contingencies of time, place, and audience. If this is the bar to be met or cleared, how can racist and sexist arguments be judged as false, illogical, inhumane, and non-democratic?[9] If the judgment of human arguments abandons "formal logic's adherence to soundness" and "platonistic absolutism" as "irrelevant" so they may support and endorse "informal logic's adherence to [audience] acceptability," such an informal approach knowingly or unknowingly falls victim to "a pernicious relativism" that makes their theories and criteria "duplicit" and "useless" in trying to "settle disputes . . . in an increasingly polarized world."[10]

These seemingly "polarized" views of how to judge human arguments, or even the rhetoric into which such arguments are embedded, if taken too seriously, may fall victim to the either/or fallacy. Yet the schism about what sort of criteria to apply makes it all too clear that evaluating human rhetoric is by no means a settled matter, any more than evaluating God's rhetoric would be.

Despite Jesus's famous injunction that we should not judge lest we be judged ourselves (Matt 7:1–2), humans remain a judgmental species; and humans' rhetorical acts, oral, written, visual, or multimodal, have always been and are likely always to be subject to judgment despite any achieved consensus about how this judgment may be reached. That said, judging human rhetoric is one thing. Judging God's is quite another. Even if we grant that the Bible has been composed, arranged, compiled, and edited by many human hands—and some devout readers may not willingly grant this—a host of problems in evaluating God's eloquence would still remain to be overcome.

Such problems are hardly new to judging human rhetoric. Writing to his brother, Quintus, Cicero conspicuously remarks on the oddity that so few men have excelled in their eloquent pleadings while many more have attained greatness in all the other human arts.[11] Cicero believed then, as perhaps Booth came to believe much latter, that the main reason Rome lacked

---

8. Johnson, *Manifest Rationality*, 104–107; Perelman and Olbrechts-Tyteca, *New Rhetoric*, 1–4.

9. Boger, "Subordinating Truth," 189–91.

10. Ibid., 229.

11. Cicero, *De Oratore*, vol. 3, 1. ii–iii. 6–12.

great rhetors was because the art is so difficult to master—a claim he goes to great lengths to defend throughout his most mature work on rhetoric, *De Oratore*. Judging rhetoric is not any easier to do than mastering it, since such judgments would depend on criteria that could be applied to any and all arguments—criteria that so far have proved as elusive as those by which to define "argument" and "rhetoric" themselves.[12]

This problem, coming so late in this book, may understandably puzzle, if not frustrate, readers. The last seven chapters have assumed that, as a rhetor, the biblical God is shown to *argue*; and that how He invents and develops arguments, selects and arranges them, and adopts a style for them can be described, analyzed, and sometimes assessed based at least on traditional, logical criteria. Those chapters, of course, were preceded by a very broad, working definition of rhetoric that allowed for a spectrum showing a qualitative range in this art's practice, from the most noble and exalted efforts to argue and persuade to far more shoddy, and even violent, efforts to achieve a rhetor's goal.

Yet that chapter came with caveats: that throughout rhetoric's long history many definitions have been offered and justified—so many these definitions at least partly account for rhetoric's having a "history" at all—and that not all would agree with the definition I outlined and justified, just as all would not agree with how that definition would be applied to God's rhetoric in later chapters. In short, in anticipating *this* chapter, I did not want to assume the definition I offered or its application rested on any general consensus among rhetorical critics or critics of the Bible's rhetoric specifically.

Yet I must now confront the more difficult question of why we do not have a consensus on criteria for judging human rhetoric and the not unrelated question of whether we have *ever* had such criteria at all. One might devote an entire book—doubtless a lengthy one—to these questions. Any scholar or critic devoted to this project might soon find that any given historical era may be marked by two or more contending definitions of rhetoric, or two or more sets of criteria to judge the quality of that rhetoric; and

---

12. See Aguayo and Steffensmeir, *Readings on Argumentation*, 69–99, 143–90, and 191–247. Readers may also consult Black's assessment of what is called the "judicial" aim of some rhetorical critics, especially rhetorical critics who consider themselves and their methods "Neo-Aristotelian," *Rhetorical Criticism*, 60–75, 77–90. The judicial aim of Neo-Aristotelian critics, Black argues, is to judge the "quality" of the texts and speeches they analyze, drawing upon Aristotle's primary criterion: the rhetor's intended "effect" on a specific audience. But Neo-Aristotelians' singular focus on a rhetor's effect on the *immediate* audience typically ignores or fails to judge the quality of what a rhetor argues, as well as why some rhetors' arguments may still be regarded and judged effective and of high quality once the immediate circumstances and the immediate auditors have long since disappeared or are no longer relevant.

might very likely discover that these two basic issues have propelled efforts both to revise and usurp this or that definition or this or that set of criteria. The basic empirical facts of these revisions and usurpations could, at least in part, be a way to trace rhetoric's history as a humanistic art of study.[13]

Even more to the point, Aristotle and Cicero probably would not have needed to wait for any *consensus* before they articulated or applied a definition of rhetoric. Nor did they *wait*. More specifically, a practicing rhetor in ancient Athens or Rome would have hoped for and actively sought consensus from any audience he hoped to persuade. A "rhetorical consensus" would have meant that a rhetor had managed to get as many as persuaded as possible so the issue might be resolved. This "rhetorical consensus" would not likely have included *every* auditor. Depending on whether a rhetor was arguing in a court of law or in a political assembly, the sheer number of those persuaded might not be as important as *who in particular was persuaded and to what extent*. That would be a far cry from trying to achieve a "scientific consensus" that is likely to seem unrealistic for the study of either rhetoric or argument.

But *why* should this be so? One very broad answer could be that the difficulty in judging today's rhetoric is but a specific symptom of a larger, cultural reluctance in the West to concede any objective, actual existence to qualitative "goods" according to which we can define what human beings should do and be and what they should value.[14] The problem of sifting good rhetoric or logically sound from simply acceptable arguments for certain audiences, obviously, presumes we humans *know* and *agree* on what it is good to be and to do and what not. Yet, for the modern world, as many now recognize, each of us seems to think that no common core of goods, no "framework" of values, exists to be invoked, and this absence appears to have sunk "to the phenomenological status of unquestioned fact."[15] The difficulty of establishing a consensus on what "rhetoric" or "argument" means and how to judge either one may be but one small instance of this larger uncertainty about what may be called "good" or "bad" at all.

Such a consensus would very likely be historically complicated and burdened with many serious social, political, and ethical implications. If scholars and critics cannot reach any agreement on a useful set of criteria by which to judge mere human rhetoric, then it is certainly tempting to dismiss the entire issue of judging God's. *Yet, if that effort is surrendered, it becomes*

13. See Arrington's attempts at this history in his *Rhetoric's Agons*, though not with the singular, detailed attention either issue demands.

14. This broader question as it connects to the modern sense of selfhood and identity is pursued and examined in Taylor, *Sources of the Self*.

15. Ibid., 17.

possible to conclude that any kind of rhetoric or argument is as good or as bad as any other kind. This conclusion would add additional confirmation to the broader collapse of values that troubles so many, devout and secular alike.

In this case, "pernicious relativism" would appear triumphant, leaving no way to sort out or separate with any degree of confidence various and competing rhetorics. We could not propose any rhetorical spectrum upon which to spread out and differentiate propaganda, smears, and lies from reasoned, public deliberation based on the best available evidence, or the decisions based on these deliberations. People who read, listen, or see this or that rhetorical act would be left to accept or reject each such speech or text based only on their own pre-conceived notions, emotions, and prejudices. They would be left to decide whether the arguments flatter and reinforce what they *already* think or believe. No one, in other words, could be reasonably persuaded to change her mind or alter in any fundamental way her position on any controversy. All would be trapped in their own ideological prisons, with no hope of parole or escape.

This imprisonment could be inevitable. *Boston Globe* journalist Joe Keohane reports on a number of psychological studies that suggest most people "interpret information with an eye toward reinforcing their preexisting views," so-called "motivated reasoning."[16] As a result, when people hear, read, or are confronted with facts or ideas that challenge their preconceptions, they become threatened—so threatened they deny inconvenient facts or distort others' different ideas. On the other hand, if they hear, see, or read facts or ideas that flatter and match their preexisting beliefs, they readily accept them, however true or preposterous the facts or ideas may be. This acceptance, Keohane reports, "makes us more confident in [our] said beliefs, and even less likely to entertain facts that contradict them." If these studies' findings are, in fact, shown to be conclusive, they represent a major blow to the study of rhetoric or its teaching, or efforts to find ways to judge it.

Yet it would seem impossible to assert that human beings *never change their minds*, that they are so ideologically motivated in their reasoning or so cynical and jaded that they cannot recognize "truthful rhetoric" or, if that is too oxymoronic for the post-postmodern world, a rhetoric that tries, as Booth recommends, to "listen" to other sides in a quest to find the "truth" along with its opposed interlocutors.[17]

---

16. Keohane, "How Facts Backfire," 24–25.
17. Booth, *Rhetoric of Rhetoric*, 1.

A Taxonomy of Criteria for Judging Human Rhetoric

If we ask, as some have, why no "history of argumentation" has yet been written, we may speculate that the reason may be because, as logic became more mathematized, logicians themselves conflated "inference, argument, and implication" as logic's own "subject matters," for which there *are* "histories," so there was no need for a separate history of "argument" itself.[18] An alternative possibility, however, would be that perhaps there have been no *separate* histories of argumentation because, at least since Aristotle, arguments or "proofs," and their invention, were and have been a part of rhetoric, its *logos*. There have been *many* histories of rhetoric, though to what extent these histories treat argumentation separate from the many other facets of rhetoric's long, rich, and sometimes tedious history is a question this chapter cannot address.

A related but different question, perhaps more relevant to my concerns here, is why scholars and critics have *no written history* of how rhetoric has been judged. Rhetoric continues to flourish, as it always has—even in times when it is harshly judged or considered useless and dangerous. Even though the art of rhetoric, its "reputation," its meaning and value as a subject of study, "has risen and fallen probably more times, and more drastically, than that of other subject," except perhaps its competitor in longevity, philosophy,[19] within these historically vacillating appraisals the question of how rhetorical theorists themselves, from classical to more recent times, thought about or even addressed this crucial problem remains unanswered.

Certainly, in its two millennia history, specific rhetorical speeches and texts would have invited—even solicited—their share of judgment, and even ridicule, from auditors and readers alike. But discovering the criteria for judgments of *specific* rhetorical acts would almost surely be a difficult, if not impossible, task for any historian to undertake. The conditions would be too various. Obviously, a historian could study the "reception" and judgments of specific speeches and texts, or types of these, or specific rhetors, or types of rhetors who produced them. But to attempt this sort of study over a two thousand year history would be a massive burden and not one most historians would likely assume. And, even if this burden were to be shouldered,

---

18. Johnson, *Manifest Rationality*, 151–52 n9. Johnson cites several histories of logic, published in the years between 1961–62, and one published in 1990, but neglects to mention such works as Howell's *Logic and Rhetoric in England 1500–1700* or his follow-up book, *Eighteenth Century British Logic and Rhetoric*, or Ong's *Ramus, Method, and the Decay of Dialogue*, all which indicate the close link between logic and rhetoric.

19. Booth, *Rhetoric of Rhetoric*, 1.

and consummately borne, the results still might not demonstrate what was hoped for.

Yet, in asking if and how God's rhetoric may be judged as humans' rhetoric, we can take a speculative short-cut around these problems. In its long history, rhetoric has been defined in many ways, and some of these definitions of rhetoric held sway for a time—even in historical periods when there may have been a far greater consensus on what it was "good" to be and what not. Some—by no means *all*—of these definitions imply criteria for judging rhetoric sufficient for a rough sketch or taxonomy of different theories associated with some of the notable thinkers associated with each criteria-set. This taxonomy of theories cannot be rigid. Nor should we expect the specific figures associated with each theory represent that theory in any "pure" sense. Some theorists' definitions may imply more than one way to judge the rhetoric so defined, in the very same or in different works. Others are more eclectic. Certainly, too, different ways of defining and judging rhetoric may co-exist in the same time-span and arise as dialectical counters to rivals and predecessors. My speculative taxonomy, however, is far too schematic to delineate nuances and subtleties in these ideas. It willingly sacrifices depth to the more practical aim of breadth and a rough chronology. Hardly complete, then, and admittedly tentative, my taxonomy is best thought of as a heuristic, a way to discover, if possible, what theoretical criteria, if any, might be applied to the biblical God's rhetoric.

If it is to be asked why or how any theoretical definition of rhetoric could be said to imply a set of criteria for judging the rhetoric so defined, or provide enough detail to extrapolate such criteria, the answer, tentative as it must be, is that these various definitions suggest both what is and what is *not* important for the terms adopted, as these terms narrow down and focus attention on what the terms emphasize and in what order. There is, to recall Kenneth Burke's "dramatistic" explanation of definition as a symbolic act, an ingenious negativity that pervades the selecting, narrowing, and ordering of the verbal elements of any definition, however "positively" it exists as a definition.[20] The evaluative criteria that would apply, even if not made explicit, would seem negatively implicit in the very definitions of rhetoric itself.

So the first approach to judging rhetoric may be called the ***Affective Theory***, perhaps the oldest of all the criteria-sets invoked to judge a rhetor's success. Glimpses of this theory may be noticed in the so-called ancient Greek sophists of fifth century BCE Greece. Gorgias and Protagoras seem

---

20. Burke, *Language as Symbolic Action*, 464–69.

to have taken this view. Other thinkers like Nietzsche in the nineteenth century, and some thinkers in later centuries, appear sympathetic to it.

This theory holds that a rhetor's argument tries to induce auditors to feel what a rhetor believes they should or must feel. Rhetors would not need to worry about making arguments based on "true" knowledge because, in many cases, that "truth" cannot be known to human beings or communicated exactly in language. Instead, human beings rely on widely-held opinions and widely accepted values and beliefs to decide whose rhetoric they should accept, believe, and act on. So a rhetor must try to invent an argument that moves an audience to decide an issue based on these accepted opinions and beliefs. Such a rhetor often exploits emotions, passions and adopts vivid, quasi-poetic language, and often depends on arguments based on probabilities. The best argument, then, is the one that sways or affects an audience to accept a given rhetor's position, regardless of whether the position is grounded in truth or even whether the rhetor's argued perspective is in an audience's best interests to accept.

Another approach for evaluating rhetoric may be described as the **Civic Function Theory**, seen in the Greek instructor of rhetoric, Isocrates (fifth century BCE), and later adopted by Cicero, Quintilian, and the many they have influenced over the centuries. This theory holds that the *best rhetoric* is that which sways public opinion to take a position that favors the maintenance and improvement of the entire state or community. Here, too, a rhetor does not always have to know what that "truth" is or what the "facts" are and may resort to arguing from probabilities, using quasi-poetic language, and so forth. In some cases, a rhetor may even have to "lie" to serve and protect the community's values and interests.

The crucial criterion here is that the best rhetoric has the entire community's or state's values, interests, and beliefs in mind. A state's survival and maintenance depend on making such decisions about war and peace, taxes, and other such issues that affect large numbers of citizens. Rhetors' success or failure would turn upon their ability to persuade audiences what is in the best interests of the state or community to believe, value, or do, avoiding issues that are too philosophical or too removed from the day-to-day business of the life of citizens.

Almost in direct reaction to both of these approaches is the **Truth and Knowledge Theory**. Adopted by Plato and many others since, this theory holds that the *best rhetoric* depends on a systematic reasoning process to find out the "truest" claim to argue, not the most probable one. This "truthful" claim the rhetor then tries to "clothe" in the most powerful language possible to persuade the auditors to accept what is good and best for the state or community, regardless of what members of that state or community already believe or value. This theory assumes the actual "truth" can always, if only eventually, be found, so its advocates typically reject both the **Affective** and **Civic Function** theories as being misleading, unethical, false, or all three.

Another way of evaluating rhetoric, at least partly found in Aristotle and the many thinkers he has influenced over the centuries, is the *Instrumental Theory of Persuasion*. In this theory, the *best rhetoric* depends on being able to discover the available means (or "instruments") to persuade audiences for any given issue, *even if a rhetor fails to attain the goal of persuasion*. Unlike his teacher, Plato, Aristotle understood, as did the sophists before him and the Roman thinkers after the sophists, that rhetors could not always be expected to find out the "truth" before they tried to persuade others. The pressures of time and the difficulties of recovering whatever evidence would be necessary to argue a truthful claim mitigate a rhetor's task and hence may be "unavailable." Certainly, if true knowledge or "facts" are attainable, rhetors should find and exploit both in arguing a particular case, since these are the easiest, most ethically responsible arguments to make. Yet this is not always possible or even likely, so a rhetor may have to argue based on probable reasoning and accepted opinions, without which no issue could be resolved and no action, taken. In either case, the best rhetor seeks to achieve persuasion through whatever means are available. If he does *only that*, his rhetoric will be judged effective, even if an audience is not always persuaded. From this viewpoint, the effectiveness of a speech or a text turns upon a rhetor's inventive powers, but not necessarily the practical or affective outcome of that inventiveness—persuasion.

Still another approach, adopted by Augustine and other Christian thinkers over the centuries, is the *Divine Truth Theory*. This view holds that, in matters of controversy, the source of a rhetor's "truth" already exists to be found in a sacred text based on a supernatural being or agent, ready to be cited to persuade audiences to feel, act, or believe as the sacred text suggests or commands. For Augustine and those he influenced, rhetoric, as Aristotle believed, is a means to an end but, in this case, to be adopted to defend the authority of the sacred truth against its critics and opponents or to explain and teach others what that sacred truth is and to persuade them to accept that truth as final and binding.

Another view of evaluation, very similar to the **Truth and Knowledge** theory, is the *Logical Validity Theory*. Adopted by various Enlightenment thinkers and later those influenced by mathematics, logic, and science, this theory is difficult to summarize. Basically, it holds that the *best rhetoric* makes a highly rational case to sway public opinion, with the argument following as closely as possible the strictly formal, logical path from true premises to a true conclusion. The best rhetors would not only follow this path but would also have to know the "facts" to be able to argue and persuade and avoid fallacious reasoning, emotional appeals, arguments based on arbitrary value-systems, or sacred texts or accepted authorities. They would have no need for heightened or quasi-poetic language and would avoid logical inconsistencies, contradictions, and fallacies to be considered persuasive and hence successful. Here, rhetoric would not only have to be grounded in truth and rationality, but also try to aspire to the scrupulosity of scientific demonstrations.

In reaction to those who have embraced the **Logical Validity Theory** are those who hold to the **Informal Logic or "Good Reasons" Theory**, mentioned above. This theory can be found in such twentieth century thinkers as Chaim Perelman and Stephen Toulmin, both of whom have influenced later informal argumentation theorists and scholars. This theory holds that *most arguments human beings make do not follow the rational, mathematical model of logicians, philosophers, or scientists.* In fact, most arguments in law courts, universities, and ordinary life are "informal," and the *best informal arguments* are ones in which the arguer seeks different audiences' acceptance of a claim based on reasons, evidence, and appeals from different hierarchies of values. The "criteria" for judging these different, and various, arguments are relative to the kind of argument made and the criteria acceptable for any situation, profession, or academic discipline—legal, scientific, political—and the auditors or readers for such arguments. Those who adopt this view of evaluating rhetoric forcefully reject the assumption that rhetoric, as humans use it, must follow the linear rigors and formalities of mathematical or scientific proofs, except in those fields of study where this kind of argument is expected and thus required.

The final evaluation theory shows up in a number of influential thinkers in America and Europe and is closely associated with such names as Stanley Fish, Richard Rorty, and Michel Foucault, not to mention some feminist thinkers. For lack of a better term, this **Postmodern Theory** defies easy or convenient summary, in part because postmodern thinkers dislike and often strenuously resist being defined or categorized or consider the very acts of definition and categorization suspect. Still, certain themes emerge in their thinking. In its strongest form, postmodern advocates argue that *no absolute* criteria for judging rhetoric exists or ever will be found. An argument succeeds or fails based on the accepted values and beliefs of authorities at a specific historical moment within a local context. Those which succeed are often made by agents in positions of power and authority who often control the means of producing and disseminating arguments and often ignore or reduce to invisibility other, marginal arguments.

In one sense, the **Postmodern Theory** almost brings us full circle, back to the *Affective Theory* the ancient sophists hinted at, and back to Nietzsche's thinking, so important to postmodernist views. It is quite hard to say, though, how such a view of evaluating rhetoric could be applied, since no one set of criteria or a single criterion can be identified for judging rhetoric, including the rhetorics adopted by postmodern thinkers themselves. From what I have read of these authors, they resist applying any sort of model or paradigm for either interpretation or judgment of an argument. For many of them, all rhetoric is limited by and a "construct" of either local values and interests or of values and interests that authoritative powers are bent on imposing to resolve local issues.

Once again, mine is broad taxonomy that groups together very complex clusters of ideas proposed by a wide range of authors. At the very least, though, the categories may help readers see that standards for evaluating human rhetoric vary, sometimes greatly, sometimes narrowly. The classification scheme also suggests that evaluating rhetoric is itself an issue, a controversy, among critics, scholars, and other experts. As an issue, it has a history even if that history has so far eluded explicit documentation and has inspired competing rhetorical claims within very wide and very narrow circles of experts who have attempted to address it.

The Problems in Judging God's Rhetoric

These competing views of how to evaluate rhetoric have, except in one case, all assumed that the *source and origin* of rhetoric is another, wholly fallible human being, and *not* a divine agent or person. Recognizing that *one* assumption alone would force anyone to hesitate when it comes to judging God's rhetoric in the Bible. On its face, the **Divine Truth Theory** should be the one and only criteria-set best applied to God's eloquence. Yet, in this case, judging God's persuasiveness would mean, among other things, accepting the premise that He and He alone is the *sole source and origin* of what He argues just as He is the sole source and origin of everything else. Some Christians would subscribe to this premise, believing that the Bible is the *actual word* of God; that God is the supernatural origin of all that the Bible contains, its language entire. For these Christians, what God says and what the Bible says He says are *one and the same, literally true and inerrant*. For these readers, the **Divine Truth Theory** is the only approach to evaluation that would apply and, further, to apply it at all seems ridiculously, if not viciously, circular. For these readers, too, the rest of this chapter is pointless.

No mere human being could possibly presume to judge God's rhetoric. The issue, then, is moot, if not overtly perverse and impious.

For many other Christian readers, the Bible has been seen as God's word revealed to human beings *without necessarily believing He wrote every word in it or without taking every word written as literally true or inerrant.* For these believers, God has *inspired* human beings to invent the language of the Bible, including God's and Jesus's speeches, just as other gods have inspired human beings to invent other sacred texts, and certainly not just sacred texts—poets for centuries have invoked and called upon the Muses for divine inspiration and guidance as they composed. Yet the question that lingers even here is what "theory" of truth and accuracy on this Christian reader's part would justify the distinction and guide that reader's efforts to sift God's literal from His figurative truth or to identify any errors in the truth asserted.

The agnostic stance I have taken toward God's and the Bible's "truth" prohibits completely ruling out of hand either of these views. It is admittedly difficult to *know* if what the Bible's narrators wrote down as God's speech, or Jesus's, was *actually said* to them or derived in some other fashion. Modern historical criticism of the Bible, we should recall, has for some time attempted to remind Christians of all denominations that the single book that lies on their coffee table or rests open on a church podium is not the *actual* word of God, recorded or revealed, but a textual *construction* of authors, translators, editors and redactors who have taken many liberties in inscribing and interpreting what they or someone else thought they heard God say or write, or what they thought Jesus said, and who have drawn upon or hypothesized many other ancient sources, traditions, and texts to complete the Bible's construction. But many American Christians, whether they have read much of the Bible or none at all, would not happily concede to this view. In fact, they might readily and vigorously oppose it as wholly contrary to the Bible they have experienced, through whatever media or in whatever context.

As an agnostic critic, I would sacrifice all credibility if I denied the valuable human efforts that went into the Bible's *construction*, without which we would not have the single book we read and argue about even now. By the same token, as a critic of God's rhetoric, I cannot be sure if the speeches and gestures analyzed and described in previous chapters belong to an actual divine being(s) or not.

However, it is also next to impossible to read and study God's rhetoric, much less judge it, as if it were just a patch-work of genres and texts. Whatever else the Bible may or may not be, God's and Jesus's rhetoric is, as I have argued from the start, *written* into the text. However they got there, or wherever they came from, or whoever may have written them down, edited, or redacted them, God's and Jesus's speeches and gestures *do appear* in the Bible and *are shown to appear there*, to be read as scripture, as literature and, I would argue, as rhetoric. Beyond this self-evident point, though, is the assumption that it is far easier to describe, analyze, and judge their divine rhetoric if their speeches and gestures are treated as revealed or inspired, than it is to assume they were directly recorded as they came from God's or Jesus's own lips.

To see the Bible as inspired or revelatory language further and rightly assumes that human beings do not simply distinguish themselves from other species through making tools or technologies. Rather, humankind, as Lewis Mumford so brilliantly puts it, is "a mind-making, self-mastering, and self-designing animal" which exploits its verbal capacities not just for inventing tools but for inventing "symbolic art"—in the form of religions' rituals, as well as literature, philosophy, architecture, painting, and sculpture.[21] Initially, Mumford believes, human beings had "to make something of [themselves]" before they could make much sense of the world they lived in or to make the tools to re-shape that world.

Mumford's insightful estimate of the importance of humankind's "mind-making" and its invention of "symbolic art" underlies Marilynne Robinson's more recent effort to rebut and correct what she considers the more "scientific," and "modern," view of mind.[22] This scientific view rejects the reality of "mind" and puts in its place the neo-Darwinian-inspired, accidental evolution of that pulpy organ called the human "brain." Robinson, of course, is a well-known novelist and an admitted, unapologetic Christian, who rightly contends that, in replacing "mind" with "brain," some modern, pseudo-scientific thinkers have been largely motivated by their rejection of metaphysical and religious ideas that predated by thousands of years modern science's emergence and, unlike science, appeared in many different parts of the globe. For Robinson, considerable "proof for the existence of mind" can be found in the centuries of art, philosophy, literature, not to mention religions themselves.[23] To treat religion as if it were but "an element in culture and history," Robinson believes, greatly oversimplifies its nature. Worse still, it oversimplifies the human mind that invented religion and practically ignores "the vast and unconsulted literature of religious thought and testimony" to advance a modernist, ostensibly scientific view

21. Here, I follow Mumford's view in *Myth of the Machine*, vol. 1, 9–10. Mumford, of course, is fully aware that the human capacity for symbolic expression had both benign as well as irrational impulses, 10–13.

22. Robinson, *Absence of Mind*, xiv–xv, 74–75.

23. Ibid., 120.

of our "true" human nature,[24] a human nature now bereft of the very "mind-making" inventiveness that Mumford identified not so long ago.

Robinson's and Mumford's arguments would not presumably rule out the rhetorical qualities of God's speeches as symbolic art, as mind-making. God's revelations to human beings across all denominations assume that the very the idea of a "god" lies in that god's possible "revealability" embedded in the Indo-European root, "*deiwos*," that which is "luminous" and "celestial."[25] Still, it may not be enough to say that "the rhetoric of sacred language" in the Bible or in other religious works is largely imaginative, asserting absolute "truth" without regard for thinking or human reasoning.[26] Nor does it suffice to suppose that religious language is "pre-rational" either—that is, a rhetoric which seeks to persuade humans, not through "logic," through reasons and evidence, but by appealing only to humans' imaginations, and to the problems which beset a religion's own communities at any given time.[27]

If this is how we are to define the religious rhetoric of the Bible, or God's rhetoric in that Bible, it would seem ultimately incongruent with what has been assumed about this art in previous chapters. This incongruence may explain why one scholar rejects this definition, insisting that this "pre-rational" characterization of the Bible seems more appropriate to Hindu works and Greek prophecies.[28] Only the most "radical Christian rhetoric" of the Bible tries to persuade in this way. As we have seen in earlier chapters, God's rhetoric does contain arguments made of claims, data, and evidence, just as it contains appeals to human emotions and values and includes styles rich in paradox, enigma, and figurative language.

That this God reveals His truth to human likenesses has led some to describe His statements as the rhetoric of "*kerygma*," "proclamations of Christian truth" closely associated with the ancient pagan heralds who announced to listeners "news" from political leaders and from divine messengers.[29] These truth-filled "proclamations" served much the same purpose as preaching in Christianity's beginnings. One of the aims of Mark's Jesus was to utter the "good news" to his auditors, to get them to believe and accept a different way of seeing themselves in the world. His proclamations had little or nothing to do with uttering "empirical knowledge," as "news" is thought of today, but with revealing to his auditors a different mode of life and belief.

24. Ibid., 14.
25. Derrida, "Faith and Knowledge," 46.
26. Grassi, *Rhetoric as Philosophy*, 103–4.
27. Wilder, *Theopoetic*, 7.
28. Kennedy, *New Testament Interpretation through Rhetorical Criticism*, 7.
29. Montesano, "*Kairos* and *Kerygma*," 167.

In revealing God's good news, Jesus awaits his auditors' recognition of the conflicts they are living through so they will be ready to respond to and receive his divine proclamations. God's covenant-arguments may be seen in a similar way—as timely expressions of another way to live and respond.[30] Such heraldic expressions could even be connected to Greek rhetoric's *kairos*, the revelatory moment, the "right time" to utter and proclaim a truth that offers audience members another vision of the conflicted world they live in.[31]

Yet these lived moments of revealed truth often end up becoming "dogmas"—universalized assertions whose authority cannot be easily or sometimes even safely challenged.[32] Accordingly, when these timely proclamations harden into dogmas, they cease to be rooted in the lived experience of those who hear them. They become transcendent, not immanent, utterances, untethered to any lived context or historical period. Thinking of God's rhetorical proclamations as *kerygma*, however, poses its own difficulties. It is far from clear how distinct "a transcendent, metaphysical reality" assumed within a religion's "dogmas" is from the rhetorical aim of a *kerygma*, as "a persuasion to a world view."[33] Even receptive auditors might expect the proclaimed and revealed view of the world from God to be a "true" interpretation of human problems, and "true" far beyond the immediate, temporal circumstances implied by the rhetorical idea of *kairos*. Accepting this kairotic view of the biblical God's *kerygma* must soon confront the clash between a view of language that attributes to God an absoluteness in what He proclaims and a view that the language of *kerygma* is rooted in the audience's history, its communal bonds, and in the passing tensions of the temporal moment. It would be very difficult to judge God's or Jesus's proclamations of truth at all if their rhetorical force consists, not in the "transcendent, metaphysical reality" that those rhetorical proclamations herald and reveal, but simply as "a persuasion to a world view" which makes living in that world easier for the moment.

We may certainly grant that the Bible's language depends on narrative and poetic symbols rather than hard facts and elaborate syllogisms, just as

30. Ibid., 168.

31. Ibid., 168–70. For a more extensive examination of the implications, meanings, and applications of *kairos* in rhetorical thinking, see Sipora and Baumlin's *Rhetoric and Kairos*, especially Sipora's "Introduction," 1–22, and his "*Kairos*," 114–27.

32. Montesano, "*Kairos* and *Kerygma*," 176.

33. Ibid., 166–67. Montesano's argument, which I have been outlining, seems uncomfortably caught between the more relativistic, context-bound sophistic view of rhetoric and the obviously "numinous" nature and "timeless ideas" of Christian proclamations he wishes to treat as rhetorical, in the fully sophistic sense, 169–70.

we may grant that many of God's own covenant-arguments depend on His human likenesses' acknowledging His ethos as divine authority. But granting these points does not necessarily mean that God's rhetoric, or Jesus's, is not meant to reveal and proclaim truths that are trans-contextual and trans-historical. Nor does it mean that God's and Jesus's rhetoric, however poetic or narrative it may be, lacks any bases in human reason. Human rhetors may need to invent a *narratio* to state the conjectured facts in a given case, just as they need to invent signs and examples, historical and actual, to make their arguments persuasive, and to adopt a style which shines with the luster of vivid metaphors and pulses in memorable semantic and syntactic rhythms to impress upon auditors the truths they hope will persuade them.

Obviously, the Bible's rhetoric varies, in form and genre, consisting of words which address God, which name what God proclaims as sacred or profane, and what belief in such a God feels like.[34] Every part of the Bible that preaches also argues, regardless of who does the preaching or arguing. The Bible does, indeed, try to persuade non-believing auditors or readers to accept God's rhetoric and the religious metaphysics intrinsic to it, just as it urges believing audiences to hold on to and practice the religious beliefs they have already embraced.[35] Prayers and hymns to God, in the Bible as in other sacred works, remain, in the end, human exhortations *to* God or to *a* god or gods. So are exhortations *by* God or *a* god or gods to human beings.

Yet, curiously, God's own rhetoric has not received as much attention as it deserves,[36] perhaps because very few scholars became interested in the rhetoric of the Christian tradition until the 1970s.[37] On this point, though, some very basic questions remain: *whose* rhetoric have we been exploring in previous chapters and *whose* rhetoric is to be judged, by whatever criteria-set? Finding themselves confronted with religion's renewed importance, some contemporary philosophers, it seems, have certainly struggled with

---

34. Pernot, "Rhetoric of Religion," 235.

35. Ibid.

36. Ibid., 237–39. Strangely, all of Pernot's examples about the rhetorical speeches of a god or gods refer to ancient Greek deities, especially in Homer's poems. Throughout his entire article, he never makes any further explicit references to what has concerned me in this book—God's own rhetorical strategies.

37. Hinze, "Reclaiming Rhetoric in the Christian Tradition." Professor Hinze offers a brief overview of the most important scholars who took a variety of rhetorical approaches to the Bible and the Christian tradition, all based, as Hinze correctly claims, on the "operative assumption . . . that, if one can identify the chosen rhetorical strategy, one can better determine the meaning of the text [Bible] for the author, and perhaps the audience." Hinze goes on to argue for an appreciation of the benefits of recognizing rhetoric's importance to the "dialogue" embedded in the many different traditions, approaches, and interpretations of Christianity.

these questions, since their very efforts to name or explain God immediately confront the very "crucial and inevitable," not to mention philosophical, "distinction between what exists and is present and real" and "what on the contrary lives by the phantasmal breath of myth, by the murmur of unfounded belief"—that is, God "as an idealized anthropomorphic entity that transcends" the world of space and time humans live in and the reasoning capacities they possess[38]—the God so prevalent in American culture.

It may be that Christian rhetoric, perhaps like that of other religions, can only now be legitimately seen by philosophers as a way to interpret and make sense of human life as we lead it.[39] Yet, however subtle and nuanced it may be, renewed philosophical attention to Christianity, and Christianity's God, still collides with a persistent problem: a crucial part of God's rhetoric, as we have seen again and again, depends on His own invented ethos as divine authority, as the Author of all that *is*, so that His arguments' "truth" are not to be understood as merely *one* mode of interpretation among many. Rather, God asserts His claims as the *one and only and best way* to make sense of the world—a true sense, for *this* time, all *past* times, and *all times to come*.

This assertion certainly underlies Auerbach's complaint about the tyrannical "truth" of the Bible as so many now and in the past have received and understood it; and it is doubtless why contemporary philosophers, whether schooled in the subtleties and nuances of postmodern thinking or sympathetic to science's rhetorical hold on what constitutes "truth" or a "fact," may very well agree with Auerbach or struggle in their own ways to escape this tyranny or flatly to oppose it.

To ask, then, whether it is possible to judge God's rhetoric in human terms, adopting any other criteria-set save the one that makes the question ludicrous, is again to ask whether it is God's revealed rhetoric we are to judge or the rhetoric that is the result of human hands and minds that constructed the Bible's symbolic art. Modern historical criticism of the Bible's quite human construction, if taken as the "truth" about what the Bible is,

---

38. Gargani, "Religious Experience as Event and Interpretation," 113–14.

39. Ibid., 114. Gargani's claim is quite similar to one made by scholars of biblical rhetoric such as Patrick and Scult, in *Rhetoric and Biblical Interpretation*, 19–20, except that Patrick and Scult argue that the Bible cannot quite be interpreted as a literary text, as simply a work of art in which readers suspend their disbelief "in order to temporarily inhabit the world the [literary] artist has created." Instead, Patrick and Scult claim that the Bible's rhetoric extends beyond artistry inasmuch as it "seeks to persuade its readers to accept the depicted world as their [the readers'] world" by "the shaping of the [biblical] text to elicit faith . . ." By the same token, a rhetorical approach to this faith-eliciting text assumes rhetoric is but one of several interpretive lenses a critic could employ and further assumes a particular definition of rhetoric itself.

and what God *is* in that Bible, must at least be briefly considered before any attempt is made to address the question of judging God's rhetoric. The Bible we all say we believe in, whether we have read it or not, did not emerge full-blown as a single, unified text with God and Jesus as its central rhetors. As a text, it has a history, as most texts do, in which humans prominently figure.

Textual Obstacles in Evaluating God's Rhetoric

The Bible, modern historians tell us, did not start *as a book* or even as a set of "sacred" writings; it began much as Homer's epics did—as oral proclamations uttered by human beings.[40] Only later were these proclamations written down on scrolls which the people of Israel carried into Babylonian exile after they revolted against King Nebuchadnezzer around 586–587 BCE. Later, these scrolls and other written works become the Christian Bible's Old Testament and the Hebrew Bible's Torah, the first five of which were thought to have been written *not* by God but by Moses himself.

The very word "testament" in the Christian Bible is a reminder of the term's legal origins in the witnessing of contracts and wills, even those "contract[s] between the living and the dead,"[41] contracts which recall, too, Middle Eastern covenants and the juridical contexts for forensic Greek rhetoric and the sometimes necessary *narratio* of factual conjectures. The tablets that God gave to Moses became the scrolls of the Hebrew Bible's Torah, thought to have been discovered during the rebuilding of Solomon's temple around 622 BCE.[42] Before that, oral renditions of stories make no reference to God's writing down any laws. But, by the seventh century, these newly articulated laws and teachings, added to the older stories, were being attributed to Moses *and* God. In fact, since these scrolls were not yet bound as a whole, sacred text, and since they had not yet become a "canon" of accepted, authoritative documents, various scribes and editors felt free to change, revise, comment, and elaborate on them.

As the year 539 BCE came to a close, Cyrus, the new King of Persia and ruler of an immense empire, had defeated the Babylonians and made good on his promise to let the people of Israel return to Jerusalem.[43] Not all *did* return, but those who made the trip carried with them scrolls that soon became Genesis, Exodus, Leviticus, Numbers, Deuteronomy, Joshua, Judges, Samuel, and Kings, a collection of prophetic writings, and other poetic

40. Armstrong, *Bible*, 3, 9–11; Swenson, *Bible Babel*, 38.
41. Pelikan, *Whose Bible Is It?* 4.
42. Armstrong, *Bible*, 21, 24–25.
43. Ibid., 29–30; Pelikan, *Whose Bible Is It?*, 29–47.

works. It took hundreds of years before these works were translated from Hebrew into Greek to become the Bible known as the Septuagint, so named for the seventy or more scholars who, legend has it, did the translation work. These translations became the Tanakh,[44] with the final Greek version of the Torah not completed until around 450 BCE. The people of Israel had to wait a while longer before the other writings became official parts of the Bible. In fact, the final order of the books in the Septuagint was not completed until 70 CE, after the Romans destroyed the temple in Jerusalem.[45]

The Septuagint was eventually claimed by Christians, self-proclaimed followers of Jesus who embraced the Greek translations of the original Hebrew in which they believed they had found evidence of Jesus's birth and ministry foretold in Isaiah. It was these Christians who would eventually translate the Greek Septuagint into Latin.[46] It was these Christians, too, who eventually selected and compiled the authoritative writings that became what is now known as the "New" Testament. Though arguments over what works to include in the much shorter New Testament took place over a couple of centuries, rather than the thousand years it took to assemble the Old Testament, the New Testament ended up including not only the four gospels but many other types of writing.[47] Prior to the second century, Christians had still not yet decided on what gospels to include or in what order—at least not until Lyon's Bishop Iranaeus (c. 140—200 CE) decided that *only* the gospels of Matthew, Mark, Luke, and John were to be included, and in *that* order.[48] Before the fourth century, historians find no specific mention of the now familiar New Testament canon—over two centuries later than the very latest texts it included.[49] This canon differed slightly from Iranaeus' recommended list, including Hebrews and Jude's epistle but dropping Iranaeus' selection of the Shepherd of Hermas as a companion apocalyptic work for Revelation.[50] Even then, the process of canon-formation of the New Testament did not conclude until 692 CE, and arguments among Christians over the canon of works in the Old Testament continued until the Council of Trent's decision in 1546. Even the Council's decision did not entirely mute the debate.[51] Still, modern Bible historians caution, the works that finally

---

44. Swinson, *Bible Babel*, 12-13, 48-48; Pelikan, *Whose Bible Is It?*, 56-60.
45. Ibid.
46. Swinson, *Bible Babel*, 64-65; Pelikan, *Whose Bible Is It?*, 91-96.
47. Swinson, *Bible Babel*, 49; Pelikan, *Whose Bible Is It?*, 102.
48. Armstrong, *Bible*, 66.
49. Swinson, *Bible Babel*, 50.
50. Armstrong, *Bible*, 66.
51. Pelikan, *Whose Bible Is It?*, 116-17.

made up the New Testament canon were not all written at the same time, in the same place, or even for the same, immediate audience.[52]

Quite apart from the issue of how the Bible became what we read today is the thorny problem of translation. Translators had no "single original Bible" to work from. Nor did they have "original manuscripts" for "any individual bible book."[53] Even the "earliest manuscripts" available "do not all agree or even always make sense." Add to these problems the simple fact that the original Hebrew language lacked any vowels and is no longer spoken, that scholars are not always sure of the grammar of this language, and that the declared "sacred" status of a text can predispose translators in one direction or another, and it is easy to see what sort of challenge a translator would have even if she did know the original languages.

This is, of course, a very barebones outline of how the Bible became "constructed" as the text it is now. Yet these historical processes, if accurate, bear directly on the question of whether anyone can judge God's rhetoric in the Bible. Even this very cursory survey suggests that we cannot be sure *whose rhetoric* we would be evaluating, even if we had a set of criteria upon which all critics of its rhetoric could agree. It took centuries for the Bible to become the single book we have now, as the end result of very complex processes in which many human hands and minds were involved.

This historical view of the Bible's "constructedness" leaves us with a high degree of uncertainty about how definite anyone could be about the speeches to be judged. Oral traditions are as subject to revisions as written ones, perhaps even more so. In the Bible's case, what people have said about it over these many years, as well as how it has been interpreted by Jews and Christians, and many others besides, may have fed back into, shaped, and re-shaped the texts as they were assembled, copied, translated, edited, and distributed. Certainly, if nothing else, modern historians' painstaking work on how the Bible became a single text confronts those who believe it is the actual, recorded words of God and Jesus with formidable obstacles, presuming of course they would even acknowledge this scholarship. By the same token, even if the Bible is seen as God's revealed words, this historical account hardly supports the attempts made here to describe and analyze God's rhetoric based on the traditional canons of rhetoric, much less what this chapter has yet to do—explain whether God's rhetoric can be judged by any set of criteria outlined in the taxonomy above.

---

52. Armstrong, *Bible*, 66–67.
53. Swinson, *Bible Babel*, 54.

Which God's Rhetoric Do We Evaluate?

An additional problem biblical historians present to any effort to judge God's rhetoric lies in the question of God's various names in the Bible, variations sometimes seen as evidence for different authors and sites of composition for various texts.[54] The God who first speaks in Genesis is called *Elohim*, but this Hebrew word is plural for the singular word, *El*, referring to one god, not many, as *Elohim* does. In the Bible the names appear with both meanings. So, in Genesis, God *could be* speaking to other gods, and *not* just Himself, as previously suggested, when He says, "Let *us* make man in our own image, after *our* likeness . . ." (Gen 1:26; emphasis added). The plural noun has led some biblical scholars to think that this God was thought to have lived with and ruled over an assembly of divine beings, an inference congruent with studies of other Eastern religions which assign different gods to various nations. The inference further suggests that in its earliest form, the Hebrew text was not so strictly monotheistic as the religion drawn from it would later claim. Of course, if a devout reader accepts the opening of the Gospel of John as divine "truth," the plural references may be explained as God referring to Himself and His only (and already) begotten son and *logos*, Jesus.

The biblical God is sometimes called *El*, often attached to other words to name His characteristics, or *El Shaddai*, a more frequent reference. However, historians are not quite sure how to translate this name, since its contexts invoke fertility. Scholars have discovered a Canaanite god called *El* in ancient tablets written in a language very similar to Hebrew, described as the benign creator of all the world, a leader of a divine assembly of other gods, and closely associated with the worship of cattle. A somewhat differently imagined *El* shows up in the name, Isra-*el*, despite the fact that the name YHWH appears in the Tanakh in excess of 6,000 times, translated from the original Hebrew in English Bibles as LORD, all uppercase letters, the name supposedly revealed for the first time to Moses on Mount Sinai but a name which also appears much earlier, in the Garden of Eden story.

YHWH soon led to the use of the word *Adonai*, a substitute for the magical, mysterious name God revealed to Moses, with both names fusing and changing into "Jehovah," based on Latin consonants for the Hebrew ones and the newly added vowels from *adonai*. But, just as *adonai* can be translated as "Lord," without all upper-case letters, so too can the Hebrew word *Baal*, also found in the Bible as another name for YHWH—this time as the lord, master, and husband to the bride, Israel. Yet *Baal*, mentioned

---

54. Here, I am indebted to Swinson's excellent chapter on this problem, *Bible Babel*, 247–68.

almost seventy times in the Old Testament, also happens to be a rival god in Canaan whose worship violated God's covenant-argument with Moses. *Baal* was closely identified with the calf and bull in Canaan and with the goddess, *Asherah*, both becoming important nemeses for YHWH's power and tempting rival gods for the early Hebrews.

YHWH's many names include such words as *Theos* or *Kurios*, both referring to "Lord." These synonyms soon attach themselves to the New Testament figure of "Jesus," the Greek name for the Aramaic *Yeshua*, usually written as "Joshua," a name which, in English, comes close to meaning, "Yah saves." Yet Jesus's name will eventually attach to various notions of "messiah," the Greek form of the Hebrew word *meshiach*, meaning "anointed," as does the Greek word "Christ" (*christos*), so readers will find in John's Gospel that God and Jesus have become the two faces of the same divine *logos*, a word closely associated, as we have seen, with ancient Greek rhetoric itself.

These different names for God may be further evidence for the long, complex historical process of transforming oral traditions and proclamations, variously inscribed at different times and places, for different audiences and purposes, into the finished, complete book we know as the Bible. This thickly woven tapestry of texts and genres has inspired many theologies and many religious sects within Christianity itself. But these divine names, like the historical construction of the single Bible out of a disparate miscellany of texts and genres, frustrate any attempt, however tentative, to judge God's rhetoric by any set of human criteria.

Perhaps that frustration, in the end, is completely justified. After all, it may be quite seriously argued that whatever God is called, or however He presents Himself in the Bible, has little or no real bearing on the question of His actual nature, which is quite beyond any critic or historian and so requires the "anthropomorphic character" of God in the Bible and the various root metaphors for naming Him. Regardless of any embarrassments it may cause, this biblical God must be translated into terms humans can understand, even if that understanding is limited and requires both our own intellect as well as revelation if God is to be glimpsed, however imperfectly, at all.[55] One such admittedly anthropomorphic translation has been the focus of our explorations here—God as *rhetor*.

Perhaps it is no coincidence, as Marilynne Robinson remarks, that one of the most conspicuous names for the God of the Bible—Yahweh—offers us "two deeply mysterious words" making up "one deeply mysterious

---

55. This is, at least, part of the complex argument made by Schuon in *Logic and Transendence*, 71.

utterance: I AM."⁵⁶ The "I" not only bequeaths to human beings their own singularly intellectual identity, their minds and souls, a way to speak of themselves as a "coherent self," a person. Along with "am," it allows us to make any number of more limited assertions embedded in our different circumstances, "I am a doctor," "I am ill," etc.

Beyond this fortunate circumstance, though, is the growing awareness that modern historical accounts of how the Bible was constructed, how its canon was formed, may be a historical construction itself, based not on the Bible per se but on "issues" theologians, Protestant and Catholic, have framed and been trying to resolve since the Reformation. Earlier, "pre-critical" views of the Bible as a single book simply did not see it as "an arbitrary construct,"⁵⁷ and many still do not, or will not, perhaps for very good reasons, since the Bible has been constructed to be read as a more or less unified text, rhetorically, a conjectured *narratio*.

What we have seen throughout these several chapters is that God's rhetoric, as the narrators directly present it in the Bible, often resembles human rhetoric. God *does* argue with various human audiences, *invents* ways to make His case that we humans can and have understood as arguments, as rhetoric. He *adopts* various stylistic devices to make those arguments—devices for which we already have rhetorical labels based on human uses of these same devices. And He *frames* many of these arguments within a story, a basic, largely linear narrative of events ordered in a way humans can follow. Many of His strategies of invention are, for the most part, fully within the bounds of humans' rhetorical strategies, including His violent rhetoric and the divine violence He enacts. God's overarching *narratio*, the story He is telling, is in many ways the STORY of story-making within which His rhetorical choices and stylistic modes of expression, even His memory and delivery, have relevance for the argument this story makes. All the *humanness* of His rhetoric does not, obviously, limit the significance of His arguments, insofar as the ideologically-driven narrators are concerned. These limits are, presumably, our own: they exist *for* us and *because* of us, because we human likenesses must have God say something to us in some way so He must resort to the intrinsic rhetorical dimensions of human language to get it said so that other human likenesses might stand a chance of understanding and being persuaded by His arguments and the narratives supporting them.

At the same time, we have also seen that God's arguments sometimes exceed the verbal limitations of rhetoric's art. However eloquent God may

---

56. Robinson, *Absence of Mind*, 110.
57. Josopivici, *Book of God*, 11.

be, however compelling, He is shown to resort to other, extra-verbal means to make His arguments believable and persuasively felt. If this were not so, we could not account for God's theophanies, His variously rhetorical revelations of Himself, His own recourse to violence or threats of violence, to His toppling or suspending the laws of nature as we humans, bound by our own limited and limiting reasoning powers, understand them. These may be extra-verbal strategies, inartificial proofs, by Aristotle's and others' definitions, except that He chooses them for quite obvious rhetorical purposes—to persuade and keep His human likenesses persuaded.

Add to these strategies God's own invented ethos, as the Rhetor of rhetors, and we can see again why His rhetoric would be difficult to evaluate, no matter what criteria we might think best applies. His very nature as "God" brooks little to no opposition, yet some of His human inventions do try to oppose Him. The arguments He makes from the absolute sovereignty of His ethos could never be claimed or presumed by a mere human rhetor. Yet our own human history is littered with instances where human rhetors have presumed to claim exactly that sovereign power, often with disastrous results.

Failing to Succeed, Succeeding to Fail

Yet, if we step back from the Bible, with God's argument fully made and bound as one, single work, it is quite impossible to ignore the vast amount of internal evidence that shows how often His own human likenesses judge His rhetoric and find it deficient, how often they simply forget about the covenant-arguments made and act as if God never made them, and how often they find reasons and excuses for their failing to stay persuaded by His pleas, vehement tirades, and astonishing, sometimes violent, theophanies. The recalcitrance of God's various audiences has been a notable theme in previous chapters. Nor is it too much of an overstatement to say that without the fluctuating tensions between God's rhetorical efforts and those He would convince and persuade, the power of His overall narrative would greatly diminish for human readers.

So, in one crucial respect, God's rhetoric *must fail* or, if that is too strongly put, at least its effects must weaken or wear off for a time, in order to justify His continuing attempts to keep His auditors, be they individuals or groups, faithful to the different covenants He invents. Equally crucial to the rhythmic patterns of God's rhetorical failures and His invention of further arguments and continued successes is the wavering, disbelieving nature of His all-too-human likenesses.

CAN GOD'S RHETORIC BE JUDGED? 239

Consider the famous scene in Exodus. Having delivered Israel out of Egyptian bondage, the narrator tells us, God delivers to Moses "two tablets of [His] testimony" written in His own hand (Exod 31:18). Meanwhile, the people of Israel have grown restless in Moses's absence and force Aaron to make a "molten calf" as one of several "gods" to "go before" them as they travel (Exod 32:1–2). It is not at all clear from the narrator's reports exactly how long Moses met with God on Mount Sinai, but it could not have been very long; for God commands Moses to "[g]o down [the mountain]; for your people whom you brought out of the land of Egypt, have corrupted themselves; they have turned aside *quickly* out of the way I commanded them . . ." (Exod 32:7–8, emphasis added). Confronting Israel's impatience, and the people's sudden recourse to making graven images of older, rival gods, such as *El*, linked to the calf and bull, God tells Moses: "I have seen this people, and behold, it is a stiff-necked people; now therefore let me alone, that my wrath may burn hot against them and I may consume them; but of you [Moses] I will make a great nation" (Exod 32:9). Moses has the temerity to talk God out of his angry vengeance, yet God's brief but scalding epideictic rhetoric clearly judges Israel's lapse of faith and character, even as He concludes to destroy them all, except for Moses, the saving remnant, who is promised exactly what God had earlier promised Abraham.

The "stiff-necked people," repeated again in the very next chapter (Exod 33:3), may be read as God's own condemnation of His elect. But, inasmuch as the Bible's interpretive reach and application as a sacred text far exceeds Israel, His judgment is hardly restricted to them alone. God had tried to persuade Adam and Eve; but they, too, do not stay persuaded very long before they are doing the exact opposite of what God commanded. Israel's stubbornness and impatience with God's exhortations, and Moses's efforts to keep His elect persuaded, suggest the pervasive weakness in all of God's human likenesses, not just Israelites.

In some ways, this later weakness is even more remarkable than Adam and Eve's violations of God's initial covenant-argument. Readers, devout or no, can certainly find in this scene and in many others in the Old Testament the repeated failure of God's rhetoric to keep Israel, a synecdoche for the whole of humanity, convinced. Hardly have the words and music of Moses's and Israel's praise of God's "terrible" and "glorious deeds" stopped vibrating in their ears before Israel seems to forget all the "wonders" of His fierce theophanies, His turning the very forces of nature into proofs that freed them from Egyptian slavery (Exod 15:11).

God's rhetoric against Pharaoh, of course, did not have a lasting effect either, intentionally so, since God hardened his heart so that he would order his armies to chase the Hebrews escaping across the Sea of Reeds. Of course, the hubris of Pharaoh's act was part of God's argument all along, but the same cannot be said for the people He saved. They, too, seem no longer persuaded, even though His awful presence glows and rumbles over them as a pillar of cloud and thunder at the top of Mount Sinai.

Certainly, God's many prophets confront the same recalcitrance in Israel as God Himself. When God speaks to Isaiah, as Isaiah reports it in the very opening verses, He confesses to have "reared and brought up . . . sons" who "have rebelled against [Him]" (Isa 1:2). He calls Israel "a sinful nation, / a people laden with iniquity, / offspring of evildoers," corrupted and "estranged" from Him (Isa 1:4). This is a curious critique, largely because God initially seems to blame Himself for making human likenesses so resistant to persuasion, only then to shift this self-blame to inherent human corruption and evil. Yet God then turns from the fiery epideictic rhetoric of curses and judgments to deliberative entreaty. Isaiah quotes His plea:

> Come now, let us reason together . . . / though your sins are like scarlet, / they shall be white as snow; / though they are red like crimson, / they shall become like wool. / If you are willing and obedient, / you shall eat the good of the land; / But if you refuse and rebel, / you shall be devoured by the / sword; / for the mouth of the Lord has spoken. (Isa 1:8)

Here, as in so many other instances, God's "mouth" is a synecdoche that repeats His long-standing covenant-argument as a conditional promise, predicated on His own human likenesses' seeing that His offer is reasonable, the best they are going to get from the God who invented them and, in terrible moments, has been and will continue to be willing to destroy them.

The pattern is by now familiar: God often blends promises with threats, quite consistent for covenant-arguments. To less devout readers, the speech may sound more like extortion than a well-reasoned case: Obey me and rewards will follow; rebel, and punishment is sure and certain. These poles, or better the *movement* between them, generate the unfolding *narratio* of God's case across the Pentateuch, through the historical stories recounting Israel's judges and kings, and across the prophets, major and minor. Order and disorder, obedience and rebellion, unfold within the broader dialectic of God's many rhetorical acts—a dialectic of opposite and contrary forces. God tries to keep His human likenesses persuaded, despite their impulses to reject, dismiss, and rebel against whatever arguments He makes and whatever form, however violent, His appeals take.

Readers can see this same pattern in the New Testament. If Jesus is God's final argument, to Israel and the entire humanity it represents, he too must be rejected and refused, only to be reborn and restored, even unto his apocalyptic promise of a return. Jews and gentiles alike seem divided about Jesus's meaning and his godhood and authority. Resistance and rebellion on the parts of figures in the four Gospels propel a similar narrative pattern. Jesus's rhetoric *must fail*, just as God's does, if for no other reason than to keep the narrative unfolding and to ensure its ultimate symmetry as a story, *narratio* as argument. Reasons for each failure, the consequences of each—these are as various as waves against the rocks, and just as constant.

But the repeated failures in God's persuasive powers must be set against His many successes. God's narrative case demands those who, like Saul-become-Paul, turn from their doubt and skepticism and find themselves wholly persuaded by God's rhetoric. It demands the obedience of Abraham, the tenacity of Moses, the visionary surrenders of the prophets, and graceful patience and sacrifice of Jesus. These and many other figures are God's faithful and devoted progenies. His rhetoric sustains and tests them, overwhelms and nurtures them. Even God's most pitiable, probing servant, Job, cannot in the end resist His power and finds in his most wretched subjugation that God's rhetoric, however evasive, cannot be denied or ignored.

So does all this mean we must abandon the question of judging God's rhetoric as fruitless? Asking this question leads us to recognize that God's rhetoric fails as much as it succeeds from within the *narratio* the Bible encompasses. It succeeds *because* it fails and fails *because* it succeeds. Like our own merely human rhetoric, His arguments beget our own, and our arguments carry His within them. To the extent that each person who bothers to read the Bible recognizes the arguments God makes there, the rhetorical means He adopts, that person should also see that God would make each of us judges of His rhetoric and, in that sense, judges of *who* we are and *who* He is to judge us.

It is doubtful that this conclusion will satisfy all readers, for some may still wonder what it is about God's rhetoric that accounts for His persuasive successes and His failures; and what criteria for judgment, beyond the apparent dialectical necessities of opposition and resistance between God's rhetoric and His human likenesses that propel the Bible's *narratio*, are to be applied to distinguish the successes from the failures. If my taxonomy of rhetorical criteria, outlined at the start of this chapter, tentative, speculative, and heuristic as it is, has any practical value, a better answer to these final questions must be offered.

In offering one, however, I must remind readers again that, historically speaking, there is no one criteria-set that has withstood the test of time or garnered any theoretical consensus across the over two millennia that the art of rhetoric has been in existence. I would further remind readers that the answers offered below will be as tentative and speculative as the taxonomy and will consist of generalizations across God's various covenant-arguments in both the Old and New Testaments, including Jesus as His final covenant-argument.

One possible reason that God's rhetoric tends to be unpersuasive for His human likenesses may lie precisely in His invention of a stubborn, skeptical audience which, as many theologians have argued, must have the capacity for "free will," the capacity *not* to be persuaded. As likenesses, God's human auditors have, it seems, been imbued with the same negative verbal genius of their inventor, insofar as both God and His likenesses have the freedom to say "No" to whatever exists or does not exist by virtue of the symboling abilities they share, though humans' symbolic capacities have limits God's is shown not to have. Without this negative capacity, the power to turn away from a rhetor, human or divine, the persuasive goal of rhetoric loses all meaning.

Nor is this capacity to say "No" to God's "No's" completely erased even in the face of God's threats, His violent rhetoric, or in His use of violence as rhetoric's last and final resort. Violence or its threat is no absolute guarantee that God's exhortations will be followed, any more than His verbal arguments are. Human beings are so made to resist both verbal and extra-verbal persuasive means, even to the point of dying or suffering great pain and hardship rather than obeying a command, or remaining persuaded by verbal arguments alone. "Free will," whatever else it may mean, must be presupposed by the art of rhetoric, even when rhetoric devolves into its worst, most damaging and coercive forms, or else a rhetor's auditors must be seen as utterly submissive automatons incapable of even an animal's resistance to a cruel master.

A second reason God's rhetoric may fail is because God often seeks to persuade His human likenesses with verbal arguments that sometimes violate the reasoning capacities of His invented human auditors. Many of His arguments do offer reasons for His exhortations. Some, however, do not supply enough reasons to justify what God commands His likenesses to do, believe, or value. God's readiness to threaten, to punish, when His verbal arguments fail, coupled with His typical unwillingness to accept any responsibility for the human creatures He has invented, their limitations and weaknesses, can make Him as well as His exhortations appear tyrannical and despotic from His likenesses' perspective. In short, God often does not seek or invent all the "available" means of persuasion to achieve His rhetorical goals or provide sufficient reasons for His commands.

A third reason for God's persuasive failures may lie in the length of time it is shown to take to satisfy the promises He makes to His likenesses. Being the supposed inventor of time, of history, He has the power to intervene in that time, that history, which His likenesses, being bound to both, cannot alter or even fully understand. A covenant-argument, once made to human beings, needs to be realized in a time-frame humans can comprehend, or else it may appear that God has retreated from His promises, forgotten them, or broken them altogether. God, presumably, does not experience at all the long delay human beings must endure between a divine promise and its being kept. Whatever causal link God is shown to have made between a divine exhortation and the promise to be fulfilled if the exhortation is heeded may weaken over time for His human likenesses or be dismissed or forgotten.

A final reason God's eloquence may fail may arise from His often invoked ethos. Since that ethos is authoritative and authorial, from its invention in Genesis, to appeal to it so often as the ground or reason for what He commands may prove tiresome and subject to doubt among His human likenesses. Since part of God's unpredictability and mystery arises from His "I am" becoming or not becoming directly present before His human auditors, His absences may very well be seen as abandonment by His likenesses. Just as God's directly spoken rhetoric is shown to diminish as the Bible unfolds, mediated by prophets speaking from or for Him, or displaced by Jesus's rhetoric as the final covenant-argument, so, too, does the power of His ethos.

So how does God manage to succeed as a rhetor? To some extent, and paradoxically, for some of the same reasons He can fail. God certainly succeeds in inventing an ethos whose persuasive effect on certain of His human likenesses cannot be easily or conveniently denied. God's spoken presence often seeks to inculcate awe and fear in His auditors, and the power of His theophanies greatly aids in inculcating those emotions. To that extent, the often capricious, arbitrary nature of His ethos strengthens the pathos of His divine manifestations. So powerful are those manifestations, they become inseparable from the effect He seeks to have on His auditors, fusing His ethos with the pathos He seeks to engender. Jesus's rhetoric extends the awe and mystery of God's ethos, though the effect he often seeks to inculcate is compassion, love, and forgiveness of the flaws in the very human likenesses God's ethos seeks to make fearful and more submissive to His exhortations. Such appeals as Jesus makes seem more aimed at the hearts, not the heads, of his auditors, though Jesus's appeals to pathos often appear in more sophisticated verbal arguments than God's.

Another reason for God's rhetorical success may lie in His ability to predict future events with extra-human accuracy. Doubtless this gives to God's arguments the appearance of profound truthfulness that His other verbal appeals to human reasoning sometimes lack. But the appeal of His *narratio* largely depends on God's knowledge of how the world of human existence began and how it will end, though when that ending will come is, like the promised rewards, often deferred to a future only He claims to know. Jesus's appeal as the final covenant-argument in God's comprehensive *narratio* seems to be an extension of God's knowledge of a human life beyond the ending of the one His human auditors have so far experienced, though what kind of life follows the ending of the current one and where it will be lived are also deferred, demanding His human auditors ground their belief, their faith, and their hope in the renewal of life that at least John's Jesus seems to represent as God's *logos*.

The continuing success of God's rhetoric for many American Christians might be cited as another, final reason for its past successes. The biblical God grounds the existence of the present world upon indisputably true axioms even an agnostic critic cannot doubt: a world full of fear, decay, destruction, and malicious malefactors intent on making others suffer to avoid suffering themselves. Time, death, history, human weaknesses and human appetites—all these are parts of God's *narratio*. So, too, is the human desire for love, compassion, peace, justice, and the pleasures this life offers. This desire is sometimes satisfied in the present world—enough at least to sustain the hope and faith that life may continue, and that another life to come may be lived without the malignancies of the present. God's rhetoric, then, depends for its continuing success as persuasion on both the tragic realities it both establishes and acknowledges and the comic, utopian reassurances of a better reality that it promises yet defers.

No claim of originality can or should be made for these tentative generalizations about why God's rhetoric succeeds as much as it fails. Many have recognized the dialectical interplay between a God of fear and a God of love and hope in the Christian Bible—so many they cannot be named or cited. Yet most do not see these emotions as either a "dialectical interplay" or as the rhetorical means by which God strives to persuade His likenesses. Some of the criteria-sets extrapolated from rhetorical theories at the start of this chapter *do* apply to judging God's rhetoric, but certainly not *all* of them, and no one set will *systematically* aid in such a judgment.

God, as so many imagine Him to be, and His rhetoric, as so many may not admit that He uses, resists any clear-cut assessment based on human theories of rhetoric, just as it sometimes frustrates any critic's efforts to describe that rhetoric according the art's traditional canons.

So a brief account of what has been gained from this book's explorations, and what has not, is the focus of the next, and final, chapter.

9

The Perils and Promises of Exploring God's Rhetoric

Explorations, real or written, bring rewards and risks, with no real assurances that what is sought is worth the finding or the obstacles suffered in the search. When I began this book some years ago, I could not be sure what might be gained in exploring the rhetoric of the biblical God's direct speeches. Nor was I certain whether the rhetorical canons that guided my explorations of these speeches would be as fully productive as I supposed they were. Few critics of biblical rhetoric, so far as I knew, had taken such approach before, so I had only so much to guide my search.

But no exploration starts out utterly innocent about what might be discovered, or without considerable preparations. I had already read a good deal about God and the Bible before I began writing, and grew up in a part of United States known for its religious preoccupations, so that certainly shaped and re-shaped my thinking. I began, too, quite aware of over two thousand years of thinking about rhetoric as a subject and a practicable human art. This awareness, obviously, determined my approach to some of those speeches directly attributed to the God and the Jesus whom so many Americans, Christian or no, take to be active agents and personalities of the Bible. So I thought myself at least reasonably prepared to study these speeches as rhetorical acts—how "reasonably" or "prepared" must be left for others to judge.

The study of the Bible's rhetoric is certainly not original to this book. Even if "rhetorical criticism is a comparative newcomer to the field of biblical studies,"[1] I had hoped to contribute to this criticism by drawing upon the full range of rhetoric's parts, its traditional canons, to describe and analyze and, where possible, assess God's rhetoric—a noticeably neglected subject, it seemed. This approach soon collided with inherent obstacles in analyzing how God invented and developed His arguments, since the very premises of rhetorical invention, however contested the concept, typically start with a human rhetor attempting to address and argue an issue or question for a human audience. The inventiveness of the God in the early chapters of Genesis complicates these premises—perhaps radically so. God's motive to invent His initial rhetorical speech, the issue He was trying to address, and the long-standing idea that He made something (the "world") from nothing are not readily or easily explicable from the biblical accounts. Its mysteries invite a host of speculations about how we might understand God's inventive capacity before He had a human audience—speculations that cluster around the ethos God invents for Himself and the rhetorical power of the names for the parts of the world He invents.

God's inventive power after He makes a human audience is easier to analyze in rhetorical terms, but here, too, obstacles arose. To the extent that God's rhetoric has been *written into* the Bible, those who wrote what He said and argued, whoever they may have been, and however truthful and accurate they were in representing what He said, certainly seemed to show a God eager to exhort and command His many audiences—including Himself. In those covenant-arguments to human auditors, God is often shown to rely heavily on His invented ethos for much of what He claims. But many of those arguments are so brief, God does not always fully articulate reasons to persuade His auditors to accept or believe them, though they often did, without any or much rebuttal. Once Jesus becomes the central rhetor of the Bible, and presumably God's final covenant-argument, he, too, posed a number of challenges—primarily which Jesus to select as the *logos* God wanted to make of Jesus's *narratio*.

Yet God does invent rhetoric of various types—epideictic (to curse and praise), deliberative (to command what should happen and to predict what will), and forensic (to recall what happened and who was responsible). He often draws on many of the common *topoi* or "places" Aristotle and many others have since believed important for human rhetors to frame assertions. The one common *topos* from which God *does not invent very many arguments* is the one Aristotle lists as the possible and the impossible.[2] For Aristotle, arguments from this *topos* typically permitted a rhetor to reason

---

1. Martin Warner, "Introduction," 3.
2. Aristotle, *Rhetoric* 2.xviii–xix.2–22.

that if a beginning is possible, so is its ending, and if the parts are possible so is the whole, and if the whole, so too the parts. The impossible, Aristotle explains, assumes the possible as its contrary or opposite; yet human beings "love or desire" what is "naturally . . . possible; for as a rule no one loves the impossible or desires it."

Perhaps no other statement that Aristotle or any other theorist of rhetoric, past or present, might make seems so contrary to God's own rhetoric. That rhetoric certainly unfolds within the possibilities of a beginning and an ending, both of which He invents, and its frequent recourse to synecdoche certainly shows possible parts implying wholes, and wholes, their various parts. Yet many of God's appeals depend on His claiming to *do* and *be* the impossible, expecting His human likenesses in fact to "love and desire" His ethos as the Impossibly Possible—to love and desire what cannot be understood, what appears and disappears as a presence in human lives, what is promised as rewards often delayed for long stretches of time and, ultimately, deferred to a future time that never arrives. God's appeals to this ethos often recall for auditors the unalterable fact that He is the impossible they must love, starting with the impossible act of making something from a supposed nothing.

God certainly tries to appeal to the different emotions and values of His audiences, notably to induce in them fear and awe, order and obedience, sometimes love, pity, and hope, especially through Jesus's *narratio*. Yet, as I have noted, He does invent arguments that exceed any human's persuasive abilities. His rhetoric, as the biblical narrators must have realized or intuited, must show a full and commanding knowledge of past and future facts, of the minds, if not always the hearts, of the human likenesses He has made. God's signs and wonders, His various theophanies, are shown to transcend any rhetorical strategies available to His human likenesses. So, while much of God's argument, even His threats and acts of violence, resemble humans' rhetorical inventions, other inventions surpass anything a human rhetor could accomplish or even imagine. These, too, argue for His own Possible Impossibilities.

This discovery may not, of course, come as a great surprise. Those who wrote God's speeches into the Bible obviously knew some of His rhetorical ingenuity would have to be human-like to be understood. The anthropomorphic qualities of God, while perhaps an embarrassment for many, believers and unbelievers alike, are wholly necessary if God is to communicate and persuade His auditors at all, limited and imperfect as they are strangely made to be. Likewise, some of God's rhetorical inventiveness must transcend human inventiveness to differentiate His own divine power from His likenesses'.

Analyzing the *dispositio* of God's rhetoric broaches a number of questions for a critic of His rhetoric, not least among them whether to examine God's arrangement speech by speech, or whether to see His entire argument arranged as the single Bible presents it, from the Old to the New Testament. Other critics of biblical rhetoric have taken great care to focus on the rhetorical structures and forms of specific prophets or single narratives, admonishing that this is the best way to examine the Bible's various forms and genres. Yet these same critics seldom acknowledge that *dispositio* is as contested a concept as *inventio*, so, against their warnings, I followed Kenneth Burke's lead and chose a wider scope, to include under *dispositio* the Bible's arrangement as God's entire argument.

Still, this breadth did not avoid obvious problems. Scholars and historians have for some time recognized that, if the Bible's order is God's order, this supposition collides with the simple fact that the Christian and Hebrew Bibles are quite different in their order, and the long, complicated process that led to the canonical shape of the Christian Bible read or ignored today inevitably affected how the *dispositio* of God's rhetoric could be explored. Even the canonical order of the Christian Bible further shows that God's rhetoric diminishes as Jesus's enlarges.

What emerged out of this exploratory effort, however, was the most basic narrative pattern imaginable—a pattern that includes both God's and Jesus's rhetorics. That *narratio* relies on the structure of unfolding covenant-arguments within the smaller narratives, from Adam's to Jesus's, as the Christian Bible moves from an absolute beginning to an absolute end, from the beginning of beginnings and to the end of endings, the Story of all stories, sacred or secular, with the added promise of another beginning without end in the controversial Book of Revelation.

While other critics of biblical rhetoric have argued that too much attention has been lavished on the Bible's style, or argued that God's most sublime speeches are stylistically obscure, I found that God's style, while usually lofty and eloquent, is fully amenable to rhetorical analysis and description. In fact, rhetorical analysis shows just how eloquent God could be. His style changes as He argues, depending on whether He exhorts auditors to believe in His covenants, or instructs them on how to build an ark. But He remains a dangerously ironic interrogator, fully prone to hyperbole as much as paradox, often addressing His likenesses through intricate patterns of repetition, syntactic variations, and vividly resonant tropes and figures. Jesus's style often resembles God's, but sometimes seems even more enigmatic—so much so that part of his ethos arises from offering seemingly simple parables whose meanings his disciples sometimes cannot fully understand.

Sometimes, too, his style, like his arguments, seem more complicated than God's more sweeping exhortations.

Initially, it seemed that of the all the parts of rhetoric, memory and delivery would be the least useful to explore. Other critics of biblical rhetoric dismiss these final canons as useless to examine. It is certainly true that the Bible seems content to let readers imagine most of what God's and Jesus's speeches sound like, and neither God nor Jesus would have any use for the memorizing strategies found in classical rhetorical manuals. Yet even here I did not find these canons as useless as other critics make them appear. The Bible as a single book can serve as God's remembering of Himself to His human likenesses, even when they seemed to forget or ignore His covenants or are no longer persuaded by them, and even though He too, at times, seems to forget or fears He will forget His covenants, just as His human likenesses do. Moreover, while God delivers most of His arguments orally, He does, unlike Jesus, deliver some of the most important exhortations in writing. His spoken and written words often find their full expansion in a wide range of extra-verbal theophanies meant to persuade His auditors of the truthfulness and power of what He says and writes. Even Jesus's manner of delivery, once he displaces God's, varies from one gospel to the next.

All of this makes God's rhetoric extremely difficult to judge by any human standards, past or present, since these standards have fluctuated over time and remain elusive still. Even if these standards can be tentatively classified based on definitions of rhetoric itself, our judgment of God's eloquent pleas and commands are fully complicated by the many human hands involved in translating and assembling the canonical Bible we read and the many names God has been given in that Bible. What seems more important, though, are the vacillating human judgments of God's and Jesus's rhetoric implicit in the Bible's overall *narratio*. God's story depends on the push and pull between His efforts to keep His human inventions convinced and persuaded and His human audience's skeptical, stubbornly perverse resistances. There, it seems, lies both the narrative tension which pushes the Bible to its always promised end and the dialectical energy that drives God's rhetoric forward even as it transforms into Jesus's. Beyond the necessities of dialectical and narrative tensions, other possible reasons why God's rhetoric may fail or succeed for His auditors appear largely embedded in His own ethos as "God."

The diminishment of God's rhetoric in both the Hebrew and Christian Bibles is certain to prompt questions for any critic of His eloquent pleas and commands. Treating God as the literary protagonist of the Tanakh, one critic suggests that the silence after the Book of Job shows that this God loses interest in His human likenesses because He has at last understood why He made them in the first place—to reproduce Himself through them. After that, God's "motivation to continue is undercut" by His own inventions' recalcitrance.[3] In this interpretation, it is Job, "being God's most perfect image" in the Hebrew Bible and "the supreme image of God's desire to know" Himself, "who loses interest" in God, so much so that God loses interest in Himself.[4] Accordingly, God ought to have died at that very moment, and almost does. But neither the Tanakh nor the Christian Bible can end as a tragedy like *Oedipus Rex*. It may more resemble the West's other great model of tragedy, Shakespeare's *Hamlet*. Like Hamlet, the God of the Tanakh remains trapped in His own contradictory character—tender and merciful and yet a ruthless warrior and judge, unable to escape the contradictions because He is "the divided original whose divided image we remain."[5]

For a critic such as myself, more interested in God and Jesus as the primary rhetors of the Christian Bible, this interpretation falls short and invites a different response. While it is true that God's direct rhetoric diminishes and is displaced by Jesus's, that fact need not mean that God loses interest in His human likenesses. Quite the contrary. Although Jesus's rhetoric largely—but not entirely—displaces God's, that displacement need not mean that Christian believers thereby no longer have any relationship to the God of the Old Testament, since God may be trying one last time to maintain His rhetorical relationship to His all-too-human, "stiff-necked" audience through Jesus himself, an even more perfectly rendered version of Job's degradation than Job can ever be. Since Jesus's rhetorical *narratio* culminates in resurrection, not in just having his life restored as Job's was, it promises a future to-come, a utopian rhetoric, as I have called it, that continues to have great appeal to those who bear witness to it and are persuaded by the argument that at least John's Jesus seems to make.

Not all, of course, will be so persuaded. Utopian rhetoric, whether from the mouth of Jesus or the pen of Karl Marx, will not convince everyone because some of God's human likenesses are unwilling to sit and wait for their heavenly rewards. Skeptics and non-believers may very well be willing to cast aside any and all utopias as mere *ideologies* in disguise, ultimately as partial and biased as any other ideology human beings might construct. Kenneth Burke would wisely remind us, though, that "'[u]topias' are but a special case of ideologies," since "[u]topian bias is progressive, futuristic . . . ," while "ideological bias" may be quite the opposite—regressive or conservative. If we treat utopian rhetoric such as Jesus's "on par with" other,

3. Miles, *God*, 403–4.
4. Ibid., 404–5.
5. Ibid., 406–8.

biased ideologies, and reject it along with all other utopian biases, "a motivational problem arises...": where will human beings derive their "primary motive power"? "For though bias is false promise," Burke concedes, "it is promise."[6] If we reject *any* utopian rhetoric because of its inherent biased promises, we humans would lack any reason for adopting or inventing rhetorical appeals that strive to rise above the status quo and seek ways to improve our earthly lives.

Throughout previous chapters, God has embedded promises into His covenant-arguments. The promises differ, but promises they remain. Even Jesus, presumably God's last argument, is a promise and shows the utopian bias toward what is always not-yet-come. We humans cannot seem to live without the promises, false or no, utopias offer. This fact about our nature as humans may well go beyond the merely intuitive and express our "great thirst" for an "'otherness' out of reach" and beyond all the facts and philosophical postulates we invent—since these too may arise out of the same thirst.[7] This may explain why Christianity enjoys the worldwide appeal it still has. Even the nightmarish destruction of Revelation that so many expect—and some Christians even *yearn* for—is not bereft of the promise John's Jesus offers to those who will be or remain persuaded by it. In that sense, God is still trying to appeal to those who will listen, who will believe in a future always elsewhere, at some other time. That is *not* the act of a God who has lost interest in the humans He rather imperfectly made.

In the end, this exploration of God's eloquence has made no effort to reconstruct or infer the actual intentions and rhetorical motives of those who may have written, edited, and assembled the Bible now read in its many translations, or the actual audiences and circumstances these authors and editors may have been trying to affect and change. I have not dwelled on these many historical factors, though I have mentioned them as relevant to challenges of analyzing God's rhetoric given the Bible's *constructedness*. Other critics of biblical rhetoric have tried to analyze and interpret specific texts based on the various historical contexts which shaped the stories, poems, and prophecies. Yet, however beneficial their analyses have been to my own, this book's focus from the start was the biblical God in whom so many Americans believe, often without being very familiar with the Bible itself, and what and how this God and Jesus argue *within* some of their most notable persuasive speeches. Frank Kermode is, I think, right to argue that trying "to reproduce the tacit understandings that existed between this dead writer and his dead audience," or between the many, largely unknown

---

6. Burke, *Rhetoric of Motives*, 199, 201.
7. Steiner, *Grammars of Creation*, 19–20.

authors and editors of the Bible and "the community for which it [the Bible or some part of the Bible] was originally written" is quite "beyond" most scholars and rhetorical interpreters,[8] myself included. "Those accords," Kermode adds, "are lost" to critics and scholars now, "and the evidence" to identify who those authors and editors were and who they were writing to, and why, would still have to "come largely from" the Bible "itself, in [a] defeating circularity."

I cannot be sure how "defeating" this evidentiary "circularity" is to my own attempts here. I am more sure that what drew me to this subject was not any desire to find and reconstruct the historical particulars external to God's rhetoric or those narrators who portrayed it but my desire to see how far, and to what extent, the arguments God makes within the Bible were amenable to the traditional ways of parsing human rhetoric. In all that I had read, I saw very few critics of biblical rhetoric try to account for and describe God's inventiveness, His arrangement of His case, His styles, or His memory and delivery.

Obviously, my effort suffers from its own admitted limitations even as it reveals obstacles for rhetorical criticism of the Bible, or at least God's rhetoric in that Bible. These obstacles may suggest why so little attention has been paid to God's eloquent pleas, critics instead preferring to examine, say, the rhetoric of the Old Testament prophets or Jesus in the New Testament. Yet, for all the limitations and obstacles, I have now a deeper respect for the Bible, in all its textual and rhetorical complexities, than I did before I began. Even as an agnostic about God's existence, I have always acknowledged the Bible's utmost importance as a book Americans need to read if they want to understand the great art, literature, and philosophy that make up both our own history as well as our shared culture, whatever is left of it. In this sense, the Bible is indispensable to our understanding of ourselves as inheritors of this culture.

Certainly, it is not the *only* book Americans need to or should read. But, having explored some of the arguments its principal rhetors—God and Jesus—make in it, I must now say that I am a more appreciative agnostic than before. I cannot help but think that many (certainly, not *all*) of the pleas and exhortations that God and, later, Jesus, make to their recalcitrant human likenesses seem compelling and persuasive, *not because God or Jesus makes them*, but because the appeals themselves goad us, as utopian rhetoric often does, to go beyond ourselves, to rise up above our clearly fallen, corrupt natures.

---

8. Kermode, *Genesis of Secrecy*, 138.

What troubles me still is why we are so corruptly and badly made in the first place that we should *have to rise up*, that we *should have to be persuaded to act as the biblical God wants us to*. Yet that would seem to be the essential, all-too-human yearning that has led us to recognize the religious impulse in our symbol-making natures—that desire for more, for the possible impossible, for the best, or for the better. Our symbolizing capacity, of which religion is so important a part, far exceeds any technological application ever likely to be manufactured. And, if for no other reason, that capacity, so fully and eloquently and often frighteningly realized in God's own rhetoric, should make us more resistant to those who would diminish, ignore, or simply ridicule it.

Yet rhetorical symboling, as an art, has always been open to and receptive of ridicule. God, as we've seen in Job's story, is fully capable of the rhetoric of ridicule. American history is, as it so happens, often punctured by the ridicule of religion, of Christianity, and of God's, if not Jesus's, rhetorical exuberance in the Bible. In *Nature's God*, author Matthew Stewart has recently made a detailed, often eloquent case that America's founding deistic principles derived from the transmission and transformation of radical ideas from such ancient philosophers as Epicurus and Lucretius, all the way through Spinoza and Locke and down to Jefferson and such lesser-known American revolutionaries as Ethan Allan and Thomas Young—all of whom variously aided in weakening the persuasiveness of God's rhetoric in the name of reason, law, and natural rights. Near the end of his book, Stewart openly acknowledges these founders' roles in establishing what he calls the "essentially atheistic public religion of the modern liberal world."[9] He rightly credits this "public religion" for liberating Americans from "common misconceptions" promulgated by many religious and Christian thinkers who had long persuaded human beings to "participate in their own enslavement" and to believe this was sanctioned by the "truth" of the Bible and the Bible's God. Though Stewart does not say so, America's deistic philosophers were among the first to recognize and criticize God's words as rhetorical suasion that had to be resisted if human beings were to escape their own political, moral and metaphysical enslavement. In fact, Stewart believes America's founders were so thorough in their rebuttal to Christian rhetoric, "[t]here is no alternative to [the] radical philosophy" of natural reason that Epicurus' bequeathed to America's great experiment of self-government. These radical ideas did not, of course, generate the counter-rhetoric necessary to free America's slaves immediately or to give women the vote, or to offer justice to Native-Americans, or to block those "malefactors of great wealth" who even

---

9. Stewart, *Nature's God*, 428–51, 435.

now seek to purchase and poison the fruits of America's radical heritage. Nor did this radical rhetoric of reason and nature dull the "the persistence in modern America of supernatural religion and the reactionary nationalism" that often follows from it. This "persistence," he concludes, remains "a piece of unfinished business of the American Revolution."

As an agnostic by-product of these radical ideas and of postmodern critiques of deistic, Enlightenment rhetoric, I cannot be so sure that this "business" will ever be finished or that there is "no alternative" to the founders' Lucretian "radical philosophy." For that is to say there is no freedom to resist and displace this or any other rhetoric. Even now, it seems, some of today's advocates for a "supernatural religion" treat the marvels of God's theophanies and His often violent ethos as *literal* sanctions and justifications for their own prejudices and sometimes violent actions rather than the rhetorical strategies God adopts trying to persuade a recalcitrant human world. Already we can see how busy these "supernatural religionists" are to find persuasive ways to co-opt the more radical, atheistic "public religion" of American founders' laws and beliefs in freedom and turn it to their own spiritual and religious ends to "re-enslave" certain people who do not believe in this God's veracity. The faith in the "land of the free" that Stewart celebrates as the inevitable result of America's radical philosophy is now become a rallying cause for some proponents of a "supernatural religion" and their reactionary supporters as much as it was for the "atheists" who sought, in their various ways, to free humanity from Christianity's hold on the American imagination. The always important human desire for symboling, for alternative rhetorical stances, for belief in a rhetorical power beyond our own, cannot be permanently satisfied or finally displaced. Nor are the darker edges of that desire for counter-symbols ever very far from the borrowed eloquence that might be exploited to end rhetoric in the ironic name of religious "freedom" upon which rhetoric, even and especially God's, must always depend.

Bibliography

Abrams, M. H. *The Mirror and the Lamp: Romantic Theory and the Critical Tradition.* 1953. Reprint, New York: Norton, 1958.
Aguayo, Angela J., and Timothy R. Steffensmeir, eds. *Readings on Argumentation.* State College, PA: Strata, 2008.
Anderson, R. Dean. *Glossary of Greek Rhetorical Terms Connected to Methods of Argumentation, Figures and Tropes from Anaximenes to Quintilian.* Contributions to Biblical Exegesis and Theology 24. Leuven: Peeter 2000.
Arendt, Hannah. *On Violence.* New York: Harcourt, 1970.
Aristotle. *"Art" of Rhetoric.* Translated by John Henry Freese. Vol. 22. Loeb Classical Library. 1926. Reprint, Cambridge: Harvard University Press, 1982.
Armstrong, Karen. *The Bible: A Biography.* New York: Atlantic Monthly Press, 2007.
———. *The Case for God.* New York: Knopf, 2009.
———. *A History of God: The 4000 Year Quest of Judaism, Christianity and Islam.* New York: Knopf, 1993.
Arrington, Phillip. "Content(ious) Forms: Trope and the Study of Composition." In *Farther Along: Transforming Dichotomies in Rhetoric and Composition,* edited by Kate Ronald and Hephzibah Roskelly, 149–67. Portsmouth, NH: Boynton/Cook, 1990.
———. "Feigned Soliloquy, Feigned Argument: Hamlet's 'To Be or Not to Be' Speech as Dissoi Logoi." *The Ben Jonson Journal* 22.1 (2015) 101–18.
———. "Reflections on the Expository Principle." *College English* 54.3 (March 1992) 314–32.
———. *Rhetoric's Agons.* Charleston, SC: Booksurge, 2008.
———. "The Traditions of the Writing Process." *Freshman English News* 14.3 (1986) 2–4, 9–10.
Auerbach, Erich. *Mimesis: The Representation of Reality in Western Literature.* Translated by Willard Trask. 1946. Reprint, New York: Doubleday, 1957.
Augustine. *On Christian Doctrine.* Translated by D. W. Robertson Jr. 1958. Reprint, Indianapolis: Bobbs-Merrill, 1979.
Austin, Gilbert. *Chironomia.* In *The Rhetorical Tradition: Readings from the Classical Times to the Present,* edited by Patricia Bizzell and Bruce Herzberg, 889–97. 2nd ed. Boston: Bedford/St. Martin's Press, 2001.

Bacon, Francis. *The Advancement of Learning*. In *Francis Bacon: The Major Works*, edited by Brian Vickers, 120–299. New York: Oxford University Press, 1996.

Bain, Alexander. *English Composition and Rhetoric*. In *The Rhetorical Tradition: Readings from Classical Times to the Present*, edited by Patricia Bizzell and Bruce Herzberg, 1145–48. 2nd ed. Boston: Bedford/St. Martins, 2001.

Bar-Efrat, Shimon. "Some Observations on the Analysis of Structure in Biblical Narrative." In *Beyond Form Criticism: Essays in Old Testament Literary Criticism*, edited by Paul R. House, 186–205. Winona Lake, IN: Eisenbrauns, 1992.

Barnstone, Willis, ed. *The Other Bible: Jewish Pseudepigrapha, Christian Apocrypha, Gnostic Scriptures, Kabbalah, Dead Sea Scrolls*. San Francisco: HarperSanFrancisco, 1984.

Barilli, Renato. *Rhetoric*. Translated by Giuliana Menozzi. Minneapolis: University of Minnesota Press, 1989.

Barrett, Cyril. "The Language of Ecstasy and the Ecstasy of Language." In *The Bible as Rhetoric: Studies in Biblical Persuasion and Credibility*, edited by Martin Warner, 205–21. London: Routledge, 1990.

Barton, John. "History and Rhetoric of the Prophets." In *The Bible as Rhetoric: Studies in Biblical Persuasion and Credibility*, edited by Martin Warner, 51–64. London: Routledge, 1990.

Bizzell, Patricia, and Bruce Herzberg. "Alexander Bain and Adams Sherman Hill." In *The Rhetorical Tradition: Readings from the Classical Times to the Present*, edited by Patricia Bizzell and Bruce Herzberg, 1141–43. 2nd ed. New York: Bedford/St. Martins, 2001.

Black, Edwin. *Rhetorical Criticism: A Study in Method*. 1965. Reprint, Madison: University of Wisconsin Press, 1978.

Blair, Hugh. *Lectures on Rhetoric and Belles Lettres*. In *The Rhetoric of Blair, Campbell, and Whately*, edited by James L. Golden and Edward P. J. Corbett, 106–28. New York: Holt, Rinehart & Winston, 1968.

Boomershine, Thomas E. "The Structure of Narrative Rhetoric in Genesis 2–3." *Semeia* 18 (1980) 113–29.

Booth, Wayne C. "Rhetoric and Religion: Are They Essentially Wedded?" In *Radical Pluralism and Truth: David Tracy and the Hermeneutics of Religion*, edited by Werner G. Jeanrond and Jennifer L. Rilke, 62–80. New York: Crossroad, 1991.

———. *The Rhetoric of Rhetoric: The Quest for Effective Communication*. Malden, MA: Blackwell, 2004.

Bloom, Harold. *The Book of J*. Translated by David Rosenberg. New York: Vintage, 1990.

———. *Jesus and Yahweh: The Names Divine*. New York: Riverhead, 2005.

———. *Wallace Stevens: The Poems of Our Climate*. Ithaca, NY: Cornell University Press, 1976.

Boger, George. "Subordinating Truth—Is *Acceptability* Acceptable?" *Argumentation* 19 (2005) 187–238.

Brown, Peter. *Augustine of Hippo: A Biography*. New ed. with Epilogue. Berkeley: University of California Press, 2000.

Burke, Kenneth. *Counter-statement*. 1931. Reprint, Berkeley: University of California Press, 1968.

———. *A Grammar of Motives*. 1945. Reprint, Berkeley: University of California Press, 1969.

———. *Language as Symbolic Action: Essays on Life, Literature, and Method.* Berkeley: Los Angeles: University of California Press, 1966.

———. *The Philosophy of Literary Form: Studies in Symbolic Action.* 3rd ed. 1941. Reprint, Berkeley: University of California Press, 1973.

———. *A Rhetoric of Motives.* 1950. Reprint, Berkeley: University of California Press, 1969.

———. *The Rhetoric of Religion: Studies in Logology.* 1961. Reprint, Berkeley: University of California Press, 1970.

———. "Words as Deeds." *Centrum* 3 (1975) 147–68.

Butler Paul, ed. *Style in Rhetoric and Composition: A Critical Sourcebook.* Boston: Bedford/St. Martin's, 2010.

Caplan, H[arry]. "Introduction." In *Rhetorica ad Herennium*, vii–xl. Loeb Classical Library. 1954. Cambridge: Harvard University Press, 1981.

Cicero. *De Inventione.* Translated by H. M. Hubbell. Vol. 2. Loeb Classical Library. 1949. Reprint, Cambridge: Harvard University Press, 1976.

———. *De Optimo Genere Oratorum.* Translated by H. M. Hubbell. Vol. 2. Loeb Classical Library. 1949. Reprint, Cambridge: Harvard University Press, 1976.

———. *De Oratore.* Translated E. W. Sutton and H. Rackham. Vols. 3–4. Loeb Classical Library. Cambridge: Harvard University Press, 1976.

———. *Rhetorica ad Herennium.* Translated by H[arry] Caplan. Vol. 1. Loeb Classical Library. 1954. Cambridge: Harvard University Press, 1981.

———. *Topica,* Translated by H. M. Hubbell. Vol. 2. Loeb Classical Library. Cambridge: Harvard University Press, 1976.

Clines, David J. A. "Deconstructing the Book of Job." In *The Bible as Rhetoric: Studies in Biblical Persuasion and Credibility,* edited by Martin Warner, 65–80. London: Routledge, 1990.

———. "Story and Poem: The Old Testament as Literature and as Scripture." In *Beyond Form Criticism: Essays in Old Testament Criticism*, edited by Paul R. House, 25–38. Winona Lake, IN: Eisenbrauns, 1992.

Coe, Richard M. "An Apology for Form: Or, Who Took the Form Out of the Process." *College English* 49.1 (1987) 13–28.

Cohn, Ruby. "Outward Bound Soliloquies." *Journal of Modern Literature, Samuel Beckett Special Number* 6.1 (Feb. 1977) 17–38.

Craig, Kenneth M. Jr. *Asking for Rhetoric: The Hebrew Bible's Protean Interrogative.* Biblical Interpretation Series 73. Boston: Brill, 2005.

Crosswhite, James. "Universality in Rhetoric." *Philosophy and Rhetoric* 22.3 (1989) 157–73.

Crowley, Sharon. "Invention in Nineteenth-Century Rhetoric." *College Composition and Communication* 36 (1985) 51–60.

———. *The Methodical Memory: Invention in Current-Traditional Rhetoric.* Carbondale: Southern Illinois University Press, 1990.

Culpepper, R. Allan. *Anatomy of the Fourth Gospel: A Study in Literary Design.* Philadelphia: Fortress, 1983.

Curtius, Ernst Robert. *European Literature and the Latin Middle Ages.* Translated by Willard R. Trask. 1953. Reprint, Princeton: Princeton University Press, 1983.

D'Angelo, Frank. "Prolegomena to a Rhetoric of Tropes." *Rhetoric Review* 6 (1987) 32–40.

Dawkins, Richard. *The God Delusion.* Boston: Houghton Mifflin, 2006.

Day, Henry N. *The Art of Discourse*. In *The Rhetorical Tradition: Readings from the Classical Times to the Present*, edited by Patricia Bizzell and Bruce Herzberg, 864–73. Boston: St. Martin's, 1990.

Deans, Thomas. "The Rhetoric of Jesus Writing in the Story of the Woman Accused of Adultery." *College Composition and Communication* 65 (2014) 406–29.

de Romilly, Jacqueline. *Magic and Rhetoric in Ancient Greece*. Cambridge: Harvard University Press, 1975.

Derrida, Jacques. *Acts of Religion*. Edited by Gil Anidjar. New York: Routledge, 2002.

———. "Faith and Knowledge: The Two Sources of 'Religion' at the Limits of Reason Alone." In *Acts of Religion*, edited by Gil Anidjar, 40–101. London: Routledge, 2002.

———. *Specters of Marx: The State of the Debt, the Work of Morning and the New International*. Translated by Peggy Kamuf. New York: Routledge, 1994.

[Anon]. "*Dissoi Logoi*." Translated by T. M. Robinson. In *The Rhetorical Tradition: Readings from the Classical Times to the Present*, edited by Patricia Bizzell and Bruce Herzberg, 47–55. 2nd ed. Boston: Bedford/St. Martin's, 2001.

Duke, Rodney K. *The Persuasive Appeal of the Chronicler: A Rhetorical Analysis*. Journal for the Study of the Old Testament Supplements 88. Sheffield, UK: Almond, 1990.

Ehrman, Bart D. *Jesus, Interrupted: Revealing the Hidden Contradictions in the Bible (and Why We Don't Know about Them)*. New York: HarperOne, 2009.

———. *Misquoting Jesus: The Story of Who Changed the Bible and Why*. San Francisco: HarperSanFrancisco, 2005.

Elbow, Peter. "The Music of Form: Rethinking Organization in Writing." *College Composition and Communication* 57 (2006) 620–66.

Evans, Craig A. "Jewish Scripture and the Literacy of Jesus." In *From Biblical Criticism to Biblical Faith: Essays in Honor of Lee Martin McDonald*, edited by William H. Brockney and Craig A. Evans, 41–54. Macon, GA: Mercer University Press, 2007. www.craigaevans.com/evans,pdf.

Farnsworth, Ward. *Farnsworth's Classical English Rhetoric*. Boston: Godine, 2010.

Fish, Stanley. *Doing What Comes Naturally: Change, Rhetoric, and the Practice of Theory in Literary and Legal Studies*. Durham: Duke University Press, 1989.

———. "One University Under God." *The Chronicle of Higher Education*, January 7, 2005. http://chronicle.com/jobs/news/2005/010701c.htm.

Foley, Megan. "*Peitho* and *Bia*: The Force of Language." *Symplokē* 20.1–2 (2012) 173–81.

Foucault, Michel. *The Punitive Society: Lectures at the Collège De France 1972–73*. Translated by Graham Burchell. Edited by Barnard E. Harcourt. New York: Palgrave, 2015.

Fox, M. V. "The Rhetoric of Ezekiel's Vision of the Valley of Bones." *Hebrew Union Council Annual* 51 (1980) 1–15.

Frankfurt, Harry G. *On Bullshit*. Princeton: Princeton University Press, 2005.

Fredal, James. "Rhetoric and Bullshit." *College English* 73 (2011) 243–59.

Frei, Hans. *The Eclipse of Biblical Narrative: A Study in Eighteenth and Nineteenth Century Hermeneutics*. New Haven: Yale University Press, 1974.

Friedman, Richard Elliot. *Who Wrote the Bible?* New York: Summit, 1987.

Gans, Eric. "The Rhetoric of God." *Chronicles of Love and Resentment*, May 30, 1998. http://www.anthropoetics.ucla.edu/views.

Gargani, Aldo. "Religious Experience as Event and Interpretation." In *Religion*, edited by Jacques Derrida and Gianni Vattimo, 111–35. Stanford: Stanford University Press, 1996.

Girard, René. *Violence and the Sacred*. Translated by Patrick Gregory. Baltimore: John Hopkins University Press, 1977.

Gitay, Yehoshua. *Prophecy and Persuasion: A Study of Isaiah 40–48*. Forum theologiae linguisticae 14. Bonn: Linguistica Biblica, 1981.

———. "A Study of Amos' Art of Speech: A Rhetorical Analysis of Amos 3:1–15." *Catholic Biblical Quarterly* 42 (1980) 293–309.

Gorgias. *Encomium of Helen*. Translated by George A. Kennedy. In *The Rhetorical Tradition: Readings from Classical Times to the Present*, edited by Patricia Bizzell and Bruce Herzberg, 44–46. 2nd ed. Boston: Bedford/St. Martins, 2001.

Grassi, Ernesto. *Rhetoric as Philosophy: The Humanist Tradition*. University Park: Pennsylvania State University Press, 1980.

Greenstein, Edward L. "In Job's Face/Facing Job." In *The Labour of Reading: Desire, Alienation, and Biblical Interpretation*, edited by Fiona C. Black, Roland Boer, and Erin Runions, 301–17. Semeia Studies 36. Atlanta: Society of Biblical Literature, 1999.

Gross, Alan. "A Theory of Rhetorical Audience: Reflections on Chaim Perelman." *Quarterly Journal of Speech* 85 (1999) 203–11.

Gross, Alan, and Laura J. Gurak, guest eds. "The State of Rhetoric of Science and Technology." *Technical Communication Quarterly* 14 (2005) 241–351.

Gross, Paul R., and Norman Levitt. *Higher Superstition: The Academic Left and Its Quarrels with Science*. Baltimore: John Hopkins University Press, 1994.

Halloran, S. M. "Tradition and Theory in Rhetoric." *Quarterly Journal of Speech* 62 (1976) 234–41.

Hamblin, C. L. *Fallacies*. London: Methuen, 1970.

Handa, Carolyn, ed. *Visual Rhetoric in a Digital Age: A Critical Sourcebook*. Boston: Bedford/St. Martin's, 2004.

Harper, Douglas. "Soliloquy." *Online Etymological Dictionary*, 2001–2004.

Harris, Randy Allen, ed. *Landmark Essays on Rhetoric of Science: Case Studies*. Mahwah, NJ: Hermagoras, 1997.

Harris, Sam. *The End of Faith: Religion, Terror, and the Future of Reason*. New York: Norton, 2004.

Hashimoto, Irvin. "Structured Heuristic Procedures: Their Limitations." *College Composition and Communication* 36 (1985) 73–81.

Hedges, Chris. *When Atheism Becomes Religion: America's New Fundamentalists*. New York: Free Press, 2008.

Heidegger, Martin. "Being and Time." Translated by Joan Stambaugh, J. Glenn Gray, and David Farrell. In *Martin Heidegger: Basic Writings*, edited by David Farrell Krell, 41–87. New York: Harper Perennial, 2008.

Hinze, Bradford E. "Reclaiming Rhetoric in the Christian Tradition." *Theological Studies* 57 (1996) 481–99.

Hirsh, James. *Shakespeare and the History of Soliloquies*. Madison, MA: Farleigh Dickinson University Press, 2003.

Hitchens, Christopher. *God Is not Great: How Religion Poisons Everything*. New York: Twelve, 2007.

Horn, Laurence R. *A Natural History of Negation*. 1989. Reprint, Stanford, CA: Center for the Study of Language and Information, 2001.
Howard, David M., Jr. "Rhetorical Criticism in Old Testament Studies." *Bulletin for Biblical Research* 4 (1994) 87–104.
Howell, Wilbur Samuel. *Eighteenth-Century British Logic and Rhetoric*. Princeton: Princeton University Press, 1971.
———. *Logic and Rhetoric in England 1500–1700*. Princeton: University of Princeton Press, 1956.
Hughes, Richard. "The Contemporaneity of Classical Rhetoric." *College Composition and Communication* 16 (1965) 157–59.
Hunter, Lynette. "Considering Issues of Rhetoric and Violence." *Parallax* 6.2 (2010) 2–8. http://dx.doi.org/10.1080.
Isocrates. *Against the Sophists*. Translated by George A. Nolin. Vol. 2. Loeb Classical Library. 1929. Reprint, Cambridge: Harvard University Press, 2000.
Jabès, Edmund. *The Book of Questions: Yael, Elya, Aely*. Translated by R. Waldrop. Middleton, CN: Wesleyan University Press, 1983.
Johnson, Ralph H. *Manifest Rationality: A Pragmatic Theory of Argument*. Mahwah, NJ: Erlbaum, 2000.
Jorgenson, Christine. "Interpreting Perelman's Universal Audience: Gross versus Crosswhite." *Argumentation* 23 (2009) 11–19.
Josipovici, Gabriel. *The Book of God: A Response to the Bible*. New Haven: Yale University Press, 1988.
Kellner, Hans. "The Inflatable Trope as Narrative Theory: Structure or Allegory?" *Diacritics* 11 (1981) 14–28.
Kennedy, George. "'Truth' and 'Rhetoric' in the Pauline Epistles." In *The Bible as Rhetoric: Studies in Biblical Persuasion and Credibility*, edited by Martin Warner, 195–202. London: Routledge, 1990.
———. *Classical Rhetoric and Its Christian and Secular Tradition from Ancient to Modern Times*. Chapel Hill: University of North Carolina Press, 1980.
———. *New Testament Interpretation through Rhetorical Criticism*. Chapel Hill: University of North Carolina Press, 1984.
Keohane, Joe. "How Facts Backfire: Researchers Discover a Surprising Threat to Democracy, Our Brains." *The Boston Globe*, July 11, 2010. Reprinted in *Writing Logically, Thinking Clearly* by Sheila Cooper and Rosemary Patton, 24–25. Upper Saddle, NJ: Pearson, 2012.
Kerford, G. B. *The Sophistic Movement*. Cambridge: Cambridge University Press, 1981.
Kermode, Frank. *The Genesis of Secrecy: On the Interpretation of Narrative*. Cambridge: Harvard University Press, 1979.
———. *The Sense of an Ending: Studies in the Theory of Fiction*. New York: Oxford University Press, 1966.
Kinneavy, James L. *The Greek Rhetorical Origins of Christian Faith: An Inquiry*. New York: Oxford University Press, 1987.
———. "Restoring the Humanities: The Return of Rhetoric from Exile." In *The Rhetorical Tradition and Modern Writing*, edited by James J. Murphy, 19–28. New York: Modern Language Association, 1982.
———. *A Theory of Discourse: The Aims of Discourse*. 1971. Reprint, New York: Norton, 1980.

Knoblauch, C. H. "Modern Composition Theory and the Rhetorical Tradition." *Freshman English News* 4 (1980) 3–4, 11–16.
——— and Lil Brannon. *Rhetorical Traditions and the Teaching of Writing*. Upper Montclair, NJ: Boynton/Cook, 1984.
Koptak, Paul E. "Rhetorical Criticism of the Bible: A Resource for Preaching." *Covenant Quarterly* 54.3 (1996) 26–37. http:www.religion-online.org.
Kugel, James. *The Idea of Biblical Poetry*. New Haven: Yale University Press, 1981.
Kuhn, Thomas S. *The Structure of Scientific Revolutions*. 2nd ed. Chicago: University of Chicago Press, 1970.
Lee, Bernard J., SM. *Jesus and the Metaphors of God: The Christs of the New Testament*. Studies in Judaism and Christianity. New York: Paulist, 1993.
Leroy, Herbert. *Rätsel und Missverständis: Ein Beitrag zur Formgeschichte des Johannesevangelitiums*. Bonner biblische Beiträge 30. Bonn: Hanstein, 1968.
Lanham, Richard A. *A Handlist of Rhetorical Terms*. 2nd ed. Berkeley: University of California Press, 1991.
Locke, John. *An Essay Concerning Human Understanding*. Edited by Roger Woolhouse. London: Penguin, 1997.
Lotier, Kristopher M. "Around 1986: The Externalization of Cognition and the Emergence of Postprocess Invention." *College Composition and Communication* 67.3 (2016) 360–84.
Lundbom, Jack R. *Jeremiah: A Study in Ancient Hebrew Rhetoric*. SBL Dissertation Series 18. Missoula, MT: Scholars, 1975.
Lunsford, Andrea A., and Lisa S. Ede. "On Distinctions Between Classical and Modern Rhetoric." In *Essays on Classical Rhetoric and Modern Discourse*, edited Robert J. Connors, Lisa S. Ede and Andrea Lunsford, 37–49. Carbondale: Southern Illinois University Press, 1985.
Mallinak, Dave. "Is Rhetoric Christian?" *To Be a Pilgrim*, May 19, 2006. http://www.tobeapilgrim.wordpress.com/2006/05/19/is-rhetoric-christian-a-guest-entry-by-pastor-dave-mallinak.
Marion, Jean-Luc. *God Without Being: Hors-Texte*. Translated by Thomas A. Carlson. Religion and Postmodernism. Chicago: University of Chicago Press, 1999.
Martin, Wallace. "Floating an Issue of Tropes." *Diacritics* 12 (1982) 75–83.
Mawson, C. O. Sylvester. *Dictionary of Foreign Terms*. 2nd ed. New York: Crowell, 1975.
May, Herbert G., and Bruce M. Metzger, eds. *The New Oxford Annotated Bible, Revised Standard Version Containing the Old and New Testaments*. New York: Oxford University Press, 1962, 1973.
Meacham, Jon (with Eliza Gray). "The End of Christian America." *Newsweek*, April 13, 2009, 34–38.
Milac, Louis T. "Theories of Style and Their Implications for the Teaching of Composition." *College Composition and Communication* 16 (1965) 66–69, 126.
Miles, Jack. *God: A Biography*. New York: Vintage, 1995.
Milbank, John. "The Double Glory, or Paradox versus Dialectics: On not Quite Agreeing with Slavoj Žižek." In *The Monstrosity of Christ: Paradox or Dialectic*, edited by Creston Davis, 110–233. Cambridge: MIT Press, 2009.
Montesano, Mark. "*Kairos* and *Kerygma*: The Rhetoric of Christian Proclamation." *Rhetoric Society Quarterly* 25 (1995) 164–78.
Moore, Stephen D. "Afterward: Things not Written in This Book." In *Anatomies of Narrative Criticism: The Past, Present, and Futures of the Fourth Gospel as*

Literature, edited by Tom Thatcher and Stephen D. Moore, 253–58. SBL Resources for Biblical Study 55. Atlanta: Society of Biblical Literature, 2008.

Muckelbauer, John. *The Future of Invention: Rhetoric, Post-modernism, and the Problem of Change.* Albany: State University of New York Press, 2008.

Muilenburg, James. "Form Criticism and Beyond." In *Beyond Form Criticism: Essays in Old Testament Literary Criticism,* edited by Paul R. House, 49–52. Sources for Biblical and Theological Study 2. Winona Lake, IN: Eisenbaun, 1992.

Mumford, Lewis. *The Myth of the Machine: Technics and Human Development.* 2 vols. New York: Harcourt, Brace, 1966.

———. *Technics and Civilization.* New York: Harcourt, Brace, 1934.

Murphy, James J. "Rhetorical History as a Guide to the Salvation of American Reading and Writing." In *The Rhetorical Tradition and Modern Writing,* edited by James J. Murphy, 13–18. New York: Modern Language Association, 1982.

Ong, Walter J. *Ramus, Method, and the Decay of Dialogue.* 1958. Reprint, New York: Farrar, Strauss & Giroux, 1974.

Pagels, Elaine. *The Origin of Satan: How Christians Demonized Jews, Pagans, and Heretics.* New York: Vintage, 1995.

Patrick, Dale, and Allen Scult. *Rhetoric and Biblical Interpretation.* Journal for the Study of the Old Testament Supplements 82. Sheffield: Almond, 1990.

Pelikan, Jaroslav. *Whose Bible Is It? A History of the Scriptures through the Ages.* New York: Viking, 2005.

Pepper, Stephen C. *World Hypotheses: A Study in Evidence.* 1942. Reprint, Berkeley: University of California Press, 1970.

Perelman, Chaim. "The New Rhetoric: A Theory of Practical Reasoning." In *The Rhetorical Tradition: Readings from Classical Times to the Present,* edited by Patricia Bizzell and Bruce Herzberg, 2nd ed., 1384–1409. New York: Bedford/St. Martins, 2001.

———. *The Realm of Rhetoric.* Translated by William Kluback. Notre Dame: University of Notre Dame Press, 1962.

Perelman, Chaim, and Lucie Olbrechts-Tyteca. *The New Rhetoric: A Treatise on Argumentation.* Translated by John Wilkinson and Purcell Weaver. Notre Dame: University of Notre Dame Press, 1969.

Pernot, Laurent. "The Rhetoric of Religion." *Rhetorica* 24.3 (2006) 235–54.

Pinker, Steven. *The Stuff of Thought: Language as a Window into Human Nature.* New York: Penguin, 2007.

Plato. *Gorgias.* Translated by W. D. Woodhead. In *The Collected Dialogues of Plato, Including the Letters,* edited by Edith Hamilton and Huntington Cairns, 229–307. Princeton: Princeton University Press, 1961.

———. *Phaedrus.* Translated by R. Hackforth. In *The Collected Dialogues of Plato, Including the Letters,* edited by Edith Hamilton and Huntington Cairns, 475–525. Princeton: Princeton University Press, 1961.

Podis, JoAnne M., and Leonard A. Podis. "Identifying and Teaching Rhetorical Plans for Arrangement." *College Composition and Communication* 41.4 (1990) 430–42.

Poland, Lynn. "The Bible and the Rhetorical Sublime." In *Bible as Rhetoric: Studies in Biblical Persuasion and Credibility,* edited by Martin Warner, 29–47. London: Routledge, 1990.

Prothero, Stephen. *Religious Literacy.* New York: HarperOne, 2007.

Quinn, Arthur. *Figures of Speech.* 1982. Reprint, London: Routledge, 1995.

Quinn, David. "The Four Master Tropes as Informing Principles." *Hispania* 66 (1983) 242–52.
Quintilian. *Institutio Oratoria*. Translated by H. E. Butler. 4 vols. Cambridge: MA: Loeb Classical Library, 1980.
Rankin, Elizabeth. "Revitalizing Style: Toward a New Theory and Pedagogy." *Freshman English News* 14 (Spring 1985) 8–12.
Robertson, D. W. "Introduction." *On Christian Doctrine* by Augustine, ix–xxi. Indianapolis: Bobbs-Merrill, 1979.
Robinson, Marilynne. *Absence of Mind: The Dispelling of Inwardness from the Modern Myth of the Self*. New Haven: Yale University Press, 2010.
Robinson, T. M. "Introduction." In *Contrasting Arguments: An Edition of the Dissoi Logoi*, 1–81. Translated by T. M. Robinson. New York: Arno, 1979.
Schiappa, Edward. "Did Plato Coin *Rhētorikē*?" *American Journal of Philology* 111 (1990) 457–70.
———. "Sophistic Rhetoric: Oasis or Mirage?" *Rhetoric Review* 10.1 (1991) 5–18.
Schuon, Frithjof. *Logic and Transendence*. Translated by Peter N. Townsend. New York: Harper & Row, 1975.
Shakespeare, William. *King Lear*. In *William Shakespeare: The Complete Works*, edited by Alfred Harbage. Baltimore: Penguin, 1969.
Sheridan, Thomas. *A Course of Lectures on Elocution*, Lecture VI. In *The Rhetorical Tradition: Readings from the Classical Times to the Present*, edited by Patricia Bizzell and Bruce Herzberg, 881–88. 2nd ed. Boston: Bedford/St. Martin's, 2001.
Sipiora, Phillip. "Introduction: The Ancient Concept of *Kairos*." In *Rhetoric and Kairos: Essays in History, Theory, and Praxis*, edited by Phillip Sipora and James S. Baumlin, 1–22. Albany: State University of New York Press, 2002.
———. "*Kairos*: The Rhetoric of Time and Timing in the New Testament." In *Rhetoric and Kairos: Essays in History, Theory, and Praxis*, edited by Phillip Sipora and James S. Baumlin, 114–27. Albany: State University of New York Press, 2002.
Sipiora, Phillip, and James S. Baumlin, eds. *Rhetoric and Kairos: Essays in History, Theory, and Praxis*. Albany: State University of New York Press, 2002.
Slater, Susan. "Imagining Arrival: Rhetoric, Reader, and the Word of God in Deuteronomy 1–3." In *The Labour of Reading: Desire, Alienation, and Biblical Interpretation*, edited by Fiona C. Black et al., 107–121. Semeia Studies 36. Atlanta, GA: Society of Biblical Literature, 1999.
Smith, Craig R. *The Quest for Charisma: Christianity and Persuasion*. Westport, CT: Praeger, 2000.
"Soliloquy." *Oxford English Dictionary*. Compact ed., 1971.
Sommers, Nancy. "Revision Strategies of Student Writers and Experienced Adult Writers." In *Rhetoric and Composition: A Sourcebook for Teachers and Writers*, edited by Richard L. Graves, 328–37. New ed. Upper Montclair, NJ: Boynton/Cook, 1984.
Sorensen, Roy. *A Brief History of the Paradox: Philosophy and the Labyrinths of the Mind*. New York: Oxford University Press, 2003.
Staykova, Julia D. "The Augustinian Soliloquies of an Early Modern Reader: A Stylistic Relation of Shakespeare's Hamlet." *Literature and Theology* 23.2 (2009) 121–22.
Steiner, George. *Grammars of Creation*. New Haven: Yale University Press, 2001.
Sternberg, Meir. "The Bible's Art of Persuasion: Ideology, Rhetoric, and Poetics in Saul's Fall." In *Beyond Form Criticism: Essays in Old Testament Literary Criticism*, edited

by Paul R. House, 234–71. Sources for Biblical and Theological Study 2. Winona Lake, IN: Eisenbaun, 1992.

Stewart, Matthew. *Nature's God: The Heretical Origins of the American Republic*. New York: Norton, 2014.

Sutherland, Stewart. "History, Truth, and Narrative." In *Bible as Rhetoric: Studies in Biblical Persuasion and Credibility*, edited by Martin Warner, 105–16. London: Routledge, 1990.

Swales, John. *Genre Analysis: English in Academic and Research Settings*. Cambridge Applied Linguistics Series. New York: Cambridge University Press, 1990.

Swenson, Kristen. *Bible Babel: Making Sense of the Most Talked about Book of All Time*. New York: HarperCollins, 2010.

Taylor, Charles. *Sources of the Self: The Making of Modern Identity*. Cambridge: Harvard University Press, 1989.

Thatcher, Tom. "Anatomies of the Fourth Gospel: Past, Present, and Future Probes." In *Anatomies of Narrative Criticism: The Past, Present, and Futures of the Fourth Gospel as Literature*, edited by Tom Thatcher and Stephen D. Moore, 1–35. Resources for Biblical Study 55. Atlanta: Society of Biblical Literature, 2008.

Thurén, Lauri. "Is There Biblical Argumentation?" In *Rhetorical Argumentation in Biblical Texts: Essays from the Lund 2000 Conference*, edited by Ander Eriksson et al., 77–78. Emory Studies in Early Christianity 8. Harrisburg, PA: Trinity, 2002.

Tietge, David J. "Rhetoric Is not Bullshit." In *Bullshit and Philosophy: Guaranteed to Get Perfect Results Every Time*, edited by Gary L. Hardcastle and George A. Reisch, 229–40. Chicago: Open Court, 2006.

Tindale, Christopher. *Reason's Dark Champions: Constructive Strategies of Sophistic Argument*. Studies in Rhetoric/Communication. Columbia: University of South Carolina Press, 2010.

Toulmin, Stephen. *The Uses of Argument*. In *The Rhetorical Tradition: Readings from Classical Times to the Present*, edited by Patricia Bizzell and Bruce Herzberg, 1417–28. 2nd ed. New York: Bedford/St. Martins, 2001.

Trible, Phyllis. *God and the Rhetoric of Sexuality*. Overtures to Biblical Theology. Philadelphia: Fortress, 1978.

———. *Rhetorical Criticism: Context, Method, and the Book of Jonah*. Overtures to Biblical Theology. Minneapolis: Fortress, 1994.

Trigg, Roger. "'Tales Artfully Spun.'" In *The Bible as Rhetoric: Studies in Biblical Persuasion and Credibility*, edited by Martin Warner, 117–32. London: Routledge, 1990.

Vico, Giambattista. *The New Science*. Translated by Thomas Goddard Bergin and Max Harold Fisch. 3rd ed. Ithaca: Cornell University Press, 1970.

———. *The Study Methods of Our Times*. Translated by Elio Gianturco. In *The Rhetorical Tradition*, edited by Patricia Bizzell and Bruce Herberg, 865–78. 2nd ed. Boston: Bedford/St. Martins, 2001.

Vattimo, Gianni. *After Christianity*. Translated by Luca D'Isanto. New York: Columbia University Press, 2002.

Warner, Martin. "Introduction." In *The Bible as Rhetoric: Studies in Biblical Persuasion and Credibility*, edited by Martin Warner, 1–28. Warwick Studies in Philosophy and Literature. London: Routledge, 1990.

Wead, David W. *The Literary Devices in John's Gospel*. Theologische Dissertationen 4. Basel: Reinhardt, 1970.

Wess, Robert. *Kenneth Burke: Rhetoric, Subjectivity, Modernism*. Literature, Culture, Theory 18. Cambridge: Cambridge University Press, 1996.
Whitehead, Alfred North. *Science and the Modern World*. New York: Free Press, 1925.
Wilder, Amos. *The Language of the Gospel: Early Christian Rhetoric*. 1964. Reprint, Eugene, OR: Wipf & Stock, 2014.
———. *Theopoetic: Theology and the Religious Imagination*. 1976. Reprint, Eugene, OR: Wipf & Stock, 2014.
Yates, Frances A. *The Art of Memory*. 1966. Reprint, Chicago: University of Chicago Press, 1974.
Young, Richard. "Paradigms and Problems: Needed Research in Rhetorical Invention." In *Research and Composing: Points of Departure*, edited by Charles R. Cooper and Lee Odell, 29–47. Urbana, IL: National Council of Teachers of English, 1979.
Ziman, John. *Real Science: What It Is and What It Means*. Cambridge: University of Cambridge Press, 2000.
Žižek, Slavoj. "The Fear of Four Words: A Modest Plea for the Hegelian Reading of Christianity." In *The Monstrosity of Christ: Paradox or Dialectic*, edited by Creston Davis, 25–109. Cambridge, MA: MIT Press, 2009.
Zulick, Margaret D. "Prophecy and Providence: The Anxiety over Prophetic Authority." *Journal of Communication and Religion* 26 (2003) 195–207.
———. "Rhetoric and Religion: A Map of the Territory." In *The Sage Handbook of Rhetorical Studies*, edited by Andrea A. Lunsford, 125–38. Los Angeles: Sage, 2009.